The American History Series

SERIES EDITORS
John Hope Franklin, *Duke University*
A. S. Eisenstadt, *Brooklyn College*

Thomas R. Wellock
CENTRAL WASHINGTON UNIVERSITY

Preserving the Nation

The Conservation and Environmental Movements

1870–2000

HARLAN DAVIDSON, INC.
WHEELING, ILLINOIS 60090-6000

Copyright © 2007
Harlan Davidson, Inc.
All Rights Reserved

Visit us on the World Wide Web at www.harlandavidson.com.

Library of Congress Cataloging-in-Publication Data

Wellock, Thomas Raymond.
 Preserving the nation : the conservation and environmental movements, 1870/
2000 / Thomas R. Wellock.
   p. cm.
 Includes bibliographical references and index.
 ISBN 978-0-88295-254-3 (alk. paper)
 1. Nature conservation—United States—History—20th century. 2. Environmentalism—United States—History—20th century. 3. United States-
Environmental conditions—History—20th century. I. Title.
 QH76.W45 2007
 333.720973'0904—dc22
                          2007002508

Cover photograph: El Capitan, Yosemite, by Carleton E. Watkins, ca. 1879.
Library of Congess, LC-DIG-stereo-1s01354.

Manufactured in the United States of America
10 09 08 07 1 2 3 4 5 VP

For Tommy and Angela

FOREWORD

Every generation writes its own history for the reason that it sees the past in the foreshortened perspective of its own experience. This has surely been true of the writing of American history. The practical aim of our historiography is to give us a more informed sense of where we are going by helping us understand the road we took in getting where we are. As the nature and dimensions of American life are changing, so too are the themes of our historical writing. Today's scholars are hard at work reconsidering every major aspect of the nation's past: its politics, diplomacy, economy, society, recreation, mores and values, as well as status, ethnic, race, sexual, and family relations. The lists of series titles that appear at the back of this book will show at once that our historians are ever broadening the range of their studies.

The aim of this series is to offer our readers a survey of what today's historians are saying about the central themes and aspects of the American past. To do this, we have invited to write for the series only scholars who have made notable contributions to the respective fields in which they are working. Drawing on primary and secondary materials, each volume presents a factual and narrative account of its particular subject, one that affords readers a basis for perceiving its larger dimensions and importance. Conscious that readers respond to the closeness and immediacy of a subject, each of our authors seeks to restore the past as an actual present, to revive it as a living reality. The individuals and groups who figure in the pages of our books appear as real people who once were looking for survival and fulfillment. Aware that historical subjects are often matters of controversy, our authors present their own findings and conclusions. Each volume closes with an extensive critical essay on the writings of the major authorities on its particular theme.

The books in this series are designed for use in both basic and advanced courses in American history, on the undergraduate and graduate levels. Such a series has a particular value these days, when the format of American history courses is being altered to accommodate a greater diversity of reading materials. The series offers a number of distinct advantages. It extends the dimensions of regular course work. Going well beyond the confines of the textbook, it makes clear that the study of our past is, more than the student might otherwise understand, at once complex, profound, and absorbing. It presents that past as a subject of continuing interest and fresh investigation. The work of experts in their respective fields, the series, moreover, puts at the disposal of the reader the rich findings of historical inquiry. It invites the reader to join, in major fields of research, those who are pondering anew the central themes and aspects of our past. And it reminds the reader that in each successive generation of the ever-changing American adventure, men and women and children were attempting, as we are now, to live their lives and to make their way.

John Hope Franklin
A. S. Eisenstadt

CONTENTS

Foreword / VII
Acknowledgments / XI

INTRODUCTION / 1

CHAPTER ONE: **Roots and Progressive Era Conservation** / 13
Early Conservation in the Country and City / 18
Preserving the Urban Environment / 29
The Lungs of a City / 32
National Conservation / 34
Preserving America's Wildlife and Lands / 45
The Battle for Hetch Hetchy / 60
Sanitary Reform / 65
Conclusion / 72
Endnotes / 74

CHAPTER TWO: **Environmental Reform in the 1920s, 1930s,
  and 1940s** / 79
*Natural Resource Conservation in a Conservative Era:
  1921–1933* / 82
New Deal Conservation / 96
Pollution Control / 108
The Wilderness Debate / 114
Toward a Land Ethic / 124
Conclusion / 128
Endnotes / 130

CHAPTER THREE: **The Emergence of an Environmental Movement, 1945–1973** / 135
Air Pollution Issues, 1945–1965 / 139
Damming a National Monument / 143
The Wilderness Act of 1964 and the Fight for the Grand Canyon / 151
Of Nukes and Pests: Fallout and Silent Spring / 157
Women in the Movement / 166
After Silent Spring / 167
Legislative Victories / 178
Conclusion / 183
Endnotes / 185

CHAPTER FOUR: **Institutionalizing Environmentalism and Protecting Gains, 1970s to 1990s** / 189
The Energy Crisis / 194
The Antinuclear Movement and Appropriate Technology / 197
The Endangered Species Act and Wildlife Preservation / 204
Ecosystem Protection: The Everglades and Marjory Stoneman Douglas / 209
The Love Canal and Toxic Wastes / 213
The Reagan Revolution / 217
The Third Wave and Alternative Movements / 222
Environmental Politics after Reagan / 237
Conclusion / 242
Endnotes / 249

Bibliographical Essay / 253
Index / 287
Photographs follow page 188

ACKNOWLEDGMENTS

When I first pitched the idea for this book to Harlan Davidson's publisher, Andrew Davidson, he grasped its value immediately and advised me to move forward on the project. Since that time, he has been very supportive of my goals for the book and understanding of my need to balance work on it with my other professional duties and personal responsibilities. I appreciate his encouragement and advice. Series editors John Hope Franklin and Abraham S. Eisenstadt provided sound advice on how to improve the manuscript and make it more engaging for the reader. Referees Paul Sutter and Char Miller's wonderfully incisive comments pointed to important areas where my argument could be strengthened. I especially appreciate Professor Sutter's ideas on New Deal conservation. Lucy Herz did a wonderful job with copy editing the final draft and collecting photographs.

My colleagues at Central Washington University took a keen interest in the project and provided me with much encouragement. Roxanne Easley, John Herum, Daniel Herman, and Karen Blair were valuable editors and readers. They offered astute comments about my argument and narrative. Central Washington University generously supported me with a summer research leave and a sabbatical that were essential in bringing this book to a conclusion.

In producing a synthetic work such as this, I racked up a considerable intellectual debt to other scholars in the field. After several decades, environmental history has become rich in extra-ordinary scholarship with new works coming out all the time. I dreaded receiving the latest issues of environmental journals, wondering what new articles and books I would need to rush off and consult, thereby making revision of the manuscript necessary. My debts are evident in the footnotes and bibliography, but there are a few scholars who deserve particular mention. Clayton Koppes, Samuel Hays, Richard Judd, Martin Melosi, Richard Grove, Char Miller, Stephen Fox, David Schuyler, John Cumbler, Glenda Riley, Jennifer Price, and David Stradling were essential to my understanding of the origins of conservation and the Progressive era. Paul Sutter, Kendrick Clements, Donald Swain, Thomas Dunlap, Richard West Sellars, Sarah Phillips and Neil Maher have done some groundbreaking work on the relatively neglected 1920–45 period. Samuel Hays, Adam Rome, Scott Hamilton Dewey, Mark Harvey, Allan Winkler, Kirkpatrick Sale, Robert Gottlieb, Richard Andrews, Langdon Winner, Mark Dowie, Philip Shabecoff, and Hal Rothman have covered well the environmental movement in the post–World War II period.

My greatest debt, of course, is to my family. I am grateful to my father, in-laws, sisters, and aunts who have supported my immediate family in so many ways. Their generosity has been humbling. My wife, Pamela, sacrificed the most in supporting me in this endeavor as I sat hunched over a computer screen for hours on end. She will be happy to know that she has her husband back. I will get started on that to-do list right away. My children, Angela and Tommy, have also waited patiently, and sometimes not so patiently, even if they did not understand why their dad could not play with them. It has been a joy watching them grow up, and it is to them that this book is dedicated.

INTRODUCTION

In the canon of the conservation movement, John Muir, Gifford Pinchot, and Theodore Roosevelt, stand as a dysfunctional Holy Trinity. Their story has been told many times. Muir, the Scottish hermit and prophet of the Yosemite Valley in California, led what historians have labeled the *preservationist* wing of the conservation movement. Muir's preservationists sought to protect wilderness areas for their aesthetic, rather than economic, value by establishing national parks and wilderness refuges. His friend and ally, Gifford Pinchot, founded the U.S. Forest Service and the forestry profession itself. Serving as Theodore Roosevelt's chief conservation advisor, Pinchot helped to convince the president to create most of the country's protected national forests, but he also helped craft a modern state capable of managing and regulating natural resources. Muir had his influence on the president, too. They struck up a friendship when Muir led Roosevelt on a tour of Yosemite. There he encouraged the president to set aside more land for parks. While Pinchot and Muir shared a commitment to saving nature, they differed in critical ways. As chief forester, Pinchot was a "utilitarian" *conservationist*, who protected resources for their commercial value. "There are just two things on this material earth," he wrote, "people and natural resources. . . . [A] constant and sufficient supply of natural resources is the basic human problem."[1] Muir did not see resources as coming from nature, but from the hand of God. Nature was "open to the Divine Soul, dissolved in the mysterious incomparable Spirit of holy Light!"[2] Tragically this difference between the two men defined and fractured the conservation movement. When Pinchot supported the construction of San Francisco's dam in Yosemite National Park, John Muir repudiated his old camping partner and rallied preservationists around the country to fight construction of the dam. Caught between two feuding friends, Teddy Roosevelt proved himself a utilitarian by coming down on Pinchot's side. The Hetch Hetchy Dam was approved in 1913. Heartbroken over the betrayal by his friends, John Muir died a year later. The conservation movement did not recover from its divisions for decades, and Pinchot and Roosevelt saw their own policies blunted by subsequent administrations.

The close and conflict-ridden relationship of Muir and Pinchot laid down lines of division in the movement that endured for a century and now forms the soul of every standard narrative of the conservation (later environmental) movement. Captivated by the drama of the story and following their own interest in nature protection, historians have tended to focus on Muir's wilderness preservation and Pinchot's natural resource management. By contrast, pollution and urban environmental problems received limited attention from them. Big trees and grand vistas mattered more to scholars than filthy city streets, sewage-choked rivers, and smog-bound skies. Historians have also portrayed the conservation movement as an American-born phenomenon, generated by federal administrators such as Pinchot. Because conservationists such as Pinchot and Roosevelt came from privileged backgrounds, historians argued that the movement emerged from the interests of wealthy elites around the turn of the twentieth century.

In the last fifteen years, historians are rethinking the sources and diversity of conservationism and environmentalism, and especially how race, class, and gender influenced the movements. The new environmental history pushes back the movement's beginning to the mid-nineteenth century, tracing its birth to more humble circumstances. Historians have exposed the layers of class and racial conflict involved in the movement. Scholars have also found extensive international ties between conservationists in America and Europe. Consequently, a new synthetic study is essential for the student of history to gain a richer perspective.

Preserving the Nation argues that the contemporary conservation and environmental movements grew out of America's particular, and even peculiar, responses to nature and the dynamics of global industrial expansion and political modernization. In the late-nineteenth century, three related movements developed in response to the depletion of natural resources, damaged land in rural areas, and blight in the cities caused by population growth, the international market, and industrialization. What linked these movements was popular support for government involvement in environmental decisions, rather than simply relying on private interests and the market for solutions. People now wanted to conserve natural resources and the environment so that future generations could enjoy a healthy comfortable lifestyle. The first of the three new movements, conservationism, favored the efficient management of natural resources for production. The second, preservationism, sought to preserve scenic and wilderness areas. The third movement, urban environmentalism, was driven by reformers to control industrial pollution and cure urban decay. These three movements succeeded in expanding government authority over resources and environmental issues and used scientific expertise to solve problems. Politically powerful and widely admired, conservationism's resource management overshadowed the other two movements until the 1950s. Conservation reached its apex in the 1930s when the Great Depression led to Franklin Roosevelt's New Deal programs designed to spur employment and rehabilitation of impoverished areas both urban and in the wild. The success and popularity of FDR's programs expanded the constituency for conservation beyond elites to working-class Americans, setting the stage for a mass movement after World War II. While advocates of resource conservation contributed to modern environmental thought their concern with the depletion of natural resources and advocacy for government solutions to environmental problems, it was the preservation movement and urban environmentalism that coalesced to form a different movement from its conservation-minded predecessor. This renamed "environmental" movement emerged out of the accelerating effects of modernization, affluence, scientific discovery, and suburbanization that led the public to value outdoor amenities and a healthy environment. Movement advocates focused less on the efficient use of resources that conservationists called for and more on creating healthy ecosystems and healthy people free of risks from pollution and hazardous wastes. Environmentalism enjoyed widespread popular support and bipartisan appeal by 1970. The movement won legislative victories in the interests of its wealthy and middle-class members, creating a large government regulatory apparatus at the local, state, and federal levels. But it gave short shrift to the environmental needs of the poor and racial minorities. Only in recent decades have environmentalists reached out to these marginalized groups. Under the influence of 1960s antiwar and civil rights activists, environmental groups questioned the value of unchecked economic expansion and population growth on the environment. Their critique of America's growth ethic and call for restrictions on use of resources put environmentalists on a collision course with political conservatives who championed capitalism unfettered by environmental regulations and conservationists who supported using natural resources, not locking them up. By the end of the twentieth century, the environmental movement had lost its bipartisan appeal and some of its influence in a Republican-dominated federal government, leaving the movement unsure of its future course.

A word is necessary about the terms used in this book. *Conservationism* is the term that contemporary people gave to environmental activism at the turn of the twentieth century. Conservationists were individuals who were troubled by the effects of America's rapid industrialization, urbanization, and use of resources and sought to moderate their impact on the environment. They rejected the long-held belief that the nation's resources were inexhaustible. To preserve America's way of life, conservationists sought to regulate the consumption of resources. For example, they favored the controlled harvesting of timber in order to sustain the supply for generations, rather than leaving the decision to mow down forests to unregulated capitalism.

As historian Clayton Koppes argued, two values motivated conservationists: efficiency and equity. Conservationists valued the efficient consumption of resources under the oversight of trained experts in government agencies. Engineers were to use applied science to look at problems with a long-term perspective rather than the short-term one favored by business interests. Conservation sought to restrain unchecked capitalism with a modicum of government oversight. By 1900, the conservation movement was led by efficiency-minded experts such as Gifford Pinchot, who sought to rationalize resource use.

The goal of efficient management was to be equity—the ideal of being just, impartial, and fair. All citizens owned the nation's natural resources, conservationists argued, and these should not be used to profit a few capitalists. Gifford Pinchot asked rhetorically, "For whose benefit shall they [natural resources] be conserved—for the benefit of the many, or for the use and profit of the few?"[3] Equitably managed resources, then, could liberate the masses economically and politically. In practice, the ideal was often sacrificed to efficiency and probusiness development when equity proved incompatible with them. But there were times, such as during the New Deal programs, when conservation policy was used as the means to redistribute wealth to Americans in need of work and rehabilitate impoverished areas.

At the same time that the conservation movement started, Koppes argues, defenders of "wilderness" whose aesthetic values drove their political activism launched a second movement. These activists sought to preserve wildlife and scenic areas for recreation and contemplation. As wildlife and pristine areas disappeared due to economic and physical expansion, middle-class Americans from the nation's urban areas rose up to protect them. Members of this *preservation* movement feared that the loss of America's scenic resources would lead to a loss of the nation's frontier identity and the virility of American men. Preserving these resources ensured that future generations of men could test their American manhood through sport in the wild. After the 1930s, ecological arguments began to augment the preservationist emphasis on the scenic in their arguments for saving nature. Thus the movement shifted away from anthropocentric (or human-centered) justifications for preserving wilderness and wildlife to biocentric (meaning that all life forms have value) rationalizations that had more scientific legitimacy. As a result, science became as vital to the preservationists, especially after 1945, as to the conservationists. Now there was a great deal of overlap between preservationists and resource conservationists. People often thought of themselves as favoring both, and leaned one way or the other depending on the issue at hand. Preservationists even called themselves conservationists until the 1960s, which made for a great deal of confusion and debate over who was a true conservationist. The term *preservationist* will be used to denote the defenders of aesthetics. *Conservationist* will be reserved for those advocating the efficient use of natural resources. *Conservationism* will describe the movement as a whole up until the 1960s when activists started to refer to the movement as *environmentalism*.

A third group consisted of *urban environmental reformers*. Like resource conservationists and preservationists, who often supported urban reform, these activists came from the educated middle class and shared a moral, Progressive ideology. The goals of urban reformers were often seen as distinct from those of conservationists and preservationists because of their limitation to improving urban conditions. The cleanup of garbage, sewage, pollution, and the establishment of city parks were the issues that animated urban reformers. Believing that sordid environments led to social decay, this group was the most likely of the three to cross class boundaries to improve conditions for the poor and other marginalized groups.

By the 1960s, activists began to use the term *environmentalism* as a way to differentiate between the concerns of the older movement and values that emerged after World War II. As historian Samuel Hays has noted, where conservation focused on resource efficiency, the new movement stressed quality-of-life issues such as controlling damage from pollution and pesticides and aesthetic and ecological preservation. The movement shifted away from the heavy emphasis on efficient production (conservation) to human consumption of a healthy and pleasing environment. The new movement represented a fusion of those who favored wilderness preservation with those who had fought for a cleaner urban environment. Although urban environmentalists had been active since the nineteenth century, their issues became national concerns mainly after World War II. Conservationists contributed their own concerns for industrialization's ill effects and the use of natural resources to the worldview of environmentalists. But, the values of preservationists and those focused on urban industrial problems were elevated above those of resource conservationists, favoring the efficient use of resources, alienating the latter group from the others.

My work brings to light a number of historical themes. First, America's economic modernization played a formative role in conservationism and environmentalism. Commercial and industrial growth created scarcities of resources and environmental degradation both in the countryside and the city. The public responded to modernization by trying to restore an earlier age when resources were abundant and to a degree equitably distributed, and the environment contributed to the well being of white Americans. The growth of a consumerist, leisure-based society and the vicissitudes of a capitalist economy in the 1920s and 1930s led to further changes in the movement, as its activists tried to adapt to the widespread use of the automobile and the resulting recreational abuse of the environment by sightseers, campers, and sportsmen. The Great Depression supplied the justification for a massive federal commitment to conservation programs as a spur to job creation and a stimulus to economic expansion in poor communities. Further economic changes altered the nature of conservationism to evolve into an environmental movement after World War II. Postwar affluence and suburbanization created a new society that focused less on its subsistence and more on its amenities, such as an aesthetically pleasing and healthy environment.

This book also emphasizes the important role of the international community as a source of inspiration and ideas for the American conservation movement. Industrialized before America and confronting resource problems in their colonies, European nations developed conservation policies early on. European countries became the destination for many a reformer researching solutions to America's persistent environmental problems. Through 1920 and even later, there was a regular exchange of ideas and experts between Europe and America. Conservation was an international phenomenon.

Class, race, and gender were also important in the evolution of conservationism and environmentalism. Conservation had humble origins, but swiftly changed into a hobby of the well-to-do. Thereafter some reformers alternately tried to cross class boundaries to solve the environmental problems of the poor, while others lived up to their elitist image and focused on the needs of the wealthy and middle-class Americans. In the twentieth century conservationism and environmentalism were largely racially and class exclusive. Environmentalists have only recently sought to address issues important to people of color, such as toxic-waste disposal in poor and minority communities. Women too played a significant role in the evolution and success of environmentalism. Women were not only foot soldiers; they altered the agenda of the movement in response to issues important to them, particularly those that affected their homes and families. More recently, women have used a feminist analysis to offer a critique of environmentalism.

Many scholars have pointed to the important role the conservation and environmental movements have played in state-building. In struggling to control mighty economic and demographic forces that degraded the environment, the public repeatedly turned to local, state, and, finally, the federal government for redress. Government regulation of the environment expanded at all levels, not just the federal. As resource and environmental problems grew in complexity and crossed city and state boundaries, interstate cooperation and later federal intervention was necessary to solve them. The movement, then, in developing government policies and programs that improved the environment while fostering economic security, personal happiness, and well-being, helped the American people have faith in and favor greater government power in their lives.

Preserving the Nation is divided into four chapters. The first details the story of the conservation movement from the mid-nineteenth century to 1920. It demonstrates that moves to conserve natural resources and preserve the country's primal forests and scenic wonders started earlier than standard histories admit and drew extensively on international sources for inspiration and ideas. The movement included not only the conservation of the country-side, forests, and lakes, but also urban concerns about hygiene and places of respite. This early movement emerged out of the ill effects of industrialization in the cities and the rapid consumption of natural resources. Progressive era–politics favoring government activism provided a means of implementing conservation policies and the creation of resource bureaucracies. Conservation was, then, an instrument in crafting the modern American state.

Chapter Two describes conservationism of the interwar period. Efficiency-minded conservationist experts in various fields took the initiative away from citizen activists. The burgeoning economy of the 1920s and technological developments such as the automobile ferried many more Americans out to see and play in nature, but they abused it once there. This development alarmed people fighting to preserve a wilderness, and they sought to restrict public access to wild country by limiting road construction. With the onset of the Great Depression in the 1930s, Franklin D. Roosevelt's New Deal used conservation projects to employ millions of citizens and rehabilitate rural areas. Increased leisure time, technology such as the automobile, and New Deal–conservation policy expanded the constituency for conservation and outdoor recreation, which set the stage for dramatic growth in these areas in the postwar period.

The evolution of the environmental movement between 1945 and 1973 is the subject of the third chapter. Concerns over rising levels of affluence, suburbanization, and the Cold War marked a shift away from an emphasis on supplying basic human needs to the values of a consumer society, where a healthy environment was seen as part of a new standard of living and a growing awareness of the fragility of life on earth. Atmospheric testing of nuclear weapons was a key trigger to mass awareness of the insidious nature of contaminants in the environment. Matters that had once been peripheral subjects for most people, such as pollution and pesticides, became central concerns. As more citizens became part of the middle class, the environmental movement grew substantially. The protests and activism of the sixties broadened the movement's constituency to America's youth and diversified its tactics. Some of these activists, however, brought with them an antibusiness attitude that began to alienate political conservatives and businesspeople from the movement. Nevertheless, Earth Day 1970 marked the culmination of two decades of rising environmental activism, greater federal regulation, and the beginning of a mass movement unified around the need to control the worst effects of modern living.

Chapter Four studies environmentalism from 1973 to 2000. Unlike the previous period of abundance, economic decline, rising fuel prices, and constrained federal budgets defined this era early on. While environmentalism had once been a bipartisan issue, after 1973 the movement's base narrowed as Republicans grew more conservative and less friendly to the regulation of private and business activity. The environmental movement now found itself best represented by the Democrats. This limited environmentalism's influence and marked the beginning of a countermovement bent on rolling back environmental gains to spur economic growth. Also troubling was that while environmental organizations became key players in Washington, they had to deal with dissent from within their own ranks. The influx into the environmental movement of activists from the 1960s and the population at large created a more diverse movement but also exacerbated conflict over ideology and tactics. Radicals, feminists, and people of color criticized the movement for its acceptance of the capitalist system, patriarchal values, and its lily-white history. The result of the conflict was the formation of a bewildering array of organizations that offered a variety of critiques of American society and focused on multiple issues and tactics. Such diversity was often an asset, but it also meant that the movement lacked coherence and unity. As the federal government was taken over by environmentalism's enemies in the 1990s, the movement struggled over how best to respond. In the new century, the environmental movement has become a paradox. Organizationally, it has never been broader in appealing to all strata of society. But not since the 1920s has the movement been so impotent. Americans voiced support for environmental goals, but their substantive commitment remained weak. This has led to a debate over the usefulness of the movement's founding principles and direction, with some activists declaring that after more than a century of development, environmentalism should die so that a new progressive movement could be born. Escaping the past, however appealing that might be, has rarely been easy or desirable.

Endnotes

1 Gifford Pinchot, *Breaking New Ground* (New York: Harcourt Brace, 1947; reprint, Washington, DC: Island Press, 1987), 325.

2 Michael P. Cohen, *The Pathless Way: John Muir and American Wilderness* (Madison: University of Wisconsin Press, 1984), 65.

3 Clayton R. Koppes, "Efficiency/Equity/ Esthetics: Towards a Reinterpretation of American Conservation," *Environmental Review* 11, no. 2 (Summer 1987): 130.

CHAPTER ONE

Roots and Progressive Era Conservation

His time serving the William Howard Taft administration had been difficult for Gifford Pinchot. The nation's head of the Forest Service had operated successfully, pushing reform of natural-resource management under presidents William McKinley and Theodore Roosevelt, but by 1910 he doubted the commitment to conservation of the new president and his secretary of the interior, Richard Ballinger. The chief forester concluded that Taft and Ballinger were at least partly complicit in what he believed was a fraudulent transfer of federal coal land in Alaska to the Morgan-Guggenhiem syndicate. Pinchot believed that such a transfer was a violation of "the people's interest."[1] During the Roosevelt administration, the president had often prevented such transfers by executive order. But Taft and Ballinger did not take such an expansive view of presidential authority and refused to investigate the claims of fraud. Pinchot believed that aggressive use of presidential power was necessary to implement his envisioned conservation program. Taft and Ballinger's intransigence was at best because they did not believe in a Rooseveltian view of power and at worst because they were in cahoots with special interests. Either way, Pinchot thought that the "people's interest" was being sacrificed. Taft, he later wrote, was the "accomplice and the refuge of land grabbers, water-power grabbers, grabbers of timber and oil—all the swarm of big and little thieves and near thieves." For his part, Taft dismissed the meddlesome Pinchot as "too much a radical and a crank" who saw conspiracies everywhere.[2] The president was inclined to think that his role was to encourage private initiative through a judicious distribution of public resources. When asked by a reporter what Pinchot thought the stakes were in his conflict with Taft and Ballinger, he replied that the conservation of public lands was a matter of economics and morality. First, he stated, "The forest is not alone useful for the timber we get from it: there are streams, recreation grounds, shade and comfort, and fertile soil." He asked, "[W]ho is to get the benefit of conservation of the forests?" That second question is not one of economics, it is greater, for it is primarily a question of morals." Pinchot warned that "the time fast approaches when we shall have to decide whether men or dollars control the country." If it was to be dollars, he continued, "we shall ourselves destroy the equality of opportunity" that was at the heart of the American story.[3]

Eventually, Taft decided to remove Pinchot from his post for insubordination, but the chief forester was proud of it. Pinchot was informed in a letter from the president that "by your own conduct you have destroyed your usefulness as a helpful subordinate of the Government." He displayed the letter to his mother announcing, "I'm fired." "[M]y mother's eyes flashed, she threw back her head, flung one hand high above it, and answered with one word: 'Hurrah!'"[4] "Great Rejoicing," Pinchot's mother recorded in her diary. Savoring the moment, she noted, "Lots of reporters," which was exactly what her son wanted. Being removed from his post allowed Pinchot to freely attack the Taft administration. He went on to lead a rebellion within the Republican Party against Taft's perceived failure to live up to Roosevelt's legacy of conservation.

The Ballinger-Pinchot controversy, as it came to be known, eventually brought down the Taft administration. With the urging of Pinchot and others, Theodore Roosevelt came out of retirement and challenged Taft for the presidency in 1912. But Woodrow Wilson defeated both of them, and the movement for a broad, integrated conservation program that Pinchot advocated was never quite the same again.

More than the intrigue of it, the Ballinger-Pinchot affair was important in revealing the central place conservation had assumed in executive administration and national politics. Just twenty years earlier, there was no Forest Service, nor for that matter were there any national forests. But by 1910, the conservation issue could bring down a president. In the nineteenth century, most Americans assumed that the function of the federal government was to place public lands and resources in private hands, as Ballinger and Taft had allowed. By the early twentieth century, a large section of the population supported Pinchot's view that the federal government was to keep, administer, and manage the public lands for the benefit of the greatest number, a huge extension in federal power and a remarkable shift in public opinion. Conservation became a means to expand federal, especially executive, authority and convince the public to embrace a more robust central authority.

Pinchot's analysis of what conservation stood for in the controversy was illuminating, although not necessarily as the chief forester intended. The twin and often conflicting elements of economics and morality were constantly in play in conservation outcomes, and often conservationists were not on the side of the people, as Pinchot liked to think. Conservation was often practical economics: simply a means of using resources more efficiently to ensure their long-term use. One historian argued that "the crux of the gospel of efficiency lay in a rational and scientific method of making basic technological decisions through a single, central authority."[5] This frequently did not lead to democratic outcomes. Conservationists often found it easier to achieve their objectives by working with large corporations rather than with small landowners. While claiming to pursue efficiency, conservation bureaucracies were also swayed by powerful political interests and their own desire to grow. Conservation, in this view, was not, as its practitioners claimed, a democratic initiative of the people versus big business, but a messier process imposed from above that bowed to political reality and economic imperatives. Some scholars have even gone so far as to claim that the needs of the poor mattered little: "Americans often pursued environmental quality at the expense of social justice."[6]

And yet, morality mattered. Conservation was rooted in a moralistic impulse to achieve equity in resource use. Pinchot oversimplified the issue as one of good versus evil when he said that conservation was to prevent "the useless sacrifice of the public welfare, and to make possible hereafter the utilization of the natural resources and the natural advantages for the benefit of all the people instead of merely for the profit of a few."[7] But there was some substance to his statement. Many conservation policies crossed class boundaries. They actually benefited the poor more than the middle class by focusing on environmental problems that inordinately affected poor communities. There were many reformers like Pinchot who were troubled by the course of industrialization and sought to control it. Popular support for conservation had been building for some time. Although conservation was controlled by the elites by 1900, it had more humble origins in America's farms and cities, which led to the formation of state and local bureaucracies to deal with environmental issues. By the time of the Ballinger-Pinchot controversy, there was a large constituency in favor of the kind of conservation Pinchot preached and the government apparatus that went with it. In sum, the impetus for conservation was a broad reaction by Americans of all classes to the new commercial and industrial realities of the nineteenth century. Conservation, as historian Richard Judd contends, "was a grass-roots phenomenon."[8]

Grassroots in origins, but global in scope, conservationism was an international process that affected America's rural communities and expanding cities. Conservation began in Europe in the mid-eighteenth century, as the growth of market economies and industrialization heightened the demand for scarce resources and created appalling urban conditions. The environmental degradation of European colonies due to resource extraction accelerated the calls by scientists for government management of essential resources such as timber, coal, and water to produce sustained economic growth. America's rise to conservationism must be seen in part as a response to Euro-American colonial expansion. Conservation was part of the conquest of colonial lands desired for their abundant natural resources to fuel economic expansion and industrialization. Focused on continental expansion, America lagged behind European nations in industrial and economic development. Its citizens came late to conservation and turned to Europe for solutions, as Pinchot did in studying forestry in France and Germany.

Similarly, European urban reformers inspired Americans to clean up their cities. As the world's leading industrial nation, England was the chief destination for Americans searching for answers to sewage and garbage disposal, city-park design, and pollution clean-up. This sharing of ideas between Europe and the United States continued to be particularly active in the early decades of the twentieth century. Urban environmental reformers, like other Progressive activists of the era, argues historian Daniel Rogers, served as "brokers and intermediaries" of social policy and ideas exchanged between countries.[9]

Nevertheless, American conservationism was more than a carbon copy of its Atlantic neighbors. American conservation bore the unique stamp of national identity and democratic politics. Perhaps in no other country was nature seen as such an essential part of a nation's identity. Americans believed that their wild country served as the basic material that formed their republican government. European policies, moreover, were ill-suited to American laissez-faire capitalism and its decentralized governance. The rise of powerful nation-states in Western Europe and the unrestrained discretion government officials enjoyed in their colonies allowed them to formulate policy with little regard for democratic consensus-building. This was not true of America. Daniel Rogers noted of New World reformers that "every imported idea and scheme was by necessity, multiply transformed" by the reformer's own sense of what was politically possible and by the "distinctive pressures of American political circumstances that came to bear on it."[10]

American conservationists, like other reformers of the period, had their work cut out for them. They needed to build a public consensus around two propositions. The urban and natural environments, they argued, were a commons—property owned by all citizens—to be managed for the general good. The power and scope of state and federal government, they added, needed to be expanded to manage the commons. Accomplishing this was no small feat in a nation whose citizens believed that their economic prosperity and freedom came from unfettered control of private property and a light touch by politicians. That reformers like Pinchot were partly successful in this endeavor was their most important legacy.

Early Conservation in the Country and City

Scholars have argued that Americans did not practice conservation before the movement emerged in the late nineteenth century. Garret Hardin argued that Darwinian struggle ruled "common" lands, or land that was owned by colonial towns and not yet subdivided for individual use. On these lands, residents grazed their animals, hunted, fished, and collected resources such as timber. In his famous essay "The Tragedy of the Commons," Hardin argued that this arrangement was environmentally unstable. Residents' self-interest, he claimed, compelled them to take more than their fair share of resources. Greed prevented collective regulation to avoid depleting the land. But Hardin's analysis, at least when applied to America, did not fit. Residents did govern the commons, and there was much local law and custom controlling resource use. Conservation was a very old concept in rural America.

In his study of rural communities in northern New England, Richard Judd found that residents regulated their commons communally to allow them to live "less expensively and more democratically." In Europe, royalty controlled many common resources, especially game animals and timber. In America the commons became a source of individual freedom, but one subject to local control. New Englanders believed that the commons should be used equitably to preserve their long-term value. Residents who violated this code could find themselves pariahs. One resident of Lancaster, New Hampshire, tried to hunt down nearly one hundred moose in one winter, a "diabolical waste" according to other residents. He was banished from town.[11] As this example suggests, until the nineteenth century, conservation was a local affair. The state and federal governments rarely intervened.

Similarly, historian Steven Stoll argues that early nineteenth-century reformist farmers along the eastern seaboard were forerunners of ecological thought, though they never thought of themselves as ecologists. They were the first to recognize the interdependence of organisms and that systems in nature were interconnected. They believed that there had to be a balance between their cleared fields and forest space. One reformer in New York stated that "husbandry, or rural economy, is a science which involves the vegetable and animal economy of the whole creation, and their dependence on each other."[12] They even saw human communities as part of this interdependence.

From these early tendencies, modern forms of conservation emerged from the breakdown of local systems of commons management. It was not individual greed, as Hardin claimed, that undid local control, but increased demand on the commons from population growth, new competitors for the resources like mills and factories, and the penetration of a global market. The abundance of frontier life disappeared, as logging companies overcut forests, hunters killed off wildlife, and mill dams depleted fish runs. Residents responded by trying to restore a past where resources were managed for community benefit. Unable to keep out new competitors, residents appealed to state and federal authorities to protect the commons. In the process, they established a moral case for conservation and began building a government bureaucracy.

In some cases, towns managed to carry out conservation efforts themselves. Fish restoration projects were some of the earliest forms of conservation. Fishing had once been an essential part of foraging practices by New Englanders. One editor remembered better times: "The little brooks and ponds of the country were once alive with . . . pickerel . . . perch, and trout [which] . . . cost [no] more time to take . . . than they were worth." Marked decline in fish runs pushed communities into restocking efforts. As early as 1803, Damariscotta, Maine, stocked ponds and controlled the harvest through a fish committee. Experiments by other towns in New England in stocking pickerel and trout yielded gratifying results.[13]

Communities tangling with large industrial enterprises usually required the intervention of state and federal courts. New England residents and state fish commissions challenged the right of mill operators to erect dams without constructing fish ladders to allow migratory fish to pass. In a landmark case in 1872, Massachusetts won a surprising victory in the U.S. Supreme Court over the Holyoke Waterpower Company. Nineteenth-century courts usually restricted public regulation of dams. But the court argued that the use of rivers "may be regarded as public rights, subject to legislative control" and mandated that the company erect a fishway for shad and salmon.[14] The victory was not enough to rehabilitate New England fisheries, which suffered from poor interstate cooperation and resistance from manufacturers. Still, the widespread efforts to restore fishing runs demonstrated the popularity of conservation.

Conflicting claims to fish harvests required the intervention of higher authorities in the state and federal government. But the management system that evolved reflected the prevailing faith in limited government. By 1876, nineteen states had fish commissions to help settle disputes over fishing rights between farmers, prosperous sports fishermen, and industries whose operations often polluted rivers or impeded fish migrations. Invariably, the commissions lacked strong enforcement power and favored solutions that were popular rather than scientifically sound. Unable to satisfy competing interests, fish commissions opted to make the pie bigger for all by breeding more fish through the science of fish culture.

Fish culture at the state level, however, usually failed due to interstate rivalry and limited resources. Eventually the federal government took over. In 1871, Congress created the U.S. Commission on Fish and Fisheries, one of the first federal conservation agencies in the nation's history. The Fish Commission became the national leader in fish culture. Fish hatcheries were pioneered in Europe and hailed as a panacea in America. Spencer Baird, head of the U.S. Fish Commission, bragged that when salmon "come under the hands of the fish-culturist, it is acknowledged . . . to exceed all other species which are propagated, in hardiness, in tenacity of life, and in freedom from tendency to disease."[15]

But scientists soon discovered that they could not create a fisherman's utopia. Their understanding of the life cycle of fish was primitive. Fish culturists in the Pacific Northwest had not even established that different types of salmon existed. Even if they had worked from solid knowledge, their options to save fish were limited. The federal government could not force states to limit fishing, and so the Fish Commission's only option was to breed more fish. But hatcheries came nowhere near the success predicted of them. Atlantic and Pacific salmon runs continued to plummet throughout the century.

When fish hatcheries failed, conflict ensued. Economic developments often determined the outcome. The number of farmers engaged in subsistence production declined, as did the power of commercial fishermen. By contrast, the number of sports fishermen expanded dramatically, as economic prosperity increased leisure time. Regulators moved into an alliance with sportsmen who seemed more willing to abide by game laws. By the end of the century, fish conservation had devolved into supplying sports fishermen with game fish, and the laws tended to favor them over the needs of commercial and subsistence fishermen.

Despite a decline in their power, New England's rural residents were able to establish the principle of common access to resources. When states tried to preserve fisheries by limiting access to fishing, subsistence users rose in protest. Private property owners supported limited access to streams in hopes of establishing private fishing and hunting clubs. Vermont passed a law in 1876 restricting public fishing rights to navigable bodies of water, which opponents attacked as favoring wealthy sportsmen. Ultimately courts limited the reach of the law and gave fishermen access to most waters, even when they flowed across private property.[16]

Farmers also influenced evolving concepts of forest conservation. Agricultural concerns for maintaining a balance between forest and field fit with studies on deforestation. It was the son of a Vermont farmer, the knowledgable George Perkins Marsh, who wrote the most important environmental study of the nineteenth century, one that justified the establishment of major forest reserves throughout the United States and the world. Marsh, better than any figure of his time, embodied both the native and foreign sources of the conservation impulse in America. He was born in 1801, the son of a prominent lawyer and farmer. Like many later environmental advocates, Marsh was a precocious child who spent much time outdoors and was drawn to nature study. He claimed he was "forest born." "The bubbling brook, the trees, the flowers, the wild animals were to me persons not things."[17] An avid fisherman and outdoorsman as a young boy, he collected plant and animal life for study, a hobby he carried into adulthood. From these varied experiences he drew connections between the extensive cutting of timber and the desiccation (drying out) and erosion of soils. But natural sciences alone could not hold his interests. By the time he attended Dartmouth College at the age of fifteen, he was an accomplished linguist, having mastered French, Greek, Italian, Latin, Portuguese, and Spanish—he eventually became fluent in twenty languages—enabling him to read the European conservation writers. After a stint as a lawyer, Marsh ran for the House of Representatives and served Vermont from 1843 to 1849. As good a naturalist as he was, his most notable achievement in Washington was to help establish the Smithsonian Institution.

Congressman Marsh's writing already exhibited a strong understanding of the links between human action and environmental change. In a speech before his farming constituency, he hailed the role of farmers in maintaining a balanced environment and warned of the consequences of excessive tree cutting. Undoubtedly aware of the conservation efforts of European governments, he exhorted his Vermont neighbors to manage forests as was done across the Atlantic. It was a message his constituents were ready to hear. Farm journals spoke of their concern for deforestation. One farmer warned of a "desolation as awful as that of the Sahara" if New England was cut over by logging interests. Farmers, too, understood the interdependence of forest and field and their economic dependence to a balance of nature. When Marsh spoke of nature as "capital" and its produce as "interest," his farming constituency understood him completely.[18]

Marsh brought his gospel of conservation to wildlife management in Vermont. Several years after leaving Congress and between stints as a diplomat, he served as the Green Mountain State's Fish Commissioner. In 1857 he wrote a report linking the decline in fish stocks on the Connecticut River to economic development. In the report, Marsh gloomily concluded, "We cannot destroy our dams, or provide artificial water-ways for the migration of fish . . . ; we cannot wholly prevent the discharge of deleterious substances from our industrial establishments into our running waters."[19] Regulation he noted might be desirable, but it was politically impossible. Like other fish culturists, Marsh's only solution was fish stocking. Despite its negative tone, the study justified state-level efforts at fish conservation throughout the Northeast.

In the 1850s and 1860s, Marsh completed his environmental education during his extensive diplomatic service in Turkey and Italy. He arrived to find Europe bubbling over with protoconservation thought that surpassed anything the Vermonter had encountered in his home country. France and Germany had long established forestry professions. The French had been particularly active in trying to manage the resources in their colonial holdings, especially after their devastating loss to the British in 1763 in the Seven Years War cut their empire and access to raw materials. Thus, European conservation, and later its American counterpart, emerged from the imperial policies of mature nation-states to control less-developed nations and their peoples. Particularly important to French conservation was the island of Mauritius in the Indian Ocean. The French had routinely scoured the island for teak to serve their navy.[20] After 1763, the French changed their approach. Significantly, Pierre Poivre, a former Jesuit priest who had studied Dutch, Indian, and Chinese forestry and horticultural practices, received the appointment as governor of Mauritius. In 1769, over the objections of some colonists, Poivre established an ordinance to limit timber harvests and initiate the replanting of cutover areas. By 1800 Poivre and his successors had a fully staffed forest service. They limited pollution from indigo factories and sugar mills and established regulations to revitalize fish stocks.[21] Based on the perceived link between deforestation and desiccation of the soil, Poivre's policies were the first to address ecological change and human action.

The colonial example soon spread throughout Europe. Despite its remoteness, Europeans copied the Mauritian experience, creating an international exchange of ideas. The French drew heavily on German expertise for forestry techniques. In the 1840s, imported German foresters labored to restore areas eroded by grazing and logging. In Tobago, the British established what might be considered the first forest reserve to control local climate, erosion, and desiccation of soils. In India, first through the British East India Company, the British sought to manage the country's vast forest resources using the same environmental arguments introduced in Mauritius. England borrowed German forest expertise too. The crown made scientific management of the forests a public responsibility by establishing the Indian Forest Department under the guidance of Dietrich Brandis. This German-born forester was a formative influence on the first American trained as a forester, Gifford Pinchot.

Marsh benefited from the European communication network of scientists who traded and published their findings on forestry, soil erosion, and rainfall extensively in books and European journals. But Marsh ranged beyond these narrow studies to analyze the connection between history and environmental change. His conclusions were again pessimistic: "Action by man has brought the face of the earth to a desolation almost as complete as the moon." Fearing the same might happen in America, Marsh predicted that continued excesses might "threaten the depravation, barbarism, and perhaps even extinction of the species."[22]

In 1864, Marsh published his findings in *Man and Nature; or, Physical Geography as Modified by Human Action.* Drawing on works in many languages and examples taken from ancient times, Marsh took issue with the accepted notion that humans always improved upon nature. "Man is everywhere a disturbing agent. Wherever he plants his foot, the harmonies of nature are turned to discords." The decline of empires such as Rome around the Mediterranean Sea and the severe soil erosion there, he speculated, were related to the extensive cutting of forest timber and soil desiccation. Forests held the soil in place and acted as watersheds that allowed for the slow melting of winter snows, thus preventing excessive flooding in the spring. Deforestation led to severe soil erosion, a loss of moisture in the soil, and destructive floods that could wipe out an empire's agriculture. Marsh issued an apocalyptic admonition to his generation that sounded much like the warnings of modern environmentalists. "We are, even now, breaking up the floor and wainscoting and doors and window frames to our dwelling, for fuel to warm our bodies and seethe our pottage, and the world cannot afford to wait till the slow and sure progress of exact science has taught it a better economy."[23] While predicting calamity, however, Marsh did not completely despair. An Enlightenment thinker, Marsh called for new "triumphs of mind over matter" and stewardship of nature.

Some recent scholars have dismissed Marsh's work as derivative or merely synthetic of common knowledge. It is true that many scientists had already noted the destructive link between human action and the environment, but Marsh offered a much more sweeping and interdisciplinary study. Only someone with Marsh's local and global experiences could have done it. Moreover, Marsh displayed ecological insights that there was interdependency among organisms in an ecosystem. "All nature is linked together by invisible bonds; every organic creature . . . is necessary to the well-being of some other." Nor did Marsh's contemporaries minimize his accomplishments. As one reviewer noted, Marsh's thesis came "with the force of a revelation." Decades later Gifford Pinchot declared *Man and Nature* "epoch-making." Foresters in countries as diverse as Italy, France, Australia, South Africa, and Japan admitted the path-breaking importance of the work. Italy passed forestry laws in 1877 and 1888 that heavily copied Marsh's recommendations, and legislators in New Zealand cited his book in calling for legislation to halt the timber cutting that might turn their "land of milk and honey" into a "howling desolation."[24]

By the 1870s, a modernizing America was ready to listen to Marsh's prescriptions. *Man and Nature* became the central text for those trying to justify forest conservation and reforestation efforts. In fact, protecting watersheds (regions draining into river systems) became the key rationale for the 1891 Forest Reserves Act. The legislation empowered the president to set aside tracts of land at the headwaters of watersheds to protect urban water supplies. Using the same logic in part, Theodore Roosevelt's administration tripled the amount of acreage in forest reserves. Even before the federal government could act, states set an example. In New York, Marsh had cited the Adirondack region as an important watershed that was in danger of destruction from deforestation. In 1872 a coalition of sportsmen seeking wildlife protection and industrialists concerned about maintaining year-round water supplies supported legislation to make the Adirondacks, as Marsh suggested, "the inalienable property of the commonwealth."[25] Legislation for creating a forest reserve languished until 1883, when a drought dropped water levels so low that it threatened navigation on the Erie Canal. Legislators halted land sales and in 1892 established the 3-million-acre Adirondack State Park.

The Adirondack legislation enjoyed support from mill owners, wealthy hunters, and forestry advocates. But like their counterparts in New England, residents near the park favored conservation, too. They believed state ownership could protect their subsistence lifestyle. As one resident noted, "People through this valley are very much in favor of the work of the Forest Commission. We need the protection, as the woods are our one source of income."[26] It was only when foresters implemented their own ideas about forest and wildlife conservation that conflict emerged among interest groups with very different ideas of the meaning of conservation.

The Adirondack State Park had been established to protect its tree canopy, but residents refused to relinquish their right to timber cutting for subsistence. Like rural folk elsewhere, residents near the park continued to hold onto the idea that they had a right to the resources on undeveloped, common land. Communities might favor conservation, but they believed that local subsistence use was exempt. In practice, if not in law, such was the case. Although foresters eventually forced an end to illegal logging by timber companies, they were never able to suppress local cutting. Community pressure on foresters and a refusal to testify against neighbors limited the police power of the state. Such flouting of timber and wildlife laws earned locals the condemnation of conservation officials and historians. For example, John Reiger argued that conservation started with elite sportsmen. Farmers and others who scratched out a living "usually made poor nature lovers, primarily seeing wildlife as competitors or sources of profit."[27]

Was conservation solely a project of the affluent? The protection of wildlife in the Adirondacks, like the regulation of fisheries in New England, demonstrated the difficulty of class categorization in conservation fights. Outside sports hunters had a significant impact on wildlife populations, especially on their huge private game reserves. Adirondack residents bitterly resented excesses by the "sports." It was the locals who often formed organizations to protect game from the wealthy.[28] Nor did the state protect only the wealthy interests in the Adirondacks. In response to pressure from less affluent hunters and local communities, the state purchased a number of private game reserves and opened them up for public access. The result was that the Adirondacks served the interests of many classes. Policies evolved through political give-and-take.

Give-and-take was not, however, the universal result of conflicts over common lands. There were significant regional variations. In the post–Civil War South, for example, conflicts erupted over common lands between landowners and subsistence farmers. The clash was a result of the growing penetration of commercial forces into what had been mostly subsistence areas, especially in upcountry regions. After the Civil War, the South was becoming ever more integrated into the international cotton economy. Antebellum agricultural and hunting practices did not fit in. Poor whites and blacks viewed the common lands as "freedom hills," because these people could supplement their crops through hunting and by allowing their cattle and pigs to forage on this land. To support this use of common lands, American colonies as early as 1759 passed "fence laws" requiring farmers to enclose their crops, at great expense, to prevent damage by roaming livestock. But plantation owners pushed game laws and grazing restrictions to reassert control over these lands and, by extension, the freed slaves. The most common solution was to pass "stock laws," which forced owners of livestock to fence in their animals. The Virginia assembly admitted that restriction of this right would cause problems for the less affluent: "Many poor persons have derived advantage from grazing their stock on the commons and unenclosed lands, and to whom the obligation to confine them . . . would operate as a great hardship." Game laws, too, became prevalent in the years after the Civil War. Planters, the *Richmond Times* complained, "suffer great annoyance and serious pecuniary loss from the trespasses of predacious negroes and low pot hunters, who with dogs and guns, live in the fields . . . as if the whole country belonged to them." To restore the plantation system, a Memphis newspaper called for laws limiting "ranging livestock . . . hunting, fishing, trapping, netting, or seining on another's land without permission." The great fear was that blacks might be able to live independently apart from the white economy. An Alabama paper warned that the freed slaves would raise their own food and animals "and will work no more in the cotton, rice, and sugar fields."[29] Thus, agricultural reformers and conservationists had a receptive audience from the wealthier classes in the South to their proposed solutions. As Reconstruction governments came to an end in the South, state legislatures and county governments passed a host of stock and game laws. Conservation became a means of reinforcing racial and class inequality and control in the region. The Southern example demonstrates how conservation became intimately bound up with the drive for white supremacy.

These regional differences in the nineteenth century set an important precedent for the conservation movement of the Progressive era. The early practices, leadership, and public support for conservation policies emerged in the Northeast. Theodore Roosevelt of New York and Gifford Pinchot of Connecticut and Pennsylvania were only the most famous examples of eastern conservationists. It created a paradox, as Richard Judd put it, in "the political geography of the conservation movement, which was so eastern in its formulation and so western in its application."[30] A conservation philosophy formulated in the East was bound to run into trouble when implemented west of the Mississippi.

Nevertheless, the outlines of a republican form of conservation had emerged. Industrialists and affluent sportsmen had some success in limiting the rights of the poor, commercial hunters, and fishermen. Some conservation laws carried the odor of class and, particularly in the South, racial bias. But in critical ways, rural folk refashioned the ideal of the commons to fit a new individualistic age, and laws and court decisions reflect a compromise between old and new tradition. As one New York forester noted, "A forest law to effect its purpose must rest on a broad and solid basis of public interest."[31] Conservation policy was a product of social conflict and negotiation.

Preserving the Urban Environment

In urban areas, overcrowding, disease, and the loss of open space led to a movement to restore the agrarian ideal of a healthy, pastoral lifestyle through sanitary services and parks. Urban reformers shared several traits with those who advocated conservation of natural resources. They viewed the environment as a commons where the public good prevailed over private interest. In 1870, the Massachusetts Board of Health asserted, "all citizens have an inherent right to the enjoyment of pure and uncontaminated air, and water, and soil, that this right should be regarded as belonging to the whole community, and that no one should be allowed to trespass upon it by his carelessness and avarice."[32] In offering solutions, urban environmental reformers relied on science and the state to solve social conflict. Like their rural counterparts had done in the fishing controversies, urban activists turned first to Europe for ideas.

America's start on urbanization was slow: only 7 in 100 Americans lived in cities in 1820. As a result, American cities suffered from environmental degradation later than their European counterparts and had less experience in solving such problems. The easiest answer to many environmental predicaments could be borrowed from experts in France and England. As early as 1799, in response to yellow fever epidemics, Philadelphia imported Great Britain's Benjamin Henry Latrobe to build a clean water supply system.[33] Latrobe was one of many European experts who helped American city governments resolve sanitation issues. Despite the Philadelphia example, urban environmental reform came in halting steps. That city governments should be responsible for sanitation services was a new concept. Most city fathers saw as their duty the encouragement of private enterprise. Few had taken on a project as large as creating a city water supply system. Most governments had bidden out services to private companies.

Critical to changing attitudes about urban filth was Englishman Edwin Chadwick's study that linked human wastes and garbage with urban epidemics.[34] Chadwick, a barrister who became an environmental activist, was a devotee of Jeremy Bentham, who believed that it was a government's responsibility to promote the general happiness, in his famous phrase, "the greatest good for the greatest number." In the wake of a series of devastating cholera and influenza epidemics, Chadwick joined a commission to investigate sanitary systems. The commission's 1842 study, *Report on the Sanitary Conditions of the Labouring Population of Great Britain*, made the British "sanitary idea" the guiding philosophy of urban clean-up.

Chadwick's report upended traditional notions of disease transmission. The public generally wrote off disease as the fault of the individual or God's will. Since the poor generally suffered more from disease than the rich, their improvidence was thought to have caused their ailments. By arguing that disease had environmental roots, Chadwick concluded the opposite; ill health helped cause poverty. As a Benthamite, Chadwick argued that it was government's responsibility to develop sewerage systems for the public good.

As much as the sanitary idea was an advance in disease prevention, it was based on faulty science. Mid-nineteenth century health reformers incorrectly concluded that miasmas—deadly gases—from garbage and sewage were the cause of disease. The "germ theory" of disease transmission did not take over until the end of the century. But in advocating sanitation, reformers did the right thing albeit for the wrong reason.[35] Chadwick and his American counterparts helped create what John Cumbler claims was a "transatlantic intellectual community" of sanitation reformers who anticipated the international reformist community of the Progressive era.[36]

Inspired by Chadwick's report, American reformers pushed for government sanitation services for waste treatment, garbage collection, and pollution. In the 1850s, Brooklyn and Chicago became the first municipalities with planned sewer lines. As in forestry, however, the reform impulse was strongest in New England, a densely populated and industrialized region. Just eight years after Chadwick's report, Massachusetts repeated the study in its *Report of the Sanitary Commission*, documenting the link between filth and disease. The study was widely circulated, but practical measures did not come until after the Civil War.

In the 1860s and 1870s, Northeastern states established boards of health to deal with pollution and refuse collection. Health boards represented a fundamental shift away from the traditional hands-off role of the government. The Connecticut board discerned "a conviction on the part of those acquainted with the rapidly growing pollution of our streams that the time had arrived when the interference of the state jurisdiction was imperatively needed."[37] Despite their affluent backgrounds, the health board members were particularly concerned about protecting the health of marginalized groups. In 1884 the New Hampshire board worried that "pure air and pure water are essential to the perfect development and good health of every individual . . . . [But the poor] usually are obliged to rely on the most dangerous sources."[38]

Massachusetts led the way with one of the most aggressive health boards. Physician Henry Ingersol Bowditch chaired the commission. Bowditch was a self described "radical" who believed he was destined "to do battle for justice and the oppressed."[39] Bowditch became an ardent advocate of government activism in defense of the poor. Like other sanitary reformers, Bowditch drew heavily on studies and legislation emanating from Europe to form his own ideas about reform in America. Following his recommendations, the state legislature passed a pollution bill in 1878 that effectively prohibited the dumping of untreated human and industrial waste into rivers. The bill exempted some of the state's most important industrial centers on the Connecticut and Merrimack Rivers and met with fierce resistance to its enforcement, but in words, if not in substance, it elevated the public good over corporate interest.[40] Later Progressive reformers built on this legacy.

The Lungs of a City

The British sanitary idea along with nostalgia for America's agrarian roots provided the key rationales for creating more open space in cities. The wave of epidemics that gave rise to sewage and garbage disposal reform impelled Americans to reevaluate the lack of open space in urban areas. Following the 1842 Chadwick report's emphasis on miasma as the cause of disease, medical authorities advocated more city parks to "absorb deleterious gases." Parks, too, offered a solution to the paradox that an egalitarian agrarian republic was becoming an urbanized nation replete with inequality. Reformers hoped parks would restore agrarian republican values and recreate America's pastoral landscapes, "likening a city to the country."[41]

As with other environmental issues, park advocates turned to Europe for ideas. While most parks in Europe were reserved for the aristocracy, by the mid-nineteenth century many were opened for public use. Parks, reformers concluded, were the "lungs of a city" and promoted health. Americans who visited Europe were chagrined to find that all social classes mixed more freely in these public spaces than in those of their own republic. One European observer noted of U.S. cities an "almost total absence of public gardens or pleasure-grounds in the large cities" for the working classes.[42]

American park designers attempted to create spaces appropriate to a democratic republic. The most important of the park designers was Frederick Law Olmstead who, along with his partner Calvert Vaux, created some of America's most venerated urban landscapes including New York's Central Park and the Boston Fens. Thought by most visitors to be natural landscapes, Olmstead's parks were almost pure artifice. They reflected his notion that open spaces could promote America's experiment in democracy: "We need institutions that shall more directly assist the poor and degraded to elevate themselves." Olmstead was also an early advocate of the value of national parks for enjoyment by all Americans. He argued that places like Yosemite would become "rich men's parks" without government protection. Vaux, a British architect, agreed, arguing that elevating the condition of the poor was critical to the "social progress of the spirit of republicanism." The role of a park designer was "the translation of the republican art idea in its highest form" onto the landscape.[43]

Olmstead and Vaux reproduced America's pastoral landscapes to provide the general public with a refuge from urban pressures. They argued that Central Park should be more than "a mere exemption from urban conditions." The park should "supply to the hundreds of thousands of tired workers, who have no opportunity to spend their summers in the country, a specimen of God's handiwork. . . ." Olmstead believed the contemplation of rural scenery induced an "unbending of the faculties." Olmstead blocked out views of the city by ringing the park with trees and created inside it a landscape of an "open and pastoral character" with "open glades of grass," "secluded walks," and a "great country green." This unique approximation of the country in the city, historian David Schuyler argues, made Central Park "the most important landmark in the emergence of an American tradition of landscape design and urban planning."[44] Contemporaries clearly understood the significance of the park. In 1861, just a few years after the construction began in New York, the cities of Philadelphia, Baltimore, Brooklyn, Hartford, and Detroit began significant park projects of their own.

Olmstead left three important legacies to urban park planning. First, he called for citywide park systems rather than individually designed parks. Second, his convictions that parks have a restorative influence on urbanites and could represent democratic spaces of class reconciliation dominated the thinking of later planners. Third, Olmstead solidified a tradition of hiring expert consultants for urban problems. Park reformers like Olmstead have been criticized because their creations were often enjoyed more by the affluent than the poor. They sought to induce a measure of social control by "civilizing" immigrants and the poor to follow middle-class Protestant norms of behavior. Olmstead was so concerned that citizens "be trained in the proper use" of his park that he convinced park commissioners to create a force of park police to educate and discipline parkgoers to avoid unspecified behavior of the lower classes. But in an age when the typical response of government officials to the plight of the needy was to ignore them, Olmstead argued that "the poor and wicked need more than to be let alone." Park designers crossed class boundaries to improve the condition and health of all Americans.[45]

The result of sanitary reform and park construction was the growth of government power. Well before 1880, state and city governments committed themselves to regulating and creating a healthy public commons for city dwellers. Administrative structures emerged to deal with environmental issues and serve as an arbiter of the public interest.

National Conservation

By the 1890s, conservation efforts were widespread but most were the product of state and local initiatives. America's modernization and its chief feature, centralization, changed all that. Centralization of political, economic, and social life made conservation a national issue and a federal responsibility. National management of resources flowed logically from greater systematic and functional organization in American society. Corporations that emphasized efficiency, expertise, and systematic organization drew Americans into ever larger forms of human organization. Organizations such as labor unions, professional associations, and interest groups led Americans to think about issues in a national context. Conservationists had made tentative steps toward centralization in establishing state resource and public health boards, but there were many issues that called for deeper national leadership, such as watershed protection, fisheries management, and forestry.

Theodore Roosevelt's presidency (1901–09) unified the disparate and often conflicting efforts to establish irrigation projects, scientific forestry, range management, and wildlife protection. Roosevelt's administration gave them a national focus around the Progressive belief in restraining capitalism with government regulation. Roosevelt's "utilitarian conservationists" represented a new professional class that was bent on crafting policy for resources particularly in the West. The experts saw themselves as the generators of these policies for the general good. Public initiative and notions of laissez-faire capitalism were not up to the task of conserving resources; university-trained experts would be the generators of these policies. Scientific forestry, dam projects, and irrigation proposals were a way of returning small farmers to the land and revitalizing an independent citizenry that seemed to have disappeared with the rise of large corporations. Conservationists like Gifford Pinchot sought to achieve efficiency and equity in Progressive America.

The profession of forestry came of age during the Progressive era. In no small part this was due to the efforts and financial support of Gifford Pinchot, Theodore Roosevelt's chief of the Forest Service. Pinchot was hardly the only force behind the rise of conservation. In fact, his influence was limited to national forests, but he indisputably gave his profession and the idea of conservation national visibility and federal support. Born in 1865, Pinchot, like his boss, was one of the few men of patrician background to select public service as his vocation. His grandfather had made a fortune in Pennsylvania timber, logging it in ways that Pinchot later restricted. He grew up with a passionate love of the outdoors and strong religious and moral convictions, so much so that he was selected deacon for Yale's class of 1889. Pinchot considered becoming a minister and served in the settlement-house movement where so many of the era's advocates for the poor worked. He declined an intensely religious life but retained sympathy for the poor and disdain for corporate power.

In 1885, Pinchot was ready to start his studies at Yale. "How would you like to be a forester?" his father asked him. By Pinchot's account, it was "an amazing question for that day and generation" since professional forestry did not even exist in America. But his father "understood the relation between forests and national welfare." His son would be "breaking new ground" as Pinchot put it in his autobiography. To learn forestry, he had to travel to Europe, which he did after graduating from Yale. Most British foresters studied in France and Germany, and Pinchot traveled to both countries. Pinchot later said of his German mentor, Dietrich Brandis, "I owe [him] more than I can ever tell."[46]

Pinchot's teachers encouraged him to pursue a Ph.D., but he stayed just a year. It was long enough to absorb the basic elements of silviculture (care of forests), such as performing an economic evaluation of a forest, efficient planning, and maintaining a sustained yield of timber.

Pinchot also absorbed what would not work in America. He found the French and Prussian forestry systems autocratic. Bureaucrats there had no commitment to equity. Pinchot knew he could not act with the unrestrained discretion that Poivre had in Mauritius or that the British had in India. Only in Switzerland, "the most democratic country in Europe," did Pinchot see a system that "brought together all the qualities a pioneer public forester must have to succeed in a country like ours—practical skill in the woods, business common sense, close touch with public opinion."[47] America's national forests, Pinchot resolved, would be hallmarks of its capitalist and republican heritage; they would be profitable and equitable.

But the nation's forests embodied a bit of American huckster-ism, too. Creating a massive federal forest management system in decentralized America required someone with extraordinary sales-manship and superb political connections. Pinchot possessed both in abundance. Having been born and bred to lead a powerful life, Pinchot learned at his parents' knee the value of cultivating key friendships among the influential.[48] Pinchot's first job as a "consulting forester" in America revealed more about his promotional abilities than his skill at forestry.

Pinchot founded forestry on a lie. It was an ill omen that in one of the nation's first experiments in scientific forestry, Pinchot had to cook the books to demonstrate a profit. Tapped in 1892 by family friend George Vanderbilt to operate the commercial logging operations at Vanderbilt's Biltmore estate, Pinchot discovered how difficult it could be to manage America's hodgepodge landscape of trees scientifically. He boasted that he would show that it was simple "business common sense" to engage in selective cutting. This emphasis on expert management to obtain profitability, ratio-nality, and efficiency was preached widely by conservationists. It became what Samuel Hays called the "Gospel of Efficiency." It was thought that rational management of a forest would correct capitalism's excesses. Bemoaning the wasteful practices of the past, Pinchot predicted, "it is not necessary to destroy a forest to make it pay."[49]

But apparently it was, since Pinchot lost money at Biltmore. Realizing he had a public relations fiasco on his hands, Pinchot altered his accounting. To support his claim that he had turned a profit, he left off the ledger his own salary, taxes on the land, and the fact that Vanderbilt had to purchase much of the timber himself because there was no local market for it.[50] Pinchot later set the same pattern at the Forest Service. The service routinely sold timber at a loss, but hid the numbers through Byzantine accounting practices. Claiming victory nonetheless, Pinchot escaped his Biltmore responsibilities and moved on to greener red ink in the federal government.

Over the next decade, Pinchot established forestry as a profession within the federal bureaucracy and cultivated influence among important politicians. Pinchot used his energy and money to promote himself. With the family fortune, Pinchot established at Yale the preeminent school of forestry in the country. Pinchot became the head of the Department of Agriculture's Division of Forestry in 1898, succeeding Bernard Fernow, a German forestry expert. Fernow had done pioneering work in the United States, a fact that Pinchot downplayed to build up his own accomplishments. But the bureau's very existence was in question when Pinchot took over as its chief, largely due to Fernow's lack of initiative. As historian Char Miller has pointed out, Fernow understood forestry only as a scientific and economic endeavor. Pinchot added an essential third element: politics. Where Fernow had despaired of America's readiness for federal management of forests, Pinchot knew how to use promotion and family connections to make the bureau far more than a simple dispensary of information on forestry practices.

In cultivating important allies, Pinchot could not have done better than when he established a close friendship with New York governor and soon-to-be vice president Theodore Roosevelt. The two men shared patrician backgrounds, a noblese-oblige view of public service, a love of the outdoors and a vigorous life, and a common commitment to protect America's natural resources from land speculators and corporations. Pinchot's star rose with Roosevelt's, when the latter became president after William McKinley's assassination. In no time, Pinchot became the "crown prince" of Roosevelt's "tennis court cabinet" of personal advisors. As such, he dominated conservation policy.

With Pinchot at his side, Roosevelt established five national parks, sixteen national monuments, and fifty-three wildlife reserves.[51] Roosevelt ran with the wide latitude afforded him under the 1906 Antiquities Act to designate as national monuments "objects of historic or scientific interest." While Congress intended the law to protect only small areas around artifacts such as Indian cliff dwellings in the Southwest, Roosevelt used it for scenic preservation, establishing hundreds of thousands of acres of the Grand Canyon and Washington's Olympic peninsula as "monuments." Monuments often became national parks, once political sentiment caught up with Roosevelt's actions. But the chief winner of the president's actions was the forest reserve system. When Roosevelt moved into the White House in 1901, there were 41 national forest reserves encompassing 41 million acres. By 1909, there were 159 national forests containing 150 million acres.

The national forests were Pinchot's to manage, but not until he engineered a congressional bill in 1905 that transferred responsibility for the forest reserves to the renamed U.S. Forest Service. This action demonstrated Pinchot's political acumen. He made the mountains come to him. With Pinchot's forest division ensconced in the Department of Agriculture and the national forests, 63 million acres of them, under the control of the Interior Department, he needed to convince the latter department to relinquish its control of the forests, hardly an action that a bureaucracy would be likely to take. Pinchot also faced resistance from a reluctant speaker of the house, Joe Cannon, the Western congressmen, and the forestry associations. With persistent lobbying, Theodore Roosevelt gave his approval to the idea first in 1903 and the Interior secretary also signed on, admitting that the transfer made administrative sense. Cannon followed along two years later. It was a signal moment of empire-building by Pinchot. The Forest Service staff bloomed to over 500, up from just 60 when Pinchot became its chief.[52]

Conservation, Pinchot and Roosevelt demonstrated, was not simply resource management; it was a means to build up the power and structure of the federal government. They replaced market mechanisms with government action over resources, but to do so they used the rhetoric of capitalism. Pinchot understood how important it was to justify his actions in terms of market profitability, and he spoke repeatedly of "efficiency" in forestry practices. Promising to make the national forests pay, Pinchot was rewarded with a kingdom. As historian Brian Balogh noted, "The roots of the modern American state might indeed be built on talk, not results."[53]

But how could the forester administer such a far-flung empire in a republic? Westerners spoke out vehemently against federal control of forest reserves. Pinchot needed to govern with a deft touch. Critical to his success was the fact that once he gained control, he gave some power back to local communities. Having rejected the German autocratic system of forest management, Pinchot knew that the Forest Service's success depended on popular approval. He devised an administrative system that placed responsibility in the hands of rangers and regional supervisors. Pinchot sought out the best men and let them do their jobs. Their mission was to administer the forests to maximize local benefits. "Local rules," he said, "must be framed to meet local conditions, and they must be modified from time to time as local needs require." But it must be done in a sustainable way, he warned. Like Chadwick in sanitation reform, Pinchot was a Benthamite. Pinchot and an associate modified Bentham's famous quotation to fit the conservation mission of protecting natural resources for the future. They were to do "the greatest good, for the greatest number, for the longest run."[54] Pinchot designed a service whose main duty was to serve the long-term interests of local resource users.

It did. The Forest Service told its rangers that national forests existed to protect "local residents from unfair competition in the use of forest and range. They are patrolled and protected, at Government expense, for the benefit of the Community and home builder."[55] Pinchot pushed for a Forest Homestead Act that excluded land speculators but opened the reserves to permanent settlers wishing to put the land to its "highest economic use" by farming it. When national hunting groups, including Pinchot's own Boone and Crockett Club, sought to create game reserves within the national forests, Pinchot fought them. The economic value of using a forest, he argued, must trump the elite impulse to preserve them "because they are beautiful . . . or because they are refuges for wild creatures."[56]

But conservation and democracy did not necessarily match. Although the Forest Service saw itself as committed to equity and working for "the people" near each forest, it often relied on larger interests to carry out effective conservation practices. This was particularly the case regarding grazing rights. Open grazing rights, Forest Service officials complained, had wrecked public lands. Cattle ranchers and sheepherders warred for the best spots, often turning animals loose on meadows with growth that was too young to survive intensive grazing. In turn, these groups came into conflict with small farmers who wanted to open up range land to agricultural settlement. To protect the land, the Forest Service proposed a leasing policy. While Pinchot wanted a policy that favored small cattle concerns, he and the service made common cause with large cattle operators to lobby for passage of a lease scheme.[57]

The same was true in forestry. Large corporations sought to bring rationality to lumber markets by promoting conservation practices. The National Lumber Manufacturing Association, for example, supported the expansion of the entire forest reserve system. The National Wholesale Lumber Dealers Association supported a forest reserve in the Appalachian Mountains "for economic reasons." When Theodore Roosevelt expanded the reserve system in 1907, the lumber journal, *The Timberman,* praised the move saying that the "future will demonstrate the wisdom of the reserve policy." This led to accusations by congressional critics that the Forest Service was colluding with major timber corporations such as Weyerhaeuser at the expense of the "common people."[58] They claimed that the goal of this combine was to limit additional competition by controlling the timber harvest in forest reserves. The Forest Service faced a paradox; it was supposed to serve the small resources user, but it often found that large operators made the best conservationists. The Forest Service was not alone in facing this contradiction. Federal irrigation managers often found themselves favoring large operators and the wealthy. Equity was sacrificed to efficiency.

More popular among Westerners than national forest conservation were federal reclamation projects designed to bring the agrarian ideal to desert lands. By the time of the Roosevelt administration, Western states were frustrated with private irrigation schemes. In the nineteenth century, the federal government had tried to spur the private sector to develop irrigation schemes with the inducement of extra land for homesteaders. The Desert Lands Act of 1877 offered settlers a square mile of desert land, 640 acres, if they agreed to irrigate it. Fraud rather than vegetables grew from this law. Speculators simply dumped a barrel of water on land and had a witness sign that it was irrigated. Eleven million acres of land passed into private hands, very little of it irrigated, before Congress, in disgust, repealed the law. The Desert Lands Act proved a hard truth. Even with the lure of almost free land, private enterprise did not have the resources to irrigate desert land. Only the federal government had the money, expertise, and disregard for the bottom line to do it.

Enter Francis Newlands, the West's savior. Newlands came from heavily watered Mississippi to the nation's most arid state, Nevada. Successful in mining, he won the state's House seat in 1892. Newlands waited for an opportunity to push water reclamation legislation to bring settlers to his sparsely populated state. McKinley's assassination provided an opening. Roosevelt favored reclamation for domestic and international reasons. The Rough Rider's time as a rancher in the Dakotas and his conservation instincts made him particularly agreeable to reclamation. Anxious, too, about the rising power of Japan, Roosevelt hoped to ensure America's dominance of the Pacific Rim through population growth. "The western half of the United States would sustain a population greater than that of our whole country today if the waters that now run to waste were saved and used for irrigation," he proclaimed in a speech.[59]

Newlands wasted no time in his pursuit of water. With Roosevelt still unpacking at the White House, he introduced legislation to finance irrigation projects through the sales of Western lands. After substantial revision, farmers received interest-free loans and a ten-year repayment schedule, a substantial subsidy that only grew larger over time. To encourage small family farms, the bill limited each farm to 160 acres of irrigated land. The Reclamation Service, later the Reclamation Bureau, would design, engineer, and build the projects. The Newlands Reclamation Act of 1902 exemplified the spirit of Roosevelt's Progressivism. Experts reclaimed desert land to serve those of modest means. By populating the West with small farmers, the bill attempted to create an independent citizenry and reinvigorate democracy, while keeping out corporations, large operators, and land speculators.

No conservation reform missed its mark as much as did the Newlands Act. Despite the intentions of its author and Roosevelt, the bill led to a West dominated by large farms dependent on federal subsidies. Small farmers could not repay the generous loans they had received. The federal government stretched their repayment schedule to twenty, then fifty, years. While small farmers often found it difficult to repay loans, large operators could. Recognizing this hard truth, the Reclamation Service began ignoring the 160-acre limit for family farms. While the Reclamation fund was meant to be self-supporting, it regularly needed infusions of cash from the federal treasury. Nonetheless, reclamation became a political end in itself. Every Western congressman wanted a project in his district and logrolling (vote trading) ensured that each politician was happy. But that was all for later administrations to handle. The Reclamation Service joined Pinchot's Forest Service in Roosevelt's administration as the harbingers of a new era of federal conservationism.

Having willed federal lands management into existence, Gifford Pinchot sought to extend his vision of conservation beyond forestry. In 1907, he had a revelation while out riding one February evening. He had long dealt with forestry, grazing, irrigation, mining, wildlife management, and soil erosion, but always as separate issues. "Suddenly the idea flashed through my head that there was a unity in this complication," Pinchot wrote. These were not separate problems, but "one single question with many parts. . . . The one great central problem [was] the use of the earth for the good of man. . . . When the use of all the natural resources for the general good is seen to be a common policy with a common purpose, the chance for the wise use of each of them becomes infinitely greater than it had ever been before."[60] This meant unifying the balkanized structure of federal and state resources agencies, a seemingly impossible task given agency turf wars. Pinchot labeled his efforts to unify and efficiently manage resources "conservation." The term had been used by George Perkins Marsh and others, but in appending it to Roosevelt's resource management practices, Pinchot put the term into popular use.

To encourage his conception of conservation, Pinchot organized the 1908 Conference of Governors. The conference was the first major national gathering of state and national politicians and conservation organizations devoted to issues of resources. The conference recommended the creation of a National Conservation Commission to perform an inventory of national resources in timber, water, soil quality, grazing lands, and public health. Most state governments created their own commissions to carry out similar state inventories and coordinate the activities of their resource agencies. President-elect William Howard Taft attended a second governor's conference in December and pledged to continue Roosevelt's conservation policies. At the end of Roosevelt's term, it seemed that Pinchot's conservation philosophy would continue to grow and flourish.[61]

It was not to be. The National Conservation Commission never received congressional funding—a deliberate slap by Congress at Roosevelt's arrogation of power. And ten months after Taft's inauguration in March 1909, Pinchot was fired by the president for his role in what became known as the Ballinger-Pinchot controversy. Publicly, Pinchot's conflict with Secretary of the Interior Richard Ballinger arose over what the chief forester alleged was the secretary's cover-up of a fraudulent land-title transfer of Alaskan coal lands in the Chugach National Forest to the Morgan-Guggenheim syndicate. Fundamentally, the controversy revealed Pinchot's lost faith that Taft would fulfill Roosevelt's conservation legacy. Favoring a narrow reading of the Constitution, Taft rejected his predecessor's expansive view of executive power. Ballinger and Taft tended to favor private leasing of potential water-power sites, rather than government development of them. Pinchot believed this was giving "government lands to the water power trust."[62] His moralistic attacks on Taft and Ballinger revealed how far the chief forester had shifted from his earlier focus on efficiency. The Taft administration did not seem as committed to social justice as had Roosevelt, and Pinchot adjusted his position accordingly. A concern for social equity now dominated his philosophy. This was evident in the way he defined conservation:

> Conservation is the application of common sense to the common problems for the common good. Since its objective is the ownership, control, development, processing, distribution, and use of the natural resources for the benefit of the people, it is by its very nature the antithesis of monopoly. . . . Monopoly on the loose is a source of many of the economic, political, and social evils which afflict the sons of men. Its abolition or regulation is an inseparable part of the Conservation policy.[63]

When Taft would not admonish Ballinger for the coal-land transfer, Pinchot fumed. When, in responding to a congressional inquiry, Pinchot by implication criticized Ballinger, and, by extension, Taft, who publicly supported his Interior secretary, Pinchot was fired.

The controversy eventually brought down Ballinger and Taft, too. Roosevelt returned from retirement to wage another campaign for the presidency. The split in the Republican Party succeeded only in getting Woodrow Wilson elected. Conservation continued under Wilson, but Pinchot's larger hopes of achieving social equity and unifying conservation remained unfulfilled. While it is easy to see Pinchot in a heroic light fighting to save nature from monopolies, it should be remembered that in some ways Ballinger was more a friend of nature than the chief forester. Ballinger favored more protection of national parks than did Pinchot. In the Hetch Hetchy battle to be discussed later, Ballinger sided with the preservationists—"nature lovers" as Pinchot derisively called them—those who wanted to exclude development from the national parks.[64]

Preserving America's Wildlife and Lands

Led by the Sierra-Club founder John Muir, "preservationists," who sought to protect scenery and wildlife for their aesthetic or leisure value, enjoy a positive public image for their seemingly uncompromising politics and intellectual purity. But of all the subgroups that made up the conservation movement, such as foresters, irrigation specialists, and fish culturists, preservationists were the most elitist of all. A small affluent segment of society, preservationists drew their views of nature from the pursuit of leisure activities. Sportsmen and lovers of wildlife believed that it was not simply conquest but preservation of America's pristine nature that gave it superiority over older civilizations. Contact with nature had regenerative powers for civilized people. In protecting scenic locations and wildlife, wilderness advocates denigrated the work of commercial fishermen, Native Americans, and local residents who hunted for subsistence or the market. They tried to limit the access of these groups to wildlife and wild lands. They may have been small in numbers, but they were powerful and articulated the hopes of an expanding class.

Wealthy hunters were one of the first organized groups to fight for wildlife preservation. Since the 1840s, hunting and fishing clubs sponsored initiatives to create game preserves and limit commercial fishing. The relatively affluent members of these clubs saw in hunting a way to identify with the seemingly contradictory qualities of manly frontier independence and the genteel habits of the English hunting aristocracy. Attracted to the rough qualities of such legendary hunters as Daniel Boone, backwoods hunters and their urban middle-class counterparts had a common bond that united them in a hunting brotherhood. As historian Daniel Herman has demonstrated, this class alliance began to dissolve after the Civil War as increased hunting and loss of habitat led to a scarcity of game animals. Wealthy sportsmen sought to imitate a code of conduct taken in part from the British aristocracy that distinguished "gentlemen" sports hunters from lower-class and market hunters. The former group emphasized the skill of the hunter and fair play. Birds, for example, must be taken on the wing rather than with an easy ground shot. The goal of one sports manual was "to diffuse throughout the community a taste for genteel and sportsman-like shooting, and to abolish that abominable poaching, game destroying, habit of ground shooting, trapping, and snaring, which prevails throughout our country in the neighborhood of all cities and large towns." The decline in game, then, was blamed on the behavior of the lower classes. As one sportsman noted, the general public was reflexively opposed to the game laws hunting clubs sponsored. They immediately raised "the senseless cry of aristocracy!—privileged orders!—oppression of the poor by the rich!"[65] But the "cry of aristocracy" was not wholly unearned, as game laws drafted by sportsmen hindered hunting by those engaged in market or subsistence hunting.

Industrialization after the Civil War tipped the numerical scales in favor of sportsmen over their lower-class competitors. An expanding urban middle class with its growing leisure time made hunting a far less exclusive pastime. Indicative of the growing popularity of hunting and fishing was the explosion of national sports journals, hunting clubs, and national organizations to promote wildlife protection. A few hunting clubs had existed as early as the 1840s in lobbying for game laws, although most of these laws were not enforced until after the Civil War. By 1891, there were nearly a thousand rod-and-gun clubs in the United States, with most in the Midwest and Northeast. These groups made up a powerful lobbying constituency for game laws. One of the most important advocates for sportsmen's interests in the late nineteenth century was George Bird Grinnell. Born of a wealthy Eastern family, Grinnell condemned the excessive materialism of modern society, in which "the mighty dollar is the controlling agency in every branch of social and public life." Grinnell took over as editor of

Forest and Stream in 1880 and remained in control of the publication for thirty-one years. From his editorial perch, he, like several earlier editors of sporting journals, inundated his readers with condemnations of the "pot-hunter" and "trout-hog" (those seeking food) who made conservation measures impossible.[66] Grinnell's crusade was to eliminate many of the hunting practices of market and lower-class hunters, such as "jacking," in which hunters froze an animal by shining a blinding light into its eyes.

Grinnell was not content to issue screeds against the lower classes. He and Theodore Roosevelt founded the Boone and Crockett Club in 1887 at a dinner party at Roosevelt's home to promote "manly sport with the rifle" and to lobby for wildlife legislation.[67] There had been many sportsmen's clubs fighting for game legislation, but the Boone and Crockett Club was the best-known, most visible, and exclusive organization. The club is a useful example of the kind of activity such organizations sponsored. Its membership included some of the most powerful men in America. Roosevelt, Grinnell, Gifford Pinchot, Senator Henry Cabot Lodge, and administration officials like Elihu Root and Henry Stimson were members. Grinnell and the club had been influential in advocating the creation of national forest reserves, shaping wildlife policy in national parks, and passing legislation protecting the remnants of America's once-great bison herds. For many of the club members, conservation was about more than preserving specific species. The clubs also saw conservation as protecting America's frontier heritage and culture of masculinity. For example, bison embodied for wealthy whites wild nature and the frontier. The very masculine activity of conquering the frontier might be lost if the bison disappeared. Roosevelt summed this position up when he warned that "it would be a real misfortune to permit the [bison] to become extinct" because the animals "most deeply imprest the imagination of all the old hunters and early settlers." This came at a time when Americans worried that industrialization and urbanization was leading to a decline of virility in Anglo-Saxons. Roosevelt wrote to naturalist John Burroughs that by the mid-nineteenth century "the physical type in the Eastern States had undoubtedly degenerated." Saving the bison, then, was for the benefit of the white race, as such. Burroughs wrote of Roosevelt, "It is to such men as he that the big game legitimately belonged." [68] Preserving masculinity, the white race, and large animals for Anglos to hunt were more an impetus for saving the bison than were arguments for species preservation and diversity, as are made by modern environmentalists.

Nevertheless, the reasoning of these individuals led to saving much of America's large game. The Boone and Crockett Club was most famous for pushing through legislation in 1894 to restrict hunting in Yellowstone National Park.[69] This legislation was the foundation for wildlife policy followed by the National Park Service for decades afterwards. The club also played a role in eliciting support for the 1916 Migratory Bird Treaty with Britain that superceded state hunting laws and set standard bag limits (restrictions on the number of animals taken by a hunter) and hunting seasons. Through sportsmen's organizations, regulation of hunting became a national and international responsibility. But not all classes appreciated the new legislation and treaties. Some saw the hypocrisy of the well-to-do forcing game laws on the backwoodsman. One Adirondack hunting guide lamented,

> In the old days I could kill a little meat when I needed it, but now they're a-savin' it for them city dudes with velvet suits and pop-guns, that can't hit a deer if they see it, and don't want it if they do hit it. But they'd put me in jail if I killed a deer 'cause I was hungry. I dunno what we're a comin' to in this 'ere free country.[70]

By the 1890s, sportsmen were not speaking out alone in preserving wilderness and wildlife. Many nonhunting members of the middle class in urban America had joined them. With sectional tensions resolved after the Civil War and the rise of the nation's status to a world power, many Americans felt a sense of national pride. Nevertheless, they also felt a general unease with modernization in fin-de-siècle America. Historian Frederick Jackson Turner best articulated his fellow citizens' concerns in a speech at the 1893 Columbian Exposition (the Chicago World's Fair). Turner highlighted the 1890 census, which declared that the American frontier had ceased to exist. Turner noted the "transforming influence of the American wilderness" on the nation's character and institutions. Democracy, he contended, had emerged from subduing wilderness. Turner wondered what would become of the nation now that this chapter in its history was over. Many Americans wondered how youth could retain virility and a commitment to the nation's values without a frontier to conquer. The novelist Willa Cather warned, "We must face the fact that the splendid story of the pioneers is finished, and that no new story worthy to take its place has yet begun. . . . Will the [next] generation . . . be fooled? Will it believe that to live easily is to live happily?"[71]

The answer to this dilemma for many affluent Americans was the "wilderness cult," a national group fascinated with experiences in wild country. As historian Roderick Nash noted, those who advocated wilderness adventures believed that such activity retained American values and institutions, enhanced youthful vigor, and provided aesthetic experiences for people seeking places of contemplation. Wilderness organizations stressed the link between citizenship and outdoor activities. Some people sought to instill these values in children through outdoor organizations. Some had names with direct links to frontier heroes, such as the "Sons of Daniel Boone." The Boy Scouts became the nation's largest youth organization, and its handbook became a best-selling publication, second only to the Bible. Scouting aimed to teach children the American values of religion, citizenship, and patriarchy through outdoor experiences. It was a particularly urban organization, intended to instill manly values and keep youth out of gangs and other trouble. One early scout pamphlet asserted that the organization was essential "because the boys in our modern life, and especially in our cities and villages, do not have the chance, as did boys of the past . . . to become strong, self-reliant, resourceful and helpful, and to get acquainted with nature and outdoor life, without special guidance and training."[72]

For adults, mountaineering was a particularly popular wilderness outlet. For men, scaling peaks reinforced their manliness, individualism, and the triumph of civilization over barbarity. Through such activity, men could link themselves to past explorers in the frontier tradition. Around the turn of the century, a host of climbing clubs, such as the Sierra Club and the Mazamas, popped up around the country. These organizations also proved to be particularly useful in turning members into committed conservationists. For women, the mountains had more complex and even contradictory meanings that sometimes subverted gender conventions that the wilderness was supposed to reinforce. Women joined mountaineering clubs in large numbers, sometimes outnumbering the men on such outings. New England women even started the Alpine Club of Williamstown, Massachusetts, an exclusive women's group, to climb peaks in the White Mountains. But how did women interpret this outdoor activity? Some women found such outings opportunities for their own liberation from female stereotypes. By climbing the same heights as their male counterparts, they challenged society's notions of their fragile nature. In scaling peaks, women had to discard some of the conventions of the day, such as wearing less clothing to make the climb, eventually discarding dresses altogether and switching to bloomers. Women were able to expand ideas about femininity and seek "joyous freedom." One woman climbing in the Sierras wrote, "We learned . . . to wear our short skirts and high hob-nailed boots . . . as though we had been born to the joy of them . . . , to be a barbarian and a communist, a homeless and roofless vagabond, limited to one gown or one suit of clothes; to lose one's last hat pin . . . ; to make one's toilet on a slippery bank, after a brave plunge into an icy river—all these breaches of convention became commonplaces. . . ." Some women even went bathing in the nude, shocking their elders. As historian Susan Schrepfer has pointed out, "Women emphasized the sensuality of nature, the pleasures of equity, and the desire to escape social strictures."[73]

For less adventuresome adults, tourism played a critical role in linking wilderness experiences with good citizenship. With advances in transportation and communication by 1880, tourism became a major industry. A mostly white, affluent clientele visited points around the country identified as uniquely American sites. Touring was more than fun; it helped create a national identity. Historian Marguerite Shaffer has argued that tourism promoters "insisted that by seeing the sights and scenes that embodied the essence of America . . . tourists would become better Americans."[74] The wilderness experience embodied the nation's identity and values, while satisfying the frontierlessness of modern society.

Traditionally, preserving American values and inculcating them in children was the job of women, and they were also at the heart of the preservation movement. By the turn of the century, women's clubs led efforts to save nongame animals, forests, historic sites, and scenic vistas. Eschewing the rational language of efficiency, women grounded their crusade on spiritual, moral, and maternal values. Women were important to the movement not simply for the political support they provided but in altering the movement's priorities and language to serve their interests. Conversely, preservation issues influenced the women's rights movement by creating an acceptable public role for women that did not challenge their position as wives and mothers. Women's clubs emerged in major cities shortly after the Civil War. Although they often started as social clubs and promoters of the arts, the clubs took on an increasingly political cast by the 1880s and 1890s. Ironically, expanding women's opportunities often came at the cost of reinforcing their traditional roles as housekeepers and mothers. As one club activist explained, "conservation is particularly a woman's job."[75] It was a woman's duty, the General Federation of Women's Clubs averred, to preserve parks "unimpaired for the enjoyment of future generations."[76]

In pursuing reforestation initiatives and establishing bird sanctuaries, wildlife refuges, national parks, and monuments, the work of women's clubs was diverse. Women preservationists were active in many parts of the country. One of the earliest women's preservation movements started in Colorado. In 1887, the women's Colorado Cliff Dwellings Association called for a "national reserve" around the cliff dwellings at Mesa Verde. The Colorado Federation of Women's Clubs waged a campaign over two decades that culminated in national park designation for Mesa Verde in 1906. Western women's clubs dominated conservation activity in their states by purchasing lands for protection against development, particularly in Washington, Idaho, Nevada, Utah, California, and Arizona.[77]

Just as white men saw conservation as a way of preserving their masculinity, the women in clubs saw their activism as a way of preserving nineteenth-century conceptions of "womanhood." Just as men chose the bison as a manly symbol worthy of protection, women fixed their attention on a more feminine icon, nongame birds. This was most evident in the clubs' pursuit of an antifeather campaign to pressure women of their class to "choose some other decoration" than feathers for their hats.[78] For some time, birds were considered feminine symbols and so feathers and sometimes whole birds adorned the hats of women. This was no trivial campaign. The slaughter of birds for fashion was enormous. One hunter in Florida claimed he had killed over 130,000 birds in one year for the feather market. By the turn of the century 5 million birds were being killed each year for their feathers.[79] The "murderous millinery" trade, as one activist put it, was threatening the survival of some species. Club women and gentlemen hunters condemned the market hunters. These "mauraders," they claimed, wandered "the forests of the earth to ravage and depopulate them."[80] To club women the very definition of womanhood was at stake and much of the debate centered on definitions of femininity. Women of the nineteenth century were traditionally considered repositories of domesticity, morality, and culture for society. Destroying defenseless birds for fashion struck many as immoral. "Do women who wear birds ever stop to think what an injury to the . . . moral influence of our sex they are inflicting?" asked one clubwoman. Wealthy and middle-class conceptions of women were at stake if women were seen to thoughtlessly accept the slaughter of birds for frivolous ends. Bird activists won this battle by redefining standards of beauty. One woman asked, "Does any woman imagine these withered corpses . . . are beautiful?" "The place for dead birds," another proclaimed, "is not above a pretty woman's face." As bird hats fell out of favor, they became a style only for the lower classes, something to be mocked. Editors at *Bird-Lore*, the Audubon Society's magazine, looked down their noses at those who wore bird hats. Bird hats were for "the 'real loidy' who . . . with hat cocked over one eye . . . haunts the cheaper shops, lunch[es] on beer . . . rides a man's wheel, chews gum, and expectorates with seeming relish."[81] Those who wore bird hats were now accused of being unwomanly and a threat to the moral fiber of the nation.

Women's clubs, the American Ornithologists Union, and the Audubon Society launched a campaign to pass state and federal laws restricting the sale and hunting of nongame birds. In 1900, they along with sporting clubs succeeded in pushing through Congress one of the first major conservation measures, the Lacey Act, that effectively outlawed during mating season the market slaughter of herons, egrets, and other nongame birds, whose feathers made popular fashion statements.[82] The onset of the movement to preserve nongame birds was the first time that Americans sought to preserve animals for aesthetic reasons rather than for their usefulness as a game species. The campaign demonstrated the power that women wielded in conservation politics.

In response, politicians cultivated the support of women's clubs. Gifford Pinchot courted them as an essential component of his coalition favoring national forests. The chief preservationist of the Sierra Nevadas, John Muir, also sought the influence of women and led them on many outings to Yosemite Valley. When Pinchot and Muir came into conflict over a proposed dam in the Hetch Hetchy Valley in Yosemite National Park, women tended to side with Muir and other preservationists in opposing construction.

Women's club members were not the only ones in the movement to favor John Muir. Muir has attained legendary status as a founding father of the conservation movement, largely eclipsing Pinchot. This is unfair to Pinchot. The public has forgotten that the chief forester was responsible for setting aside far more land as reserves than Muir ever managed to create in national parks. Muir's rise was the result of the growing popularity of wilderness preservation and the decline in public support for Pinchot's utilitarian conservationism after World War II. Nonetheless, Muir's fame is well earned. Unlike virtually every conservation advocate who preceded him, Muir believed that nature existed in its own right, not merely for human use. And unlike Henry David Thoreau and Ralph Waldo Emerson, Muir was not content to write about na-

ture: he founded the Sierra Club and contributed to the establishment of six national parks. Historian Max Oelschlaeger argued that
"[Muir] is best understood as one of that rare breed whose life uni-
fies *theorie* and *praxis*: an American scholar who not only speculated about but also changed the world."[83] The American preservation movement, in thought and action, began with Muir.

If so, preservationism can chalk its birth up to bad parenting
skills. Daniel Muir, John's father, was the caricature of a puritani-
cal patriarch whose zealotry drove his son to reject the dour, pious
life he had been raised to lead. Born in 1838 in the town of Dunbar,
Scotland, John Muir endured a childhood of relentless work, spar-
tan living, and ritual beatings for small sins. A preacher, Daniel
Muir broke with Presbyterianism and moved his family to the Wisconsin frontier to join the Campbellite sect, whose religious primi-
tivism he found attractive. A man of absolute convictions and no
tenderness, he drove his family to misery. "Old Man Muir works
his children like cattle," neighbors said of the sixteen-hour days
Daniel exacted out of his children. The elder Muir banned as un-
godly all books from his home save the Bible. He forbade the
highland ballads his wife liked to sing and even the lace and em-
broidery that his daughters liked to work on for fear such things
would instill vanity in them. With switch in hand Daniel monitored
his children's Bible study. He was particularly hard on John, perhaps seeing in him the future rebel. "The very deevils [sic] in that
boy," he worried. By eleven, John knew the New Testament "by
heart and sore flesh." When he could, he escaped to the woods
where he was fascinated by its flora and fauna. The peace and solitude he enjoyed in the forest was a wonderful respite from the
abuse heaped on him at home.[84]

Muir hungered for the intellectual sustenance that his father
did not allow. Predictably, in adolescence his mutiny began. He
wore down his father who eventually permitted him to read history,
religious theory, and literature. Night after night John rose after
midnight to study. Later, he found escape for a few years at the
University of Wisconsin where he absorbed literature and the latest
scientific discoveries, particularly botany. Freed of his father's influence, Muir's studies were again stalled by the Civil War. Muir

fled to Canada to avoid the draft. He took up several factory jobs there and later in Indianapolis when he returned to the United States after the war. His superiors recognized Muir's inventiveness, and he was quickly promoted. But success seemed to block his way to his true love, botany. "I suppose I am doomed to live in some of these noisy commercial centres," he mourned. "Circumstances over which I have had no control almost compel me to abandon the profession of my choice and take up the business of inventor."[85]

Fatefully, Muir suffered a horrible accident. Working late one evening in 1867, the point of a file pierced his right eye and the left went blind from shock. Muir spent weeks wondering if he would recover his sight and contemplating the direction of his life. "My days were terrible beyond what I can tell," he wrote, "and my nights were if possible more terrible. Frightful dreams exhausted and terrified me every night without exception." In time, he recovered his sight, but he was forever changed. During his convalescence he returned to nature study. "I am thankful that this affliction has drawn me to the sweet fields rather than from them," he wrote to his friend Jeanne Carr. Muir decided to take a "grand Sabbath day three years long" by wandering through the Gulf states.[86] It was a trip that would take him away from his father's Protestant zealotry into a new religion of wilderness.

While traveling through the wilds of Florida, Muir had a defining insight. Surrounded by exotic plants, Muir concluded that Christianity teaches "that plants are not like man immortal, but are perishable—soul-less. I think that is something that we know exactly nothing about." Of the awful but remarkable alligators, animals that seemed to serve no clear human purpose, Muir realized that perhaps God's creations were not there for human use, but for their own purpose. Muir commented, "Fierce and cruel they appear to us, but beautiful in the eyes of God. . . . How narrow we selfish, conceited creatures are in our sympathies! How blind to the rights of all the rest of creation."[87] The equal "rights" of other creatures was a heretical insight to his father's beliefs. Rather than seeing God by looking to heaven, as his father would have him do, Muir found the Divine in all things on earth. Muir rejected the anthropocentrism of Christianity in favor of what is now called a biocentric worldview. It was a revelation that took him deeper and deeper into the wilds of nature and eventually to Yosemite Valley.

Muir arrived in the Sierra Nevada in the late 1860s, and for the next five years lived there, studied it, and honed his new religion on it. "I am bewitched, enchanted," he admitted. He slept outdoors as much as possible, even in winter. He kept a journal of his observations, and made scientifically important studies of the region's glaciers. He became so detached from civilization that the other occupants of Yosemite thought he was crazy. "I have run wild," he wrote. As he ran further from society and the religion of his father, his writings indicated that he was still a minister's son. He fumed that "the gross heathenism of civilization has generally destroyed nature and poetry, and all that is spiritual." Muir offered, instead, a new religion of nature. "I feel like preaching these mountains like an apostle."[88]

And preach he did. Muir eventually left Yosemite, married, and called the San Francisco Bay area his home for the rest of his life. He returned to Yosemite only to visit. He earned his fame in writing a mountain of books and articles on the Sierra and other regions he visited in the West and Alaska. The Scotsman was not content to merely preach. Unlike Thoreau's fatalistic sense that nature could not be saved through political action, Muir campaigned to save Yosemite by making it a national park. Although the valley had been made a state reserve in 1867, by the late 1880s Yosemite was overrun by a motley collection of business establishments, including a butcher shop, markets, saloons, and hotels. Muir recruited Robert Underwood Johnson, editor of *Century* magazine, to visit the valley. The trip had the desired effect. Johnson campaigned for the creation of Yosemite National Park, and John Muir supplied two articles for the effort.[89]

The drive to establish Yosemite created some unusual alliances. Predictably, businesses catering to tourism in the valley opposed a bill that would kick them out of the park. But Muir and Johnson found a key backer among their assumed enemies, the Southern Pacific Railroad. The Southern Pacific ran a rail line near the park and, à la George Perkins Marsh, was concerned about the

Sierra watershed to protect its land holdings in the California Central Valley. This was more than an alliance of convenience. Muir was a close friend of the Southern Pacific's head Edward H. Harriman and its chief counsel, William F. Herrin. Both were sympathetic to wilderness preservation, Herrin in particular. A major corporation helped create the national park for conservationist, even preservationist, reasons, as it would on many other occasions. Through the invisible hand of railroad corporate lobbying, over 700,000 acres surrounding Yosemite Valley became the second national park in the United States. For the moment, however, the valley floor remained under state control.[90]

Muir's success in cultivating alliances with business underscores the reality that the dividing line between preservationists and conservationists was not nearly as clear as some histories would have it. Writer Stephen Fox believed that conservation fights were a "stark alignment of white hats and black hats," but, in reality, coalitions of pragmatists and idealists dominated both sides. Often portrayed as the hardheaded realists, conservationists of Pinchot's stripe were motivated by a strong moralistic fervor that underlay many Progressive era–reform movements. Muir, the supposed idealist, was also a hardheaded and successful farmer who did not despise capitalism or corporate power. It was not far-fetched, then, that he could form an alliance with the most hated corporation in California. Similar coalitions were behind the establishment of many other national parks, including Yellowstone, Glacier, and Mt. Rainer.

Muir's skillful cultivation of friends in high places indicated that he understood the realities of American politics better than his saintly image indicated. Muir blended the idealism of Henry David Thoreau with the political activism befitting a modern lobbyist. Muir used his friendship with powerful men, including Theodore Roosevelt, to advance wilderness preservation. In 1903, Muir spent four days with the president on a pack trip through Yosemite. The two men hit it off. "I fairly fell in love with him," Muir confessed. The president was only slightly less effusive. Upon leaving the valley, Roosevelt preached the gospel according to Muir: "We are not building this country of ours for a day. It is to last through the ages."[91] His first act back in civilization was to extend the Sierra reserve from Yosemite to Mount Shasta. Roosevelt also resolved to work toward combining Yosemite Valley with the national park surrounding it. There was a powerful coalition of economic interests opposed to transferring the valley from state to federal control. Fearing defeat in the state legislature of the transfer bill, Muir used his influence with Harriman, whom some called "the most powerful man in America." Harriman lobbied quietly for the bill, and it passed by one vote. Muir wrote later, "we might have failed to get the bill through the Senate but for the help of Mr. Harriman, though of course his name or his company were never in sight through all the fight." Harriman's assistance was even more direct in passing a similar bill in Washington, DC. The railroad man persuaded Joe Cannon, speaker of the house, to reverse his opposition and let the bill come up for a floor vote. Roosevelt signed the Yosemite bill on June 11, 1906. The fight to save Yosemite, Muir exalted, was "at last fairly gloriously won, every enemy down derry down."[92] Down but not out, Muir, it turned out, had more to fear from his friends than his enemies.

The creation of America's national parks was not an entirely noble undertaking. The drive to create them revealed a great deal about the place of Native Americans in modern society. The establishment of national parks was part and parcel with the Anglo conquest of the continent. Historically, westering Americans had expected a wilderness filled with wild Indians, as part of their frontier experience. But by the late nineteenth century, Americans envisioned a clean, safe wilderness appropriate for tourist viewing. For people such as Theodore Roosevelt and John Muir, *wilderness* was defined as the opposite of *civilization*, land that did not contain any evidence of human occupation. John Muir even saw Indians as intruders in Yosemite. As early as 1868, Muir had contact with Yosemite Indians and concluded that they did not *fit* with the wilderness and animals around him. "A strangely dirty and irregular life these dark-eyed dark-haired, half-happy savages lead in this clean wilderness," he wrote.[93] Others agreed and sought to dispossess the Indians of their traditional homes to make way for "wilderness." In Yellowstone, Glacier, and Yosemite national parks,

Native Americans were evicted from their lands and confined to reservations to prepare for white tourism. Hence, conservation and preservation activities were at times a means of oppression of minorities and poor whites. The establishment of the national parks indicated that white America's "pristine" wilderness was a social construct that had no place for minority groups such as Indians, and whites molded the parks to fit their idealized image.

Given the racial attitudes of America at the turn of the century, it is not surprising that white supremacists found their way into wilderness preservation movements. What is more remarkable is that some of them saw a direct link between nature preservation and the supremacy of Caucasians in America. Eugenics, the "science" dedicated to the better breeding of the human race and the elimination of inferior species, had links to some preservationist and conservation activity. With the influx of immigrants from eastern and southern European nations who had more children than did native-born whites, some Anglo-Saxons worried that America was committing "race suicide," as Theodore Roosevelt put it. Even Gifford Pinchot was a member of the Race Betterment Foundation of Battle Creek, Michigan. Some in conservation saw a clear link with preserving superior native species such as redwood trees on the west coast and preserving the white race. Madison Grant, a noted preservationist and eugenicist who wrote the racist tract *The Passing of the Great Race*, saw the redwoods as representing a "great race."[94] As one author noted, "the great white race which dominates the world today had made its entrance on the stage of history when the Grizzly Giant [sequoia tree] began its existence."

Organizations such as the Save the Redwoods League, of which Grant was a member, saw conservation, as historian Alexandra Stern notes, as "a metaphor for defending racial purity and ensuring the survival of white America."[95] Others viewed the matter in similar terms. The President General of the Daughters of the American Revolution said at the 1909 National Conservation Congress, "We, the mothers of this generation—ancestresses of future generations—have a right to insist upon the conserving not only of soil, forest, birds, minerals, fishes, waterways, in the interest of our future home-makers, but also upon the conserving of the supremacy of the Caucasian race in our land. This Conservation, second to none in pressing importance, may and should be insured in the best interests of all races concerned; and the sooner attention is turned upon it the better [great applause]."[96] Some believed preservation of western nature was a way of celebrating the white conquest of the continent and the rightful displacement of the "inferior" Mexican races. Preservation of certain "noble" species and park land fit in very well with efforts to improve and propagate the white race. This sentiment was perhaps best put forward by one California preservationist who said, "Perhaps the greatest national gains from a really completed National Parks system interlocks [sic] with State Park's chains, can be expected in the accelerated building of a eugenically-better nation. This would include gradual elimination of imbeciles, those insane through inheritance, carriers of congenital diseases, such as Huntington's chorea, haemophilia. This would further reverse the tragic decline of the leadership type's birthrate."[97] Whether eugenics sits at the "heart" of environmentalism, as Stern claims, or was just so common that it inevitably had some connections to conservation is very debatable, but what is clear is that the conservation and environmental movements have never been able to rid themselves of the taint of racism. In fact, some claim that recent debates within the environmental movement over immigration policy and overpopulation show that the movement has not shaken off its "inherited" eugenic traits.

The Battle for Hetch Hetchy

Muir and other preservationists had not set out clear legal limits on the extent to which national parks could be developed. This spawned a conflict within the conservation movement and revealed a fundamental ideological difference among its members. Pinchot's utilitarian conservationism could not be reconciled with John Muir's preservationism in the battle over the construction of San Francisco's Hetch Hetchy Dam in Yosemite National Park. The conflict unfairly cast the two men as extreme exponents of their respective positions. But while the Hetch Hetchy battle may not be useful for a full understanding of Muir and Pinchot, it defined the terms and rhetoric of debate within the movement for a century.

The conflict started with friendship, as Muir and Pinchot first met in 1893 when the Pinchot family invited Muir, who was visiting New York City, for dinner. The older man captivated the younger Pinchot with his famed story-telling ability. The friendship grew, and Pinchot invited Muir to many social functions. It was something of a father-son relationship with Muir dispensing advice and Pinchot playing the obedient novice. Muir and Pinchot grew even closer when in 1896 they both served on the National Forest Commission in an extended survey of Western timber. "Like a pair of school boys," Pinchot admitted, he and Muir delighted in going off alone together and camping under the starlight of the Grand Canyon.[98] Over the next several years, the two men hatched plots to meet up. Even as Muir criticized Pinchot's forest policies in 1899, they still found time to camp together.

The goodwill endured many policy disagreements. A popular story claims that Pinchot and Muir had their falling out suddenly in 1897. When Pinchot said to a reporter that he supported sheep grazing in national forests, Muir confronted him and was reputed to say, "In that case, I don't want anything more to do with you. When we were in the Cascades last summer, you yourself stated that the sheep did a great deal of harm." This tale was useful to historians. It presented Muir as an uncompromising defender of nature and Pinchot as a utilitarian conservationist. But the account is almost certainly apocryphal. Muir and Pinchot retained warm relations for years afterwards. Muir supported the idea of using the national forests: "It is impossible in the nature of things to stop at preservation," he wrote in 1895, indicating that he saw a place for forest development. Forests "like perennial fountains, may be made to yield a sure harvest of timber, while at the same time all their far-reaching uses may be maintained unimpaired."[99] Muir believed scientific forestry was an improvement over the chaos that preceded it, and he praised Pinchot's work. For his part, Pinchot did recognize the damage that sheep did to grazing lands and sought to limit their impact. The final break came down less to policy than to something personal: Muir's beloved Sierras.

The Hetch Hetchy Valley has been called a sister to its better-known relative Yosemite because of its beautiful meadows, granite cliffs, and waterfalls. At John Muir's urging, Congress included it in the final borders of Yosemite National Park. But in looking to break free from a much-despised private water company, officials in San Francisco proposed damming the valley for a public water supply. Muir and the Sierra Club protested, but in 1903 city officials applied to the Secretary of the Interior to grant them an easement to build a dam. The secretary rejected the request and the city's reapplication in 1905 because they violated the preservationist mission of the parks.[100]

Pinchot disagreed. He weighed in on the side of San Francisco, claiming the dam would not "detract from [the park's] beauties or natural grandeur," even though he had never seen the Hetch Hetchy Valley. The forestry chief argued that the park had to accommodate the needs of "a great group of communities" in the Bay Area.[101] When the 1906 earthquake severed water lines, and fire destroyed much of San Francisco, the city reapplied for the easement and the Department of Interior approved the dam in 1908 with a strong prod from Pinchot. Congress was not so accommodating. Responding to a furious assault on the project by Muir, the press, and preservationist organizations, politicians shelved authorizing legislation. Both sides turned to the press to make their case.

Preservationists fought the rhetorical war by presenting Hetch Hetchy as a shrine and a playground. To Muir, the Sierras were "Mountains holy as Sinai." Although some historians have claimed that the preservationists fought to save wilderness, Robert Righter has shown that the activists really wanted to develop the valley as a tourist attraction complete with hotels, camp grounds, and other tourist amenities. The idea that nature might be saved for its own sake, occurred to very few. Muir himself argued that wilderness should be used when he declared that "everybody needs beauty as well as bread, places to play in and pray in where Nature may heal and cheer and give strength to body and soul alike."[102] The conflict was really over two different visions of human use of the valley.

Preservationists believed that the key support for the dam came from politicians like Pinchot and former San Francisco mayor James Phelan, who, they claimed, stood to gain if the project was built. In his blasts against "Satan and Co." as he called his enemies, Muir acted more like the minister's son than he might have cared to admit. The "temple destroyers" were men who cared only for the "Almighty Dollar," he raged. "Dam Hetch Hetchy! As well dam for water tanks the people's cathedrals and churches for no holier temple has ever been consecrated by the heart of man."[103] His language was brilliant, but it was also alienating. Dam supporters, too, gave as good as they got claiming that their opponents were dupes of private utility companies. They sought to portray men who opposed the dam as sentimental and effeminate. In one cartoon, John Muir was depicted in women's clothes using a broom labeled "Sierra Club" to sweep back the dam. Supporters claimed that preservationist ranks were filled with "short-haired women and long-haired men."[104] Many of Muir's traditional supporters deserted him. Congressman William Kent, the man who created Muir Woods National Monument, noted that Muir was "a man entirely without social sense. For him, it is me and God and the rock where God put it. And that is the end of the story."[105]

But that was not the end of the story for Kent and other dam supporters. The dam represented to them a triumph over an old Progressive bugbear, private monopoly. Pinchot was a particularly ardent foe of private utilities. Fearful that private corporations might control water resources in the state, advocates saw the dam as an affirmation of democracy. Kent agreed with Pinchot that "real conservation meant proper use and not locking up of resources."[106] The practical and democratic uses of Hetch Hetchy outweighed using the valley as a tourist attraction.

In the end, Congress agreed. A vote on the dam finally came up in 1913. The results typified the regional conservation attitudes of the era. Development-minded Westerners and Southerners tended to favor construction. In New England, one congressman noted, "the opposition has become a frenzy."[107] Although preservationists saturated the House and Senate with letters, the dam advocates' lobbying effort carried the day. The bill easily passed the House, and in December, the Senate passed it with a 43-to-25 vote. Typical of water projects, the water system came on line in 1934, late and at double its estimated cost.

From the perspective of a modern environmentalist, the damming of Hetch Hetchy seems an intolerable insult, especially since alternative sites existed. But the national park system, at its founding, carried a utilitarian element in its mission. In 1916, Congress wrote this utilitarian view into law when it passed the National Parks Service Act, which said that the new parks service administration was to "conserve the scenery and the natural and historic objects and the wild life therein . . . [and] leave them unimpaired for the enjoyment of future generations." Using "conserve" rather than "preserve" and "unimpaired" instead of "untouched" implied the park could be managed and modified. Further provisions demonstrated that the Park Service was to fulfill what Director Stephen Mather called its "double mandate" of using and preserving parks. Park rangers were authorized to eliminate predators to maximize the presence of popular species. Congress allowed cattle grazing to continue inside parks, and even permitted the granting of the right-of-way for pipelines, power lines, and reservoirs.[108] Although Congress eliminated the latter allowance in 1920, the founding legislation for the parks demonstrated that despite the mandate to protect the scenery, the parks were also to serve the very practical ends of Gifford Pinchot's conservationism.

For the next fifty years, the Park Service carried out functions of conservation as well as preservation. Lacking ecological insights, Park Service leaders advocated management practices that appealed to their key constituency, the tourists who visited the parks. They manipulated stocks of fish, game populations, and forest resources to cultivate the tourist-friendly look and feel that visitors came to expect. To pacify local residents, they allowed cattle, but not sheep, to graze in areas of the park not frequented by visitors. Ecological considerations took a back seat to human use. Parks, then, carried with them a multiple-use mission that caused much friction between government agencies and environmental groups after World War II.

Given the prevailing attitudes about national-park use, the Hetch Hetchy battle was more a victory for preservationism than it appeared in 1913. As Roderick Nash pointed out, the most amazing part of the controversy was that it had occurred at all. Many

Americans fought for a valley they had never seen. Even politicians who voted for the dam felt compelled to point out their great love of wilderness. The cult of the wilderness continued to grow through the rest of the century. Preservationists lost the valley, but they set the precedent that parks should, for the most part, remain off-limits to large-scale development. After World War II, environmentalists pushed to limit utilitarian uses of national parks aggressively.

But that was far in the future. The defeat of the preservationists in the Hetch Hetchy controversy inaugurated a three-decade domination of conservationism by male, efficiency minded experts of Pinchot's ilk. The Hetch Hetchy controversy alerted many men in the forestry profession of the pitfalls of allowing women into forestry debates. Because women tended to support Muir's emotional, sentimental preservationism, men concluded that women's thinking was too feminine; that they were too sentimental and illogical. Hence, the close alliance of the forestry profession, that prided itself on its dispassionate expertise, and women's clubs broke down. The American Forestry Association, for example, had once encouraged women to be involved in forestry issues. Gifford Pinchot even hired an employee of the Forest Service to be a liaison with women's clubs. After 1908 or so, such support began to dry up. With women's clubs fighting him on Hetch Hetchy, Pinchot fired the liaison. The AFA accused the women's clubs of "immature thought" and "insufficient knowledge" of forestry issues, which the AFA argued undermined the cause of conservation. The group began excluding women from submitting articles to its publications. In later years women's arguments about resources and scenery were downplayed by men, who feared that they would be labeled effeminate.[109]

Sanitary Reform

Experts also came to dominate urban pollution reform. Until the late nineteenth century, Edwin Chadwick's English sanitary system had gained only a few adherents on this side of the Atlantic. Based on the flawed miasma theory of disease transmission, sanitation reform might have withered with the rise of bacteriology, or the "germ theory" of disease, that emphasized finding cures to diseases rather than preventing them. But the sanitary movement flourished because urbanization and industrialization increased the demand for a clean environment. Progressives believed that only reform could cure urban ills, and city governments expanded their administrative capability. Nonetheless, bacteriology eventually shifted the control of sanitary reform away from citizen groups, especially women's clubs, to experts who understood the science of disease transmission.

The urban reformers of Gilded Age and Progressive era are especially instructive of the risks of categorization in this study. Although this book has, for clarity's sake, neatly divided activists between conservationists, preservationists, and urban environmentalists, these categories were far more fluid than meets the eye. Many activists of the period operated in a number of areas, Theodore Roosevelt being only the most obvious example of someone who easily skipped from resource conservation, to preservation, to urban clean-up. Gifford Pinchot's interest in urban settlement-house issues and conservation, moreover, was no coincidence. Women activists in particular through their club activities could work on nature preservation one moment, trash clean-up the next, and morals legislation later. Progressive era–activists, moreover, operated in an international milieu where reformers in many countries shared ideas on a host of issues. Categories such as the ones selected in this study are more representative of a constellation of ideas and political positions than labels that can be affixed to specific individuals.

Urban growth was so rapid that many doubted a modern city could stay clean. In 1880, 14 million Americans lived in cities. By 1920, 54 million did so, more than half the population of the country. Industrialization was closely linked to the growth of cities. More than 90 percent of America's industrial capacity was located in urban centers, with predictable results. Filth, disease, fouled air, and polluted water dominated America's cities. Typhoid epidemics regularly claimed thousands of lives, mostly among the poor. Those who turned to the courts for redress usually found themselves with a losing case. In the late nineteenth century, judges followed the legal logic that pollution was a risk that city dwellers had to bear for industrialization to flourish.

In calling for change, reformers carried out a two-pronged offensive. One line of attack sought to carry out specific and practical legislative reforms, while the other focused on overhauling city bureaucracy by eliminating municipal corruption and the boss system. Immigrant politicians, who doled out government jobs as a reward for political service, largely operated machine politics. Native-born, middle-class Americans despised political machines and argued that government should be run by the "better sorts" who made it "efficient, organized, [and] cohesive."[110]

Reformers trusted in solutions proffered by elite experts and did not usually include the opinions of the poor, immigrant, and minority groups they helped in their political coalitions. Despite the classism that such a view entailed, reformers, like Edwin Chadwick before them, emphasized the environmental causes of disease and poverty—a notable advance over the Social Darwinist belief that poverty, crime, and disease were inevitable among "inferior" classes. As the head of the Chicago Women's Club stated, "Chicago's black pall of smoke, which obscures the sun and makes the city dark and cheerless, is responsible for most of the low, sordid murders and other crimes within its limits. A dirty city is an immoral city, because dirt breeds immorality."[111] By improving the urban environment, reformers hoped that illiteracy, disease, crime, and social conflict might be eliminated too.

Urban environmentalists who focused on sanitary reform came from two groups. Professionals with a variety of technical skills, including physicians, efficiency experts, engineers, and public health officials entered expanding municipal bureaucracies. Supporting them on the outside of government were citizen groups that influenced policy through protest, education, and voluntary programs. These "civic environmentalists" came from organizations with broad interests, such as women's clubs, or from specialized groups that focused on specific problems such as smoke abatement and sanitation. Regardless of their organization, urban environmentalists came mostly from the middle and upper classes. They readily identified with the Progressive movement's moralism, its belief in human goodness and the environmental causes of social problems, and its faith in expert solutions to urban problems.[112]

Women's organizations and clubs were at the forefront of the drive to morally and physically clean up cities, often called "municipal housekeeping." As early as 1877, the sanitarian George Waring argued that the job of cleaning up cities was "especially women's work" since it fit with the "habit of good housekeeping." Women saw their activism as an extension of their domestic roles. As one activist put it, "Woman's place is Home, but Home is not contained within the four walls of an individual house. Home is the community."[113] In the circumstances, such arguments provided women with a logical entry into public activism. The Women's Christian Temperance Union leader Frances Willard told women that to protect their families, they needed "to make the whole world homelike."[114] Therefore, women's public activism was simply an extension of their roles as wives and mothers. Women also turned to activism because they believed pollution affected them more directly than their middle-class husbands, since they were primarily responsible for keeping their homes clean.

Women's activism began with something as prosaic as a pile of manure. Offended that an enormous mound of stinking, dust-blown dung had not been removed from their neighborhood, fifteen women of the exclusive Beekman Hill area of New York City founded in 1884 the first women's urban environmental group, the Ladies Health Protective Association. Their success through court action emboldened them to appeal to the mayor for cleaner streets.[115] By the 1890s, women's sanitary groups had emerged all over the country. Women launched high-profile efforts to clean up Chicago in time to host the 1893 Columbian Exposition and to reform New York's street cleaning and refuse removal system.

As they had with preservationist issues, women justified their public activism by its relevance to their domestic duties. Men, they claimed, were "derelict in the matter of street cleaning" because it was women, not men, who cleaned "from floors and walls, furniture, utensils and clothing, the dirt and soil" that attack "the household at every hour." They suggested that women inspectors be named to oversee street-cleaning operations since "keeping things clean, like the training of children and the care of the sick, has ever been one of the instinctive and recognized functions of women."[116]

Women were, in no small measure, responsible for expanding the role of government in environmental and social issues. Women usually advocated government solutions to urban problems more than their male counterparts. In Chicago, for example, the men's and women's city clubs offered very different solutions to the trash-disposal problem. Seeing the problem strictly in business terms and trusting in solutions offered by the private sector, the men's city club recommended a private contracting service, which, they claimed, was economical. For women's clubs, economics was a secondary consideration to the health of all residents. Enlisting the aid of settlement-house women, the club sponsored a study that concluded that a municipally operated trash service would improve the health of all Chicagoans. For these women, the term "municipal housekeeping" carried a deeper meaning than simply cleaning up the city. Just as all members of a household should benefit from housekeeping, all members of a city should benefit from reform.[117]

Municipal housekeeping made it possible for women to cross economic boundaries to protect the men and women of the laboring classes. Usually composed of businessmen, men's clubs did not care to cross the labor divide. Jane Addams who ran Hull House, Chicago's famous settlement house, bridged class borders in attacking Chicago's political machine. She linked the city's corrupt health department to the deadly typhoid outbreaks that inordinately affected tenement neighborhoods. Tapping the expertise of Dr. Alice Hamilton, Addams demonstrated that poor sewerage systems and the prevalence of houseflies in lower-class neighborhoods were responsible for the epidemic. By 1905, Addams generated enough public support to effect modest reforms. Addams's passion to bring justice to the poor made this campaign one of the first environmental justice movements in the United States.[118]

Women did not always stand on the outside of municipal government. They often became public officials charged with overseeing sanitation services in cities. Even here, however, women were careful to describe their work in terms of the domestic ideal. Mildred Chadsey, Commissioner of Housing and Sanitation in Cleveland, defined municipal housekeeping as "the science of making the city clean, healthy, comfortable and attractive."[119]

To succeed, however, women needed to recruit male experts to speak in the language of science. Men controlled the scientific professions, and as sanitation became more of a scientific and technical field, women found themselves excluded. In 1895, women's groups in New York backed the appointment of George Waring to the post of street-cleaning commissioner. Along with Theodore Roosevelt as police commissioner, Waring was expected to reform a corrupt city government. Waring brought technical expertise to his position and soon turned Gotham's refuse management system into a model that was copied throughout the country. Waring's system required the hiring of trained sanitation engineers, invariably men. By 1920, women often found themselves isolated from the technical debates over the refuse problem.[120]

This trend was even more evident in pollution and wastewater issues. While women often made these problems public issues, physicians and engineers usually took command of finding solutions. In Cleveland, St. Louis, Pittsburgh, New York, Cincinnati, and Milwaukee, women succeeded in pushing antismoke ordinances, although many of these ordinances were overturned in courts as excessive exercise of state power. To pass muster, judges demanded clear proof of damage. Women were at a disadvantage in these legal disputes. They grounded their arguments in distinctly feminine terms, such as morality, cleanliness, and aesthetics, which were unlikely to sway men. Invariably, the most important argument in a courtroom was health. Since courts required proof that smoke did harm to the public, women's groups had to enlist the cooperation of and cooptation by physicians. Similarly, doctors and sanitary engineers dominated debates over sewage treatment. Eventually these experts found their female allies to be a detriment. The men did not want to be thought of as effeminate by justifying their support for feminine reasons such as city beautification. They focused on the more masculine and "rational" argu-

ments of health and efficiency. They claimed that smoke represented waste and could be eliminated with a more efficient burn.
After 1900, those with technical or medical expertise controlled
the movement's direction. Women were less important to pollution
campaigns after 1910 and did not regain the initiative until the
1960s.[121] Although such isolation seems regrettable to the modern
observer, women at the time welcomed the involvement of experts
in their campaigns and did not display resentment at the situation.

Not all women were excluded from public health debates.
Addams's campaign began Alice Hamilton's career as an industrial environmentalist. Hamilton went on to establish a connection
between disease and a worker's environment as a researcher for an
Illinois labor commission and later for the U.S. Bureau of Labor.
In researching the effects of lead on workers' health, Hamilton recognized that women researchers enjoyed an advantage over men
when interviewing victims. "It seemed natural and right that a
woman should put the care of the producing workman ahead of the
value of the thing he was producing. In a man it would have been
[seen as] sentimentality or radicalism."[122] By the 1920s, Hamilton
initiated numerous studies on workplace contamination. Linking
health to the chemical products of the industrial revolution, Hamilton pioneered the modern understanding of the environmental
risks of industrialism that was critical to the work of Rachel
Carson and others after World War II.

Addams's and Hamilton's work was part of a large movement
to undertake comprehensive studies of environmental problems.
The Russell Sage Foundation's groundbreaking survey of Pittsburgh's urban environment set a standard for the use of the sciences in effecting social reform. The steel city had a well-earned
reputation as a place of environmental catastrophe. Described as
"hell with the lid off," Pittsburgh had a working class which suffered from terrifying hazards on and off the job. Allegheny County
had over 500 fatal workplace accidents each year, and Pittsburgh
had one of the highest typhoid rates in the world. In 1900, the
death rate from typhoid was thirty times that of Berlin, ten times
that of London, and even twice that of the nation's swampy capital.
The Sage Foundation brought in experts who documented the un-

healthy conditions of the city, its nonexistent parks, poor water and sewerage, and poverty. The refusal of the city fathers to take these problems seriously, the report concluded, was the result of a "public moral adolescence" and an "overwrought materialism" by the city's middle and wealthy classes. Pittsburgh did not leap on the reform bandwagon, but the extensive coverage of the Foundation report goaded the city to curb its worst abuses. By 1922, improved sewage treatment lowered the city's typhoid rate by 96 percent.[123]

By the end of the Progressive era, urban environmentalism had established a beachhead. It had raised public awareness, curbed the worst environmental abuses, and pushed for substantial reform of municipal governments. But America's cities remained unhealthy places to live. Nor had the reformers empowered the poor to push for environmental reform themselves. Leadership remained in the hands of professionals and the wealthy. But such criticism can be overstated. Urban environmentalists were some of the first reformers to work for improvements that crossed class, racial, and gender divisions. If the social gospel that guided many Progressives was an Anglocentric view of the future, it also carried with it the possibility to transcend social divisions and advocate environmental rights for all. When one Cincinnati activist preached that "to breathe pure air must be reckoned among man's inalienable rights," many urban activists responded with a hearty amen.[124]

Conclusion

The drive to conserve resources, preserve nature, and clean up the environment was hamstrung by the dominance of property rights in this era, and its adherents suffered from a lack of ecological insight. They tended to manage resources in isolation from the rest of the environment. For example, they did not understand the value of balancing predator and prey populations. Thus women's groups and the Audubon Societies treated predators such as hawks as "bad" birds and called for limiting their population to allow "good" songbirds to flourish.

Reformers also carried with them the biases of their class and ethnicity. Theodore Roosevelt, for example, looked to the gentleman sportsman as the "true hunter" and the men of lower classes who made their living in market hunting as "butchers" who set about their "brutal work of slaughtering the game. . . ."[125] Mabel Osgood Wright, an author and a leader in the Connecticut Audubon Society, condemned people of other "races with instincts concerning what are called lower animals, quite beyond the moral comprehension of the animal-loving Anglo-Saxon." Protecting nature, Thomas Dunlap asserted, was "most popular among the descendants of the pioneers—the white, 'Anglo-Saxon,' Protestant people who dominated American society—and their commitment was in part an effort to preserve their culture and its virtues in a new world."[126] In this respect, they were little different from other middle-class and wealthy native-born Americans in their view of those of differing backgrounds and race.

But the accomplishments of the early conservationists, preservationists, and urban environmentalists were profound. As the idea of a local commons was breaking down in the late nineteenth century, they constructed a democratic consensus around the need to treat parts of the environment as a national commons. In doing so, they expanded the power and scope of state and federal governments, particularly the executive branch. They created an infrastructure of state and federal agencies, expert professions, and citizen organizations concerned with environmental reform. Moreover, the establishment of the National Parks opened the way for a growing constituency of middle-class and wealthy Americans to visit and appreciate nature, influencing their votes to preserve it in the future.

Endnotes

1 Char Miller, *Gifford Pinchot and the Making of Modern Environmentalism* (Washington, DC: Island Press, 2001), 216.

2 Char Miller, "The Greening of Gifford Pinchot," *Environmental History Review* 16, no. 3 (1992): 10 and Samuel P. Hays, *Conservation and the Gospel of Efficiency: The Progressive Conservation Movement, 1890–1920* (Cambridge: Harvard University Press, 1959; Anthenum, 1975), 169.

3 Miller, *Gifford Pinchot,* 215.

4 James Penick Jr., *Progressive Politics and Conservation: The Ballinger-Pinchot Affair* (Chicago: The University of Chicago Press, 1968), 142 and Miller, *Gifford Pinchot,* 217.

5 Samuel P. Hays, *Conservation and the Gospel of Efficiency,* 271.

6 Karl Jacoby, *Crimes Against Nature: Squatters, Poachers, Thieves, and the Hidden History of American Conservation* (Berkeley: University of California Press, 2001), 198.

7 Miller, *Gifford Pinchot,* 222.

8 Richard W. Judd, *Common Lands, Common People: The Origins of Conservation in Northern New England* (Cambridge: Harvard University Press, 1997), 12.

9 Daniel T. Rogers, *Atlantic Crossings: Social Politics in a Progressive Age* (Cambridge: Harvard University Press, 1998), 24.

10 Ibid., 31.

11 Judd, *Common Lands, Common People,* 7–8, 49.

12 Steven Stoll, *Larding the Lean Earth: Soil and Society in Nineteenth-Century America* (New York: Hill and Wang, 2002), 168.

13 Judd, *Common Lands, Common People,* 50.

14 John T. Cumbler, *Reasonable Use: The People, the Environment, and the State, New England 1790–1930* (Oxford: Oxford University Press, 2001), 99.

15 Joseph E. Taylor, *Making Salmon: An Environmental History of the Northwest Fisheries Crisis* (Seattle: University of Washington Press, 1999), 82.

16 Judd, *Common Lands, Common People,* 188–89, 147.

17 David Lowenthal, *George Perkins Marsh: Prophet of Conservation,* 2d ed. (Seattle: University of Washington Press, 2000), 19.

18 Judd, *Common Lands, Common People,* 95 and Stoll, *Larding the Lean Earth,* 175.

19 Taylor, *Making Salmon,* 70.

20 Richard Grove, *Ecology, Climate, and Empire: Colonialism and Global Environmental History, 1400–1940,* (Cambridge, UK: White Horse Press, 1997), 54.

21 Ibid. 57–63.

22 Lowenthal, *George Perkins Marsh,* 282.

23 Ibid., 278, 283.

24 Ibid., 283, 303–05.

25 Jacoby, *Crimes Against Nature,* 14–15.

26 Ibid.,18–19.

27 John F. Reiger, *American Sportsmen and the Origins of Conservation,* 3d ed. (Corvallis: Oregon State University Press, 2001), 91.

28 Jacoby, *Crimes Against Nature,* 62.

29 Steven Hahn, "Hunting, Fishing and Foraging: Common Rights and Class Relations in the Postbellum South," *Radical History Review* 26 (1982): 42, 44, 46, 57.

30 Judd, *Common Lands, Common People,* 194.

31 Ibid., 11.

32 Cumbler, *Reasonable Use,* 3.

33 Martin V. Melosi, *The Sanitary City: Urban Infrastructure in America From Colonial Times to the Present* (Baltimore: Johns Hopkins University Press, 2000), 17–18, 31.

34 An introduction to Chadwick's efforts is in Melosi, *Sanitary City*, 43–57.

35 Ibid., 46–47.

36 Cumbler, *Reasonable Use,* 129.

37 Ibid., 114.

38 Ibid., 114.

39 Ibid., 104.

40 Ibid., 104, 117–18.

41 David Schuyler, *The New Urban Landscape: Redefinition of City Form in Nineteenth-Century America* (Baltimore: Johns Hopkins University Press, 1986), 61.

42 Ibid., 60, 64.

43 Anne Whiston Spirn, "Constructing Nature: The Legacy of Frederick Law Olmstead," in *Uncommon Ground: Rethinking the Human Place in Nature,* William Cronon, ed. (New York: W.W. Norton, 1995), 92; and Schuyler, *New Urban Landscape,* 7.

44 Schuyler, *New Urban Landscape,* 85, 89–94.

45 Ibid., 7, 85, 94.

46 Gifford Pinchot, *Breaking New Ground* (New York: Harcourt Brace, 1947; reprint, Washington, DC: Island Press, 1987), 1, 17.

47 Miller, *Gifford Pinchot,* 90.

48 Ibid., 79.

49 Ibid., 111–12.

50 Brian Balogh, "Scientific Forestry and the Roots of the Modern American State: Gifford Pinchot's Path to Progressive Reform," *Environmental History* 7, no. 2 (April 2002): 214–15.

51 Stephen Fox, *The American Conservation Movement: John Muir and His Legacy* (Madison: University of Wisconsin Press, 1985), 128.

52 Miller, *Gifford Pinchot,* 156, 196–97.

53 Balogh, "Scientific Forestry," 212.

54 Miller, *Gifford Pinchot,* 155, 168.

55 Harold K. Steen, *The U.S. Forest Service: A History* (Seattle: University of Washington Press, 1976), 79.

56 Hays, *Conservation and the Gospel of Efficiency,* 42.

57 Ibid., 49–65 and Steen, *U.S. Forest Service,* 163.

58 William G. Robbins, *American Forestry: A History of National, State, and Private Cooperation* (Lincoln: University of Nebraska Press, 1985), 23–24, 29.

59 Marc Reisner, *Cadillac Desert: The American West and Its Disappearing Water,* 2d ed. (New York: Penguin, 1993), 112.

60 Pinchot, *Breaking New Ground,* 322–24.

61 Hays, *Conservation and the Gospel of Efficiency,* 127–33.

62 Miller, *Gifford Pinchot,* 208.

63 T. H. Watkins, *Righteous Pilgrim: The Life and Times of Harold L. Ickes* (New York: Henry Holt and Company, 1990), 454.

64 Hays, *Conservation and the Gospel of Efficiency,* 197–98.

65 Daniel Justin Herman, *Hunting and the American Imagination* (Washington: Smithsonian Institution Press, 2001), 239–40, 247, and Reiger, *American Sportsmen,* 9–10.

66 Herman, 239; and Reiger, 52.

67 Reiger, *American Sportsmen,* 150–51.

68 Andrew C. Isenberg, *The Destruction of the Bison: An Environmental History, 1750–1920* (Cambridge: Cambridge University Press, 2000), 169–70, 180.

69 Reiger, *American Sportsmen,* 163.

70 Herman, *Hunting and the American Imagination,* 259.

71 Katrina Vanden Heuvel, ed., *The Nation, 1865–1990 : Selections From the Independent Magazine of Politics and Culture* (New York: Thunder Mouth Press, 1990), 52.

72 Peter J. Schmitt, *Back to Nature: The Arcadian Myth in Urban America* (New York: Oxford University Press, 1969), 109.

73 Susan R. Schrepfer, *Nature's Altars: Mountains, Gender, and American Environmentalism* (Lawrence: University Press of Kansas, 2005), 69, 78–79, 114–15, 121.

74 Marguerite Shaffer, *See America First: Tourism and National Identity* (Washington, DC: Smithsonian Institution Press, 2001), 4.

75 Glenda Riley, *Women and Nature: Saving the "Wild" West* (Lincoln: University of Nebraska Press, 1999), 102.

76 Polly Welts Kaufman, *The National Parks and the Woman's Voice: A History* (Albuquerque: University of New Mexico Press, 1998), 32.

77 Riley, *Women and Nature,* 98–102.

78 Ibid., 103–04.

79 Mary Joy Breton, *Women Pioneers for the Environment* (Boston: Northeastern University Press, 1998), 256.

80 Lisa Mighetto, *Wild Animals and American Environmental Ethics* (Tucson: University of Arizona Press, 1991), 57.

81 Jennifer Price, *Flight Maps: Adventures with Nature in Modern America* (New York: Basic Books, 1999), 73, 79–80, 82–83.

82 Robin W. Doughty, *Feather Fashions and Bird Preservation: A Study in Nature Protection* (Berkeley: University of California Press, 1975), 109–110.

83 Max Oelschlaeger, *The Idea of Wilderness: From Prehistory to the Age of Ecology* (New Haven: Yale University Press, 1991), 172.

84 Fox, *The American Conservation Movement,* 31–32.

85 Ibid., 48.

86 Ibid., 49.

87 Ibid., 51–52.

88 Ibid., 10–13.

89 Ibid., 86–99.

90 Richard J. Orsi, *Sunset Limited: The Southern Pacific Railroad and the Development of the American*

West (Berkeley: University of California Press, 2005), 366.

91 Fox, *The American Conservation Movement,* 126.

92 Orsi, *Sunset Limited,* 367–69; and Fox, *The American Conservation Movement,* 128.

93 Carolyn Merchant, "Shades of Darkness: Race and Environmental History," *Environmental History* 8, no. 3 (July 2003): 382.

94 Alexandra Minna Stern, *Eugenic Nation: Faults and Frontiers of Better Breeding in Modern America* (Berkeley: University of California Press, 2005), 124.

95 Ibid., 124.

96 Gray Brechin, "Conserving the Race: Natural Aristocracies, Eugenics, and the U.S. Conservation Movement," *Antipode* 28, no. 3 (1996): 238.

97 Stern, *Eugenic Nation,* 134, 148–49.

98 Miller, *Gifford Pinchot,* 126–27, 133.

99 Ibid., 121, 137.

100 Ibid., 138.

101 Ibid., 139.

102 Michael P. Cohen, *The Pathless Way: John Muir and American Wilderness* (Madison: University of Wisconsin Press, 1984), 65; and Roderick Nash, *Wilderness and the American Mind,* 3d ed. (New Haven: Yale University Press, 1982), 165.

103 Nash, *Wilderness and the American Mind,* 167–68.

104 Robert W. Righter, *The Battle Over Hetch Hetchy: America's Most Controversial Dam and the Birth of Modern Environmentalism* (Oxford: Oxford University Press, 2005), 91;

and Adam Rome, "'Political Hermaphrodites,' Gender and Environmental Reform in Progressive America," *Environmental History* 11, no. 3 (July 2006): 441.

105 Nash, *Wilderness and the American Mind,* 174.

106 Ibid., 173.

107 Ibid., 180.

108 Richard West Sellars, *Preserving Nature in the National Parks: A History* (New Haven: Yale University Press, 1997), 38, 43–45.

109 Rome, "Political Hermaphrodites," 450–51.

110 Melosi, *Sanitary City,* 105–06.

111 David Stradling, *Smokestacks and Progressives: Environmentalists, Engineers and Air Quality in America, 1881–1951* (Baltimore: Johns Hopkins University Press, 1999), 45.

112 Melosi, *Sanitary City,* 106–07.

113 Catherine Gudis, *Buyways: Billboards, Automobiles, and the American Landscape* (New York: Routledge, 2004), 164.

114 Suellen Hoy, *Chasing Dirt: The American Pursuit of Cleanliness* (New York: Oxford University Press, 1995), 73.

115 Ibid., 74.

116 Ibid., 74–75.

117 Maureen Flanagan, "Gender and Urban Political Reform: The City Club and the Woman's City Club of Chicago in the Progressive Era," *American Historical Review* 95, no. 4 (1990): 1036–39.

118 Harold L. Platt, "Jane Addams and the Ward Boss Revisited: Class,

Politics, and Public Health in Chicago, 1890–1930," *Environmental History* 5, no. 2 (2000): 194–222.

119 Melosi, *Sanitary City,* 184.

120 Ibid., 190–94.

121 Rome, "Political Hermaphrodites," 454–55.

122 Robert Gottlieb, *Forcing the Spring: The Transformation of the American Environmental Movement* (Washington, DC: Island Press, 1993), 49–50.

123 John Opie, *Nature's Nation: An Environmental History of the United States* (Fort Worth, TX: Harcourt Brace, 1998), 283–84; and Melosi, *Sanitary City,* 138.

124 Stradling, *Smokestacks and Progressives,* 59.

125 Daniel J. Philippon, *Conserving Words: How American Nature Writers Shaped the Environmental Movement* (Athens: University of Georgia Press, 2004), 51.

126 Ibid., 101–02.

CHAPTER TWO

Environmental Reform in the 1920s, 1930s, and 1940s

It was one of the more important conversion experiences in conservation history. In the 1920s Aldo Leopold, an employee of the Forest Service responsible for game management in the Southwest, was eating his lunch with some others on a rimrock overlooking a river. They observed what they thought was a deer crossing the waterway, but to their surprise a wolf emerged on the bank and its pups from hiding to play with their mother. "In those days we never heard of passing up a chance to kill a wolf," Leopold recalled. In fact, Leopold and the Forest Service were locked in a campaign to extirpate wolves from the region to increase deer populations for hunters. They fired many rounds at the wolves hitting the mother and one of the pups, then climbed down to inspect their kill. As Leopold recounted in an essay entitled "Thinking Like a Mountain,"

> We reached the old wolf in time to watch a fierce green fire dying in her eyes. I realized then, and have known ever since that there was something new to me in those eyes—something known only to her and the mountain. I was young then, and full of trigger-itch; I thought that because fewer wolves meant more deer, that no wolves

would mean hunters' paradise. But after seeing the green fire die, I
sensed that neither the wolf nor the mountain agreed with such a
view.[1]

For Leopold it was a realization that led him away from the
game management practices of the past and eventually to a more
ecological point of view that emphasized maintaining diversity and
making sure predators and prey were in balance within the environment. In the Forest Service he learned that eliminating predators was his main duty to increase the "crop" of deer. But during
the interwar period, he gained a sense that there were consequences to this policy. By 1949, when his words were posthu-
mously published, his conversion to an ecological "land ethic" was
complete. *A Sand County Almanac* became the bible for a new environmental philosophy in the postwar period.

Some historians have described the interwar and World War II
era from 1920 to 1945 as a lull between two dynamic conservation
eras: the Progressive era–conservation movement and the modern
environmental movement. There is some truth to this judgment.
The era lacked populist vitality, in which citizen organizations led
the movement. Experts in the private sector and government agencies, like Leopold, dominated. Myriad local groups and organizations that gave the Progressive era its diversity and energy found
themselves coopted. Activists accepted and often promoted institutional reform that placed power in the hands of new agencies, commissions, and technical experts. The Progressive movement enlarged the power of the state, leaving a smaller role for citizens.[2]
Although some women's groups continued to push for air-pollution reform, women's organizations went into decline with the
end of the fight for suffrage. There were individual women who
worked for change, such as Rosalie Edge of New York who created the Emergency Conservation Committee and led the fight to
save raptors (birds of prey) and in 1938 establish Olympic National Park in Washington State. More often, however, middle
class men and women allowed public officials and technical experts to handle environmental problems. However, several new
citizen conservation organizations emerged in this era to replace
the losses, such as the Izaak Walton League, the National Wildlife

Federation, and the Wilderness Society. But even in these organizations, leaders often came from the ranks of conservation agencies rather than the general public. The involvement of ordinary citizens, what writer Stephen Fox called the "radical amateur" tradition, was limited.

As Leopold's story attests, however, the interwar and World War II period was a time of important change in the thinking of conservationists. While there were many continuities between the Progressive era and interwar movements in philosophy and issues, the latter movement was unique and influential in important ways. Conservationists dealt with unprecedented threats from America's modern economy and culture. First, the rise of a modern consumer culture and greater leisure time led to an unparalleled level of tourism, camping, hunting, and fishing. In addition, new technology, mainly the automobile, allowed the public to penetrate and scar wilderness areas on a much wider scale. Leopold, for example, was trying to satisfy demands for game by hunters who drove into the national forests. Where conservationists had once promoted public access to wilderness, they now called for restrictions and the creation of wilderness areas where roads could not go. Assumptions about wildlife management were also challenged. A number of episodes of wildlife population crashes and changing scientific thought forced many conservationists and agencies to take ecological considerations into account in formulating policy, as individuals such as Leopold advocated. Finally industry's appetite for natural resources and the development of the petrochemical industry led to the emission of greater amounts and varieties of pollutants. All of these considerations spurred on government regulation, some of which was actually effective. In natural-resource conservation, pollution control, and wilderness preservation, public officials and experts expanded their responsibilities. The Great Depression temporarily stymied the expansion of conservation in the latter half of the Herbert Hoover administration. With the ascension of Franklin Delano Roosevelt to the presidency in 1933, however, conservation was transformed into a jobs program to aid economic recovery, particularly in agricultural areas. These programs expanded the base of the movement to include more people from working-class backgrounds, built support for a Democratic majority, and broadened government involvement in conservation issues in a way that Theodore Roosevelt could only have imagined. By the end of the 1930s, state and federal governments were more involved in conservation activities than at any time. World War II slowed but did not derail these gains, leaving a legacy of increased government oversight, expert control, scientific-based management, and increased public enthusiasm for conservation and outdoor recreation. And a small but influential group of activists began groping toward a new ecological way of thinking that would flourish in the postwar period.

Natural Resource Conservation in a Conservative Era: 1921–1933

An examination of the early years of this era seems to confirm the judgment that there was a lull in conservation activity. The twelve years of Republican administration from 1921 to 1933 have been dismissed as a low point for conservationists. One historian argued that Warren Harding and Calvin Coolidge "generally ignored conservation issues."[3] Harding entered office promising to do as little as possible, and he did it. The former senator from Ohio promoted removing regulatory shackles on resource use. Efficiency, it seemed, trumped equity. Conservation agencies learned that they could best survive in this new lax atmosphere by deemphasizing regulation and focusing on services to private industry. This laxity, however, came at a price. The Teapot Dome scandal sent Harding's Secretary of the Interior Albert Fall to jail for secretly leasing naval oil reserves in Wyoming to his cronies in exchange for gifts. Coolidge avoided scandal but took even less interest in conservation issues. Only with Herbert Hoover did conservationists find a friend in the White House. Even then, the Depression and Hoover's beliefs in individualism, voluntarism, and decentralization limited his initiatives.

Below the level of presidential politics, however, the federal government extended conservation programs. Conservation agencies adapted to the priorities of GOP presidents and sought programs that avoided federal regulation in favor of cooperation with private industry. Although New Deal–programs dwarfed these initiatives, conservation became a bipartisan issue. Conservation policies in the 1920s anticipated the reform measures of the 1930s.

In several ways, historian Kendrick Clements argued, the 1920s were an era of conservation: (1) federal officials favored natural resource development; (2) opportunities for outdoor recreation grew with park development, greater leisure time, and access to the outdoors, made possible by the automobile; (3) government agencies became more involved in wilderness and wildlife preservation; and (4) government officials tried to eliminate waste to minimize pollution and conserve resources while helping troubled industries.[4] Republican administrations demonstrated some commitment to all of these programs, especially under the guidance of Herbert Hoover, who served as a member of Harding's and Coolidge's cabinets and then as president.

The Forest Service pursued policies that meshed well with the hands-off philosophy of the Harding and Coolidge administrations. It pressed for a policy of cooperation rather than extensive regulatory oversight in dealing with timber and ranching interests. The service's new head, William B. Greeley, was a conservative Yale-trained forester. He argued that "the task of keeping our forest lands productive should not be attempted by federal control of forest industries or of the use of private property, but rather through the encouragement of local initiative."[5] Greeley opposed federal regulation of private land and called instead for education and persuasion.

This approach bothered some interested observers. No longer with the Forest Service, Gifford Pinchot had turned against cooperation with the timber industry. Pinchot called for mandatory regulation of all timberland by the Forest Service. Pinchot derided the cooperative efforts of the Forest Service and claimed that it was "degenerating into a routine bureau, grown old and stale on the job." The lumber interests, he claimed, had spent millions "to fool the American people into believing that the industry is regulating itself and has given up the practice of forest devastation. . . . We are still sowing the wind and the whirlwind is not far off."[6] Responding to predictions of a "timber famine" caused by unregulated cutting by timber companies, Pinchot used his political skill to encourage legislation to regulate private lands.

Despite Pinchot's opposition, the Forest Service continued its cooperative approach. Greeley formulated a plan to win support for his policies. Controlling the machinery of the Forest Service and enjoying the support of private industry, Greeley turned aside Pinchot's challenge. He pushed through several pieces of legislation that expanded the service's ability to consolidate the holdings of the national forests and enacted cooperative initiatives with the states to promote tree plantings and expand forest-fire prevention. Most of all, he stymied the passage of any bill that regulated private lands, as Pinchot wanted.

The Forest Service also won from Congress additional funds to expand its scientific programs. Although the service claimed that it engaged in scientific forestry, it actually paid little attention to basic research for forests. Economic and political considerations played a larger role in its decisions. As Aldo Leopold, an associate director for the Forest Service, noted, most foresters were administrators and there were few scientifically trained employees. There was minimal support for basic research. But in the 1920s, the service won increases from Congress that allowed it to expand its research stations from four to nine. In 1928, the service won a long-term commitment from Congress: $3 million over ten years for basic research into insect pests, tree diseases, wild animals, the causes of forest fires, and forest management.

Even the onset of the depression in 1929 did not slow work in the National Forests. Anticipating the activities of the Civilian Conservation Corps in FDR's New Deal, the Forest Service in the years after World War I launched a program of roads and trails construction to provide jobs. By early 1933, the service had constructed numerous firebreaks, lookout towers, roads, and trails.

Despite these accomplishments, the Forest Service faced a challenge from another federal conservation agency, the Park Service. The younger agency sought to enlarge the park system, often at the expense of national forests that surrounded national parks. The NPS-USFS battle was certainly a turf war, but it was more than that. The two agencies operated with different mandates and philosophies.

The Forest Service was a Progressive era–agency that emphasized, at least publicly, efficiency and scientific management for the greater public good. The USFS's emphasis on serving local communities and a more utilitarian brand of conservation made it difficult for the service to respond to national leisure trends. Forest Service leaders had established themselves as managers of timber, not as tour guides.

The Park Service operated with different values and constituencies. It emerged in response to a market for leisure activities. It did not stress scientific management of the parks as much as it promoted and advertised the parks for public enjoyment. Park Service officials sold their goods, scenic vistas, in competition with sports events, movies, and radio; the Park Service was good at promoting itself. But the Park Service developed a split personality. It was supposed to preserve parks from abuse, but to survive it had to attract tourists who abused the parks in using them. In practice this meant the parks had two kinds of supporters. Purists favored minimal human intrusion in the parks and light-impact activities. They wanted the parks to educate the masses. Boosters emphasized making the parks entertaining. They sought to expand access to the parks and improve accommodations through aggressive building programs.

The Parks Service's promotional side dominated its early years. Its director, Stephen Mather, was a wealthy business executive. Mather recognized that for a small agency like his to survive, he needed to cultivate a national following. Together with his chief assistant Horace Albright, Mather used his promotional skills to market the national parks. Between 1917 and 1919, he put out over 1,050 articles on the parks and countless maps, booklets, and films. With automobile transportation, Americans flooded the parks, and Mather improved road access to them. The Park Service was so aggressive in its recreation expansion that a purist like Newton Drury, executive secretary of the Save the Redwoods League, complained that the Parks Service had become little more than "a glorified playground commission." The Redwoods League was so alarmed at the Park Service activity that they withdrew their support for a redwood national park, no longer trusting the Parks Service to do it right. But the "cheap showmanship" (as Drury saw it) of the Park Service endeared it to the American people.[7] People liked to turn out for the bear shows where park goers could see bears rooting through the park dump. The Forest Service, by comparison, responded slowly in promoting the national forests as a recreational resource and instead served its traditional constituency in local communities.[8] When the Parks and Forest services came into conflict, the Park Service had a national constituency to draw on and superior promotional skills.

Conflict came often. In 1925, Mather proposed major extensions of Yellowstone, Sequoia, Grand Canyon, Crater Lake, Mount Rainer, and Rocky Mountain National Parks. The Park Service was not able to get all it wanted but gained enough to show its political muscle. Changes in leadership and an overstepping of its bounds during the New Deal–era blunted the drive of the Park Service, but until 1937, it held the upper hand against the Forest Service. In 1937, the Department of the Interior tried to take over the Forest Service from the Department of Agriculture. Allies of the Forest Service, such as hunters, ranchers, sheep raisers, and mining interests, reacted with alarm to the proposal and organized to defeat it. The fear was in no small part due to the concern that the Park Service would expand dramatically at the expense of the Forest Service or that the Department of the Interior would limit access to forest resources. The National Woolgrowers Association predicted that "such a move would remove once and for all the main barriers to unlimited expansion of the National Parks, which in turn would automatically eliminate future use of national-forest lands for prospecting, grazing use, and hunting."[9] Even conservation organizations, such as the Izaak Walton League and the General Federation of Women's Clubs, rallied to the Forest Service side, in part due to a lingering mistrust of the Department of the Interior from the days of the Pinchot-Ballinger controversy. The Forest Service lobby handed the Department of the Interior and the Park Service a stinging defeat.

Despite the prominence of the conflict between the NPS and the USFS, the interwar years marked a period in which the two agencies no longer dominated the conservation movement anyway. An expanding economy and leisure time brought other environmental issues to the fore, such as game management and water reclamation. One of the chief game agencies in the federal government was the U.S. Biological Survey. The survey's research function changed in 1918 when Congress passed the Migratory Bird Treaty Act, which put the federal government in the business of regulating bird populations. It abolished spring shooting, limited the selling of game, closed seasons altogether on certain nongame birds, and set bag limits on hunters at a generous twenty-five ducks, eight geese, and eight brant per day. The Biological Survey administered this act and managed bird refuges.

The Biological Survey was a weak agency. Caught between advocates of game protection and hunting and gun manufacturers, the survey found it difficult to take a politically acceptable position in controlling game populations. Meanwhile, the population of game birds was dropping under the combined pressure of decreasing habitats and over-hunting. Increased leisure time and automobile access led to an explosion in the number of hunters. In 1911, 1.5 million state hunting licenses were issued. In 1922, the figure increased to 4.5 million, and it reached 6.5 million by 1928.[10] Complicating regulation was a labor shortage in the survey. The agency had only thirty-one wardens to enforce bag limits for the entire nation.

Solutions to the problem of declining game bird populations revolved around those who wanted to restrict the hunt and others who wanted to enlarge the hunting pie. Advocates of game protection, led by the Izaak Walton League and William Hornaday, director of the Bronx Zoo, called for Congress to establish lower bag limits. Hornaday zealously advocated game protection, but as noble as that was, he largely hoped to save game for elite hunters who could afford to follow game laws. Hornaday complained of the game taken by the lower classes, "Italians, negroes and others who shoot song-birds for food." He concluded that "all members of the lower classes of southern Europe are a dangerous menace to our wild life."[11] Thus, Hornaday's was an not entirely selfless crusade.

Hunting interests spearheaded by the gun industry–backed American Game Protection Association (AGPA), rejected the idea and called for the establishment of more sanctuaries to increase the bird supply, a strategy reminiscent of the efforts to breed more salmon. The AGPA called for opening game refuges to hunting, a proposal that Hornaday violently opposed. In Congress, the two sides fought each other to a standstill. With both sides stymied, the fighting turned ugly. Hornaday accused the Biological Survey's chief of engagement in a conspiracy with hunting interests to kill his bill setting bag limits. The gun manufacturers fought back, eventually encouraging the Bronx Zoo's board of directors to force out the vituperative Hornaday from his position as director, succeeding in 1926. Hornaday, however, won the day. When documents emerged linking the AGPA to gun manufacturers, the embarrassed industry withdrew from the fight. Congress passed bills in 1929 supporting Hornaday's bag limit and one expanding bird sanctuaries, without opening them to hunting.

Hence, the irresolute Biological Survey grew, despite itself. The Biological Survey expanded the number of wildlife refuges in its control. In 1921 the survey oversaw a total of 70 refuges; by 1933 that number had increased to 102 refuges.[12] The main problem the survey had was keeping the game populations down so as not to overextend the refuges. The survey thinned herds of deer, elk, and buffalo. Some preservationists objected to the practice, but the policy did keep herds within acceptable limits.

By the end of the 1920s, a rough policy of game management was in place. Bag limits were reduced, wildlife refuges had been established, and a program of exterminating predators was followed. But the system did not work. The duck population fell precipitously in 1931 due in part to conditions game managers did not control: drought and drainage of wetlands by farmers. Deer populations fluctuated markedly too. The swings revealed that managers knew little about controlling game populations. Game management operated in response to the political pressures of hunters not of scientists. As Aldo Leopold complained, "So far we have the scientist, but not his science, employed as an instrument of game conservation."[13] Game managers still tended to focus on controlling the hunt rather than seeing the problem in ecological terms and trying to manage animals and their habitat. It would not be until Franklin Roosevelt's New Deal that managers would try a more holistic approach to management.

A catalyst for change was the management failure in the Kaibab National Forest on the north side of the Grand Canyon. After becoming a game preserve in 1906, the deer population grew rapidly as managers sought to maximize the herd's size for hunting. Predator control was zealously pursued, as Biological Survey hunters eliminated 4,849 coyotes, 781 mountain lions, 554 bobcats, and the region's entire population of 30 wolves. The policy seemed to have produced the desired result. By 1920, the Forest Service reported that the herd was growing out of control. For several years, survey biologists called for a thinning of the herd to prevent overgrazing on the range. Because of interdepartmental squabbling, nothing was done. The National Park Service and state officials objected to herd reduction because the deer were a tourist attraction. By 1924, the deer had eaten nearly all the browse within reach. The forest, Leopold noted, looked "as if someone had given God a new pruning shears and forbidden Him all other exercise." That winter, the cold and lack of food caused the deer population to crash, with scores of carcasses showing up in the spring. Even after the decline, Arizona officials opposed herd control and took the Forest Service to court when it raised the bag limit. The Supreme Court ruled against Arizona in *Hunt* v. *The United States*, and the Forest Service received undisputed sanction to control wildlife populations on federal lands. Nevertheless, explosions in deer population increased throughout the country.[14]

Although this explanation of the Kaibab problem has some critics, the story has been elevated to a myth in environmental circles. Foes of predator control claimed that the story taught two lessons. First, it showed that predators were essential in balancing game populations. The story also demonstrated the negative consequences of human meddling in nature. Scholars enshrined these lessons in environmental and game management textbooks for decades.

Even after the Kaibab episode, change came slowly. By the late 1920s, deer populations spiked regularly, but predator extermination was such an ingrained policy that many resisted abandoning it. Throughout the 1920s, the Biological Survey continued to poison 35,000 coyotes per year.[15] Part of the problem was the that the public traditionally had a negative view of predators. The public and game managers often ascribed evil motivations to them as if they were humans. They complained that "varmints" were involved in the "murder" of "innocent" animals. Others called predators "criminal" and claimed they killed "for sheer bloodlust."[16] But some people countered that predators protected the "balance of nature," that they were essential for scientific study, and that they had a moral right to exist. Scientists began investigations that put predators in a positive light.

Reform eventually trickled up to conservation agencies. The National Park Service amended its policy of eliminating predators to enhance the number of "beautiful" species that were popular with visitors. In 1928 park superintendents condemned predator control. In 1931 the service declared an end to its use of poison saying that it would "give total protection to all animal life."[17] The Park Service also launched public education programs in the 1930s designed to teach a more positive image of predators as being essential to the balance of nature. It was not a complete victory, however. The Park Service promised only that it would engage in "no widespread campaign" against predators. Throughout the 1930s, it continued to control coyote populations with poison.[18] Nevertheless, the Park Service was inching toward a scientific understanding of predators. Even the Biological Survey, which was responsible for eliminating predators, no longer spoke of "exterminating" them, but only of their population "control."[19] New Deal agencies made wildlife preservation a part of their mission and employed many wildlife scientists. Science had, for the most part, won the day.

Science was less important in water reclamation policy. By the 1920s, the limits of the Newlands Act had become evident. The act limited irrigated land to 160 acres per farmer and required settlers to repay the cost of irrigation construction within ten years. Congress established a fund for irrigation projects, and repayments replenished it. But few farmers settled on the government lands, and most could not repay the loans. By 1922, farmers had repaid less than 10 percent of the $135 million appropriated by Congress. Sixty percent had defaulted on their interest-free loans.[20] Still, evicting the settlers was politically unthinkable.

Disturbed by the failure of reclamation, the new Secretary of the Interior, Hubert Work, created a fact-finding commission in 1923. The commission presciently condemned "Federal paternalism" which encouraged water users to look at themselves "as wards of the Government, a specially favored class with special claims on the government bounty." It called for a scientific approach to reclamation, in which an equitable system would be worked out for settlers to repay their loans and take over management of water projects. Despite the commission's work and the passage of supporting legislation, the Reclamation Service (renamed the Bureau of Reclamation at this time) only modestly increased repayment rates, as settlers continued to pay less than half of construction costs of irrigation works. The onset of the Great Depression made matters worse. Representatives of existing farm regions complained that in a time of drastic oversupply, the last thing the nation should be doing was bringing more land into production. Allies of the bureau responded that the actual acreage brought into production was small, and that the crops produced by reclamation lands did not compete with existing farms since they harvested at different times of the year. Despite the opposition and the fact that the bureau was behind in its repayment schedules, Congress continued to authorize more reclamation projects.[21] The projects were politically popular and the bureau's failure did not decrease the demand for its services.

The bureau was, in fact, about to get much bigger. The story of the world's largest dam, Hoover Dam, began at the turn of the century, with an irrigator's scheme to divert part of the flow of the Colorado River into the Imperial Valley, a virtually uninhabited dry sink in the corner of southeast California. By 1904, the region hosted several boomtowns and railroad spurs. The only problem was with the Colorado River. The river fluctuated wildly and carried one of the heaviest silt loads on earth, which could overwhelm irrigation works. As the irrigation channel silted up, developers tried to cut a new one, but storm waters broke through before the developers could build an adequate control gate. Practically the entire river turned out of its bed and poured through the gap. Ninety thousand cubic feet of water spilled into the Imperial Valley every second, threatening the entire settlement. Only the heroic efforts of engineers financed by Southern Pacific Railroad tycoon E. H. Harriman, whose price was to take control of the irrigation company, stopped the flood in 1907 after two years of effort. The flood waters emptied into the Salton Sink, a dry seabed lacking an outlet. The resulting body of water became the Salton Sea, a salt-water lake fifty miles long and fifteen miles wide.[22]

The episode made it clear that the Colorado was too dangerous a river to be tamed by private interests. Only the government could control the river's vast irrigation and hydroelectric potential. To protect the region from the river's fury and other rivals for its water, the Imperial Irrigation District aligned with the Bureau of Reclamation. The bureau built a new canal for $30 million, but the repayment terms were interest-free and spread out over many years. In return, Imperial Valley farmers agreed to join in reclamation's "unified Colorado River project," which included building storage dams upstream to smooth out the flow of water between drought and flood seasons.[23]

Several impediments remained before a dam the size of Hoover could be built. All the states bordering the Colorado River had claims to its water, and each state's politicians opposed dam construction unless there was a settlement favorable to that state. The politicians were especially worried that fast-growing California would get most of the water. The federal government sponsored negotiations between all interested parties in New Mexico in 1921. Brokered by Secretary of Commerce Herbert Hoover, the states agreed to divide the river into two basins. The upper basin included the states of Colorado, New Mexico, Utah, and Wyoming, and the lower basin, California, Nevada, and Arizona. Each received half of the river's 15 million acre-feet of estimated water flow. As events proved, the estimate of acre-feet was too high, which made for further political battles in the years to come. Private interests who did not want to see the federal government get into the electric-power business fought the compromise, as did Arizona, which feared that the deal favored California.[24] Nevertheless, California's phenomenal growth, the Imperial Valley's need for protection, and Herbert Hoover's election to the presidency in 1928 ensured passage of the bill authorizing the dam. The age of dam building, most commonly attributed to FDR's New Deal, began during the Hoover years. Dam construction was a bipartisan issue. Hoover's presidency marked the beginning of the federal government's domination over Western water development.

Hoover's role in water reclamation was no accident. Unlike his predecessors, Harding and Coolidge, the Stanford University graduate was a committed conservationist. Hoover came to conservation through his leisure activities and professional work as an engineer and businessman. He was an outdoorsman and a fanatical fisherman. "The most vivid and joyous recollections of my Iowa boyhood days are of patient angling in Iowa streams for the very occasional fish, with a willow pole and a properly spat-upon worm."[25] His devotion to fishing earned him the presidency of the Izaak Walton League, the nation's leading fishing conservation society.

As a business executive, Hoover also saw conservation as essential to a successful economy. The wise use of resources could guarantee prosperity for all Americans. He anticipated that the rise in affluence would elicit demands for more outdoor opportunities and a healthy environment. Environmental protection was needed to take advantage of the benefits of a growing economy.[26] While it is tempting to say that Hoover came from the mold of Gifford Pinchot and Theodore Roosevelt, his was a brand of conservation that emphasized voluntarism and government decentralization, while his predecessors had favored more direct government regulation of industries. Hoover proposed to "centralize ideas and decentralize execution."[27] He was a unique conservative, George Nash argues. He favored an activist government that would "stimulate the private sector to organize and govern itself."[28]

Hoover's conservation also had a moral component to it. As historian Kendrick Clements argues, Hoover "had enormous practical experience in the efficient use of resources and deep personal convictions about the moral use of leisure."[29] His zeal for fishing and rural upbringing made him sensitive to the ways an urban-industrial society separated humans from nature. Properly exercised leisure, he thought, restored people and made them better citizens. Hoover believed that "the blessings of fishing include discipline in the equality of men, meekness and inspiration before the works of nature, charity and patience toward tackle makers and the fish, a mockery of profits and conceits, a quieting of hate, and a hushing to ambition."[30] Hoover's support for conservation embodied economic, scientific, and ethical aspects.

Hoover recognized that modern society could bring people in contact with nature. By the 1920s, America's consumer economy had come of age as wages rose and work hours fell. The technology of the age brought people closer to nature. Hoover noted, "The automobile has begun a new era of wholesome contact with open air and nature whose benefit to the physical, mental, and spiritual welfare of the American people are inestimable."[31] By 1926, the number of fishermen swelled to 10 million, an increase of ten times during twenty years.[32] The growth of outdoor recreation pleased Hoover, but he raised concerns about declines in fish stocks resulting from overfishing by private and commercial fishers. He called on hatcheries to increase production of game fish. Conservative that he was, Hoover asked sports clubs rather than government agencies to take on the task of raising fish.

Hoover's efforts to regulate commercial fishing were not successful. Although he managed to push through legislation to protect Alaskan salmon fisheries, Hoover's emphasis on cooperative solutions failed to revive fishing. He believed that federal power extended only to sponsoring interstate agreements on fishing resources. If parties could not come to terms, there was nothing that the federal government could do but to educate the public.

Concern about fish also led Hoover to advocate controls on pollution. Public awareness about pollution had flared anew in the twenties when oil in several harbors caught fire, and bathers found themselves coated in oil. As Commerce Secretary, Hoover called for conferences of state fish commissioners to address the problem

of oil pollution in interstate waters and argued for corrective legislation. Opposition from shipping interests and oil companies, however, limited the scope of the legislation. The 1924 Oil Pollution
Control Act empowered the Secretary of the Army to regulate oil
discharges from ships. The act only applied to coastal waters, limited the regulation to ships, and exempted land-based pollution
sources. Furthermore, Hoover was unable to secure an agreement
on international dumping of oil at sea. In 1926, conferees from ten
nations gathered to discuss the issue. They negotiated a half-
hearted, vaguely worded agreement. Germany, Italy, and Japan opposed it, killing the initiative.[33]

Hoover's emphasis on voluntary initiatives continued to suffer
setbacks during his presidency. With the success of the Colorado
River Compact, Hoover hoped to duplicate its formula of central-
izing planning and decentralizing administration of agreements in
the timber and oil industries. Both suffered from problems of temporary overproduction, falling prices, and possible shortages in the
near future. Hoover called on voluntary industrial associations to
agree to regulate production and lift sagging prices.

For timber, Hoover saw standardizing lumber milling as the
key to eliminating waste and improving efficiency. But the overall
goal of limiting production remained elusive. A committee dominated by large timber interests did little to solve the problem,
and by 1930, the industry, as one wood spokesman admitted, was
"threatened with economic chaos."[34] Small operators fearing economic catastrophe during the depression expanded production and
drove prices still lower. Hoover formed a new Timber Conservation Board to solve the overproduction problem, but some industry
spokesmen actually preferred federal control of production rather
than Hoover's self-regulation. No clear policy emerged.

The oil industry was in even worse trouble. At the beginning
of the twenties, an oil shortage loomed over the country. Discoveries of oil in California, Oklahoma, and East Texas turned the shortage into a glut. Oil prices fell, and small companies faced economic ruin. The Harding administration's corruption in handling
oil reserves at Teapot Dome created disarray. As with the timber
industry, larger companies favored production controls, but smaller

operators resisted. A Federal Oil Conservation Board was formed, but no agreements emerged until Hoover became president. In September 1929, Oklahoma, Kansas, and Texas settled on oil production quotas, but new discoveries in East Texas upset the agreement. Overproduction worsened and the price of oil plummeted from ninety-five cents a barrel to ten.[35] Hoover instituted measures to limit exploration and reduce imports, but he rejected as unconstitutional federal regulation of production. The measures were not enough as consumption fell, leaving the oil industry awash in surplus crude.

The general failure of Hoover to gain agreement on regulating fishing, pollution, timber, and oil underlined the weakness of conservative conservation. Although the conservatives had notable successes such as the Colorado River Compact where the states saw it in their interests to agree on a solution, they could not compel a resolution when parties would not come to terms. The Republicans' emphasis on cooperation and voluntary solutions had only limited success. They had even less success in solving the economic crisis that gripped the nation after 1929.

New Deal Conservation

By 1933, the American economy had reached its nadir. About half of the nation was unemployed or underemployed. With thousands of banks failing each year, Americans rejected Hoover's seemingly timid response to the Great Depression. Many believed Hoover's market-friendly approach had failed, giving those who favored federal regulation the upper hand. For the first time in twelve years, Americans voted a Democrat into office, Franklin Delano Roosevelt. Since the turn of the century, most noted conservationists had been Republicans. GOP members dominated conservation agencies, such as the Parks Service and Forest Service, and organizations, such as the Audubon Society, the National Parks Association, and the American Planning and Civic Association. Conservation under the Republicans was probusiness. What Democrats might offer was uncertain.

But in FDR, Americans had the most committed conservationist in the White House since his distant relative Teddy. FDR was once blamed for considering all policy problems in terms of conservation. "I must plead guilty to that charge," he admitted.[36] Roosevelt's devotion to conservation was passionate, especially when it came to birds and trees. When he was young, FDR had led a sheltered existence at the family's secluded Hyde Park estate along the Hudson River, even being schooled at home. Alone much of the time, he turned to the outdoors as a refuge and a place to play. By the age of nine he had taken up ornithology and kept a specimen collection of over three hundred birds. As president, he continued to go on birding expeditions around his home.

Like Gifford Pinchot, who was a source of inspiration, Roosevelt took to forestry after exposure to German practices. In 1891 he visited a forest tract near Bad Nauheim that had produced regular timber yields for two hundred years. In 1910, Roosevelt tried his own hand at forest management. He bought 1,200 acres of exhausted farmland and reforested it for commercial sale. Like a good conservationist, he declared, "Growing trees is a long-time proposition. We are looking to the human race, which we hope won't end in fifty years." As president, he boasted "Forestry pays from the practical point of view. I have proved that."[37]

Throughout his public life, Roosevelt pushed for the conservation of trees as a community virtue. FDR entered politics in 1910, when he joined the New York legislature. As chair of the Forest, Fish and Game Committee, he introduced bills to control fishing and hunting. He tried to prevent unregulated timber-cutting on private lands. Unlike his GOP predecessors, FDR believed in the primacy of group rather than individual rights. Allowing individual companies to cut down trees without restriction, he argued, damaged group rights to a healthy environment. The liberty of the individual, he declared, must give way to "the liberty of the community."[38] When Roosevelt became governor of New York in 1928, he sought to blend conservation and employment of the poor. Taking more than ten thousand men off relief rolls, Roosevelt employed them in a program planting trees.[39]

With much of the conservation movement in the other party, FDR, as president, selected two renegade Republicans to head the most important conservation departments in the federal government. Roosevelt tapped Henry Wallace, a GOP leader from Iowa, to be Secretary of Agriculture, and Harold Ickes, a Progressive from Illinois, to run the Department of the Interior. In late 1933, FDR replaced the heads of the Park and Forest Services with Democrats, the first party members to hold these posts. FDR stole the conservation issue from the Republicans, but even GOP stalwarts applauded his efforts. Gifford Pinchot expressed delight in the new appointments, noting that the Forest Service had once again become "the aggressive agent and advocate of the public good, and not the humble little brother of the lumbermen." Ickes agreed, arguing that to help the impoverished the nation needed to conserve "our natural resources and provide for a more equitable distribution of their bounties."[40] New Deal advocates tried to ensure that electricity was distributed to public power entities, called for more equitable distribution of Alaskan fishing grounds between small and large operators, and tried to enforce the Newlands Reclamation Act's 160-acre limitation on irrigation, favoring small farmers. Equity, it seemed, had become the equal of efficiency in conservation matters.

Roosevelt's initiatives abandoned Hoover's emphasis on cooperation and voluntarism in favor of a more direct government role. There were three fundamental components to FDR's conservation programs: to restore damaged environments through initiatives such as the 1934 Taylor Grazing Act, which placed 80 million acres of rangelands under more rigorous management and provided funds from user fees to restore damaged land; to "improve" on existing environments to maximize human benefits through programs such as developing river basins with hydroelectric dams for electricity, irrigation, and flood control; and to create new government institutions and governing mechanisms, such as the Soil Conservation Service, which shared governance of erosion programs with local organizations.[41] New Deal conservation copied similar ideas from the Progressive era–movement, but FDR added new elements that expanded the scope of federal involvement and brought more environmental awareness to policy. In a 1935 message to Congress, the president demonstrated his own very modern sounding environmental awareness: "It is an error to say we have 'conquered Nature.' We must, rather, start to shape our lives in a more harmonious relationship with Nature."[42]

What tied the three strands of FDR's conservation policy together was the Great Depression. He linked America's need for work and economic recovery with his own interest in conservation. As historian Hal Rothman noted, depression era–conservation became a jobs program for millions of Americans. Sarah Phillips has taken Rothman's observation further and claimed that New Deal–conservation was "a set of federal strategies aimed at rehabilitating the economies of agricultural areas. . . . Behind the conservation programs lay the assumption that sustainable and equitable use of the nation's resources would put the countryside on a more equal footing with cities, thereby preventing future depressions." As early as 1931, FDR captured the essence of this logic: "I want to build up the land as, in part at least, an insurance against future depressions." The new administration claimed that the depression was partly the result of the low–living standards in rural areas. When farmers earned an "American standard of living," industrial workers would benefit from their purchases of consumer items. "One-half of our population, over 50 million people, are dependent on agriculture," Roosevelt said when accepting the Democratic nod for president. "And, my friends, if those 50 million people have no money, no cash, to buy what is produced in the city, the city suffers." New Deal advocates argued that economic depression in rural areas, which had been going on through most of the 1920s, was due to wasteful resource consumption and unfair allocation of resources. New Deal conservationists tried to reinvigorate rural areas economically and socially through conservation measures, such as taking marginal lands out of use, controlling soil erosion, restoring forests, controlling floods, and generating inexpensive electricity from dams.[43] This program was, some believed, a "New Conservation." The emphasis on using conservation to rehabilitate impoverished areas was new, but in many ways the New Conservation touched on themes of equity and efficiency voiced by Gifford Pinchot twenty years earlier. Admittedly some New Deal programs favored wealthy farmers, but others specifically targeted those impoverished by the depression.

The conservation programs developed during the New Deal reflected this emphasis on jobs and rural rehabilitation. The most famous and romanticized New Deal conservation agency was the

Civilian Conservation Corps (CCC). Drawing on his own experience as governor of New York, his work in supporting Boy Scout conservation activities, and a similar program sponsored in Germany, FDR proposed to employ hundreds of thousands of young men in "simple work, not interfering with normal employment, and confining itself to forestry, the prevention of soil erosion, flood control, and similar projects."[44] Employing mostly young unmarried men, the CCC provided the recruits room, board, and $1 a day, of which $25 a month had to be sent to their families. In return, the young men agreed to work on conservation projects supervised by the army. Over 3 million men served in the CCC between 1933 and 1942.[45]

As Franklin Roosevelt intended, the corps took young men out of unhealthy urban environments and remade them. Although some elites in conservation and environmentalists in the postwar era looked down on those who made their living off the land, such as the wealthy sportsmen who opposed market and subsistence hunters, FDR believed that working with the environment restored health and cultivated an appreciation of nature. Like conservationists of the Progressive era, New Deal administrators worried that the urban environment damaged city residents, making young men lazy and weak. Roosevelt claimed that for "the city boy living in crowded conditions, artificial interests have been substituted. Normal, natural growth is threatened." New Dealers believed that work in nature could cure what ailed city boys, and they were right. Countless recruits remarked on how the outdoor physical activity transformed them. One enrollee said of his comrades in 1936 that they were "thin, hollow-chested, sharp-faced products of our big cities' slums with the threat of tuberculosis hovering over them." The army, which ran the program, noted the change as well. Upon entering the CCC, the recruits exhibited terrible physical health. "Thousands of these 'light-weights,'" the army noted, "possess[ed] well developed or incipient ailments which—within a few months to a few years—would have produced total permanent disability or death." However, within a few months of joining the program, the average recruit gained eleven to fifteen pounds and the incidence of diseases such as tuberculosis dropped dramatically. As one recruit gushed, "my health was renewed."[46]

Conservation agencies benefited from the manpower supplied by the CCC. The CCC was best known for its forestry activities. Recruits performed a host of activities relating to fire prevention, constructing nearly 120,000 miles of new roads and erecting 1,147 new lookout towers.[47] The CCC bridged the divide between preservationism and conservation by doing work in the national forests and national parks. In 1940 alone, CCC recruits worked in over 323 camps in national forests and 177 in state forests. They reforested over 2 million acres with approximately 2 billion trees.[48] The recruits also worked in park development, building roads, trails, campgrounds, and visitor centers. The CCC was also active with the Soil Conservation Service in the Dust-Bowl states of the Great Plains and with the Tennessee Valley Authority's farming constituents. Its programs educated farmers to engage in soil conservation measures, such as contour plowing, gully control, and tree planting.

The CCC was a mixed blessing for America's state and national parks. On the positive side, CCC workers advanced national park development two decades beyond where it would have been.[49] Eight hundred state parks were developed, including many in states that previously had no park system.[50] Typically, CCC activity included road- and trail-building, administrative and visitor facility construction, and sewerage and water development. But intensive construction activity created more tourist pressure on the parks and negatively affected wildlife. Over 200 men usually occupied a single CCC camp, and the workers themselves created hazards for wildlife. The National Park Service Director Horace Albright warned National Park supervisors that they must ensure that crews "safeguard rather than destroy" wildlife. The Park Service tried to minimize the impact on wildlife by hiring more biologists, but this could not compensate for the damage done by CCC projects that were utilitarian and sought to increase park attendance. Over the objections of biologists, the CCC cleared forests and roadsides of brush to eliminate fire hazards, built fire roads, and launched programs to control insects and other pests. All of this was done, not for ecological reasons, but "to improve the appearance of the immediate landscape." Years later, one park biologist complained that the negative effect of CCC projects was "still very evident on the land."[51] Only World War II and the elimination of the CCC ended the agency's extensive pruning of the national forests and parks.

As far as Democratic and conservation politics went, however, the CCC was an unqualified success. As historian Neil Maher has pointed out, the men of the CCC generated widespread support for the New Deal and conservation activity breaking through the class barrier that defined the previously elite movement. FDR intended for the New Deal programs to benefit his constituents, such as the poor, minority, and immigrant groups. Most of the CCC recruits came from the working class and minorities, although African Americans were put in segregated units. Eighty percent of poor Americans voted for FDR in 1936, and 5 of 6 million first-time voters did as well. Not surprisingly, most of the 3 million recruits became avid conservationists. Where conservationism had been most popular among elite Americans, the CCC and other New Deal programs drew in working-class elements. "The work we do in the Great North woods gives us greater understanding of what the word 'Conservation' meant," one enrollee noted. "I am now a firm believer that conservation is necessary for the preservation of our forests." Thus, the CCC was a major conservation recruiter for the New Deal era and the postwar period. The CCC's work on parks and promoting recreational opportunities also expanded the definition of conservation by popularizing preservationism, the idea of ecological balance, and outdoor recreation, which became key issues in postwar environmentalism. In broadening the movement, the CCC helped lay the basis for the mass movement of environmentalism after 1945 and served to bridge the two eras. CCC recruits themselves saw a link between their work and the rise of a modern environmental movement. The motto of the Association of Civilian Conservation Corps Alumni is "Before There Was Earth Day, There Was the CCC."[52]

Another great conservation experiment of the New Deal was the Tennessee Valley Authority. The Tennessee River Valley, a

40,000-square-mile basin, covered parts of Tennessee, Virginia, North Carolina, Georgia, Alabama, Mississippi, and Kentucky. It was one of the poorest regions of the country, with a per capita income of $163, less than half the national average. Of the 3.5 million people in the region, private electric companies served only 300,000.[53] The region was 78 percent rural compared to the national average of 44 percent. Farming on marginal lands and heavy rainfall caused severe erosion problems for 70 percent of the region's farm families.[54] The river itself was unruly in wet seasons and unnavigable in dry.

The seeds of the TVA were rooted in World War I, when President Woodrow Wilson authorized the construction of a federal dam at Muscle Shoals, Alabama. After the war, public and private power advocates battled over whether the dam should be sold or made part of a regional power and navigation project on the Tennessee River. The dam's fate remained bottled up in Congress throughout the twenties. Roosevelt transformed the single dam into a basin-wide project. Signed within FDR's first hundred days in office, the act creating the TVA envisioned one agency responsible for reforestation, flood control, power generation, industrial development, rural planning, and employment projects in the Tennessee River Valley. The TVA was an agency that embodied the three elements of FDR's conservation programs: restoration, improvement, and creating new government conservation agencies.

Roosevelt was fascinated with the idea of planning, a term he never defined clearly. He believed fervently that depressed farming regions needed to be rehabilitated while their natural resources were preserved. His thinking was influenced by the Regional Planning Association of America. The key goal of this small group of experts was to make living and working more fulfilling for the average American. The RPAA contended that "regional planning is the New Conservation—the conservation of human values hand in hand with natural resources . . . permanent agriculture instead of land-skinning, permanent forestry instead of timber mining, permanent human communities." Similarly, Roosevelt spoke about the larger aims of the TVA for equity. "What we are doing there is taking a watershed with about three and a half million people in it, almost all of them rural, and we are trying to make a different type of citizen out of them. . . . TVA is primarily intended to change and improve the standards of living of the people of that Valley."[55]

The TVA did not fulfill the most grandiose dreams of regional planners, but its accomplishments were nonetheless real. By 1946, the TVA had constructed sixteen dams and produced 2.5 million kilowatts of electricity for a valley that had been locked in a nineteenth-century existence.[56] That electricity also was used for wartime nitrate, aluminum, and uranium production. The authority extended the navigable portion of the river to Knoxville and promoted the general welfare of the region through a host of smaller programs. It eliminated malaria from the region, sponsored agricultural demonstration projects, and helped establish a state park system in Tennessee. The TVA came closer to Gifford Pinchot's vision of conservation as integrated planning than had any other government agency.

In addition to the Tennessee Valley, the New Deal dealt with another stricken area, the Dust Bowl. The depression era was particularly cruel to Plains farmers. They had not participated in the exuberant economic times of the twenties, so many thought they would avoid the long fall into depression that the urban portions of the country felt. "Farm prices were not high anyway," one Kansas resident recalled, "and they did not immediately plummet. . . . And besides, there were no skyscrapers from which ruined farmers could jump."[57] But drought conditions began to affect rural communities in 1930. A band running from Virginia to Arkansas was the hardest hit, with record lows for rainfall in many states. In 1931, the drought shifted west into the Great Plains. Heat followed the drought. Temperatures in Nebraska hit 118 degrees and in Iowa, 115. By 1936 farm losses cost $25 million a day. Every year there were dust storms, many due to all the sod being plowed up in recent years. In 1931, one third of the Oklahoma and Texas panhandles, western Kansas, southeastern Colorado and northeast New Mexico were plowed up, exposing the soil to wind erosion. Over 179 storms were reported in April 1933, but the biggest hit in May 1934. Approximate 350 million tons of some of the country's best topsoil was picked up in the Plains and hurled eastward. A couple of days later people from Boston to Atlanta saw darkness at noon. The dust that did not fall on the eastern United States headed for the Atlantic Ocean. Ships 300 miles out to sea reported dust covering them.[58] While many blamed God and nature for the catastrophe, a federal committee report, *The Future of the Great Plains,* blamed the American agricultural system and the fact that farmers did not accept that there were environmental limits to how much plowing the land could take. "There is no evidence that in historic times there was ever a severe enough drought to destroy the grass roots and cause wind erosion. . . . That phenomenon is chargeable to . . . plowing and overcropping." The "Plainsman . . . must realize that he cannot 'conquer Nature'—he must live with her on her own terms, making use of and conserving resources which can no longer be considered inexhaustible."[59]

Farmers tried to cope with the crisis but failed. Some tried an alternate form of plowing called *listing,* but it did not limit moisture loss. A man-made disaster of this scale cried out for federal intervention, and it came. To deal with soil erosion, the federal government created institutions that emphasized cooperation and assistance between federal administrators and local organizations. In 1933, the Department of the Interior allocated 5 million dollars through its Soil Erosion Service for erosion control in the Dust Bowl.[60] Hugh Hammond Bennett, director of the SES, which was later renamed the Soil Conservation Service and moved to the Department of Agriculture, established demonstration projects in which he called for new techniques to solve the problems of the Great Plains. Hailing from a North Carolina cotton family, he had seen early on the destructive practices that had gullied many a Southern farm field. Bennett attended the University of North Carolina where he majored in the study of soils and agriculture, then joined the Department of Agriculture, where he was charged with doing an inventory of the nation's soils. He discovered that America's farmland was pockmarked with eroded soils and lost fertility. To prevent further erosion, Bennett called for the maintenance of as much vegetable cover as possible to hold the soil in place. But much damage was already done. He found that even with the use of modern techniques and fertilizer, cotton production had declined between 1870 and 1920. Bennett became convinced that the erosion problem was as much a social problem as an economic one. "Eroded soils," he said, "make for eroded people."[61] This link between environmental and social problems was repeated many times later during the New Deal. But in the early 1900s, his superiors did not catch on as quickly as he did. In 1909, the Bureau of Soils announced, "The soil is the one indestructible, immutable asset that the nation possesses. It is the one resource that cannot be exhausted; that cannot be used up."[62] The Dust Bowl experience had proved that assessment wrong.

By the 1930s, agricultural experts were still not thinking systematically. Bennett had heard of a plan to build terraces (raised banks with a level top and sloped sides) to control erosion. He argued that many other techniques could be used as well such as contour plowing (the plowing of furrows perpendicular to the slope of the land rather than the more erosive practice of parallel plowing), strip cropping (alternating crops in strips to minimize damage), and grassed waterways (vegetative cover in waterways to control erosion). Bennett, the "messiah of the soil," as one publication called him, preached to whomever would listen. He spoke before a Senate committee to great dramatic effect. He heard that a dust storm out of New Mexico was headed east and would arrive in Washington, DC, on the very day of his testimony. Bennett talked as long as he could until at last the sky went dark as clouds of dust from 2,000 miles away rolled in. The senators sat dumbfounded as Bennett declared, "This, gentlemen, is what I have been talking about."[63] Congress quickly passed the world's first soil legislation forming the Soil Conservation Service.

What made Bennett so successful was that he told the farmers what they wanted to hear and created institutions that they could control. Some New Dealers believed that agriculture had to be restrained to limit productive capacity, thus boosting prices. Farmers tended to resist such restrictions, and Bennett argued that with proper techniques, American agriculture could be unleashed to feed the world. "By increasing the per-acre, per-farm, and per-nation supply of food and fiber, conservation technology can provide the basis for an improved standard of living and simultaneously reduce the hunger and discontent among peoples which so frequently leads to discord, dictatorships, and war." Moreover Bennett recognized that his gospel of conservation would be better received if the message came from fellow farmers. In 1936, the Soil Conservation Service proposed model legislation for the states that, if accepted by the states, would create soil conservation districts. The idea was that community groups would implement conservation techniques beyond the demonstration areas set up by the SCS. The role of the SCS was limited to technical advice and some financial aid. The SCS, like the Forest Service in the Progressive era, sought a decentralized system of administering its programs. "We may have been the first and only bureaucrats in history who ever voluntarily turned over their jobs to local people," Bennett bragged.[64]

The SCS and New Deal farm policy in general substituted federal agencies and institutions for local ones. Many of the farmers claimed their success was due to SCS programs. Fully 80 percent of farmers operating under SCS programs credited the rise in their income to federal conservation practices, and 95 percent planned on continuing such practices. Farmers came to depend on the advice and financial aid of the SCS more than they relied on their county agricultural extension agents. As Neil Maher has argued, the acceptance of SCS advice about practices such as contour plowing was a "coronation of an expansive federal government throughout the American West." Or, as one resident of Jewel County, Kansas, observed, "when a farmer drove by a field that had contours on it, he immediately knew that that farmer had been involved with the federal government."[65] Moreover, like the CCC and the TVA, New Deal agricultural conservation measures expanded the constituency of supporters of conservation from its traditional base of elites to the common citizenry. Conservation was a broad-based movement.

The practical benefits of New Deal soil programs were mixed. One SCS program region on the southern Great Plains estimated that the benefits accrued to farmers between 1935 and 1942 were about $37 million. Unfortunately, that was after $43 million in federal money had been expended, although benefits had finally outstripped the costs by the end of the program.[66] Still it was certainly questionable whether taxing the general public to benefit a few farmers was wise or even just. New Deal advocates argued that by raising the living standards of rural areas, urban dwellers stood to gain too. But what it also did was to accelerate the trend toward large subsidies for America's farm community.

The New Deal conservation programs unquestionably altered national politics, creating believers in the ability of government, particularly the federal government, to do good. Lyndon Baines Johnson, a young Congressman from Texas in the 1930s, built his career on that assumption. Johnson later told a television audience, "All of our rich topsoil was wasting away. And so we started to do something about it. We had to dig some wells. We had to terrace our land. We had to remove some of the small cedars and trees. . . . We built six dams on our river. We brought floods under control. We provided our people with cheap power. . . . That all resulted from the power of the government to bring the greatest good to the greatest number."[67] The Democrats had clearly captured the conservationist mantle of Gifford Pinchot, and politicians like Johnson promoted such policies for decades to come. Less noticed, perhaps, was that by transferring the initiative and responsibility for conservation to the Democrats and government, the power of the traditional elites, mostly Republicans, who relied on private initiative and philanthropy for their influence, declined. For example, conservative members of the Save the Redwoods League opposed much of the New Deal's conservation efforts on ideological grounds and fear of their waning influence. Traditionally, they relied mostly on private money to save the big trees, but the New Deal promised to replace that money for park development with federal and state dollars.[68] Government-sponsored conservation was an important element in the shift away from elite control to a mass movement in the postwar period. It also signalled that in future environmental crises, the public and the government would respond with federal regulation and the creation of new agencies.

Pollution Control

Like the conservation movement, pollution reform became the province of experts and government officials. In the interwar years, neither the quality nor the character of sanitary and pollution control changed significantly. It was an era dominated by state and local government, rather than federal control, a reliance on technical fixes rather than legislative reform, and expert management of problems. Regulators stressed cooperation with polluters.

Despite the lax regulation, the interwar years established precedents for the postwar era. Experts and the public began to take a broader view of pollution by including industrial and invisible sources of pollution rather than just focusing on smoke. The New Deal marked the beginning of federal involvement in pollution issues. Pollution also became an issue of public health rather than a question of efficiency or a nuisance.

Water pollution control was characterized by what historian Martin Melosi called a "broadening viewpoint" regarding the complexity of pollution problems. Experts saw problems in terms of entire river basins rather than single-point pollution. Hence, they looked to protect river systems and did not focus exclusively on the more human-centered concern of disease prevention.[69] Although not yet adopting an ecological viewpoint, experts now approached problems with greater environmental awareness.

Purification of drinking water demonstrated this broadening perspective. Since the Progressive era, cities focused mostly on organic rather than on industrial pollution. Given the high rates of typhoid epidemics, the concern with bacterial pollutants was understandable. With the use of water filtration systems and chlorination, however, disease rates fell markedly, from 33.8 deaths per 100,000 in 1920 to 3.7 by 1945.[70]

Public pressure forced officials to expand their purview beyond biological hazards. As one water engineer put it in 1932, "the awakened public conscience as to the conservation of water resources and abatement of stream pollution is creating demands upon some state health departments to increase their activities along these lines, upon others to inaugurate such work." The president of the National Coast Anti-Pollution League warned that water pollution was a "problem of National importance, imperiling health and food supply."[71]

Health officials and experts heeded the demand for a healthy drinking supply and expanded their study of the problem. A 1923 report found that industrial wastes had contaminated 248 water supplies. As the nation's industrial capacity expanded, the impact and types of wastes multiplied. A report saw the problem as complex. "There are many sources and many types of pollution," the study warned. "Each type has distinctive effects on human activities. Each general type requires a special technique for abatement."[72] In 1925, the U.S. Public Health Service revised its clean drinking water standards and included maximum concentrations of inorganic materials such as lead, copper, and zinc.

Wastewater treatment underwent a similarly broadened treatment. Public and official concern over pollution in streams compelled experts to take a more systematic approach to examining river basins. One official noted that the systemic view of stream pollution had "brought with it a marked change in the nature and complexity of the engineering problems to be solved" and had led to a "water-shed consciousness" among pollution experts. Other sanitary engineers warned against the traditional reliance on dilution of pollution and the profession's exclusive focus on biological rather than industrial threats. Engineers were no doubt also responding to public pressure. In the late twenties, the Izaak Walton League, a fish-sporting society began its own study of how pollution affected aquatic life. The league began a campaign called "Clean Streams for Health and Happiness," which awakened public opinion in support of industrial and domestic sewage treatment.[73] In the late 1930s, the National Wildlife Federation joined the league in campaigning to clean up rivers.

States rather than the federal government sought out ways to ameliorate pollution. Between 1917 and 1926, three states, Connecticut, Ohio, and Pennsylvania, established boards to deal with industrial pollution.[74] In the 1920s, several states required that cities provide sewage treatment rather than dumping raw sewage into bodies of water. In 1937, Pennsylvania's Anti-Stream Pollution Act attempted to broadly proscribe pollution in bodies of water. The statute defined pollution as substances that rendered waters unfit for use as domestic water supplies, by animals and aquatic life, and for industry and recreation. In Chicago, courts limited the city's ability to dump raw sewage into the Mississippi when the city of St. Louis objected to the practice. Instead, the Windy City was required to construct sewage-treatment plants. The court decision established a precedent for later court intervention in environmental disputes and made dumping of raw sewage a questionable practice.[75]

Pollution control was still largely a matter for state and local governments during the interwar years, but the federal government did expand its involvement through pollution studies, legislation, and funding of construction projects. The U.S. Public Health Service began conducting pollution studies in 1912, but the government had no power to act on its conclusions. Until 1924, the only major piece of federal legislation to deal with pollution was the 1899 Refuse Act. This legislation prohibited the discharge into navigable bodies of water of any refuse without obtaining a permit from the Army Corps of Engineers. The act only dealt with solid wastes; liquid wastes, such as sewage, were not covered under the law. The previously mentioned 1924 Oil Pollution Control Act was a typically weak piece of legislation. Congress did not take action again on pollution until after World War II, when in 1948 it passed the Water Pollution Control Act. Avoiding outright regulation, the act provided funding only for construction grants for municipal wastewater facilities.[76]

The New Deal inaugurated federal support for water supply and wastewater treatment. With income from taxes slipping during the depression, municipalities cut back on public works projects, which reached a low point in 1932. Several New Deal agencies moved to correct the decline. Between 1933 and 1937, the Public Works Administration budgeted $450 million for water and sewer systems. The Works Progress Administration expended nearly 10 percent of its labor force on water and sewer projects. Although support slipped back a bit during World War II, the federal government had committed itself to partnering with state and local government.[77]

Federal involvement was less extensive in air pollution reform. Although the New Deal sponsored some smoke-abatement projects, there were no laws passed. Even at the state level, only one statute passed and that did not come until 1947 in California.

Reform came at the local level. After World War I, lay activists picked up where their Progressive counterparts had left off. Key leaders in the movement were women's clubs and physicians, who tended to stress the idea that smoke was unhealthy. In 1928, the Milwaukee *Journal* ran a headline, "Doctors Attack Smoke as a Menace to Health."[78] Women's clubs in Cleveland and St. Louis launched campaigns to clean up their skies. Municipal leaders responded to this kind of lobbying by improving smoke-abatement departments. But the skies of most major cities did not clear much. Coal consumption rose dramatically, peaking in the 1920s, and smoke-abatement departments had only limited authority to force industry and homeowners to cut back on emissions.

Leadership of the movement shifted to experts. Experts other than physicians tended to minimize the health risk of smoke and viewed the problem as a question of efficient burning of fuels. Education efforts focused on industry, utilities, and railroads. By the late twenties, experts agreed that those entities had made progress, largely because of a desire to burn fuel economically. But given coal's abundance and inexpensive cost, industries were only willing to economize so much. The main problem lay with domestic coal use. Home heating units burned inefficiently, and the public was unlikely to change its habits unless another economical fossil fuel was found.

Some experts decided to alter tactics. They called for switching fuels to cleaner burning coal. The campaign began in St. Louis. In the late 1930s, Raymond Tucker, an assistant to the mayor, decided that the educational campaign carried out by the Women's Organization for Smoke Abatement had failed. Tucker reasoned that if the city could find coal with less fly-ash, the smoke problem would be eliminated. After several years of intense debate, the city began purchasing Arkansas coal that had a much lower content of volatile matter than did the local coal. The city distributed the coal to domestic users at reasonable prices. The results were immediate. Experts noted that the winter of 1940–41 had passed "without a really good smoke," and that the hours of thick smog had decreased by 83.5 percent.[79]

The St. Louis example spawned a fight between the coal industry and antipollution advocates over similar ordinances in other cities, especially in Pittsburgh. Notorious as the "Smoke City," pollution in Pittsburgh was so bad that mid-morning looked like night. At public hearings the traditional antismoke advocates, physicians and women, overshadowed experts. They emphasized the health threats of smoke. The city council passed an ordinance even stronger than that in St. Louis in 1941. The war, however, delayed its enforcement, and it was not until 1947 that Pittsburgh enjoyed its first smokeless winter.[80] Similar ordinances passed in New York and Cincinnati.

Still, substantial declines in smoke had to await the switch to other fuels. The improvement in Pittsburgh's air quality was in part due to the rapid switch to natural gas, driven by cheap supplies from the Southwest. Where only 17 percent of Pittsburgh homes used natural gas in 1940, 66 percent did so in 1950.[81]

Nevertheless, the antismoke debates of the 1930s and 1940s laid the groundwork for the public debates of the 1960s. Even though experts had stressed efficiency arguments in limiting smoke, it was concern for health that eventually helped pass these laws. Health concerns also shifted the balance of power within pollution-abatement circles. No longer did engineers dominate the debate. Increasingly physicians and industrial hygienists, who had long been familiar with the health risks of industrial processes, had influence.

This shift was in no small part due to the 1948 disaster in Donora, Pennsylvania. In this small mill town, smog had sickened 40 percent of the population and killed twenty people, launching a national investigation. A similar pollution episode in London killed at least 4,000 of its residents in 1952. A year later approximately 200 died in New York from smoke-related illnesses.[82] That invisible pollutants did much of the damage in Donora and elsewhere forced experts to shift their focus from visible pollutants to a broader spectrum of hazards. These events and the recognition of the complexity of the pollutants pushed pollution issues into the national spotlight.

The Wilderness Debate

Although wilderness values took a back seat to more utilitarian forms of conservation in the twenties and thirties, the era brought important changes in attitudes toward nature and leisure. Many historians point to the period between 1880 and 1920 as the key time when Americans came to know nature through their leisure activities. As Paul Sutter has noted in *Driven Wild*, nature became "a potent symbol and a foil for the dramatic urban-industrial changes overtaking society."[83] America was shifting from a Victorian society that valued self-sacrifice to one that favored consumerism and the therapeutic qualities of leisure time. Nature had once been a place to conquer and find natural resources. By 1920, it had also become a place of regeneration and contemplation.

The interwar period continued these trends in wilderness values but added new dimensions. By 1922, there were 10 million automobiles on the roads. By 1929, the number had jumped to 23 million, or one car for every five citizens. As sociologists Robert and Helen Lynd found in their study of Muncie, Indiana, the auto was an "invention remaking leisure." Responding to the growth in automobile use, federal, state, and local governments sought ways to promote leisure travel through road-building projects, state park development, and the promotion of tourist venues. Finally, American culture altered as a result of the mass production of consumer products and modern advertising. Consumerism dominated outdoor recreation in this era. Americans spent more money on travel and camping equipment and accumulated more experiences in nature.[84]

Autocamping and motor touring became two of the most popular outdoor leisure activities. By one estimate, 10 to 15 percent of the population using half of all automobiles were engaged in autocamping by the early twenties. Taking to America's back roads, autocamping, or "gypsying" as it was called, offered a liberating experience to its practitioners. As the camping craze spread, tourists became fascinated with technology that eased the burden of life in the outdoors. As one outdoor publication noted, campers could "rough it de luxe" by purchasing the right technology for the job. In 1923, the Coleman Company began producing camp stoves, the use of which was "The Smooth Way to Rough It," as the company claimed. A host of other companies produced tents, camping chairs, clothing, and specially packaged foods to support hobbyists. By the 1930s, house trailers were widely available, with 400 companies producing almost 100,000 trailers a year—a $50-million-dollar a year industry. Nineteen-thirty-four was one of the worst years of the depression, but *Fortune* magazine noted that in that year roadside support services for auto touring had become a $3 billion industry.[85] Camping and touring had truly become part of a consumerist society.

Some of the nation's most prominent wilderness organizations encouraged the craze for touring. The Sierra Club made it its mission "to explore, enjoy, and render accessible the mountain regions of the Pacific Coast." Accepting that the National Park Service needed to build a constituency if it were to survive bureaucratic fights with the National Forest Service, the club supported the Park Service's program of road building. In 1927, the club advocated a road-building plan for Yosemite that exceeded the Park Service's plan.[86] Aesthetics mattered, but it was an ideal that had to bend to the reality of politics and tourists.

Government officials searched for ways to deal with the growing demand for camping venues. State governments and the National Park Service helped launch a movement for state parks. Begun in 1921, the goal was to establish "A State Park Every Hundred Miles" to accommodate roving campers. From 1920 to 1933, 70 percent of all state parks had been established.[87] The New Deal only accelerated this trend as the CCC helped build over 700 new state parks throughout the country.

The National Parks Service also responded with a deluge of new parks, national monuments, and road-building projects in the interwar years. Park Service director Stephen Mather began viewing the park system in terms of automobile touring. He encouraged the completion of a grand 3,500-mile loop, whereby park tourists could visit all the major national parks and monuments in the West. Public accessibility and opening up the park system to new constituents were the main factors in establishing national parks in the East, including the Sieur De Monts (now Acadia National Park) National Monument in Maine. By 1931, despite the depression, the National Park Service was spending $7 million annually on road-improvement projects. The New Deal added another $17 million and over 150,000 CCC workers to National Park projects. Of all the activity, FDR boasted, "We are definitely in an era of building—the building of great public projects for the benefit of the public and with the definite objective of building human happiness."[88]

Not everyone was pleased by the government's plans to accommodate leisure activities and the automobile. As visitations to the parks and the national forests grew, a small but influential chorus of voices questioned whether the wilderness might not be overrun. In the 1920s, women's groups were particularly active in fighting the plethora of billboards that desecrated the countryside. The General Federation of Women's Clubs decried roadside billboards "as preventing the full enjoyment of outdoor beauty."[89] Others argued that it was road building itself that most threatened the backcountry. One critic argued it was the "automobile, agent of material progress, destroyer of deserts, leveler of mountains and annihilator of time and distance" that posed the greatest threat to wilderness.[90] Rosalie Edge of the Emergency Conservation Committee objected to the extensive road building of the Forest Service for the profit of lumber interests, but which also opened up the forests to excessive recreation access. "Roads and more roads are dividing, shrinking and destroying the remnants of the wilderness. . . . Only trails belong to deep forests; a road into a wild region is the prelude to its destruction."[91]

Scientists, too, in the Ecological Society of America (ESA) called for preserving lands with minimal human disturbance for study as ecological laboratories. They anticipated the ecological motivations of postwar environmentalists. The ESA's members had very different priorities than did wilderness advocates. Scientists sought "natural conditions" where humans had not significantly intervened in natural processes so that they could study the natural succession and climax of various species. Moreover, the ecologists wanted to save "representative types" of natural settings where distinct plant and animal communities could be studied. Finally, ecologists sought to preserve much smaller tracts of land than wilderness advocates, just what was necessary to preserve an ecological community. By contrast, wilderness advocates thought of these areas in human terms. For example wilderness advocates called for setting aside roadless lands large enough for people to use for extended camping trips. Ecologists did not want large wilderness areas, just ones that were ecologically pristine.[92] There were some such as Edge who embraced both perspectives:

> It is time that the nation insists on the preservation of the national forests for other and greater benefits [than lumber]. They should guard the headwaters, equalizing the stream-flow, and preserving the lower lands from floods and erosion. They should be a haven for wildlife. . . . They should be laboratories for the study of ecology. . . . Above all, the Forests should be preserved for the recreation of those whose need impels them to withdraw from time to time from conventional life. . . . To all such benefits roads are inimical.[93]

Oddly, given Edge's criticism, it was in the Forest Service, the prodevelopment agency, that the movement to protect wilderness emerged. As with the Park Service, the Forest Service had witnessed the phenomenal growth of tourism and camping on its lands. Between 1917 and 1924 the number of visitors to the national forests quadrupled. Unlike the Park Service, the Forest Service had few policies in place for dealing with tourism. Inevitably, demand for recreational facilities conflicted with the Forest Service's traditional emphasis on resource extraction.

Recognizing the need for a new approach, Arthur Carhart, a landscape architect with the Forest Service, proposed that national forest land around the popular Trapper's Lake in Colorado remain free of tourist development. Under the Term Permit Act, applicants could establish cottages in national forests. Carhart hoped to keep the shoreline of the lake free of development. The Forest Service followed his recommendations in 1919. It was the first time that the service had protected national forest land from excessive recreational development.

Carhart's actions had an important influence on Aldo Leopold, then Chief of Operations for the Forest Service's Southwest District. Leopold and Carhart discussed how the Trapper's Lake model could work in other regions. Leopold had something bigger in mind than did Carhart. Where the architect had preserved only about a half mile of forest buffer around a scenic lake, Leopold envisioned preserving huge undeveloped areas that could support campers on a pack trip for over two weeks. Leopold's main concern was to keep these areas free of auto traffic and consumer trappings. Wilderness was to be open for hunting and camping and remain "devoid of roads, artificial trails, cottages, and other works of man."[94] Thus Leopold, one of the most ecologically minded of the wilderness advocates, still thought in anthropocentric terms about wilderness.

Leopold argued that in many areas of the national forests recreational use had become the highest use of the land. He concluded that some areas of the forests had to "be preserved as wilderness."[95] Leopold laid out a plan in which an area in Gila National Forest in New Mexico would be preserved for more primitive outdoor experiences than that offered by automobile camping, boating, and touring. In 1924, the Forest Service accepted Leopold's recommendations and set aside 574,000 acres. The reservation's protected status could be reversed by administrative fiat at any time, but for the time being, the Forest Service voted to preserve some wilderness to prevent overdevelopment for recreation.[96]

Leopold spent the 1920s advocating a stronger Forest Service wilderness policy. He called for saving wilderness areas from the automobile and recreation. Arguably he was advocating an elitist approach in which only a select few could enjoy certain stretches of public land. "The majority," he admitted, "undoubtedly want all the automobile roads, summer hotels, graded trails, and other modern conveniences that we can give them. . . . But a very substantial minority, I think, want just the opposite." Critics claimed Leopold was trying to save wilderness for "himself and the elect few, and objects to roads because they inevitably bring other people."[97] There was something to this argument. Later studies showed visits to wilderness areas closely correlated to income and education with just 5 percent of all visits made by blue-collar workers, while college graduates made up two-thirds of the visitors. Leopold responded that he was merely trying to prevent the "universal motorization of the forests," but the elitist tag was one that stuck to the wilderness movement for decades to come.[98]

Eventually, the Forest Service moved to placate the preservationists with some modest steps. William Greeley, the service's chief, adopted a policy of limited wilderness preservation on national forest land. Greeley proposed a formal policy of setting aside wilderness areas. In the late 1920s, the Forest Service instituted regulation L-20, which established "primitive areas" where development and resource extraction was to be limited. "These mountain wildernesses," Greeley wrote, "may not be used by numbers of people in any wise commensurate with those who will throng the highways, but their individual service will be immeasurably greater." To satisfy the interests of the Ecological Society of America, the new regulation also established "research reserves."[99] But the protection of the new primitive areas was a limited victory. Their protected status could be overturned at any time and there were no clear prohibitions against all kinds of development.

The Forest Service's change of heart was not entirely altruistic. The service was certainly trying to protect select areas from recreational pressures and logging, but it had other motives too. Given the Park Service's voracious appetite for national forest land, unless the Forest Service did more to serve tourists, some officials feared that it would "have little valid ground for objection to a change in [national forest land] administrative supervision" to the Parks Service.[100] Without the expensive hotels, the Forest Service hoped to position itself, as historian James Glover argues, as a "blue-collar alternative" to the more elitist national parks.[101] Preservationists benefited from the bureaucratic competition between the Park Service and the Forest Service.

Congress also moved to protect wilderness areas in Superior National Forest in Minnesota. At the behest of Arthur Carhart, the region, today known as the Boundary Waters Canoe Area, was set aside as a roadless area, but logging and potential dam construction continued to threaten it. The key opponent of development was the Izaak Walton League. The organization lobbied Congress hard for passage of a bill to protect the area. In 1930, the Shipstead-Newton-Nolan Act created by statute what was the first national forest wilderness area, covering over 1.2 million acres of national forest land, more than any primitive area established by the Forest Service.[102] The area enjoyed protections that no national park had, since recreational development and road building were banned. It was not surprising that some preservationists began to prefer Forest Service protection to that of the National Park Service.

The early thirties were important for wilderness protection for another reason. Robert Marshall arose as the nation's leading voice for preservation, until his untimely death in 1939. The son of a widely respected constitutional lawyer and leader of New York City's Jewish community, Marshall was educated in the progressive Ethical Cultural School in the city, and it helped instill radical politics in him. He learned to love the outdoors from his father and grew up spending his summers in the Adirondacks. With his brother, George, he climbed all the neighboring peaks higher than 4,000 feet, a total of forty-six. The elder Marshall also set an example for his sons in wilderness politics. Louis Marshall helped lead the fight in 1915 against timber interests that sought to open up the Adirondacks to cutting. At the same time, Robert decided on a career in forestry, a profession his father called "missionary work." "I love the woods and solitude," Robert wrote. "I like the various forms of scientific work a forester must do. I should hate to spend the greater part of my lifetime in a stuffy office or in a crowded city."[103]

He did not. Marshall earned forestry degrees from Harvard and Syracuse Universities and a Ph.D. in plant physiology from Johns Hopkins. He joined the forest service and later the Bureau of Indian Affairs where he oversaw the establishment of wilderness areas on Native American lands. He made excursions into the field and took a fifteen-month break in 1930–31 to spend a year among Native Americans and white prospectors above the Arctic Circle in Wiseman, Alaska. He wrote a best-selling account of his experiences in *Arctic Village*.

When not working outdoors, Marshall became a wilderness advocate and leading critic of the Forest Service's cooperationist policies with timber corporations. Following his own socialist in-clinations, Marshall called for government regulation of private lands: "The period for voluntary private forestry is over," he noted in 1929. "The government must step in and compel the private tim-ber owner to leave the forest which he exploits in a productive con-dition."[104] Marshall joined Aldo Leopold in the wilderness debate that foresters engaged in throughout the interwar period. Like Leopold, Marshall's chief objection was to road building and the introduction of the automobile into wilderness areas. Trying to straddle the elitist concept of wilderness and his own socialist roots, Marshall was one of the few activists of his time to try and combine equity and aesthetics. Marshall called for opening up the forests so that even "the most destitute of the city population will be able to get a vacation in the forest." Marshall was unusual among preservationists in advocating for the poor. In 1930 Mar-shall sketched out his concept of a wilderness area. It had to be a "region which contains no permanent inhabitants, possesses no possibility of conveyance by any mechanical means and is suffi-ciently spacious that a person crossing it must have the experience of sleeping out." He called for a group of "spirited people who will fight for the freedom of the wilderness."[105] Marshall's image of wilderness was still tied to aesthetic considerations. In defining a wilderness area, he did not include ecological considerations. Nev-ertheless, his definition became a rough outline for the debates to come.

Eventually, Marshall's idea for a wilderness organization took shape. By 1934, a number of individuals had become alarmed at the extensive road-building and conservation activities of New Deal organizations. Benton MacKaye, the founder of the Appala-chian Trail, which stretched from Maine to Georgia, hiking enthu-siast Harvey Broome, and Harold Anderson, a leading member of the Potomac Appalachian Trail Club, exchanged ideas on how to best preserve the trail from proposals to build skyline drives nearby. In a letter to MacKaye, Anderson noted, "You and Bob Marshall have been preaching that those who love the primitive should get together. . . . That is what I would like to get started." When the group approached Marshall with the idea of a society to protect the trail, Marshall transformed the proposal into a national organization to protect wilderness. With a $1,000-grant from Marshall, the Wilderness Society began operations in January 1935 with Robert Sterling Yard, former head of the National Parks Association, as its president. But Marshall still largely ran the organization. He wanted a militant organization to push wilderness values without significant compromise. "We want no straddlers," Marshall noted of his desire to see that only the converted become members of the organization. A wilderness society was needed, Marshall wrote, "to counteract the propaganda spread by the Automobile Association of America, the various booster organizations and the innumerable Chambers of Commerce, which seem to find no peace as long as any primitive tract in America remains unopened to mechanization."[106] Although Aldo Leopold encouraged the society to admit those who favored "wilderness for ecological" reasons, most members including Leopold did so initially for aesthetic reasons and to limit the mechanization of the back country.[107]

On the issue of roads, wilderness advocates had a powerful ally in the Secretary of the Interior, Harold Ickes. Ickes decried the effect automobiles had on the national parks. "If I had my way about national parks," he said in 1933, "I would create one without a road in it. I would have it impenetrable forever to automobiles, a place where man would not try to improve upon God." Five years later he still disparaged the mechanization of the parks. "Ever since I came to Washington I have been trying to impress the National Park Service with the fact that not only do we not want any more roads but that we have too many as it is. The fewer the better as far as I am concerned. . . ." Demonstrating a bit of elitism, he sneered at the Park Service's making over the parks into "Coney Islands." "The parks are for those who will appreciate them and not merely for the hordes of tourists who dash through them at break neck speed. . . ."[108] Under Ickes' sometimes ruthless prodding, the federal government increased the number of national monuments from thirty-three to eighty-six. The size of the national parks and monuments system increased from 14 million acres in 1933 to 20 million by 1946.

The Wilderness Society took the offensive immediately. A new dispute had emerged between the Forest Service and the Park

Service over Olympic National Park. A proposal called for expanding the park by taking away some land from the surrounding national forest. Many members of the Wilderness Society were suspicious of the National Park Service and its tendency to promote tourism. To get the Park and Forest services in a bidding war for the society's support, Marshall asked both agencies what their plan was for the area. He testified before Congress that the society favored National Park Service administration of the land, since the Forest Service proposal called for some clearing of timber that the Park Service would protect. Shortly thereafter, the Park Service proposal carried the day. The Wilderness Society learned from this encounter that it could play one agency against the other as they bid for its support.[109]

Marshall saved one of his most important contributions for last. In 1936, he took a position in the Forest Service as head of recreational development. He initiated a substantial revision to the L-20 regulations that had established "primitive" areas. To wilderness advocates, the L-20 regulations had drawbacks. Although there were seventy-two primitive areas on over 13 million acres of land, road construction was allowed on fifteen, grazing on sixty-two, and logging in fifty-nine areas. Just four areas prohibited all development.[110] Marshall pushed through new "U" regulations that prohibited roads and timber-cutting in wilderness areas. Unlike the L-20 primitive areas, wilderness designations were made at the highest levels of the service and were seen as permanent. The U regulations substantially reduced the Forest Service's primary commitment to timber harvesting and fire regulation in the restricted areas. The service still permitted hunting, which the preservationists did not oppose, but more troubling was its allowance for grazing and mining in the wilderness areas. But without new legislation, the Forest Service had no authority to go further.

Just two months after the issuance of the U regulations, Robert Marshall died in November 1939 of heart failure at the age of thirty-eight. Marshall's death left a number of legacies. He divided his $1.5 million estate between his three favorite causes, socialism, civil liberties, and wilderness preservation. The last bequest secured the future of the Wilderness Society.[111] Without his guiding hand, however, the society became a more conservative organization, making few efforts to build coalitions across class boundaries as Marshall advocated. It focused instead on behind-the-scenes lobbying. Nevertheless, the Wilderness Society was the chief force in the passage of the 1964 Wilderness Act that secured the place of wilderness in the national forests.

Toward a Land Ethic

The Wilderness Society was founded on a rejection of America's consumer and motorized society. The society's founders did not give high priority to preserving unique ecological areas. In this respect, the society reflected the general tenor of the conservation movement in the interwar years. Conservation was a movement to protect resources from abuse by America's growing consumer culture. After about 1935 the wilderness movement took an ecological turn. Some game management experts and the Ecological Society of America were already espousing the protection of animals and the land for scientific purposes. These groups lacked an advocate who could articulate a new vision of how humans should relate to the land.

Aldo Leopold became that advocate. What made Leopold the greatest environmental thinker of his age was his ability to combine ethical principles with the science of ecology, a reverence for life with the practical knowledge of an expert. Initially, however, Leopold was a traditional conservationist in the mold of Gifford Pinchot. An avid hunter and naturalist as a child, he graduated from Yale's School of Forestry in 1909 schooled in the practical and economic ways of forestry. Until the 1920s, Leopold served in various posts with the Forest Service in the Southwest and Wisconsin. He became an advocate for wilderness preservation, but his work also took him into game management, a topic on which he wrote the premier textbook in 1933. Keeping with Progressive era–conservation philosophy, he advocated that game animals should be viewed in terms of agronomics—animals were a crop to be maximized by managers and harvested by hunters. Deer were the prime game animals in the Southwest, so he promoted an extensive program to exterminate their predators, "skulking marauders," especially the wolf.[112] In 1920, he told members of a conference on game animals, "It is going to take patience and money to catch the last wolf or lion in New Mexico. But the last one must be caught before the job can be called fully successful."[113]

By the 1920s, Leopold began to have second thoughts about the wisdom of the Forest Service's predator-extermination campaign. As Leopold told it, his conversion happened in his encounter with the wolf, told at the beginning of the chapter. But despite the essay's claim, this was no born-again conversion. He condensed into one story a process that actually took years for him to complete. As late as 1933, after he had joined the faculty at the University of Wisconsin, Madison, Leopold still referred to game as a "crop." But Leopold began to recognize the limits of a strictly economic approach to game management. The Kaibab episode was particularly important to his thinking. With the elimination of the wolves and other predators, he saw deer multiply and overbrowse range after range, destroying the available vegetation in the process. "In the end the starved bones of the hoped-for deer herd, dead of its own too-much, bleach with the bones of dead sage, or molder under the high-lined junipers."[114] Leopold began to see predators and a diversity of species as an essential part of a healthy ecosystem.

The year 1935 was a turning point for Leopold in several respects. He became one of the founders of the Wilderness Society. He traveled to Germany, where he was repelled by the intensive and artificial tending that forests received. He also bought an exhausted 160-acre farm in Wisconsin and proceeded to experiment with rejuvenating the devastated landscape. Over the next decade, he wrote a series of essays espousing his ethical insights about preserving game, protecting wilderness and restoring farmland. He compiled his musings in *A Sand County Almanac*, one of the most important books ever written on the environment. The book was accepted for publication in 1948, just a week before Leopold died while helping a neighbor fight a grass fire near his Sand County farm. As Donald Fleming described Leopold, he was "the Moses of the New Conservation impulse of the 1960's and '70's, who handed down the Tablets of the Law but did not live to enter the promised land."[115]

Leopold's key accomplishment in *A Sand County Almanac* was combining moral insights with ecological principles to create a new environmental ethic. Deeply influential for him were the ideas of the German physician Albert Schweitzer who argued that humans could not be truly ethical until they developed a reverence for all life. Leopold added ecological science to Schweitzer's worldview. Ecology emphasized the interdependence of living things. Using a mechanical metaphor, Leopold argued that when tinkering with the workings of nature all the cogs and wheels must be saved to ensure the proper functioning of the whole system. In his view, an "ecological conscience" respected all life forms. This "changes the role of *Homo sapiens* from conqueror of the land-community to plain member and citizen of it." But if humans were merely citizens, they were the only ones who could unalterably damage the entire community. People had to follow a "land ethic." The key tenet was that "a thing is right when it tends to preserve the integrity, stability, and beauty of the biotic community. It is wrong when it tends otherwise."[116] This ethic was not something to be left to professionals. Leopold argued that the only way the environment could be protected was if all Americans internalized these ideas and lived life with more humility toward nature.

This growing emphasis on blending ecology with aesthetic preservation found its expression in the new additions to the national park system. Isle Royale and the Everglades were apt examples of this trend toward establishing parks that were ecological units. The Everglades Park, in particular, demonstrated the new focus on ecology and the deemphasis of aesthetics or monumentalism. A movement to create an Everglades park was started by a New England transplant, landscape architect Ernest Coe. Coe was appalled at the loss of birds due to poaching and the transplanting of rare orchids from the Everglades. In 1928 he started the Tropical Everglades National Park Association and lobbied for creation of a national park in the halls of Washington. The park had no grand vistas and did not play to the typical cultural nationalism that scenic parks traditionally embodied. But it was established for the vital role that the Everglades played in south Florida's ecology. In dedicating the park in 1947, President Harry Truman highlighted the fact that it was the Everglades ecology that was important: "Here are no lofty peaks seeking the sky, no mighty glaciers or rushing streams wearing away the uplifted land. Here is land, tranquil in its quiet beauty, serving not as the source of water, but as the receiver of it. To its natural abundance we owe the spectacular plant and animal life that distinguishes this place from all others in our country."[117] Some park enthusiasts opposed the Everglades as not being park-worthy. William Hornaday, a leader in wildlife conservation, said of the Everglades, "I found mighty little that was of special interest, and absolutely nothing that was picturesque or beautiful . . . a swamp is a swamp." Nevertheless, proponents were able to ensure that the enabling legislation recognized the Everglades for its wilderness and ecological value. "The said area or areas shall be permanently reserved as a wilderness," the legislation read. And it also restricted development of the park if it might "interfere with the preservation intact of the unique flora and fauna and the essential primitive conditions."[118] The Everglades campaign demonstrated the shift toward a more ecological view of the park system.

Leopold had married science to the sentimental aesthetic viewpoint, but there was a problem; the science of ecology was changing. As historian Donald Worster pointed out, Leopold railed against seeing the environment in strictly economic terms as conservationists were wont to do, but ecology itself began to move toward a more agronomic, economic outlook. Science might not be a reliable foundation for a new ethic as Leopold had supposed. Nevertheless, by the 1950s and '60's the public was ready to hear his message. Leopold provided preservationists with new weapons to fight environmental battles. To their aesthetic, romantic, and moral arguments, he added the veneer of acceptable science. Moreover, his argument that an "ecological conscience" must be democratized and spread among the people struck a nerve with activists of the 1960s. His land ethic became the cornerstone of the new environmental movement.

Conclusion

By the late 1940s, the conservation movement was very different from what it had been in 1920. The three disparate threads of the movement—resource conservation, pollution control, and wilderness preservation—were drawing together. The most noticeable commonality was the presence of the federal government. Federal regulators increased spending and regulation in a host of areas, and the diversity of federal conservation functions expanded markedly. The federal government became even more involved after World War II.

Expertise as an idea and professional identity had gotten its start in the Progressive era, but it became the dominant force in the movement by the forties. Science, too, took its place at the center of conservation. A greater environmental and ecological under standing pervaded conservation work. In game management, it was manifest in predator control. In pollution, experts not only recognized the growing threat of industrialization, but they began to see pollution problems with greater complexity. Health experts looked at pollution not in terms of waste and efficiency, but as a health issue stemming from environmental causes. The influence of ecologists was also felt in the movement for wilderness preservation. At least part of the rationale for preserving wilderness was to save unique ecological areas. Experts and their science had proved their worth and, despite the infusion of private activists after World War II, remained critical to the success of the movement.

Science had also infused a new ethical view of the environment. Best exemplified by Aldo Leopold's work, the new ethic justified environmental policies not simply on economics, as was often done in the past, but on the necessity to maintain diversity and the right of a species to exist. Ecology spurred a new attitude toward predators and the value of wilderness. In the area of pollution, new scientific studies revealed the health threats that pollution posed to the public. Americans demanded a cleaner environment, not simply to alleviate a nuisance, but as a fundamental human right.

More Americans demanded a better environment than ever before. The automobile was at the center of a new consumer culture that valued new forms of tourism, camping, sports fishing, and hunting. Once largely the province of the wealthy, outdoor living came within reach of more Americans. As recreation increased, the government was compelled to expand the infrastructure to support it, with new parks, wilderness areas, and government-sponsored reconstruction efforts such as the Civilian Conservation Corps. What was emerging was a constituency of Americans and government administrators who favored resource conservation and preserving scenic and healthy places in which to live and play.

But in history not all is continuity. The end of World War II was a watershed for conservation. The war's end unleashed social changes, economic affluence, and suburban growth that made conservation what it had never before been, a mass movement. But the unity could not hold. Resource conservationists found themselves alienated from the preservationists and urban environmental reformers as public values switched from quantitative conservation to qualitative lifestyle issues. In the midst of change, the older elements of the movement struggled to define themselves. At times they led the movement, but at others they found themselves struggling to catch up with the social and political forces that they had not created. The redefined environmental movement of the 1960s and 1970s was a hybrid of old and new.

Endnotes

1 Aldo Leopold, *A Sand County Almanac: With Essays on Conservation from Round River* (Oxford: Oxford University Press, 1966; reprint, New York: Ballantine Books, 1970), 138–39.

2 Susan Flader, "Citizenry and the State in the Shaping of Environmental Policy," *Environmental History* 3, no. 1 (January 1998): 15.

3 Benjamine Kline, *First Along the River: A Brief History of the U.S. Conservation Movement,* 2d ed. (Lanham: Acada Books, 2000), 60.

4 Kendrick A. Clements, "Herbert Hoover and Conservation, 1921–33," *American Historical Review* 89, no. 1 (1984): 85–86.

5 Donald C. Swain, *Federal Conservation Policy, 1921–1933* (Berkeley: University of California Press, 1963), 13.

6 Ibid., 23.

7 Susan R. Schrepfer, *The Fight to Save the Redwoods: A History of Environmental Reform, 1917–78* (Madison: University of Wisconsin Press, 1983), 56.

8 William G. Robbins, *American Forestry: A History of National, State, and Private Cooperation* (Lincoln: University of Nebraska Press, 1985), 110–111.

9 Richard Polenberg, "Conservation and Reorganization: The Forest Service Lobby, 1937–1938," *Agricultural History* 39, no. 4 (1965): 234.

10 Stephen Fox, *The American Conservation Movement: John Muir and*

His Legacy (Madison: University of Wisconsin Press, 1985), 163.

11 Kevin DeLuca and Anne Demo, "Imagining Nature and Erasing Class and Race: Carleton Watkins, John Muir, and the Construction of Wilderness," *Environmental History* 6, no. 4 (October 2001): 552.

12 Swain, *Federal Conservation Policy,* 42.

13 Thomas R. Dunlap, *Saving America's Wildlife* (Princeton: Princeton University Press, 1988), 65.

14 Ibid., 66–67, 69.

15 Lisa Mighetto, *Wild Animals and American Environmental Ethics* (Tucson: University of Arizona Press, 1991), 85.

16 Donald Worster, *Nature's Economy: A History of Ecological Ideas* (Cambridge: Cambridge University Press, 1977), 277 and 279.

17 Dunlap, *Saving America's Wildlife,* 79.

18 Richard West Sellars, *Preserving Nature in the National Parks: A History* (New Haven: Yale University Press, 1997), 119.

19 Worster, *Nature's Economy,* 278.

20 Marc Reisner, *Cadillac Desert: The American West and Its Disappearing Water,* 2d ed. (New York: Penguin, 1993), 116.

21 Swain, *Federal Conservation Policy,* 81–86.

22 Donald Worster, *Rivers of Empire: Water, Aridity, and the Growth of the American West* (New York: Pantheon, 1985), 197.

23 Ibid., 208.

24 Ibid., 209.

25 Carl E. Krog, "'Organizing the Production of Leisure': Herbert Hoover and the Conservation Movement in the 1920s," *Wisconsin Magazine of History* 67, no. 3 (September 1984): 201.

26 Kendrick A. Clements, *Hoover, Conservation, and Consumerism: Engineering the Good Life* (Lawrence: University Press of Kansas, 2000), x.

27 Clements, "Herbert Hoover and Conservation, 1921–33," 88.

28 Clements, *Hoover, Conservation and Consumerism*, 128.

29 Ibid.,1.

30 Krog, "Organizing the Production of Leisure," 202.

31 Ibid., 210.

32 Ibid., 202.

33 Clements, *Hoover, Conservation, and Consumerism*, 66–69.

34 Clements, "Herbert Hoover and Conservation, 1921–33," 76.

35 Ibid., 78–79.

36 Jared Orsi, "From Horicon to Hamburgers and Back Again: Ecology, Ideology, and Wildfowl Management, 1917–1935," *Environmental History Review* 18, no. 4 (Winter 1994): 31.

37 Fox, *American Conservation Movement*, 185–86.

38 Ibid., 186.

39 John A. Salmond, *The Civilian Conservation Corps, 1933–1942: A New Deal Case Study* (Durham: Duke University Press, 1967), 8.

40 Fox, *American Conservation Movement*, 188; and Clayton R. Koppes, "Efficiency/Equity/Esthetics: Towards a Reinterpretation of American Conservation," *Environmental Review* 11, no. 2 (Summer 1987): 134.

41 Richard N. L. Andrews, "Recovering FDR's Environmental Legacy," in *FDR and the Environment*, eds. Henry L. Henderson and David B. Woolner (New York: Palgrave, 2005), 222–29.

42 Ibid., 226.

43 Sarah T. Phillips, "Acres Fit and Unfit: Conservation and Rural Rehabilitation in the New Deal Era," (Ph.D. dissertation: Boston University, 2004), 7, 95, 101.

44 Fox, *American Conservation Movement*, 189.

45 Neil M. Maher, "A New Deal Body Politic: Landscape, Labor, and the Civilian Conservation Corps," *Environmental History* 7, no. 3 (July 2002): 437.

46 Maher, "New Deal Body Politic," 440–41, 443–44; and Cornelius M. Maher, "Planting More Than Trees: The Civilian Conservation Corps and the Roots of the American Environmental Movement," (Ph.D. dissertation, New York University, 2001), 63–64.

47 A. L. Riesch Owen, *Conservation Under FDR* (New York: Praeger, 1983), 129–31.

48 Ibid., 129, 133.

49 Sellars, *Preserving Nature*, 101.

50 Owen, *Conservation Under FDR*, 137; and Maher, "New Deal Body Politic," 437.

51 Sellars, *Preserving Nature,* 100, 127, 129.

52 Maher, "New Deal Body Politic," 447, 451, 453. See also his dissertation: Maher, "Planting More Than Trees."

53 North Callahan, *TVA: Bridge Over Troubled Waters* (South Brunswick, NJ: A.S. Barnes, 1980), 27.

54 Phillips, "Acres Fit and Unfit," 119, 129.

55 Phillips, "Acres Fit and Unfit," 36; and Fox, *American Conservation Movement,* 189.

56 Richard Lowitt, "The TVA, 1933–1945," in *TVA: Fifty Years of Grassroots Bureacracy,* eds., Erwin C. Hargrove and Paul K. Conkin (Urbana: University of Illinois Press, 1983), 55, 60.

57 Neil Maher, "'Crazy Quilt Farming on Round Land': The Great Depression, The Soil Conservation Service, and the Politics of Landscape Change on the Great Plains during the New Deal Era," *Western Historical Quarterly* 31, no. 3 (Autumn 2000): 328.

58 Donald Worster, *Dust Bowl: The Southern Plains in the 1930s,* 2d ed. (Oxford: Oxford University Press, 2004), 11–14.

59 Phillips, "Acres Fit and Unfit," 174–75.

60 Sarah T. Phillips, "Lessons From the Dust Bowl: Dryland Agriculture and Soil Erosion in the United States and South Africa, 1900–1950," *Environmental History* 4, no. 2 (April 1999): 256.

61 Peter Farb, "Messiah of the Soil,"

American Forests 66 (January 1960): 19.

62 Worster, *Dust Bowl,* 213.

63 Farb, "Messiah of the Soil," 40.

64 Worster, *Dust Bowl,* 214–15, 219, and Farb, "Messiah of the Soil," 40.

65 Phillips, "Lessons from the Dust Bowl," 257; and Maher, "Crazy Quilt Farming," 338.

66 Worster, *Dust Bowl,* 223.

67 Phillips, "Acres Fit and Unfit," 216.

68 Schrepfer, *The Fight to Save the Redwoods,* 65.

69 Melosi, *Sanitary City,* 256.

70 Ibid,, 226.

71 Ibid., 225.

72 Ibid., 225.

73 Ibid., 256–58.

74 Joel A. Tarr, *The Search for the Ultimate Sink: Urban Pollution in Historic Prespective* (Akron, OH: University of Akron Press, 1996), 359.

75 Melosi, *Sanitary City,* 259–60.

76 Richard N. L. Andrews, *Managing the Environment, Managing Ourselves: A History of American Environmental Policy* (New Haven: Yale University Press, 1999), 204–05.

77 Melosi, *Sanitary City,* 219–20.

78 Stradling, *Smokestacks and Progressives,* 153.

79 Ibid., 163–67.

80 Tarr, *The Search for the Ultimate Sink,* 16 and Stradling, *Smokestacks and Progressives,* 168–69.

81 Stradling, *Smokestacks and Progressives,* 171.

82 Andrews, *Managing the Environment,* 207–08.

83 Paul S. Sutter, *Driven Wild: How the Fight Against Automobiles Launched the Modern Wilderness Movement* (Seattle: University of Washington Press, 2002), 21.

84 Sutter, *Driven Wild,* 24–27.

85 Ibid., 33–34, 37.

86 Michael P. Cohen, *The History of the Sierra Club, 1892–1970* (San Francisco: Sierra Club Books, 1988), 47, 89.

87 Sutter, *Driven Wild,* 38.

88 Hal Rothman, "Second Class Sites: National Monuments and the Growth of the National Park System," *Environmental Review* 10, no. 1 (Spring 1986): 48–49 and Sutter, *Driven Wild,* 108, 137.

89 Catherine Gudis, *Buyways: Billboards, Automobiles, and the American Landscape* (New York: Routledge, 2004), 172.

90 Sutter, *Driven Wild,* 136.

91 Madelyn Holmes, *American Women Conservationists: Twelve Profiles* (Jefferson, NC: McFarland and Co., 2004), 74.

92 Sutter, *Driven Wild,* 73–75.

93 Holmes, *American Women Conservationists,* 75.

94 Sutter, *Driven Wild,* 68–70.

95 Ibid., 69.

96 Roderick Nash, *Wilderness and the American Mind,* 3d ed. (New Haven: Yale University Press, 1982), 187; and Craig Allin, *The Politics of Wilderness Preservation* (Westport, CT: Greenwood Publishing, 1982), 70.

97 Sutter, *Driven Wild,* 70; and Daniel J. Philippon, *Conserving Words: How American Nature Writers Shaped the Environmental Movement* (Athens: University of Georgia Press, 2004), 183.

98 Joseph L. Sax, *Mountains Without Handrails: Reflections on the National Parks* (Ann Arbor: University of Michigan Press, 1980), 48; and Sutter, *Driven Wild,* 83.

99 Allin, *Politics of Wilderness Preservation,* 72–74.

100 Ibid., 81.

101 James M. Glover, *A Wilderness Original: The Life of Bob Marshall* (Seattle: The Mountaineers, 1986), 95.

102 Allin, *Politics of Wilderness Preservation,* 76–79.

103 Nash, *Wilderness and the American Mind,* 201; and Fox, *American Conservation Movement,* 206.

104 Fox, *American Conservation Movement,* 207.

105 Robert Gottlieb, *Forcing the Spring: The Transformation of the American Environmental Movement* (Washington DC: Island Press, 1993), 16.

106 Fox, *American Conservation Movement,* 210–11; and Sutter, *Driven Wild,* 233.

107 Philippon, *Conserving Words,* 192.

108 Donald C. Swain, "The National Park Service and the New Deal, 1933–1940," *Pacific Historical Review* 41, no. 3 (1972): 330.

109 Glover, *Wilderness Original,* 191–93, 199–200.

110 Allin, *Politics of Wilderness Preservation,* 83.

111 Glover, *Wilderness Original,* 267–72.

112 Mighetto, *Wild Animals and Environmental Ethics,* 102.

113 Susan Flader, *Thinking Like a Mountain: Aldo Leopold and the Evolution of an Ecological Attitude Toward Deer, Wolves, and Forests* (Columbia: University of Missouri Press, 1974), 3.

114 Leopold, *Sand County Almanac,* 140.

115 Donald Fleming, "Roots of the New Conservation Movement," in *Perspectives in American History,* eds. Donald Flemming and Bernard Bailyn (Cambridge: Harvard University Press, 1972), 18.

116 Nash, *Wilderness and the American Mind,* 197.

117 "Everglades National Park," http://www.everglades.nationalpark.com/info.htm (13 August 2006).

118 Alfred Runte, *National Parks: The American Experience,* 2d ed. (Lincoln: University of Nebraska Press, 1987), 131, 135–36.

CHAPTER THREE

The Emergence of an Environmental Movement, 1945–1973

"By use of the machine, by exploitation of the world's resources on a purely extractive basis, we have postponed the meeting at the ecological judgment seat. The handwriting on the wall of five continents now tells us that the Day of Judgment is at hand." Such was William Vogt's forewarning of potential global calamity in his 1948 book, *Road to Survival*. Overpopulation and soil erosion, he concluded, were creating the conditions for starvation, population collapse, and conflict. The book's dust jacket summed up Vogt's argument: "Man's so-called conquest of nature is shown to be a suicidal process whereby the world, a sanctuary without exits for a fast-breeding human race, is rapidly being made uninhabitable."[1] A decline in the living standard was inevitable and had already begun, he confidently predicted. In the same year, Fairfield Osborn published *Our Plundered Planet*, which made remarkably similar predictions of impending ruin.[2] Surveying the situation around the globe, the books predicted that no region of the world would escape the crisis. Writing in the shadow of World War II and the atomic bomb, the authors feared that the resulting instability might lead to cataclysmic warfare. Grounding their arguments in ecological precepts similar to Aldo Leopold's land ethic, they called for Americans to see nature as a "living web" and "interrelationships" between all forms of life."There would seem to be no real hope for the future," Osborn surmised,"unless we are prepared to accept the concept that man, like all other living things, is part of one great biological scheme."[3]

Six years later Harrison Brown published *The Challenge of Man's Future*, which, expanded on Osborn's and Vogt's message by looking at limitations on supplies of other resources, such as coal, oil, and steel. Although Brown believed that the world's population could expand more than the other authors, his message was just as dire. Writing soon after the explosion of the first hydrogen bomb, he believed that the competition for diminishing resources would lead to atomic warfare and that "industrial civilization is doomed to extinction."[4] All three authors laid some of the blame for the crisis on capitalism and the profit motive. But their main concern was overpopulation in the developing world, not realizing that the U.S. population growth was more of a concern since the average American consumed resources at a horrific rate. Some of their solutions were moderate, such as Osborn's recommendation for government regulation of private land. Vogt and Brown added more draconian ideas for trimming the world population. Vogt wrote approvingly of infanticide and later called for rethinking humanitarian aid to developing nations unless they adopted rigorous birth-control policies.[5] Brown called for a "broad eugenics program" that would "discourage the unfit from breeding at excessive rates."[6] In sum, the books asserted that without the acceptance of limits to growth and radical population reductions, advanced and developing nations alike teetered on the edge of an abyss.

It was an odd time to be such Gloomy Guses. Just a few years earlier, fascism had been destroyed. America had emerged from the conflict relatively unscathed and in an unrivaled international position. The country was beginning an economic expansion that established the first truly middle-class nation in history. Perhaps for these reasons, the books' immediate influence was limited. They sold relatively well and usually had positive reviews, although one review dismissed *Road to Survival*'s "exaggerations and inconsistencies, its apparent complete disregard for human values."[7] The books were read in environmental circles, but the American public did not respond to their call to arms. Caught up in postwar abundance, they had yet to see substantial evidence of depleted resources and overpopulation. Those problems were something for the developing world to worry about.

But Osborn, Vogt, and Brown were on to something. Their concerns became the environmental movement's concerns. Despite the rosy picture, Americans were anxious about the future and became only more so as time went on. The reality of the Cold War, atomic weapons, and radioactive fallout gave special urgency to the movement to avoid future conflicts by limiting population and economic growth that damaged the environment, depleted resources, and stimulated competition and conflict among nations. The public eventually shared the authors' apprehension about industrial expansion and population growth that exacerbated pollution problems and led to unexpected crowding in the nation's suburban refuges. The ecological outlook that Osborn and Vogt evinced in their writings became the holy scripture of the movement. The three authors were also prescient when they called on activists to think of environmental problems globally. Resource depletion, erosion, overpopulation, and later global warming were issues that connected all nations, wealthy and poor, in a common dilemma.[8] Finally, their critique of capitalism prefigured the anticorporate, anticapitalist attitudes of some sectors of the movement in the late sixties and seventies.

The books offered not just a glimpse of the movement's future but a look at its past. The postwar environmental movement would share much in common with its Progressive era and interwar predecessors. That there were limits to what humankind and technology could do with the environment and its resources was a longstanding sentiment within the movement. Activists in both periods worried about the unregulated use of private resources and looked to the government to control them. The ecological thinking of the authors and the postwar movement owed a substantial intellectual debt to 1930s scientists and activists such as Leopold. The books' warning of an impending calamity for civilization mirrored the thinking of Thomas Malthus and George Perkins Marsh in the nineteenth century, a theme which would dominate environmental writings right up to contemporary debates about global warming. Like Malthus, the authors correctly pointed out potential problems, but their prophesies of doom were notable for being, at best, premature; this was a disconcertedly common fault for environmental mystics that created a long-term credibility problem.

The public's anxieties for the future were also due in part to the social values that emerged out of the nation's newfound wealth. Affluence allowed individuals to pursue their desires instead of necessities, expand their leisure time, and settle in the suburbs. The public placed a priority on amenities such as a clean environment and personal health and safety. Concerns for health translated into demands to limit pollutants in the air and water. Affluence and suburban sprawl spurred calls for setting aside more wilderness and recreational areas. Sprawl, in particular, made many residents aware of the need to preserve open space for recreational and ecological reasons. Quality-of-life movements for wilderness, open space, and against pollution challenged the conservation philosophy that valued the efficient use of resources and economic growth. Although they contributed much to increasing public concern for the environment and creating support for government programs, New Deal conservationists found themselves at odds with this new "environmental" movement over previously popular conservation developments such as hydroelectric projects.

Increased public support for environmentalism translated into renewed political activism among wilderness organizations and anti-pollution advocates in the 1950s. This would be a different kind of political activism than earlier efforts. The environmental movement possessed a substantial grassroots base that, with some exceptions, the prewar elitist style of conservation did not. Atomic weapons fallout and the publication of Rachel Carson's exposé on pesticides, *Silent Spring*, expanded the movement to include urban/industrial issues such as pollution, pesticides, and energy use. Grassroots issues and a criticism of corporate responsibility made the movement particularly attractive to young sixties activists interested in personal empowerment and critiquing capitalism. Gaining strength from a new generation, Earth Day 1970, a catalyzing demonstration for environmentalism, highlighted the coalescence of the wilderness and industrial strands of the movement. Instinctively in favor of industrial development, the Richard Nixon administration nonetheless cunningly responded to this new political phenomenon by crafting moderate environmental legislation to attract support. The National Environmental Policy Act, the Environmental Protection Agency, and clean air and water legislation all flowed from the pen of the president.

Air Pollution Issues, 1945–1965

Although public attitudes about pollution and the environment underwent important changes prior to 1945, America's economic expansion after the war created the basis for a new social movement. As part of a rising standard of living, American society sought out recreational opportunities and healthier living arrangements. Responding to industrial abuse of the environment, Americans demanded that state and federal governments control pollution's effects.

As was the case with the interwar period, the postwar drive to control air pollution started at the municipal level. But as historian Scott Hamilton Dewey has shown, it differed from its predecessor because it led to federal involvement, a legacy of the New Deal's emphasis on and public acceptance of federal regulation. The impetus for air pollution reform came from the hazy skies of southern California. Although a London physician invented the term "smog" in 1905, Los Angeles's skies embodied the word. Smoke-trapping temperature inversions were common in the L.A. basin. The city's fate was particularly galling because its climate and pleasant atmosphere had made it a "veritable sanitarium" according to boosters. The city's sun and beaches were the lure that brought many residents west. They were rudely shocked by the persistent haze. Although the region had smog before the war, the problem became acute by the 1940s with greater automobile use.[9]

Los Angeles's citizens forced the local government to take action. By 1943, "smog town," as it was called, was deluged with complaints from residents, editorials in the *Los Angeles Times*, and pressure from the real estate and hospitality industries. In 1947, L.A. county supervisors established the Air Pollution Control District (APCD) to reduce sources of air pollution. The city had the best-funded pollution control agency in the country with a $178,000 budget and a staff of forty-seven. The APCD became the world leader in air pollution control. As one New York City official confessed, "We copy them [the APCD]. . . . Their budget is five times ours. They investigate—we check."[10]

It was one thing to establish a government agency to deal with air pollution; it was another to solve the smog problem. No one was really sure what created smog. Many people blamed emissions from stationary sources in the steel mills and foundries, oil refineries, and backyard incinerators. Attempts at regulating these sources did not work. Pollution only worsened in the fifties, so much so that the Los Angeles Chamber of Commerce resolved that new industries with pollution problems should not locate in the city. The *New York Times* noted, "Until recently, any such notion [of limited industrial growth] bordered on civic heresy." Efforts that concentrated on regulating stationary sources of pollution were misplaced. In the early fifties, scientists at Cal Tech determined that auto emissions were the prime culprits in creating smog. The public became even more alarmed when in 1955 tests also showed that not only did smog kill much of the local vegetation, it caused cancer in laboratory mice. Los Angeles, with one vehicle per 2.8 residents, compared to 7.1 for New York City, had a very difficult problem on its hands.[11] If Angelenos were going to solve the pollution problem, they would have to drive less or purchase cars with lower emissions. Predictably, they chose the latter course.

Pollution-control officials turned to Detroit for solutions, but representatives of the auto industry there tried to shift blame from themselves. A Ford Motor company official, sounding like a cigarette company executive in denial, argued that car exhausts "dissipated in the atmosphere quickly and [did] not represent an air pollution problem." General Motors' researchers suggested that "As far as we are aware, Los Angeles is the only community having this particular complaint [eye-stinging smog] . . . indicating that perhaps some other factors than automobile exhaust gases may be contributing to the problem."[12] It was years before the Motor City owned up to its role in the problem.

With the auto industry dragging its feet, L.A. county officials turned to higher levels of government. Pressure from Los Angeles and other cities resulted in the first major piece of federal legislation on air pollution in 1955. The act, however, focused on funding for research and had little impact on the city's plight. Southern California officials had more luck with state representatives. The 1960 California Motor Vehicle Pollution Control Act established an air pollution–control board to mandate auto emission standards. The state demanded that the auto industry install pollution control devices on new cars. Well on its way to becoming the nation's largest state, California had considerable clout with Detroit and in Washington. The federal government responded to California's initiative by pressuring automakers to install pollution-control devices on all cars sold in the United States. Having resisted such a move as being too expensive, the automobile industry headed off federal action by announcing that it would voluntarily install devices on all 1963 model cars. "Auto companies proved miraculously equal to the new challenge," two pollution historians wryly noted.[13]

Los Angeles's success was the great national exception. New York, Dewey has shown, had the more typical mixed results achieved at the local level. Like Los Angeles, the Big Apple started in the forties to push for pollution control with the support of civic organizations, citizens groups, the local press, and politicians. But twenty years later, the New York metropolitan region was still struggling to develop a coherent enforcement policy and probably had the country's worst air-pollution problem. Perhaps this failure was due to the fact that New York's identity was not bound up in a healthy environment as was that of Los Angeles. At any rate, the New York experience demonstrated that voluntary compliance by polluters and interstate cooperation did not work.

The drive for pollution control in New York City started out with great fanfare and high hopes. In 1947, the *New York Times* editorialized about the "serious menace" posed by smoky air, and a citizen group formed soon afterwards to lobby for legislation.[14] But they confronted businesses that resisted the cost of cleanup, an apathetic public, and politicians who hesitated to upset the status quo. As the winter heating season came to an end, politicians ignored the issue.

The problem might have remained there but for the Donora, Pennsylvania, disaster in October 1948, wherein twenty people died from industrial air pollution. The Donora deaths alerted New Yorkers to the fact that air pollution was more than a nuisance. It was alarming too that the key killer in Donora was not smoke but invisible "poison gas," as the city papers put it. A revived coalition of reform politicians, women of the Outdoor Cleanliness Association, and the press pushed through a citywide bill in February, 1949, that created the Bureau of Smoke Control (BSC). The *Times* lauded the legislation but warned that funding and enforcement were necessary for the bill to have any teeth.[15]

For the next twenty years, the Bureau of Smoke Control was in fact badly underfunded, and only timidly pursued pollution scofflaws. Its initial budget represented only 2¢ a year per New York resident. By comparison, other cities were spending anywhere from 6 to 18¢. The city's record was no better in court. A smoke control advocate argued, "not a single court summons has been issued to smoke violators since February, 1949," when the BSC was created. Even when the bureau did pursue violators, its fines were trivial, just $100 for major violators. Instead of the hardline approach adopted by Los Angeles regulators, the BSC relied mostly on education efforts to curb pollution. As the *Times* lamented, cooperation and education had "failed, as any housewife mopping up soot in the apartment knows."[16] But what undermined the crusade more than anything was the weak and sporadic effort made by the public to push reform and force politicians to do something about the problem. It revealed the weakness of pollution-control movements in the fifties. These groups often came together for brief periods, enacted some modest reforms, and then disbanded, leaving no one to police the enforcement system.

Even the 1966 Thanksgiving Weekend episode proved to be a fleeting influence. A stagnant mass of air locked in pollutants in eastern cities from Pittsburgh to Boston. The five days of pollution might have been much worse if it had not happened on a holiday when most businesses were closed. As it was, estimates ran as high as 168 deaths in New York City from the pollution. In the wake of the incident, scientists estimated that the city had the worst sulfur-dioxide levels in the nation and the worst overall air quality, with dangerously high levels of carbon monoxide and particulates. Despite these revelations, 135,000 oil burners and 17,000 garbage incinerators continued to operate, in defiance of ordinances outlawing them.[17]

To make matters worse, New York City failed to gain the cooperation of New Jersey, which contributed to the Empire State's overall pollution problem. Interstate cooperation was nearly impossible when the effects of pollution created by one state were mainly felt in another. New York's story was hardly unique. Most states and cities did nothing about air pollution. As late as 1961, not even half of all cities with air-pollution problems were spending $5,000 a year on the problem. States were no better. Only seventeen spent more than $5,000 and California alone spent 57 percent of the national total of $2 million.[18] Real reform had to await federal action later in the decade. The failure of states to control the problem and growing public concern forced the federal government to intervene.

Damming a National Monument

Air-pollution control was an issue confined to urban areas. Outside of metropolitan areas, the public's interest turned to recreation. Visits to state and national parks rose dramatically after the war, representing a potential political constituency for preservationists. A rebirth of wilderness activism in the John Muir tradition followed logically from this public interest in scenic and wild country. The galvanizing event for the preservation movement came when the Bureau of Reclamation proposed two dams for the Dinosaur National Monument in Utah and Colorado. Seeing the dams as a threat to the entire national park system, preservation organizations banded together and defeated some of the most powerful bureaucrats and politicians in the federal government. The Dinosaur episode was a coming-out party for the preservation movement, demonstrating its new power and national popularity. It confirmed the movement's sophistication in organization and tactics. It also made plain the growing estrangement of the efficiency and aesthetic wings of the conservation movement.

Established in 1915 by President Woodrow Wilson, Dinosaur National Monument was, as the name implies, a discovery site of dinosaur skeletons. Wilson designated a small eighty-acre site as a monument to protect the find, but the Carnegie Museum still managed to remove most of the valuable skeletons. Until the 1930s, Dinosaur was a monument without a purpose. Then a reporter from the *Denver Post* extolled the scenic quality of the area. "Imagine," he reported, "seven or eight Zion [canyons] strung together, end-to-end; with Yosemite Valley dropped down in the middle of them; with half-a-dozen 'pockets' as weird and awe inspiring as Crater Lake. . . . Then you will just begin to get some conception of Yampa [canyon]."[19] After touring a meadow area in the canyon called Echo Park for its near-perfect ability to reflect sound, the superintendent of Yellowstone National Park reported that the canyons were indeed worth saving. On July 14, 1938, Franklin Roosevelt signed an executive order expanding Dinosaur to over 200,000 acres. In a concession to the Bureau of Reclamation, the order left open the possibility that Echo Park might include a dam site.

The Great Depression and World War II ensured that for the next ten years Dinosaur was neglected and rarely visited, but it would have been overlooked in any event. As a national monument, it did not enjoy the same high profile as did the more prestigious national parks. Congress had not been involved in creating the monument and had no interest in improving it. And the leading groups that later came to its aid, the Sierra Club and the Wilderness Society, had played no part in its creation. As the Bureau of Reclamation cast about for dam sites, Dinosaur's protected status was vulnerable.

Economic and political factors played a key role in the Bureau of Reclamation's hatching of a grand plan for the Colorado River, known as the Colorado River Storage Project (CRSP). This was to be a ten-dam project for the river. During the depression, projects such as the Hoover and Grand Coulee Dams were the jewels in the crown of the New Deal. Dams and the cheap hydroelectricity they provided were at the heart of FDR's drive to rehabilitate rural regions. The public viewed dams as symbols of American prosperity, resolve, and civilization. The demand for dams accelerated after World War II. The Cold War contributed to the conviction that a strong federal effort in power production was imperative. The bureau had a free hand to develop the West's water however it wanted.

There were also powerful regional factors that made the construction of dams almost inevitable. States in the upper Colorado River basin—New Mexico, Utah, Colorado, and Wyoming—had been badly wounded by the depression and drought. The region's agriculture had barely survived. Their problems, upper basin officials believed, could be solved with new water projects producing cheap power and irrigation, although the Echo Park dam would provide little irrigation water. Upper basin officials looked enviously at the benefits that the Hoover Dam had bestowed on southern California and Nevada. Although the Colorado River compact ensured that the upper states were to receive half of the river's water, they worried that Los Angeles might take their share. The *Salt Lake Tribune* warned its readers that they should demand action or they were "likely to awaken to find their water in California." At the behest of local politicians and boosters, bureau personnel fanned out over the upper basin exploring sites for dams, including one at Echo Park. A dam there, the bureau concluded, was ideal for power generation and storage for irrigation. The Cold War figured heavily in the decision to approve the dam. The Atomic Energy Commission ensured that the Department of the Interior would approve the dam by citing its need for more electrical reserves in the Utah area. On June 27, 1950, Interior secretary Oscar Chapman approved the dam.[20]

The National Park Service and its head, Newton Drury, viewed all these developments with alarm, for they were part of a larger pattern of abuse of the parks justified under economic or military necessity. Efficiency once again took precedence over equity and aesthetics/ecology. This pattern had begun during World War II. The national forests and parks had been raided for resources due to wartime exigencies. After the war, timber interests proposed opening up Olympic National Park to logging. The Army Corps of Engineers and the Bureau of Reclamation produced proposals for dams in or near a number of national parks. The corps threatened Glacier National Park with a proposal for a dam on Montana's Flathead River. Although the dam was never built, the corps also talked of a dam near Mammoth Cave National Park in Kentucky. For its part, the bureau eyed dams for Marble Canyon and Bridge Canyon, both within the Grand Canyon and near the park. Rosalie Edge of the Emergency Conservation Committee warned "the despoilers await like hungry wolves the opportunity to exploit our Parks."[21] The Echo Park dam seemed like the thin end of a wedge that would pry open the parks to development. As far as preservationists were concerned, the dam violated the National Park Service Act, which stipulated that the parks be preserved "unimpaired." Howard Zahniser of the Wilderness Society predicted that American society "will eventually modify for human exploitation every last area on earth—except those that through human foresight and wisdom have been deliberately set aside for preservation."[22]

These demands on national parkland came at the same time that the parks were enjoying a boom in attendance. After a wartime lull, the number of park visits rebounded sharply. In 1954, the national parks had 47.8 million visitors, a record for the tenth straight year and double the number in 1941.[23] This newfound popularity had not yet translated into political muscle or new funding. Some preservationists inside and outside the Park Service resolved to see what kind of power they had. As one participant put it, "let's open this to its ultimate and inevitable extent, and let's settle . . . once and for all time . . . whether we may have . . . wilderness areas . . . in these United States."[24]

Newton Drury fought the Bureau of Reclamation over the Echo Park proposal, despite the fact that his boss, Secretary of the Interior Oscar Chapman, had approved the dam "in the interest of the greatest public good."[25] Drury objected so strenuously, preservationists believed, that Chapman demanded his resignation in April 1951. Preservationists counted Drury, who had been the head of the Save the Redwoods League, as one of their own, and they resented the Interior secretary's decision. But Chapman enjoyed the support of President Harry Truman, who was not the conservationist that FDR had been. Truman remarked of the Dinosaur controversy, "It has always been my opinion that food for coming generations is much more important than bones of the Mesozoic period," even though the bones were not the key issue.[26] Without Drury, preservation organizations would have to do battle alone against all the influence the Department of the Interior enjoyed.

Now preservationists made an unprecedented effort. Seventy-eight national and 236 state level organizations joined the fray. By comparison, John Muir could count on just seven national and two state level organizations in his fight to save the Hetch Hetchy Valley.[27] Two organizations, the Sierra Club and the Wilderness Society, carried the load in this campaign, led by their respective executive directors, David Brower and Howard Zahniser, who brought new energy and aggressive tactics to the movement.

Forming the Council of Conservationists to wage the campaign, preservationists crafted a battle plan that consisted of three parts. First, they highlighted the beauty of Dinosaur through a massive publicity campaign. A second part emerged when preservationists recognized that they alone did not have the power to halt the project. They recruited other constituencies that did not want to see the Colorado River Storage Project move forward: the Army Corps of Engineers; water users in California; and members of Congress from farm regions in the East who opposed the irrigated farming competition created by the CRSP. Finally, the preservationists had to take on the Bureau of Reclamation, challenging the technical wisdom of the project.[28]

The preservationists sought to publicize Dinosaur's beauty through films, pamphlets, articles, and books. Wilderness organizations sponsored numerous float trips through Echo Park, raising dramatically the number of visitors to Dinosaur. The float trips also gave rise to stunning photographs of the canyons that splashed across the pages of national publications such as *Time, Readers Digest, Life,* and the *New York Times.* David Brower came up with the idea to sponsor a professional film of Echo Park that was shown hundreds of times around the country. The Sierra Club also sponsored a picture book edited by novelist and historian Wallace Stegner entitled *This is Dinosaur: Echo Park Country and its Magic Rivers.* Alfred Knopf, the publisher, agreed to donate a copy to every member of Congress. All of these works carried the same message: Echo Park was worth preserving for its scenic qualities. It was one of America's "primeval parks" whose transcendent beauty served humankind. "Wilderness areas have become to us a spiritual necessity," one opponent of the dams insisted, "an antidote to the strains of modern living."[29] The rhetoric justifying wilderness preservation had changed very little in the four decades since the Hetch Hetchy battle.

Such publicity raised national awareness of Echo Park, but it was a hardly sufficient reason to kill a project dear to upper-basin voters. Preservationists turned to allies in several places. The Colorado River's lower basin states, especially California, were growing much more rapidly than were those in the upper basin. Some politicians in southern California hoped to renegotiate the 1922 compact and gain a greater share of the Colorado River's water. Midwestern congressmen also opposed the Echo Park dam. Illinois Senator Paul Douglas questioned the value of putting more farmland into production when the nation had large crop surpluses and falling prices. Noting the high cost of irrigation water in the upper basin, Douglas observed, "it is too bad that these fine people live in [such a dry region] with a river running through deep canyons. We are sorry for them, but I do not think that creates for them a perpetual claim on the public treasury."[30]

Douglas's point about the high cost of irrigation water raised another issue in the fight against dams in Dinosaur, the technical merit. Preservationists fought the dam with the Bureau of Reclamation's own tools. They cast doubt on the economic value of the dam, proposed alternate sites, and even questioned the bureau's scientific conclusions. In a famous moment in congressional hearings, David Brower questioned the accuracy of the bureau's estimates of water loss due to evaporation. Using what he called "ninth grade arithmetic," Brower demonstrated that Echo Park alternatives would not lose as much water as the bureau claimed, a point the bureau eventually conceded.[31] The "great evaporation controversy" was not the dagger in the heart of the project, but it did open the bureau up to challenge of its expertise.[32]

The issue came to a head in the Eighty-Fourth Congress in 1955. Despite efforts to strip it out of the bill authorizing the Colorado River Storage Project, the Echo Park dam survived in the Senate, but not in the House. With mail on the subject running eighty-to-one against the dam, representatives were more susceptible to public pressure. The bill cleared the committee without the Echo Park dam. In an amazing admission of the power of the preservation movement, a Utah congressman confessed, "We hated to lose it," but "the opposition from preservation organizations has been such as to convince us . . . that authorizing legislation could not be passed unless this dam was taken out." He admitted that dam proponents had "neither the money nor the organization to cope with the resources and mailing lists" of preservationists.[33]

Victory was at hand, but there was one last act in the drama. In November 1955, Western congresspeople met in Denver to discuss ways to reinsert the Echo Park dam back into the authorizing legislation. The Council of Conservationists learned of the meeting. In a display of political chutzpah, the council took out a full-page advertisement in the *Denver Post* the day before the meeting. The council members advised Congress that they would use all their power to oppose the entire Colorado River Storage Project if any version of the bill "encompasses, anticipates, or secretly hopes for a dam or reservoir in a National Park or Monument."[34] Howard Zahniser negotiated the final details of the compromise, in which preservationists promised not to oppose the CRSP. In turn, Western congressmen inserted language into the legislation stating that no part of the CRSP would violate the boundaries of national parks or monuments. The bill was signed into law April 11, 1956.

As historian Mark Harvey argues, the Echo Park dam controversy was the most significant episode in the wilderness movement between the founding of the Wilderness Society and the passage of the 1964 Wilderness Act. Wilderness organizations benefited immensely from the campaign. The Sierra Club doubled its membership. It transformed the club from a regional organization into a national powerhouse. It became, according to the *New York Times*, "the gangbusters of the conservation movement." David Brower's profile was similarly raised in the movement. Sigurd Olson of the Wilderness Society remarked, "Thank God for Dave Brower and his boundless energy."[35]

Echo Park also signaled a fundamental shift in values. Americans rallied to the protection of a canyon most had never seen. There had been a wholesale change in public attitudes about the environment after World War II, due to fundamental social and economic changes in American society. The expansion of the middle class, greater education, and more leisure time had decreased Americans' concerns with the basic needs that the Bureau of Reclamation was created to satisfy and had led instead to a search for amenities. Americans now wanted more vacations, camping excursions, and trips to parks. This fact alone meant growing support for the goals of those who favored preservation of scenic lands and a decline in support for traditional conservationists who were interested in resource extraction, such as those in the Bureau of Reclamation.

Nevertheless, the Echo Park controversy was more a political than a philosophical awakening for the preservation movement. The movement had, as writer Wallace Stegner noted, displayed "astonishing political muscle." But it was of a piece with an older movement whose basic goal was the defense of scenic lands and national parks. It was not part of modern environmentalism, with its emphasis on protecting biotic communities and limiting the influence of modern industrial life on the environment. Although some activists favored saving Dinosaur for ecological reasons, as Aldo Leopold would have wanted, the language of the battle was strikingly similar to that of the Hetch Hetchy battle. "The two situations are so much alike," Sierra Club member Harold Bradley observed, "that the campaign literature on both sides might be interchanged, with appropriate names added."[36] The basic question in both episodes was the same: should the national park system be inviolable? As opponents of the dam argued, if the national parks could not be protected from development, what could be?

The movement had paid an unknown price for the Echo Park victory. In agreeing to drop their opposition to the CRSP, preservationists ensured that the Glen Canyon dam would be built. The preservationists gave up on a place few had seen. Only late in the struggle for Echo Park did the preservationists begin to understand what they were relinquishing. The canyon had "the most extraordinary scenery I have ever seen," one visitor observed. David Brower in particular came to regret the trade he had made to save Dinosaur. As he had with Echo Park, Brower edited an illustrated book entitled *The Place No One Knew: Glen Canyon on the Colorado,* with captions supplied by poets. The message to the preservation movement was clear. Do not bargain away what you do not know. "Glen Canyon is gone," surmised Richard Bradley, a Sierra Club member, "and with it some of the most remarkable canyon country on the continent. It died a needless death just as people were beginning to learn of its wonders."[37] To more militant preservationists Glen Canyon became a symbol of the dangers of compromise and made the preservation movement more determined to halt further dam development on the Colorado River.

The Wilderness Act of 1964 and the Fight for the Grand Canyon

Echo Park encouraged preservationists to dream big dreams. In 1957 Howard Zahniser proposed at a Sierra Club wilderness conference that the movement seek statutory protection of wilderness areas in national forests, putting these areas once and for all beyond the reach of motorized recreationists and mining and timber companies. The resulting wilderness bill was his chief accomplishment. His activism, as his biographer Mark Harvey has shown, was animated by several factors. Zahniser's approach to wilderness preservation, like that of many other activists, had been shaped by a childhood spent in the woods. He was also taken by Aldo Leopold's land ethic."We deeply need humility to know ourselves as the dependent members of a great community of life," he wrote,"and this can indeed be one of the spiritual benefits of a wilderness experience." The brutality of World War II and the deaths of so many at the hands of Hitler and Stalin was, Zahniser believed, typical of societies dedicated to controlling nature and the lives of others. Only through Albert Schweitzer's philosophy of a "reverence for life" could a society become humane. Preserving wilderness would encourage that reverence for wildlife and humans. In this philosophy, Zahniser differed from later more extreme activists who developed a distaste for humanity and its destruction of wild places out of their love of nature. Zahniser was also one who resisted demonizing his political opponents, making him an effective lobbyist. Unlike later activists, he believed that preservation and conservation could be compatible, seeing that both groups shared a common goal of getting society to live within the limits of nature. "We must wear the mantle of conservation if we are to be effective as preservationists."[38] But the battle for the wilderness bill would sorely test his philosophy.

Zahniser knew that the Forest Service could change at any time the protected status of wilderness areas by administrative fiat. The wilderness movement no longer trusted the Forest Service to protect these areas. The service had increased timber production on federal lands dramatically after World War II. Would it open up wilderness areas to cutting and road building, too? Zahniser wanted a permanent arrangement. He wrote the first draft of a wilderness protection bill and convinced Democratic Senator Hubert Humphrey and Republican Representative John Saylor to introduce it in June 1957.

To say that the legislation was bold was an understatement. Zahniser marked off 160 areas in national forests, national parks, national monuments, Indian reservations, and national wildlife refuges and ranges, 60 million acres in all. The proposed legislation would outlaw practically all kinds of human intrusion into these areas, such as mining operations or road building. In the legislation, Zahniser called for protecting areas that were "untrammeled" by humans. By "untrammeled" Zahnisher did not mean that an area was untouched, but that human influence there had been minimal enough that the area could recover its biotic integrity. Wilderness

areas were to be those "not subjected to human controls and ma-
nipulations that hamper the free play of natural forces." Such protection was not enjoyed anywhere else, even in the national parks.
A bill so far-reaching was sure to have many enemies, and it did.
Companies dealing with wood products, oil, and mining opposed
the bill, as did professional foresters, the National Park Service, the
Forest Service, and recreationists interested in mechanized outdoor
experiences. The battle dragged out over seven years. There were
nine hearings on it, and the bill was rewritten sixty-six times.[39]

Zahniser used the same well-oiled machine that had won the
Echo Park victory. Audubon House agreed to push an education
campaign on the issue. The *New York Times* pledged its editorial
support. The Izaak Walton League endorsed the measure, as did
the Jaycees, the General Federation of Women's Clubs, FDR's
wife, Eleanor Roosevelt, and two-time Democratic nominee for
the presidency and United Nations ambassador, Adlai Stevenson.
Zahniser tapped preservation organizations' mailing lists for supporters. Congress received more mail on it in 1962 than on any
other issue.[40]

The bill benefited from delay. President Eisenhower was luke-
warm on preservation. With the election of John F. Kennedy in
1960, preservationists now had a friend in the White House. The
new president was convinced that the federal government had the
primary responsibility to protect the environment. Preservation fit
well with the liberal programs Kennedy envisioned and even more
later on with Lyndon Baines Johnson's Great Society programs.
Johnson, whose wife, Ladybird Johnson, was the most active First
Lady in the area of preservation, needed little convincing to
support wilderness legislation. "Lady-bird's pushing," asserted
Stewart Udall, Secretary of the Interior, made the president even
more active on preservation issues than he might have been otherwise.[41]

Still, there would have to be compromise. As historian Dennis
Roth claimed, the controversy over the wilderness bill hinged on
how much preservationists would compromise without themselves
being compromised.[42] And they conceded a great deal, largely because of Congressman Wayne Aspinall, chairman of the House

Committee on Interior and Insular Affairs. Aspinall was a traditional conservationist who did not see nature when he looked at woods, but resources to benefit humankind. He did not understand the growing popularity of the preservationists, saying that he did not know "when, where, or how the purist preservationist group assumed the mantle of the conservationists."[43] But Aspinall recognized that the growing power of Zahniser's forces would have to be satisfied. The congressman trimmed the bill significantly. All but fifty-four areas in the National Forests were eliminated from the bill, leaving just 9 million acres for preservation. All future additions to the system would need congressional approval. Aspinall inserted a provision allowing new mining claims in wilderness areas until 1984; existing claims could continue even after that date. To satisfy the cattle interests, controlled grazing was also to be allowed in wilderness areas. The final bill sailed through both houses of Congress, and LBJ signed it into law on September 3, 1964. Zahniser did not live to see the bill enacted. He had died of a heart attack three months earlier. When it was over, some argued the preservationists had conceded too much. But there seemed to be no other option to move the bill out of committee. Moreover, despite what some contended were crippling provisions, the wilderness system has been significantly enlarged since the act's passage. By 1995, the wilderness system had grown to 90 million acres on over 500 tracts, far beyond what Zahniser had originally envisioned.[44]

Preservationists did not have to wait long for the next battle over the Colorado River. In 1963, the Bureau of Reclamation proposed the Pacific Southwest Water Plan, a billion-dollar project. To pump Arizona's share of the Colorado River to cities like Phoenix, the bureau included two hydroelectric dams at Marble and Bridge Canyons. The resulting reservoir would back up into Grand Canyon National Monument. Saving the canyon was a fight even more formidable than that at Dinosaur. Unlike the Echo Park episode, preservationists were up against a united Colorado Basin congressional delegation. The dams enjoyed the blessings of Lyndon Baines Johnson and Secretary of the Interior Stewart Udall. The hard-driving, hard-drinking head of the bureau, Floyd Dominy, pushed the project like "an utter maniac."[45] With that kind of political weight behind them, observers expected approval of the dams to sail through Congress. But they did not count on the resistance of the Sierra Club and the American people. "If we can't save the Grand Canyon," David Brower asked, "what the hell can we save?"[46]

The Sierra Club responded with an all-out publicity campaign. Brower took out ads in the *Washington Post, New York Times, Los Angeles Times,* and *San Francisco Chronicle.* "This time," the ads declared, "it's the Grand Canyon they want to flood, the *Grand Canyon.*" The bureau responded that only a small portion of the canyon would be flooded, and that it would benefit vacationers in the canyon by giving those who floated past a closer look at its rock walls. The Sierra Club responded with an ad whose words could have come right from John Muir, "Should we also flood the Sistine Chapel so tourists can get nearer the ceiling?"[47] As much as the movement's members liked to think of themselves as being different from their predecessors in the prewar period, they relied on past rhetoric and ideology to rouse the public more than they realized.

The ads had a devastating effect on the bill. Thousands of letters poured into Congress. "I never saw anything like it," quipped one reclamation official. "Letters were arriving in dump trucks. Ninety-five percent said we'd better keep out mitts off the Grand Canyon and a lot of them quoted the Sierra Club ads." Even apolitical publications like the *Reader's Digest* came out against the dams. "Right after the *Reader's Digest* article," the reclamation official remembered, "*Life* ran a big goddamed diatribe. Then we got plastered by *My Weekly Reader.* You're in deep shit when you catch it from them. Mailbags were coming in by the hundreds stuffed with letters from schoolkids."[48]

By 1967, it was clear to everyone but Floyd Dominy that the project could not get authorization with the dams in the bill. Dominy attempted a compromise by including only the Bridge Canyon dam in the bill and, to avoid trespassing on national parkland, eliminating the Grand Canyon National Monument.

Preservationists refused to back down. They wanted no dams at all, and that is what they got. Representative Morris Udall of Arizona confessed, "I must tell you bluntly that no bill providing for a so called 'Grand Canyon Dam' can pass the Congress today."[49] When Dominy was out of the country on an inspection tour, his boss, Secretary of the Interior Stewart Udall, told his aides to come up with a power alternative to the dams. Engineers needed enough power to pump water for the Central Arizona Project 1,200 feet over a mountain pass. Their answer was to use coal plants, hardly an appealing alternative to the dams considering how much the plants would smoke up the clear skies of the Southwest, but it worked. The bill's sponsors agreed to remove the dams from the bill, and LBJ signed it into law on September 30, 1968. Bitter, Dominy later said of Udall's betrayal, "My secretary turned chickenshit on me." One Bureau of Reclamation representative concluded, "The fact is we were licked. The conservationists and the press and ultimately the public licked the Bureau of Reclamation."[50]

Or so it seemed. Numerous authors and activists hailed the victory as an indicator that preservationism had become a major lobby in Washington politics. Byron Pearson, however, concluded in a recent study that the activities of the Sierra Club were of secondary importance in the battle. The cancellation of the Grand Canyon dams was more the result of the breakdown of a complex series of deals between lawmakers. Compromise among legislators fell apart when Pacific Northwest legislators, especially Senator Henry Jackson, successfully opposed the diversion of Columbia River water to the Colorado River to support the Central Arizona Project, an idea put forward to satisfy the water needs of Arizona and California politicians. Nevertheless, the controversy was important for the "mirage of power," as Pearson puts it, created for the preservationist wing.[51] The mirage translated into real power as wilderness organizations gained thousands of new members from the publicity. That growth indicated that the balance of power had tipped away from the dam builders. The age of the high dams had come to an end. In part, this was because most major rivers had been developed, but it was also the result of shifting public opinion. Free-flowing rivers were no longer considered a waste of resources, but an amenity desired by a growing sector of the public.

The Grand Canyon victory represented the high-point for scenic preservation. It was also a symbolic parting of the ways between resource conservationists and preservationists. The latter group turned away from New Deal–style conservation programs that sought to "improve" on nature for human benefit. In the Echo Park controversy, preservationists opposed the dam because it interfered with a national monument. They did not question the need for water-reclamation projects in general and acceded to the Glen Canyon Dam. At the Grand Canyon, activists demonstrated that they were ready to fight dams in general. Rather than aiding the public, the movement now saw dams as pet projects put forward by Congress and bureaucracies such as the Army Corps of Engineers and the Bureau of Reclamation for their own interests. Their main functions in dam building and stream channelization were now seen as threats to the environment.

Activists had tapped into a burgeoning constituency of affluent Americans who favored setting aside sacred lands for permanent protection. But preservationists had not expanded the scope of issues. Those who fought for clean air and water and those who favored wilderness preservation operated on separate tracks. Preservationists did not concern themselves with urban issues or those of minorities and the poor living in squalor. For them, equity was less important than aesthetics. They had not yet learned to think environmentally, with a focus on ecological health and the threat posed to all living things posed by industrial society. Two products of the postwar period drew the two sides together: the Cold War and the widespread use of modern chemicals. By highlighting the risks of both to the nation, thinking about the environment was transformed.

Of Nukes and Pests: Fallout and *Silent Spring*

America's foreign policy pushed the conservation movement in an environmental direction. Locked in an arms race with the Soviet

Union, American civilian and military leaders developed ever-larger nuclear weapons and created an environmental crisis. On March 1, 1954, the United States detonated its first practical hydrogen bomb on Bikini atoll, a small island in the South Pacific. The Bravo test, as it was known, went terribly awry. It exposed eighty-six residents of Rongelap Island to enough radioactive fallout to make them ill and lose their hair. Ninety miles from the blast, crewmen of the Japanese fishing ship the *Lucky Dragon* experienced a rain of ash. The crew developed the symptoms of radiation poisoning, including nausea, diarrhea, and loss of hair. One shipmate died several months later. Although the United States paid restitution to the Japanese government, radioactive fallout now became a serious issue, first among scientists and then the general public.[52]

Atomic scientists were unable to reassure the public about the safety of aboveground weapons testing. In 1956, the National Academy of Sciences formed two committees to look at the fallout issue, but they returned contradictory conclusions. One warned that while fallout had produced only small quantities of radioactive isotopes in the environment, public exposure to it should be strictly limited. Another committee produced in the same year a more bullish report, maintaining that there was an "unequivocally safe amount" of the isotope strontium-90 that could be ingested by humans. While the Atomic Energy Commission minimized the risk of testing, scientists such as Nobel Prize–winner Linus Pauling estimated that nuclear tests had caused 10,000 people to die of leukemia. Publications such as *The Nation, The New Republic, The Reporter,* and the *Saturday Review of Literature* called for more studies on the subject. Public awareness rose accordingly. In 1955, only 17 percent of the public could explain what fallout was. By 1957, 52 percent thought it was a "real danger." *Public Opinion Quarterly* noted that when such divisions existed among scientists, it was "small wonder that no reduction of anxiety" was found among the public.[53]

Two studies raised the concern over fallout to a general alarm. In 1958, the Committee for Nuclear Information at Washington University in St. Louis, an antinuclear organization led by future environmental advocate Barry Commoner, demonstrated how strontium-90 entered the food chain and lodged in the teeth of growing children. An advertisement in the *New York Times* showed three smiling children and reported, "Your children's teeth contain Strontium-90." The advertisement pointed out that there had been an increase in levels of the radioactive isotope in the environment over sixteen times in five years. *Consumer Reports* followed with a study on strontium-90 in milk and found that levels, while below threshold danger levels, were rising.[54]

Perhaps even more effective in raising public awareness of atomic pollution was the movie industry. Hollywood churned out a succession of movies that played on the idea of nuclear radiation causing grotesque biological mutations. *The Beast From 20,000 Fathoms, Them!* (a story of giant mutated ants), and *Tarantula* all used nuclear radiation as the trigger for nature run amok. Other movies looked at what would happen to the survivors of a nuclear war. The best known of these films was *On the Beach*, based on Nevil Shute's best-selling 1957 novel. *On the Beach* told the tale of residents of Australia, the last survivors of the human race, who awaited a fatal cloud of radioactivity to descend on them after a nuclear war in the northern hemisphere wiped out everyone else. Producers of the movie advertised it for its relevance to the current issues of nuclear fallout and the survival of mankind in the Cold War. *On the Beach* was an instant success and made people aware of the ways in which atomic poisons could spread in the atmosphere and threaten life on earth.[55]

While Australians in the movie stoically and passively accepted their fate, Americans did not. In the late 1950s and early 1960s, a craze for backyard fallout shelters ensued during a period of heightened tensions between the Soviet Union and the United States. The shooting down of an American U-2 spy plane over Soviet airspace poisoned relations between the Eisenhower administration and the Kremlin. Things did not improve in the early years of John F. Kennedy's administration. The failed invasion of Cuba at the Bay of Pigs embarrassed the young president and furthered his resolve to be resolute in future confrontations. The Cuban Missile Crisis of October 1962 made *On the Beach* seem all too real.

Hence, Kennedy stepped up federal support for a fallout shelter system.[56]

While some citizens dug in, others sought to end the possibility of war. Opponents of nuclear weapons testing called for a moratorium on it. The National Committee for a Sane Nuclear Policy (SANE) had 25,000 members and 130 chapters. SANE leaders argued that the public had to be made aware of the "poisoning effect of nuclear bombs on international relations and on humanity." The group ran a number of effective advertisements that played up the insidious nature of fallout including a television cartoon of an atomic explosion, the resulting fallout, and its poisoning of a pasture. Cows then ate the grass and their milk was given to children. [57]

Women activists played a critical role in the fallout controversy. In 1961, some disaffected women left the largely male SANE with its relatively conservative approach and formed their own organization, Women Strike for Peace. These women were opposed to SANE's decision to expel communists from the organization. They resolved to have an open admission policy and no membership lists. Despite SANE's advertisements, the WSP's leaders also wanted even more stress on "mother's issues" such as the contamination of milk supplies. Sounding very much like an activist from the Progressive era, one woman noted, "This movement was inspired and motivated by mothers' love for children. . . . When they were putting their breakfasts on the table, they saw not only the Wheaties and milk, but they also saw Strontium 90 and Iodine 131."[58] The WSP launched milk boycotts to protest the atomic testing, an effective campaign. Women received much credit for the signing of the Treaty Banning Nuclear Weapons in the Atmosphere, in Outer Space, and Underwater, in August 1963 between the United States and the Soviet Union.

Although SANE and Women Strike for Peace were pacifist, not environmental, organizations, their critique of the arms race was most effective when using environmental arguments connected with fallout. By stressing the hazards posed by atomic testing, they educated the public on how radioactive isotopes could poison the environment through the food chain. It was not much of a stretch for people to see that other poisons such as pesticides could affect people the same way.

In 1962, just a month before the Cuban Missile Crisis, Rachel Carson published *Silent Spring*, a book on the hazards pesticides posed to the environment. The book has often been hailed as the beginning of the modern environmental movement, as the conservation movement was increasingly called in the sixties. Prior to Carson's book, conservation organizations limited themselves to preserving scenic outdoor amenities. After it, protecting the ecosphere and human beings from all the depredations of modern life became paramount. *Silent Spring* was, in the words of columnist E. B. White, the *"Uncle Tom's Cabin"* of the environmental movement. As Carson's biographer Linda Lear argued, *Silent Spring* was "a fundamental social critique of a gospel of technological progress" that dominated American society. Carson reiterated the now common theme that humans should not see themselves as separate from nature. "We still talk in terms of conquest. We still haven't become mature enough," she said, "to think of ourselves as only a very tiny part of a vast and incredible universe."[59]

From the start, Rachel Carson was made for a life in the natural world and as a writer. She was born in 1907 in the small town of Springdale, Pennsylvania, near Pittsburgh. Carson's mother encouraged her children to explore the outdoors and to read and write. From an early age Carson composed short stories about the animal world. She had ambitions to be a writer, and she went to college to be an English major. But after two years, her early love of the natural world took over, and she switched her major to biology. She worked at the Woods Hole Marine Biological Laboratory, and in 1932 earned a master's degree in zoology from Johns Hopkins University. The death of her father forced her to cut short her academic ambitions and work to support her family. She entered government service, eventually receiving a position as an aquatic biologist for the Fish and Wildlife Service. Her obvious writing talent later earned her the position of chief editor of the Department of the Interior's publications.

In her spare time, Carson pursued a writing career examining life in the sea. In 1941 she published her first book, *Under the Sea*

Wind, which was not a commercial success. Her second book, however, *The Sea Around Us,* published in 1951 was a named a Book-of-the-Month Club selection and won the National Book Award for nonfiction. With this success, Carson left government work and devoted herself to writing.

In the late fifties, Carson returned to the seed of an idea she had been germinating since 1945. At the end of the war, she proposed to *Reader's Digest* an article on the risks inherent in the pesticide DDT, a chlorinated hydrocarbon that had largely replaced old organic pesticides. The chemical was hailed as a miracle cure for everything from insect pests on farm crops to lice on humans. But the magazine did not pursue her idea, and Carson let the matter drop. In 1958, a friend wrote her a letter complaining of the lethal effect pesticides had on birds near her home. As a serious bird watcher, the letter disturbed Carson. She began investigating pest eradication campaigns that the chemical industry had launched around the country. Carson saw the larger implications of her research, drawing parallels with the ongoing fallout controversy. "Whether radiation or chemicals are involved," she wrote, "the basic issue is the contamination of the environment."[60]

The project grew in complexity and scope, taking her five years to complete, due to her suffering from breast cancer. The evidence she collected added up to a damning indictment of the influence of pesticides on the environment and humans. Her chapters were mostly about the hazards chemicals posed to wildlife, but her "principal emphasis [was] to the menace to human health." Of pesticides, she asked, "if this 'rain of death' has produced so disastrous an effect on birds, what of other lives, including our own?"[61] Carson already had an answer. The short-term hazards of pesticides were well known, but experts had not seriously studied their long-term risks. She believed she had a strong case linking pesticides to cancer.

The delay in publication actually helped Carson. In addition to the fallout controversy, a number of other scares alerted the public to the hazards of low-level poisons in the environment. In 1959, just before Thanksgiving, cranberries containing the cancer-causing weed killer aminotriazole had to be pulled from the market.

Shortly thereafter the thalidomide tragedy occurred, in which pregnant women who had taken the drug to prevent miscarriage produced horribly deformed babies. Carson admitted that it was "fortunate chance that I am a slow writer."[62]

But Carson had picked a dangerous time to be launching such an investigation. The pesticide industry had grown rapidly after the war; pesticide sales increased five times between 1947 and 1960.[63] The industry had many allies in agribusiness and academia. This coalition would surely react to *Silent Spring* with a vigorous response of its own. When the industry got wind of the serialization of her book in the *New Yorker*, some companies threatened legal action and suggested that Carson's work had links to communism.[64] Nevertheless, the *New Yorker* and Carson's book publisher released her work after bringing in outside experts to verify her research.

Silent Spring was a devastating critique of the pesticide industry. It opened with a quotation by Albert Schweitzer, who had influenced so many environmentalists: "Man has lost the capacity to foresee and forestall. He will end by destroying the earth." Chapter titles like "Elixirs of Death," "Needless Havoc," "And No Birds Sing," and "Rivers of Death" set its ominous tone. Carson warned, "For the first time in the history of the world, every human being is now subjected to contact with dangerous chemicals from the moment of conception until death."[65] She described what pesticides did to target species, and how they influenced animals and humans. Explaining how the food chain worked, she showed how pesticides could eventually take up residence in the human body. She drew a direct comparison between fallout and pesticides in one section. She compared the death of a Swedish farmer from pesticides to the Japanese fisherman who died on the *Lucky Dragon* from atomic fallout. "For each man a poison drifting out of the sky carried a death sentence. For one, it was radiation poisoned ash; for the other, chemical dust."[66] She closed with a recommendation for greater education, more government oversight, and a less chemically based method of dealing with pests.

The book was more than just a practical guide. It drove home a moral message: that society had to alter its unthinking acceptance of technological innovation and its conceited attitude that nature was to be controlled for man's use. "The 'control of nature'" she wrote in a vein similar to Aldo Leopold, "is a phrase conceived in arrogance, born of the Neanderthal age of biology and philosophy, when it was supposed that nature exists for the convenience of man." No "civilization," she argued, "can wage relentless war on life without destroying itself, and without losing the right to be called civilized." The book was an instant best-seller, reaching the top of the *New York Times* best-seller list, where it stayed for thirty-one weeks.[67]

As expected, the chemical industry counterattacked with an advertising blitz. The industry recognized that *Silent Spring* could both hurt sales of pesticides and undermine public confidence in chemicals in general. The National Agricultural Chemicals Association budgeted over $250,000 to undermine Carson's credibility. The industry tried to paint Carson as unprofessional in her presentation of the facts. With only a master's degree, they argued, she was not a qualified expert. The attacks focused on Carson's unmarried status and gender, claiming that she was an overly emotional writer. Ezra Taft Benson, former Secretary of Agriculture, was reported to have puzzled,"Why a spinster with no children was so concerned about genetics?" He concluded that Carson was "probably a Communist." *Time* called the attacks on her book "unfair, one-sided, and hysterically overemphatic." One industry drawing even portrayed her as a witch.[68]

In the end, Carson was mostly vindicated. President John F. Kennedy convened a President's Science Advisory Committee to review the pesticide issue. Released in May 1963, the committee report supported some of her positions and called for possible legislation reforming pesticide regulation and greater education efforts. The report noted that "until the publication of *Silent Spring*, people were generally unaware of the toxicity of pesticides."[69] DDT was not banned for another ten years, but Carson had started the debate.

With meticulous research and beautiful prose, Carson set an example of how the modern environmental movement should approach problems. As Philip Shabecoff wrote, she "combined a transcendentalist's passion for nature and wildlife with the cool analytical mind of a trained scientist and the contained anger of a political activist." She understood that her exposé on pesticides was just a part of a larger "picture marred by polluted rivers, by cities half hidden in a murky smog, by a world now visited by rains of radioactive fallout from the skies."[70] By stressing the interconnectedness of ecosystems, she was able to challenge the general direction of science and resource conservation. Carson taught conservationists, who used economic and technological principles to change nature, how to think environmentally and to be more careful when manipulating nature. Increasingly, those who clung to the old view of conservation, where efficiency and natural resources were paramount, were alienated from the new movement of environmentalism.

Carson also expanded the public commons, the areas of the environment that could be regulated by the public. One writer concluded: "Most important of all, Rachel Carson raises one burning question: who has the right to poison the air I breathe? The water I drink? The food I eat? I am not, nor should anyone else be, satisfied with the reply that it is done under the nebulous banner of progress, because the next obvious question is: progress toward what? Slow annihilation?"[71] Carson raised the question of whether scientists and industry had the right to release poisons into the environment and legitimated the general regulation of pollutants.

Taken together, the fallout controversy and *Silent Spring* altered the agenda for the environmental movement. Preservation of scenic resources was still a part of the movement, but more and more environmentalism espoused maintaining a healthy ecology. It also showed antipollution advocates how to think in broader terms. They needed to see pollution as more than a simple public nuisance or health hazard to humans alone. Humans, as Aldo Leopold argued earlier, could not separate themselves from their environment. It was time, Carson wrote, "that human beings admit their kinship with other forms of life."[72] She showed how the separate strands of the movement could intertwine.

Women in the Movement

The campaigns against air pollution, fallout, and pesticides underscored the resurgence of women in environmental campaigns, reminiscent of the Progressive era. Women did not disappear from the movement between 1920 and 1945. Indeed they played an important role in the antismoke campaigns of St. Louis and Pittsburgh, and Rosalie Edge proved influential through her Emergency Conservation Committee. They did, however, lose significant influence to men in the movement. The professionalization of sanitary services and pollution control had left women without a voice on pollution issues, as men with scientific credentials dominated the debate.

That began to change in the fifties when women campaigned for open space and clean air and water. In the fallout debate moreover, disagreement among scientists allowed women to reassert their role as protectors of the home and children. Their motivations reflected, in part, the concerns of Progressive era–women's groups. As one member of Housewives to End Pollution put it, her organization consisted of "concerned women . . . who have banded together to attack immediate local pollution problems that center around the home."[73] Rising levels of affluence and domestic roles gave women the means and the time to campaign for a better environment. Usually women activists were married, middle-class mothers with above-average levels of education who did not work outside the home. But environmental activism was more than an effort to protect the home for these women; they found in it an outlet for their talents and energies.

Women's clubs provided essential support for environmental controversies. No one understood this better than Rachel Carson. While she attempted to craft an argument that appealed to both men and women, much of her rhetoric spoke directly to a woman's role as a mother. She demonstrated that the home could not provide a refuge from poisons. She noted that pesticides "are now stored in the bodies of the vast majority of human beings regardless of age. They occur in the mother's milk, and probably in the tissues of the unborn child."[74] Carson spoke to an influential group of women who knew how to present an issue in terms that did not challenge women's traditional roles. This proved a successful formula. But perhaps for this reason, women in the environmental movement were often unconnected to the rising tide of feminism in the nation. As the next chapter will show, a feminist interpretation of the nation's environmental problems became an integral part of the movement in later decades.

After *Silent Spring*

As *Silent Spring* alerted the public to pollutants in the environment, suburbanization and the resulting sprawl made people aware of the costs of metropolitan growth. Whether it was septic tanks polluting groundwater or the clearing of forests and fields for new homes, people recognized that overpopulation and unregulated expansion were costing them the American Dream. With suburban construction gobbling up a million acres a year in the 1950s, an area equivalent to the size of Rhode Island, the problems for the environment were extensive. Septic tanks were one problem. Some experts estimated that septic-tank failure was responsible for 40 percent of all water-borne diseases between 1945 and 1980. Septic effluents were responsible for soap suds in drinking water from laundry detergent, pollution of nearby waters, and disease and potential stomach cancer. By the early 1960s, the number of press accounts of septic-tank problems mushroomed. One magazine warned, "The disturbing discoveries about the outbreaks of infectious hepatitis and the distasteful detergent suds problem plaguing many communities should drive home to all of us—physicians, home owners, and municipal authorities—that perils to family health from polluted water are steadily increasing. We can no longer afford to enjoy the popular illusion that because we live in America our drinking water is safe."[75] Protests by homeowners and health experts led to some moderate federal legislation and regulation in the 1960s, but real reform had to wait until the 1970s, when federal and state governments sought to limit the number of developments with septic systems.

An even greater outcry arose from suburbanites who were los-ing access to open space. Very often undeveloped land near sub-urbs attracted children to play. Many residents looked on this space as the equivalent of parkland. They were often rudely shocked when the land was sold to a major developer. As one suburban writer recalled of her own experience,"One day my little girl, Jan, ran into the house shouting, 'Mother, there's a bulldozer up the street. The men say they're going to cut down the trees. They can't do that. They're my trees! Where will we play? Please, mother, please stop them.'" The author went on to relate the destruction of the woods in dramatic terms. The bulldozers "raped the woods, filled up the creek, buried the wildflowers, and frightened away the rabbits and birds." She referred to "murdered trees" demonstrating the dramatic change in how Americans viewed and came to iden-tify with nature. Grassroots–neighborhood groups headed up by women often led the charge against unplanned development call-ing on government to "save our trees" and "stop the rape of the valley." Organizations with names like People for Open Space, the Open Space Action Institute, and the Open Space Council sprang up around the country. In 1966, the *Saturday Evening Post* wrote, "In every city and in thousands of towns and obscure neighbor-hoods, there are housewives and homeowners banding together to fight, block by block, sometimes tree by tree, to save a small hill, a tiny brook, a stand of maples." These groups focused mostly on aesthetic and recreational arguments, but by the end of the 1960s, ecological arguments that open space was necessary to maintain an "ecological balance" became popular with activists. In an indica-tion of this new sentiment, the Audubon Society weighed in in support of open-space advocates citing the essential role such spaces played in the health of the ecosystem. By the end of the 1960s, the open-space issue had led many residents of suburbia to reevaluate the benefits and costs of development. They certainly saw the suburbs as a sign of progress, but they recognized that too much of it might actually lower their standard of living.[76] The key result of this movement were calls for land purchases and regula-tion of private development. The open-space crusade also ex-panded the constituency for the environmental movement and set environmentalism against those who sought to expand suburban development.

The pollution, open-space, wilderness-preservation, and pesticide issues all reached a critical stage by the early sixties. This roughly coincided with the elevation of Lyndon Baines Johnson to the presidency. The Johnson regime represented the high point of postwar liberalism. Environmentalism, or the "New Conservation" as the administration called it, figured prominently into its agenda.[77] The Johnson administration provided a national focus to the disparate elements of the movement and helped weld them into a cohesive policy.

The New Conservation was a prime example of what historian Arthur Schlesinger, Jr., called "qualitative liberalism," which was "dedicated to bettering the quality of people's lives and opportunities."[78] The New Deal focused on their immediate needs, Schlesinger noted. Liberals should focus on using America's postwar affluence to improve the quality of people's lives through expanded government programs. Others in the Kennedy and Johnson administrations picked up Schlesinger's theme. Stewart Udall, Secretary of the Interior from 1961 to 1969, wrote a crusading book on the environment, *The Quiet Crisis.* "America today stands poised on a pinnacle of wealth and power," he wrote, "yet we live in a land of vanishing beauty, of increasing ugliness, of shrinking open space, and of an overall environment that is diminished daily by pollution and noise and blight."[79] Udall called on government to solve the crisis. Such a call to arms particularly suited Johnson's goals. He hoped to surpass his mentor, Franklin D. Roosevelt, who had been a strong conservationist president. Ultimately, Johnson achieved moderate advances in pollution control and wilderness preservation.

The Johnson administration had one foot in the older camp of scenic preservation. LBJ signed the landmark Wilderness Act into law in 1964. In addition, Johnson signed off on the Land Water Conservation Fund Act of 1964, which budgeted money to acquire private land within national forests. This was the first serious effort to add land to the National Forests system in the postwar period. Johnson also added several national parks to the system, including the North Cascades Park in Washington, the Canyonlands Park in Utah, and the Redwoods Park in California. Finally, Johnson added a significant number of national seashores and recreation areas to the park system. For LBJ, the traditional emphasis on beauty and scenic preservation were key animating factors in these efforts. He called for "the right of easy access to places of beauty and tranquility where every family can find recreation and refreshment—and the duty to preserve such places clean and unspoiled."[80]

Air pollution legislation, however, demonstrated that the administration was in tune with environmentalism's recent emphasis on human health. States and cities outside of California failed to control air pollution. When their efforts faltered, federal intervention followed. Congress responded with increasingly forceful legislation. Through the fifties, federal bills mostly had focused on research. That changed with the 1963 Clean Air Act. John F. Kennedy told the nation,"We need an effective Federal air pollution control program now." The bill budgeted $95 million for three years to start the program. In addition to funding research, the bill made grants to state and local pollution agencies to improve their enforcement policies. The act also called for the development of pollution-control devices on automobiles. Finally, the bill called for federal nonmandatory pollution standards for states looking to enact their own laws.[81] The 1963 legislation sought to maintain a balance between federal and state control.

After 1963 federal deference to local government eroded. The Secretary of Health, Education, and Welfare, John Gardner, informed the states of a new age of federal activism. He censured local government for not establishing "regional approaches demanded by a problem that ignores traditional state boundaries."[82] Amendments to the 1963 legislation, known as the Air Quality Act of 1967, sought to balance federal and state authority. Pushed through by Senator Edmund Muskie of Maine, who was dubbed "Mr. Clean" for his pollution crusading, the act called on state and local governments to develop multistate air quality control zones. The federal government was authorized to intervene to set standards, but only after a lengthy process documenting that the states had not fulfilled their duties.

Johnson maintained a similar commitment to water-pollution control and waste management. Once again, Muskie led the way in Congress as chair of the Subcommittee on Air and Water Pollution. Mr. Clean introduced substantial amendments to the 1961 water-pollution control act and created a new Federal Water Pollution Control Administration. The administration also pushed for greater funding for waste-treatment facilities, and signed into law the Solid Waste Disposal Act of 1965 to assist states in developing comprehensive waste disposal plans.[83]

The environmental movement did not content itself with legislative victories. The 1960s witnessed the growing use of one of the movement's most powerful weapons: the lawsuit. Emerging out of an opposition group to DDT, a number of Long Island scientists and lawyers joined together in 1967 to found the Environmental Defense Fund (EDF). The EDF immersed itself in a broad array of lawsuits, including those against industrial pollution, nuclear power, and lead poisoning. Pursuing a "sue-the-bastards" approach to environmental issues, the EDF pioneered the art of environmental litigation. The EDF soon had imitators in the Natural Resources Defense Council and the Sierra Club Legal Defense Fund.[84]

By the late sixties, activists began to see that environmental problems were more complex than simply stopping pollution; other factors were involved, such as population, which had to be controlled. For some time, environmentalists had worried about the impact on the Earth of overpopulation. The postwar period had brought on, in philosopher Lewis Mumford's words, "the population explosion, the freeway explosion, the recreation explosion, the suburban explosion."[85] In 1968, overpopulation became a national issue after the Sierra Club published Stanford University Professor Paul Ehrlich's *The Population Bomb*. With evidence of uncontrolled population growth all around them, the public responded avidly to Ehrlich's message in a way that they never did with the earlier books by Fairfield Osborn, William Vogt, and Harrison Brown. The book was a runaway best-seller with over 3 million copies in print. Even as Ehrlich warned that population growth had to be contained, he predicted that it was already too late to stop a major die-off, since food production could not possibly keep up with population growth. "The battle to feed all of humanity is over," Ehrlich predicted. "In the 1970's the world will undergo famines—hundreds of millions of people are going to starve to death in spite of any crash programs embarked upon now. At this late date nothing can prevent a substantial increase in the world death rate. . . ."[86]

Ehrlich detailed the environmental costs of overpopulation. He minimized the possibility of a technological solution and predicted that only a substantial reduction in population could dent the problem. America, he claimed, had a responsibility to find a solution, since its population consumed over half of the world's resources. He recommended that the country establish an agency responsible for reproduction. As if it was necessary, the agency was to promote sex for pleasure rather than reproduction. In foreign affairs, he called on American officials to cut off food aid to countries like India. Such countries, he argued, would be forced to develop population-control policies. Though population control would "demand many brutal and heartless decisions," it was the only "chance for survival."[87] Ehrlich's comparisons of population and food supply echoed the work of eighteenth-century cleric Thomas Malthus, who had made similarly dire predictions. Critics derided Ehrlich's estimates as neo-Malthusian and claimed that his warnings, like those of Malthus, Osborn, Vogt, and Brown would prove wildly premature. But his warning had a powerful influence. Along with the pollution disasters of the late sixties, Ehrlich's book contributed to the anxious feeling on the part of Americans that the nation needed to act fast on population control.

That sense of the limited time available to save the environment was heightened by a series of calamities in 1969. On January 28, the Union Oil Company suffered a blowout of one of its oil-drilling platforms near the beautiful coastal community of Santa Barbara, California. The oil spill that washed ashore on its pristine beaches received national coverage. In an utterly futile gesture, residents formed an organization named GOO (Get Oil Out), which sponsored a one-day boycott of gasoline purchases and a burning of gasoline credit cards. Such mild protests only underscored the public's heavy dependence on oil. Americans wanted cheap gas but were unwilling to accept their responsibility in such accidents. Critics also contended that the Santa Barbara spill, relatively minor compared to other blowouts and in the overall damage it caused, received publicity because it occurred in a wealthy college town, which supported those who tagged environmentalists as elitist.

The same could not be said for the next episode. Due to oil dumped into it, Cleveland's Cuyahoga River caught fire, as it often had before. The worst fires came in 1952, doing $500,000 in damage, and in 1959, when the river burned for eight days.[88] Cleveland was home to numerous oil refineries that dumped so much oil into the river that it sometimes had a slick six inches thick. So another fire did not particularly surprise the city's residents. "It was strictly a run of the mill fire," said a fire chief. But with environmental awareness on the rise, the fire received national press coverage. *Time* devoted a special section to it. The magazine described the river as "chocolate-brown, oily, bubbling with sub-surface gases, it oozes rather than flows."[89] Cleveland was a gritty city, the "mistake by the lake" as it was known, unlike wealthy Santa Barbara, and such an incident should not have aroused publicity. But by the end of the sixties, the urban environment concerned the public as much as scenic spots.

The Cuyahoga River fire highlighted the "death" of nearby Lake Erie. Untreated sewage was regularly dumped into the lake by cities such as Detroit, Cleveland, and Buffalo. The Detroit River alone dumped into the lake 1.6 billion gallons of domestic wastewater and industrial effluents each day, carrying 20 million pounds of pollutants.[90] Particularly harmful were laundry detergents containing phosphates. The detergents caused unsightly suds to form on the lake's surface. Phosphates contributed to the growth of algae blooms which depleted the oxygen in the lake. Scientists had recorded extensive areas of the lake that were practically devoid of oxygen and marine life. *Time* labeled the lake the "North American Dead Sea."[91] Such a characterization was overstated. The lake still had an abundance of life. Nevertheless, the episode contributed to a movement to limit phosphate discharges into the lake and to demand federal action for its regulation.

As important as these events were in galvanizing environmentalists, America's youth were even more consequential in taking the environmental movement in new directions. The counterculture and the New Left radical political movement of the 1960s focused their hostility and contempt on what they saw as a wasteful, corrupt society and big government and industry. The influx of baby boomers energized environmentalism, transforming it into a mass movement. The environment fit well with the issues and concerns of America's young people who often held apocalyptic visions of America's Cold War future. As anthropologist Margaret Mead wrote, "They have never known a time when war did not threaten annihilation. . . . They can understand immediately that continued pollution of the air and water and soil will soon make the planet uninhabitable and that it will be impossible to feed an indefinitely expanding world population."[92]

The counterculture was an obvious fit with environmentalism. Rejecting the artificial nature of consumer culture, hippies believed the natural world offered an antidote to a conformist civilization. By the end of the decade numerous communes sprang up in rural areas. The reasons for hippies starting these communes varied, but their rejection of modern society and concern for the environment were near the top of the list. "Right now, I'm trying to keep from being swallowed by a monster—plastic, greedy American society," one prospective communard wrote. "I need to begin relating to new people who are into taking care of each other and the earth."[93] Most communes did not last long, but the counterculture left a cultural legacy. Many members of the environmental movement came to believe that to live lightly on the land, they had to change American culture. They called for a more natural way of living and popularized the use of organic foods.

Political radicals in the New Left had a harder time accepting environmentalism. Some college-age activists who had fought for civil rights and against the war in Vietnam saw environmentalism as a middle-class movement, a detour from true revolutionary work. Many radicals did not participate in the first Earth Day demonstrations in April 1970. But others became interested in environmental politics, just as the energy went out of the civil rights and antiwar movements. Rejected by black radicals in civil rights movements, white activists turned to the next best thing. "Now a lot of us are turning to the environment," a Columbia University graduate student said. "It's right here. It's something we can do something about. And—for a change—we might just win this one."[94]

What the radicals offered to the movement was an anticorporate critique of society and a call for a decentralized power structure. The New Left believed that citizens had to tear down a "corrupt economic system" and an "unresponsive, undemocratic government." There was a "basic malfunction of the social order itself, and consequently [reform] cannot be dealt with on a piecemeal, patchwork basis."[95] Long after the New Left vanished, environmentalism retained a hint of an anticapitalist ethos and fear of centralized power.

There was no better indication of the strength of these gathering social forces than the biggest demonstration of the era, Earth Day, April 22, 1970. The idea for the demonstration was hatched by Senator Gaylord Nelson, a Democrat from Wisconsin, in a 1969 speech he made in Seattle. He proposed a nationwide "teach-in," modeled on the college events activists created to educate students about the war in Vietnam. Nelson's modest proposal took on a life of its own. Requests for information about the event overwhelmed his office. To handle the calls and plan the event, Nelson picked up a foundation grant, speaking fees, and personal contributions to set up an office staffed by three Harvard graduate students. "Planned" is not the right word for the many spontaneous demonstrations that occurred that day. "If we had actually been responsible for making the event happen, it might have taken several years and millions of dollars to pull it off," Nelson recalled. "In the end, Earth Day became its own event."[96] Earth Day was a massive outpouring of feeling by activists around the country. *Time* called it "the biggest street festival since the Japanese surrender in 1945."[97] An estimated 20 million people took part. Events took place in most major cities, on 1,500 college campuses, and at 10,000 schools.

Earth Day was largely a mainstream event. This was by design. Earth Day leaders hoped to avoid leftist politics. Middle- and working-class Americans were hostile to the antiwar movement, New Left, and counterculture, but polls showed that they supported saving the environment. Earth Day was a unifying event. "We didn't want to alienate the middle class," Dennis Hayes, the chief organizer of the event noted. "We didn't want to lose the 'Silent Majority' just because of style issues." The press and organizers emphasized the diversity of peaceful demonstrations. Corporate leaders, celebrities, and politicians joined each other on stages around the country and professed their allegiance to the new movement. Even Governor Ronald Reagan said, "there is no subject more on our minds than the preservation of the environment." Adults and children held marches, went around their neighborhoods cleaning up the trash, and planted trees. There was something for everyone to do. Jesse Unruh, Reagan's Democratic opponent in his reelection campaign surmised, "Ecology has become the political substitute for the word *mother*."[98]

Still, there was a clear bias against corporate and government representatives among some participants. They carried with them an aggressiveness that a consensus builder like Howard Zahniser would have found repugnant. At a Washington, DC, rally, Dennis Hayes warned, "politicians and businessmen who are jumping on the environmental bandwagon don't have the slightest idea what they are getting into. They are talking about filters on smokestacks while we are challenging corporate irresponsibility." One electric utility executive who participated in the day's events confessed it was "embarrassing to sit there and get booed and laughed at" for suggesting incremental reform.[99] There was a great deal of guerrilla theater, "ecotage" as it was called. Student activists cut down unsightly billboards. Florida activists dumped a dead octopus at the corporate headquarters of Florida Power and Light to protest thermal pollution at its power plants. Denver activists presented the Colorado Environmental Rapist of the Year award to the Atomic Energy Commission. In Miami, pranksters dumped yellow dye into the sewerage system, turning the canals of Dade County yellow. The disrespect for political and corporate leaders was widespread.[100] Notably, these acts did not undermine public support for the movement. By carrying out a highly decentralized campaign,

Earth Day activists were able to incorporate radical and respectable elements into the day's demonstrations.

The influence of Earth Day has been much debated among scholars. Some portray it as a breakthrough moment in environmental history that finally forced together the preservationist and urban, industrial wings of the conservation movement. Up to this point, they argue, old-line conservation organizations, such as the Audubon Society, the National Wildlife Federation, the Wilderness Society, and the Sierra Club avoided urban environmental issues. As Hal Rothman pointed out, traditional conservation organizations "took little notice of urban sprawl and pollution issues except in the most peripheral ways."[101] In his work *Forcing the Spring,* Robert Gottlieb concludes that the white, wealthy Republicans who had dominated wilderness organizations in the past were uninterested in responding to the "urban and industrial realities" of the postwar era, and had reached a political and ideological "impasse" that prevented them from thinking environmentally.[102] They were suspicious of the agenda and radicalism of the Earth Day's organizers. But the success of Earth Day forced these organizations to reorder their priorities and expand their vision.

Admittedly, the *ancien regime* of the conservation movement was notably absent from the Earth Day's festivities. And as Michael McCloskey, Executive Director of the Sierra Club, acknowledged, conservation organizations were caught flat-footed by the upsurge in popularity that environmentalism enjoyed. "We were severely disoriented suddenly to find that all sorts of new personalities were emerging to lead something new," McCloskey said, "mainly people out of the youth rebellion of the 1960s who had all sorts of notions that just came out of nowhere."[103] But McCloskey and the Sierra Club were hardly alone in their confusion. Few contemporaries could comprehend Earth Day's bewildering array of issues and organizations.

In fact, conservation organizations had been reconfiguring their outlook on environmental issues throughout the sixties. By the end of the decade, few of the major organizations focused exclusively on wilderness preservation. The Audubon Society took the lead in defending Rachel Carson during the *Silent Spring* controversy and calling for pesticide control. The society was also active in promoting the open-space movement. The National Wildlife Federation and the Izaak Walton League became immersed in water-pollution issues. And by the end of the decade, the Sierra Club had turned against nuclear power, after a fractious debate within the organization that led to the ouster of David Brower as executive secretary and his founding of the more militant Friends of the Earth. McCloskey expressed this new aggressive posture in an interview, where he warned, "Our strategy is going to be to sue and sue and sue. Eventually the [electric] utilities are going to have to take us seriously." He was hardly exaggerating. By early 1970 the Sierra Club was involved in fifty-five legal actions around the country.[104]

In large part because of this shifting emphasis, the traditional organizations benefited immensely from Earth Day. Membership in the organizations, which had grown substantially in the fifties, mushroomed in the sixties. Over the course of the decade, the Audubon Society increased its membership from 40,000 to 80,000. The Wilderness Society doubled its membership, and the Sierra Club saw its roster balloon from 20,000 to over 100,000 members.[105] The older organizations continued to lead the movement, even if they lagged somewhat in their embrace of the new environmental agenda.

It is, then, more accurate to claim, as historian Samuel Hays has, that Earth Day was as much a culmination of a decade of environmental activity as it was a cause of later activism. What can be said for Earth Day is that it infused the environmental movement with a diverse membership that had new ideas, and it quickened the pace of change.

Legislative Victories

The quickened pace caused by Earth Day was particularly evident in legislation and policy. Now a flood of environmental bills made their way through Congress in areas such as pollution control, pesticide regulation, toxic substances, and solid-waste disposal. Reform followed two lines. Some of the legislation and administrative change sought to do away with the piecemeal fashion in which the federal government dealt with environmental problems. Until 1970, separate agencies handled water and air pollution, and still another handled pesticides. Advocates called for a holistic, integrated approach to pollution control, similar to ecological thinking of the time. The worst environmental calamities, one activist said, were the result of a "failure to perceive environmental situations in comprehensive ecological terms."[106] A second area of reform sought to replace scattered and ineffective state efforts with stronger federal initiatives. The failure of the less-ambitious laws enacted during the Johnson administration led to far-reaching proposals in the early seventies.

The trend toward holistic legislation was most clearly embodied in the National Environmental Policy Act (NEPA). Passed during the run-up to Earth Day, NEPA is arguably the most important piece of environmental legislation ever enacted. Proposed by Senator Henry Jackson of Washington and aided by Indiana University professor Lynton Caldwell, an expert in public administration, NEPA sailed through Congress with bipartisan support and headed to President Richard Nixon's desk for signature. A man who wore dress shoes to the beach, Nixon was no friend of the environment. Despite Nixon's prodevelopment ethic, his administration cunningly responded to the environmental phenomenon by crafting a moderate environmental agenda. Nixon signed the NEPA bill in a televised ceremony on January 1, 1970. He called the seventies the "decade of the environment" where "America pays its debts to the past by reclaiming the purity of its air, its waters, and our living environment." He dramatically predicted, "It is literally now or never."[107] Nixon's embrace of an environmental agenda indicated that through the early 1970s, environmentalism still enjoyed bipartisan support. It would only be later as the Republican party drifted in a more conservative direction that the movement lost support of the GOP.

NEPA consisted of three parts. First, it contained a policy statement of environmental goals that federal agencies should strive to fulfill, such as "productive harmony" between humans and their environment. It mandated that federal agencies expand their criteria of evaluation for federally sponsored projects from simple cost-benefit analysis to include environmental factors.[108]

The most important section of the act sought to establish "action-forcing mechanisms" to ensure that agencies took seriously the policy statement in their regular operations. Agencies had to develop an Environmental Impact Statement (EIS) that discussed the environmental consequences of a proposed project and possible alternatives to it that might diminish the harm to the environment. Significantly, the law required that agencies distribute the EIS to other affected agencies and to the public for comment and hearings. This opened up the EIS process to legal challenge from outside entities, including activist groups. NEPA was a law that decentralized power. Federal bureaucrats never again had wide discretionary authority. In the first nine years, more than 11,000 EIS's were prepared. About 1,000 wound up in court. In about 200 of these cases, the courts enjoined agencies from continuing projects until modifications were made or the EIS was revised.[109]

The final element of NEPA was the creation of the president's Council on Environmental Quality (CEQ). The law charged the CEQ with overseeing the implementation of NEPA and to advise the president on environmental policy. But the CEQ's real impact depended on the whims of presidents. Under the Carter administration, the CEQ had significant influence on policy. Ronald Reagan, on the other hand, practically abolished the council and stripped it of most of its staff. The council did not regain significant influence again until the Clinton administration.[110]

Consistent with the holistic approach of NEPA, the Nixon administration created the Environmental Protection Agency (EPA) at the end of 1970. The administration took the agencies that dealt with pollution and pesticide control, scattered about in the Atomic Energy Commission and the Departments of the Interior, Agriculture, and Health Education and Welfare and gathered them in one entity. The EPA instantly became a major agency within the federal bureaucracy with a staff of over 6,000.

Under its first administrator, William Ruckelshaus, the EPA set a tone of aggressive enforcement of environmental laws by filing 152 lawsuits against major polluters. The EPA defined itself as a defender of the environment and an adversary of industrial and government polluters, rather than a compromiser to economic necessity.

While the failure of pollution control at the state and municipal level spurred somewhat more federal oversight in the sixties, Earth Day created a flood of legislation. Dwight D. Eisenhower had considered air and water pollution "uniquely local" problems. In the seventies, politicians recognized that the public demanded federal action. The first major statute out of the starting gate was the Clean Air Act of 1970. It empowered the EPA to set national air-quality standards. Significantly, these standards were to be determined by the best available science in evaluating the public health risk posed by six major pollutants: sulfur and nitrogen oxides, carbon monoxide, particulates, lead, and ozone. States had to come up with implementation plans approved by the EPA. New point sources (pollution that comes from a single point) had to obtain a federal permit that evaluated the technology used to control emissions. The act required automakers to achieve a 90 percent reduction in emissions by 1975. Finally, funds were provided to states for air-pollution control programs.[111] One drawback was that the law exempted or grandfathered in older sources of pollution regarding emission standards.

Nevertheless, the Clean Air Act was a nearly unqualified success in reducing industrial and vehicle emissions. Between 1970 and 1990 smoke pollution abated nearly 80 percent, lead emissions an amazing 98 percent. Other pollutants declined by one-third to one-fifth of their former amounts, despite increasing economic activity. State regulation contributed to some of the drop, but the numbers were so dramatic that few could criticize the effectiveness of the law.[112]

Even stronger than the Clean Air Act were the Water Pollution Control Act Amendments of 1972. The amendments set national goals that all surface waters be "fishable and swimmable" by 1983, and contain zero emissions by 1985. The amendments also provided for large subsidies to municipalities to upgrade their waste-water-treatment facilities. Unlike the Clean Air Act, the water-pollution control amendments did not allow for grandfathering in of older sources of pollution. The amendments dramatically reduced pollution. Organic materials that depleted oxygen dropped by 65 percent, suspended solids by 80 percent, and dissolved solids by 52 percent. Still, pollution did not disappear since nonpoint sources (pollution that comes from no single clearly definable source), such as agricultural runoff and storm-water discharges, were exempt from the law. Also municipalities could report that they were not in compliance with the law, but the federal government could not compel voters to approve bond measures to upgrade waste-treatment facilities.[113]

Taken together, Earth Day and the subsequent environmental legislation marked the transition to a new regulatory regime. Historian Terence Kehoe has characterized environmental regulation up to 1970 as "cooperative pragmatism."[114] Government regulation of industry was based on voluntary action by corporations, expertise, and state or local administration. This system, which had been developing since the Progressive era, began to break down during the 1960s. George Hoberg has called the new system the "Pluralist Regulatory Regime," that was defined by litigation and an end to the informality of the regulatory process. Instead formal procedures were put in place that permitted more groups to have an input on policy.[115] Gone were the days when corporations and regulators made policy through informal channels. Public-interest groups were successful in instituting environmental regulation, consumer protection, and workplace-safety laws and policies that shifted regulatory power to the federal level. They limited the autonomy of regulators by forcing them to follow formal procedures. Federal bureaucrats found that their responsibilities increased, but their ability to make independent decisions declined, constrained by public hearings and legal challenges. Courts became much more willing to intervene and overrule decisions made by regulators.

Much of the protest and legislation of the late sixties and early seventies focused on urban industrial issues. Seemingly lost amid new pollution statutes were the traditional foci of the old-line organizations, such as the Sierra Club and Audubon Society, on wilderness and wildlife. These concerns were not entirely forgotten, as the Endangered Species Act of 1973 demonstrated. Like other environmental legislation, the act had its antecedents in the Johnson administration, which had passed two bills protecting endangered species. The new legislation prohibited anyone from "taking" an endangered species. The Fish and Wildlife Service defined a "taking" to include not only killing a species but also destruction of its habitat. The latter decision had profound implications for later controversies, since protecting a species might mean that whole ecosystems might need to be spared from development. The Endangered Species Act demonstrated just how far opinion had changed in regard to animal protection. The bill was not passed for economic reasons or because animals were useful to humans. Animals and their habitat were protected because Americans acknowledged their right to exist. This bill set the stage for major controversies over habitat protection in the seventies and eighties.

Conclusion

In the twenty-five years after World War II, environmental values had undergone a fundamental shift. This change in values made possible the transformation of the conservation movement into a larger, more broadly defined environmental movement that incorporated the scattered efforts to protect wilderness, wildlife, suburbia, and the urban environment. Environmentalism's success in the late sixties was largely due to its unifying nature. At a time when the nation was rent asunder by civil rights, Vietnam, and cultural change, the environment was an issue to which both right and left could pledge their allegiance on some level. This unity did not last forever. Due in part to the rightward drift of the Republicans, the bipartisan consensus on protecting the environment broke down as sixties activists infused the movement with a more anti-corporate agenda than it ever had before.

The era also witnessed the institutionalization of the environmental movement. Between 1969 and 1973, major legislation enshrined environmental values within local, state, and federal bureaucracies. Environmental organizations became part of the political establishment and developed large bureaucratic structures. No longer content to maintain an ad hoc presence in Washington, the movement developed professional lobbyists and support staffs. As the movement grew, it also became more diverse, with specialized organizations providing expertise on specific issues.

The environmental movement marched into the future with broad public support and institutional sophistication. It also enjoyed the benefits of economic prosperity that made the costs of its reforms possible. But it was severely tested in the coming decades, as the economic shocks of the seventies and a backlash against the movement in the eighties tested the public's commitment to environmental values.

Endnotes

1 William Vogt, *Road to Survival* (New York: William Sloane Associates, 1948), 33, 78.

2 Fairfield Osborn, *Our Plundered Planet* (Boston: Little, Brown and Company, 1948), 35, 186–87, 293.

3 Osborn, *Our Plundered Planet,* 193, 196; and Vogt, *Road to Survival,* x.

4 Harrison Brown, *The Challenge of Man's Future: An Inquiry Concerning the Condition of Man During the Years That Lie Ahead* (New York: Viking Press, 1954; reprint, Boulder, CO: Westview Press, 1984), 235.

5 Vogt, *Road to Survival,* 58; and Vogt, *People! Challenge to Survival* (New York: William Sloane Associates, 1960), xi–xii.

6 Brown, *The Challenge of Man's Future,* 263.

7 E.G.R. Taylor, review of *Road to Survival,* by William Vogt, *The Geographical Journal* 113 (Jan.–June 1949): 93.

8 Adam Rome, *The Bulldozer in the Countryside: Suburban Sprawl and the Rise of American Environmentalism* (Cambridge: Cambridge University Press, 2001), 48.

9 Scott Hamilton Dewey, *Don't Breathe the Air: Air Pollution and U.S. Environmental Politics, 1945–1970* (College Station, Texas A&M University Press, 2000), 19, 37–40.

10 Ibid., 43–56, 84, 95.

11 Ibid., 48, 59, 91, 95.

12 Ibid., 49.

13 Ibid., 66–67, 69.

14 Ibid., 138–41.

15 Ibid., 143.

16 Ibid., 124, 143–44, and 146–48.

17 Ibid., 133.

18 Ibid., 231.

19 Mark W. T. Harvey, *A Symbol of Wilderness: Echo Park and the American Conservation Movement* (Albuquerque: University of New Mexico Press, 1994; reprint, Seattle: University of Washington Press, 2000), 11.

20 Harvey, *Symbol of Wilderness,* 29 and Mark Harvey, *Wilderness Forever: Howard Zahniser and the Path to the Wilderness Act* (Seattle: University of Washington Press, 2005), 105.

21 Harvey, *Symbol of Wilderness,* 61–62 and Madelyn Holmes, *American Women Conservationists: Twelve Profiles* (Jefferson, NC: McFarland and Co., 2004), 76.

22 Harvey, *Wilderness Forever,* 98–99.

23 Richard West Sellars, *Preserving Nature in the National Parks: A History* (New Haven: Yale University Press, 1997), 182.

24 Roderick Nash, *Wilderness and the American Mind,* 3d ed. (New Haven: Yale University Press, 1982), 210.

25 Ibid., 211.

26 Clayton R. Koppes, "Environmental Policy and American Liberalism: The Department of the Interior, 1933–1953," *Environmental Review* 7, no. 1 (Spring 1983): 28.

27 Nash, *Wilderness and the American Mind,* 212.

28 Harvey, *Symbol of Wilderness,* 130–31.

29 Nash, *Wilderness;* 212–13 and

Harvey, *Symbol of Wilderness,* 257–58.

30 Harvey, *Symbol of Wilderness,* 214.

31 Ibid., 160.

32 Ibid., 181, 191.

33 Ibid., 271; and Nash, *Wilderness and the American Mind,* 218.

34 Ibid., 277.

35 Stephen Fox, *The American Conservation Movement: John Muir and His Legacy* (Madison: University of Wisconsin Press, 1985), 280, 286.

36 Harvey, *Symbol of Wilderness,* 57, 270.

37 Ibid., 299.

38 Harvey, *Wilderness Forever,* 147, 237.

39 Ibid., 119; and Nash, *Wilderness and the American Mind,* 221–22.

40 Nash, *Wilderness and the American Mind,* 225; and Fox, *American Conservation Movement,* 288.

41 Lewis L. Gould, *Lady Bird Johnson and the Environment* (Lawerence: University Press of Kansas, 1988): 42.

42 Dennis Roth, "The National Forests and the Campaign for Wilderness Legislation," *Journal of Forest History* 28, no. 3 (July 1984): 125.

43 Harvey, *Wilderness Forever,* 235.

44 Mark Dowie, *Losing Ground: American Environmentalism at the Close of the Twentieth Century* (Cambridge, MA: MIT Press, 1995), 31.

45 Marc Reisner, *Cadillac Desert: The American West and Its Disappearing Water,* 2d ed. (New York: Penguin, 1993), 289.

46 Nash, *Wilderness and the American Mind,* 229–31.

47 Ibid., 229–31.

48 Reisner, *Cadillac Desert,* 286, 288.

49 Nash, *Wilderness and the American Mind,* 234.

50 Susan Zakin, *Coyotes and Town Dogs: Earth First! and the Environmental Movement* (New York: Viking, 1993), 166–67; and Reisner, *Cadillac Desert,* 290.

51 Byron E. Pearson, *Still the Wild River Runs: Congress, the Sierra Club, and the Fight to Save Grand Canyon* (Tucson: University of Arizona Press, 2002), 171–89.

52 Allan M. Winkler, *Life Under Cloud: American Anxiety About the Atom* (New York: Oxford University Press, 1993), 93–94.

53 Ibid., 96, 101–02.

54 Ibid., 102.

55 Ralph H. Lutts, "Chemical Fallout: Rachel Carson's *Silent Spring,* Radioactive Fallout, and the Environmental Movement," *Environmental Review* 9, no. 3 (Fall 1985): 216–18.

56 Lutts, "Chemical Fallout," 218–20.

57 Winkler, *Life Under a Cloud,* 105–06.

58 Ibid., 106; and Amy Swerdlow, *Women Strike For Peace: Traditional Motherhood and Radical Politics in the 1960s* (Chicago: University of Chicago Press, 1993), 46–48.

59 "The Silent Spring of Rachel Carson," *CBS Reports,* April 3, 1963, transscript.

60 Rachel Carson to Paul Brooks, April 11, 1960, Rachel Carson Papers, Beinecke Library, Yale University (RCP/BLYU).

61 Carson, Rachel, "Vanishing

Americans," *Washington Post*, April 10, 1959.

62 Gartner, *Rachel Carson,* 86.

63 Paul Brooks, *The House of Life: Rachel Carson at Work* (Boston: Houghton Mifflin, 1972), 300.

64 Lear, *Rachel Carson,* 417–18.

65 Rachel Carson, *Silent Spring* (Boston: Houghton Mifflin, 1962),15.

66 Ibid., 229–30.

67 Ibid., 99, 297; and Lear, *Rachel Carson,* 426.

68 Brooks, *The House of Life,* 297; Maril Hazlett, "'Woman vs. Man vs. Bugs': Gender and Popular Ecology in Early Reactions to *Silent Spring*," *Environmental History* 9, no. 4 (Oct. 2004): 707, and Lear, *Rachel Carson,* 429.

69 Lear, *Rachel Carson,* 451.

70 Philip Shabecoff, *A Fierce Green Fire: The American Environmental Movement* (New York: Hill and Wang, 1993), 110; and Brooks, *House of Life,* 300.

71 Hazlett, "Woman vs. Man vs. Bugs," 713.

72 Rachel Carson, Speech, Kaiser Foundation Symposium, "The Pollution of Our Environment," October 18, 1963, RCP/BLYU.

73 Terence Kehoe, "'Merchants of Pollution': The Soap and Detergent Industry and the Fight to Restore Great Lakes Water Quality, 1965–1972," *Environmental History Review* 16, no. 3 (Fall 1992): 32.

74 Vera Norwood, *Made From This Earth: American Women and Nature* (Chapel Hill: University of North Carolina Press, 1993), 155.

75 Rome, *Bulldozer in the Countryside,* 110 and 114.

76 Ibid., 123, 145–50.

77 Martin V. Melosi, "Lyndon Johnson and Environmental Policy," in *The Johnson Years Volume Two: Vietnam, the Environment, and Science,* ed. Robert A. Divine (Lawrence: University Press of Kansas, 1987), 117.

78 Adam Rome, "'Give Earth a Chance': The Environmental Movement and the Sixties," *The Journal of American History* 90, no. 2 (September 2003): 528.

79 Rome,"Give Earth a Chance," 532.

80 Melosi,"Lyndon Johnson and Environmental Policy," 128–31; and Rome, *Bulldozer in the Countryside,* 141.

81 Dewey, *Don't Breathe the Air,* 238–39.

82 Ibid., 240.

83 Melosi, "Lyndon Johnson and Environmental Policy," 137–39.

84 Kirkpatrick Sale, *The Green Revolution: The American Environmental Movement, 1962–1992* (New York: Hill and Wang, 1993), 21.

85 Susan R. Schrepfer, *The Fight to Save the Redwoods: A History of Environmental Reform, 1917–78* (Madison: University of Wisconsin Press, 1983), 103.

86 Paul R. Ehrlich, *The Population Bomb* (New York: Ballantine Books, 1968), prologue.

87 Jeffrey C Ellis,"On the Search for a Root Cause: Essentialist Tendencies in Environmentalist Discourse," *Uncommon Ground: Rethinking the Human Place in Nature,* ed., William Cronon (New York: W. W. Norton, 1995), 261–62.

88 Ted Steinberg, *Down To Earth: Nature's Role in American History* (New York: Oxford University Press, 2002), 239; and Martin V. Melosi, *The Sanitary City: Urban Infrastructure in America From Colonial Times to the Present* (Baltimore: Johns Hopkins University Press, 2000), 312.

89 Steinberg, *Down To Earth,* 239.

90 William Ashworth, *The Late, Great Lakes: An Environmental History* (New York: Alfred Knopf, 1986), 133.

91 Steinberg, *Down to Earth,* 248.

92 Rome, "Give Earth a Chance," 542.

93 Ibid., 543.

94 Fox, *American Conservation Movement,* 325.

95 Rome, "Give Earth a Chance," 545.

96 Robert Gottlieb, *Forcing the Spring: The Transformation of the American Environmental Movement* (Washington, DC: Island Press, 1993), 106.

97 Richard N. L. Andrews, *Managing the Environment, Managing Ourselves: A History of American Environmental Policy* (New Haven: Yale University Press, 1999), 225.

98 Gottlieb, *Forcing the Spring,* 107; and Zakin, *Coyotes and Town Dogs,* 32.

99 Ibid., 112; and Thomas Raymond Wellock, *Critical Masses: Opposition to Nuclear Power in California, 1958–78* (Madison: University of Wisconsin Press, 1998), 96.

100 Ibid., 111; and Fox, *American Conservation Movement,* 325.

101 Hal Rothman, *The Greening of a Nation?: Environmentalism in the United States since 1945* (Fort Worth, Tex.: Harcourt Brace, 1998), 55.

102 Gottlieb, *Forcing the Spring,* 41, 46; Dowie, *Losing Ground,* 30–32; and Benjamine Kline, *First Along the River: A Brief History of the U.S. Environmental Movement,* 2d ed. (San Francisco: Acada Books, 1997), 84–85, 89, 91.

103 Shabacoff, *A Fierce Green Fire,* 119.

104 Jeremy Main, "A Peak Load of Troubles for the Utilities," *Fortune* 81 (November 1969): 119; and Main, "Conservationists at the Barricades," *Fortune* 82 (February 1970): 145.

105 Sale, *The Green Revolution,* 23.

106 Matthew J. Lindstrom and Zachary A. Smith, *The National Environmental Policy Act: Judicial Misconstruction, Legislative Indifference, & Executive Neglect* (College Station: Texas A&M Press, 2001), 21.

107 Andrews, *Managing the Environment, Managing Ourselves,* 229; and Lindstrom and Smith, *National Environmental Policy Act,* 50.

108 Ibid., 286.

109 Ibid., 286–87.

110 Ibid., 289–90.

111 Ibid., 203, 233–34.

112 Ibid., 233–34.

113 Ibid., 236–37.

114 Terence Kehoe, *Cleaning Up the Great Lakes: From Cooperation to Confrontation* (DeKalb: Northern Illinois University Press, 1997), 5–6.

115 George Hoberg, *Pluralism by Design: Environmental Policy and the American Regulatory State* (New York: Praeger, 1992), 39.

Top: George Perkins Marsh was a gifted linguist, diplomat, and scientist. His Man and Nature *demonstrated that humans could irreparably damage the environment, which led to watershed protection efforts and the establishment of forest reserves worldwide. Library of Congress, LC-USZ62-109923.*

Bottom: Men of privileged birth, Gifford Pinchot and Theodore Roosevelt dramatically expanded the National Forests, the federal role in managing resources, and public support for an efficiency-minded conservation ethic. Shown here are Roosevelt and Pinchot standing on deck of steamer Mississippi, *during tour of Inland Waterways Commission. Library of Congress, LC-USZ62-55630.*

Top: Posing at Yosemite Valley's Glacier Point in 1903 during a camping expedition, John Muir (right) and Theodore Roosevelt developed a close partnership on preservation issues. Courtesy Yosemite Museum.

Bottom: Mesa Verde. In 1906, the Colorado Federation of Women's Clubs won a two-decade campaign to protect the cliff-dwellings at Mesa Verde, demonstrating the political clout of women conservationists. National Archives: Ansel Adams photographs of natural parks, ID #: 79-AAJ-3-Untitled of Mesa Verde.

Top: Dr. Alice Hamilton. Crossing class boundaries, Hamilton conducted research on and campaigned against the ill effects of lead and other toxins on the health of industrial workers. Library of Congress, LC-DIG-ggbain-29988.

Bottom: In 1933 at a Civilian Conservation Corps camp in Virginia, Franklin Roosevelt had lunch with Secretary of the Interior, Harold Ickes, Agriculture Secretary, Henry Wallace, and camp members. The CCC was FDR's favorite New Deal program. Shown here, Roosevelt (at head of table), with Ickes (third from left) and Wallace (second from right). Courtesy AP/Wide World.

1930   1934

Above: In these photos, the Soil Conservation Service highlighted the effectiveness of natural vegetation in erosion control in agricultural regions. Soil Conservation Service, Missouri State Archives. National Archives, ARC ID 286155.

Opposite top: Civilian Conservation Corps Enrollees. The first CCC enrollees arrive at Camp Roosevelt in 1933. The program made conservationists of many working-class men. U.S. Forest Service, Tennesee Valley Authority.

Opposite bottom: Early construction on the Tennessee Valley Authority's Douglas Dam. Such New Deal projects aimed to conserve resources and rehabilitate impoverished regions. Library of Congress, LC-USW361-476.

Above: New York City smog. Limiting coal smoke did not solve the nation's air pollution problem, as this 1953 photograph of the Chrysler Building proved. Local pollution control advocates sought federal pollution control legislation in the 1960s. New York City/ World-Telegram *photo by Walter Albertin. Library of Congress, LC-USZ62-114346.*

Opposite top: Pittsburgh Air Pollution on 5th Avenue. In the 1940s, air pollution in Pittsburgh was so thick that it blocked out the sun at 11 A.M. Library of Congress, LC-USZ62-76932.

Opposite bottom: Women wearing face masks in Pittsburgh. Pittsburgh's environmental activists sought to highlight the air pollution threat with this staged photo of women shopping downtown wearing surgical masks. Courtesy of the Carnegie Library, Pittsburgh.

Top: Once an advocate of predator extermination, Aldo Leopold became the conservation movement's most eloquent advocate for preserving species diversity with the publication of A Sand County Almanac *in 1949. Library of Congress, LC-USZ62-93082.*

Bottom: Robert Marshall was a founder of the Wilderness Society and a leading advocate for creating wilderness experiences for less affluent Americans. Bancroft Library—UC Berkeley.

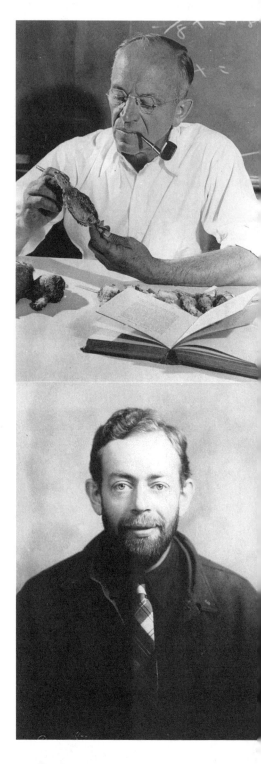

APRIL SHOWERS

Top: "April showers." In 1962, cartoonist Bill Mauldin effectively captured the public's fear of radioactive fallout from atmospheric testing of nuclear weapons. Reprinted with permission of the St. Louis Post-Dispatch, *copyright (1962).*

Bottom: Rachel Carson at a microscope. Concern over radioactive fallout turned to public alarm when in 1962 Rachel Carson published her exposé of chemical pesticides, Silent Spring. *Rachel Carson, 1962. Photograph by Brooks Studio. Used by permission.*

Above: Cuyahoga River Fire 1952. Although the 1969 fire on Cleveland's Cuyahoga River received extensive press coverage, the river actually had worse fires earlier—such as the 1952 fire pictured here—that were little noticed by the press. Public tolerance for such pollution had dropped dramatically by the end of the 1960s. James Thomas, photographer. Cleveland Press Collection, clevelandmemory.org.

Opposite top: Santa Barbara Oil Spill. In 1969, outraged residents protest against the Union Oil Corporation for its oil blowout near Santa Barbara that damaged the affluent community's beaches. Courtesy UCSB Environmental Studies Program.

Opposite bottom: Earth Day, 1970. Although there were large demonstrations for the first Earth Day in major cities, thousands of smaller activities took place all over the country, such as this one at Illinois State University. Courtesy Illinois State University Archives, Milner Library, Illinois State University .

Above: For Earth Day 1971, Walt Kelly drew Pogo and Porkypine in a trash-covered forest. It is the first time the phrase "We have met the enemy and he is us" appeared in print. Copyright 1971, 2005 OGPI. Used by permission.

Opposite top: Three-Mile Island. The 1979 accident at the Three Mile Island nuclear complex led to a surge of antinuclear activity and ensured the demise of the peaceful atom as a source of power. National Archives, ARC 540028.

Opposite bottom: Living to the age of 108, Marjory Stoneman Douglas was the key voice in the protection of the Florida Everglades. In 1993, President Bill Clinton awarded her the Presidential Medal of Freedom. floridamemory.com

Top: Love Canal Protest. Outrage at the leak of chemicals from a waste dump at New York's Love Canal spurred the passage of Superfund legislation in 1980 to clean up similar sites nationwide. epa.gov.

Bottom: Anger at logging restrictions on Federal forests in the Pacific Northwest is expressed in a bumper sticker on a pickup. Steven Holt/stockpix.com.

Top: Dave Foreman addressing a crowd. Charismatic and militant, Dave Foreman led Earth First! in its advocacy for "monkey wrenching," or sabotage, of logging equipment to save old-growth forests. Steven Holt/stockpix.com.

Bottom: In the spring of 1990, Daryl Cherney, Judi Bari (left) and Darlene Comingore led a rally in Ukiah, California, advertising their campaign for a "Redwood Summer" of protest against logging in northern California. Shortly after this photo was taken, a bomb exploded in a car in which Cherney and Bari were riding, injuring Bari severely. By permission of the Judi Bari Web Photo Gallery.

Environmental Justice Demonstration. Asian youths from East Oakland, California, campaigning against "environmental racism" in a protest in front of the Integrated Environmental Systems medical waste incinerators in 2000. In response to public opposition, the facility closed in December 2001. Courtesy Greenaction for Health and Environmental Justice.

CHAPTER FOUR

Institutionalizing Environmentalism and Protecting Gains, 1970s to 1990s

In 1983, Dave Foreman, the charismatic founder of the radical environmental group Earth First!, stood defiantly against a construction crew intent on building a logging road in Oregon's Siskiyou National Forest. While not as picturesque as the nearby Cascade Mountains, Siskiyou was considered one of the most biologically diverse ecosystems in the country and Earth First! members were determined to save it. Earth First! and local residents had been running protests in the forest for months in hopes of saving the area around Bald Mountain from the axe. There had been some hostile confrontations between road crews and the activists; tensions were high. Protesters with Foreman had dragged a downed tree across the road, but construction crews removed it, and a truck loaded with workers approached the picket line. The driver, Les Moore, tried to dodge Foreman, barely missing a demonstrator in a wheelchair. When Foreman cut him off, Moore turned back to the road, but the Earth First! leader got back in time. The truck sat for a good while as Moore decided what to do next. He dropped the truck in gear and rushed at Foremen knocking him back while picking up speed. Foreman was plastered against the grill holding onto the hood of the truck trying to maintain his balance, but he fell under the truck, grabbing onto the front bumper. The truck surged forward dragging him along. When Moore finally stopped, he got out of the vehicle and shouted, "You dirty communist bastard! Why don't you go back to Russia!" Foreman, still under the truck and lying in the mud, shot back, "But, Les, I'm a registered Republican."[1] Rather than being able to charge Moore with assault, Foreman was arrested for blocking a public thoroughfare. But Earth First! got what it wanted. Accusing Moore of attempted murder, Foreman made the nightly news along with footage of the incident. Even more important, the publicity brought in donations for a lawsuit by local groups and Earth First! that stalled the project.

Clashes over the environment had now degenerated into standoffs like this. The confrontation indicated just how different and diverse the movement had become since the first Earth Day thirteen years earlier. Up until the early 1970s, the environmental movement was notable for its conservative method of working within the system to effect change. And such methods worked. At the same time that the civil rights movement and the New Left were splintering apart, environmentalists were winning their greatest victories. This had established a long-range strategy for the movement's leaders of identifying a problem, bringing technical expertise to study it and formulate a solution, and then hiring lobbying experts to push through legislation on Capitol Hill. But the huge influx of supporters and activists to the movement after Earth Day brought more uncompromising elements in from the New Left and the counterculture. Like the civil rights and antiwar movements, environmentalism developed a revolutionary wing. Where moderate environmentalists agreed with radicals on the need for environmental reform, they disagreed on the methods and extent of change necessary to save the planet. More militant environmentalists accepted the dire warnings of Fairfield Osborn, Paul Ehrlich, and others. They called for a fundamental change in social values and the economic system. They used unconventional methods, such as nonviolent direct action, in their strategies for change that generated public awareness, but led to their own marginalization. The antinuclear power movement of the 1970s was the first major element to use nonviolent protest. Earth First! took this philosophy one step further and advocated the sabotage of equipment like bulldozers and logging trucks that destroyed ecosystems. Eventually some activists found even Earth First! too tame and moved on to more confrontational organizations that specialized in sabotage.

Earth First!'s protest dramatized the rift that had emerged between environmentalism and a traditional conservation ally: the Forest Service. The service's decision in the postwar period to maximize its timber harvest ran counter to the growing support among the American people for preservation of ecologically sensitive areas. The agency that had employed Aldo Leopold and Bob Marshall and marked out the first wilderness areas was now seen as an adversary, as were the conservation efficiency ethicists in general. For the radicals and moderates alike, maximizing sustained resource extraction was no longer the solution; it was part of the problem. Defenders of the service could point out that it had continued to support environmental positions. For example, in 2001, the service designated over 58 million acres of national forest land as off-limits to most commercial logging and road building. But for many, this gesture was insufficient. They did not trust an agency that seemed to be sleeping with the enemy: the logging industry.

In losing the conservationists, the environmental movement parted from a segment of the population that Franklin D. Roosevelt had recruited with his conservation programs, the blue-collar workers, especially those in resource industries. Elements in the movement now alienated working-class constituencies in style and substance. The movement no longer put forward a positive vision of the future as FDR had in linking conservation with prosperity. Groups like Earth First! seemed instead to appeal to the public's fears. In the 1930s, FDR had expertly yoked conservation with employment opportunities creating broad support for its programs among the working class. Their enemies claimed environmentalists did the opposite. By the 1970s, conservatives labeled environmentalists as radicals who were anti-American and opposed to economic growth and good jobs, jobs that were in short supply in the economically uncertain 1970s. The environmental successes of the previous period took place in the context of economic abundance; the public did not doubt the country could afford environmental reforms. The period after 1973 was defined by scarcity, recession, and diminished expectations. Every issue, it seemed, was a choice between the environment and the economy.

The creators of Earth Day were undoubtedly surprised at this partisan divide and change in fortunes. On the surface, environmentalism was a unifying cause in a country split by war and other social problems. It enjoyed startling success and little opposition in the early 1970s. Environmental organizations ballooned in size, from elite to mass organizations. In pressing their anticorporate critique, however, the movement alienated the GOP's base among industrialists and provided the Nixon administration with little popular backing. The hostile feelings increasingly grew mutual. By the time of Nixon's resignation in 1974, Republicans were turning against the movement for ideological reasons. The party of Theodore Roosevelt and Gifford Pinchot moved in a conservative direction that was incompatible with the movement's values and state-sponsored solutions to environmental problems. By the end of the decade, developers, industry, elements of labor, and the "Sagebrush Rebellion," a movement that favored local control of federal lands, were powerful opponents.

Despite this growing opposition, the Watergate scandal of the Nixon era appeared to open the way for further environmental gains by bringing a Democrat to the White House. Pinning their hopes on Jimmy Carter, environmentalists were disappointed. Carter's early sympathy for the environment dissipated under the influence of economic stagnation and progrowth advisors. Discouraged with limited political success at the federal level, nonviolent direct-action movements, principally those against nuclear power, sought drastic change. Protesters called for fundamental social transformation, decentralization of environmental management, and smaller scale, renewable, "appropriate" technologies that could be controlled by individuals rather than by big corporations and government agencies. With the end of the energy crisis, however, public concern over nuclear power and interest in appropriate technology collapsed.

In the 1980s, the environmental opposition found their hero in Ronald Reagan, who came to office vowing to roll back the previous decade's gains. Misreading his election as a mandate for economic growth at any price, Reagan turned the Department of the Interior over to the environmental movement's nemesis, James Watt. The movement enjoyed broad popular support, however, allowing environmentalists to check the administration's most far-reaching plans and successfully depose Watt. The George H. W. Bush presidency assumed a less confrontational stance, offering rhetorical support for environmentalism but often opposing environmental initiatives in practice.

As the environmental juggernaut ground to a halt in the 1980s, the movement squabbled over its proper course and reexamined its elitist roots. Mainline environmental organizations were an integral part of the Washington power structure, but they failed to resolve politically divisive problems such as logging in national forests and toxic-waste disposal. The latter issue, a particular concern in poor and ethnic communities, was one of several that forced the movement to confront its comfortable lily-white history and search for a more inclusive conception of environmental justice.

Among radical elements of the movement, there was no shortage of solutions to the movement's ills. Varying in their tactics and employment of class, gender, and race in their analysis, radical groups shared a belief that the environmental crisis must be solved through social and economic transformation rather than legislative reform. Believing that an industrial, patriarchal society was lethal to the environment, Deep Ecologists, ecofeminists, and environmental anarchists such as those in Earth First! argued that a biocentric, rather than an anthropocentric, view of nature would return stability to the environment. Radicals had trouble defining a coherent vision of biocentrism, and it made little headway with the general public.

By the end of the century, environmentalism was at a standoff with its enemies and without much influence in Washington. Environmental opponents enjoyed some success, but the public still expressed overall support for environmental goals. This support was broadly based but shallow. Americans backed environmentalism, but not if it threatened their livelihoods or if it impinged on their economic freedoms and consumption ethic. The stagnation of the movement led to a crisis of confidence among activists as they confronted the new century.

The Energy Crisis

By 1973, the environmental movement had won overwhelming popular support and stunning legislative victories. As the movement laid out a new agenda in the 1970s, events forced environmentalists to shift their emphasis. While activists concentrated on pollution, energy came to dominate the political debate. In October 1973 the Yom Kippur War between Israel, Egypt, and Syria started a five-month oil embargo by Arab states to punish the United States for its support of the Jewish state. Panic ensued in the U.S. Motorists held up gas stations so often that attendants carried guns. Children wearing mittens and wool hats shivered in stone-cold classrooms. Tanker trucks were hijacked, and pleasure boats and luxury automobiles, symbols of American affluence, went unsold. Those who hoped the crisis might unite the country as the Great Depression had were given pause by the Texas bumper sticker that said of Northerners: "Let the Bastards Freeze in the Dark."

The energy industry hoped to take advantage of the turmoil by calling for a relaxation of environmental regulation to spur energy development. Energy executives confidently assumed that Americans would rise up and demand whatever steps were necessary to restore their gasoline and electricity. The nuclear-power industry predicted that the boost in fossil-fuel prices would spur orders for new atomic plants. And the energy industry blamed environmentalists as the chief culprits in the crisis. "Boy what a field day the oil companies and everybody else were having with us," one environmental lobbyist remembered. "Finally after four or five years on the defensive they could come back and they were the good people, honest people trying to provide energy supplies, and we were the bad people, extremists. . . . We were just sort of cowering in the trenches while the artillery thundered overhead, and there wasn't a damn thing we could do about it."[2] Industry lobbyists joked that the country would keep warm during the winter of 1973–74 by burning environmental protection laws.

Shifting away from his earlier support for the environment, Richard Nixon proposed "Project Independence," a legislative package that was sure to warm the hearts of energy executives. Nixon envisioned a project on the scale of the Apollo space program to make the country energy self-sufficient. Nixon asked Congress for emergency powers, minor conservation efforts, a relaxation of environmental standards, and the authority to issue temporary operating licenses for new nuclear power plants without holding public hearings. The underlying assumption of Project Independence was clear: America's energy problems were the result of restrictive environmental regulation. Fearing a backlash, environmentalists tried to appear reasonable in accepting short-term variances to pollution laws.

The environmental lobby underestimated the public support for their position. Rather than indict the environmental movement, 83 percent of the public laid the blame for the crisis at the feet of the oil industry that had received windfall profits from higher oil prices. By the end of 1974, Nixon had resigned as a result of the Watergate scandal, and his Project Independence languished in Congress. In fact, no omnibus energy legislation emerged during the Nixon or Ford administrations. Rather than a boon to the nuclear power industry, the high costs of the nuclear plants led to a wave of cancellations of construction orders. No nuclear power plant ordered after 1974 was ever finished.

With the energy industry's offensive blunted, environmentalists put forward their own proposals to solve the crisis. Even before the oil embargo, environmental groups had been thinking about the role energy played in the nation's environmental problems. It was not simply population growth that contributed to pollution problems, they concluded. Even if population held constant, pollution would increase due to rising economic output and associated energy growth. Sierra Club President Phillip Berry noted, "It became obvious to us there was one big central block of issues attached to energy." Another environmental leader agreed: "Almost everywhere that environmental problems arose there were energy aspects to them."[3] Energy conservation, it seemed, could solve a host of pollution problems. Environmentalists proposed greater efficiency standards for appliances, improved home insulation, and a switch to smaller, more fuel-efficient automobiles.

Amory Lovins best synthesized these ideas in an important article in 1976 entitled "The Road Not Taken." In it, Lovins described two different ways of consuming energy. The "hard path" emphasized the large, highly capitalized power generation. He compared this to the "soft path" that depended more on conservation and small-scale renewable energy sources. He argued that the soft path was not only more environmentally sound, it was better economically and politically. Soft-path technologies had the added benefit of being more democratic, since local entities would decide what energy mix they wanted, rather than relying on a highly centralized government agency, such as the Nuclear Regulatory Commission.

Energy officials dismissed the value of conservation, but the public became attracted to energy-saving ideas. Market forces accounted for some of the savings, but the public also supported government-imposed measures such as corporate average fuel efficiency (CAFÉ) standards for auto manufacturers. A Sierra Club publication optimistically predicted, "America's attitudes toward energy conservation are changing overnight. . . . New habits of care are emerging; expectations of growth are changing. . . . Reduced energy consumption means less physical impact on the environment. . . . Energy limits may mean an end of an auto dominated culture. What could be more profound?"[4]

It was not to be, of course, but America's capacity for conservation should not be dismissed. Lovins forecasted much lower rates of energy consumption than other experts, and he was right. Between 1973 and 1986 overall U.S. energy consumption hardly changed, even though the economy grew by 45 percent.[5] The trend did not last, as an oil glut in the 1980s led to a collapse in world oil prices and a return to spendthrift ways. Americans dumped economy cars for sport utility vehicles. By the 1990s, the United States imported more oil than it produced. Nonetheless, the era proved that economic growth and energy consumption did not have to be linked.

Psychologically, the energy crisis gave credence to the idea that perhaps Western society's collapse was not far off. Even before the energy crisis, the seventies were, in the words of Kirkpatrick Sale, the "Doomsday Decade," an era where dozens of Cassandras turned out books predicting Armageddon that sounded very much like the forecasts of Fairfield Osborn, William Vogt, and Harrison Brown twenty years earlier. The titles were revealing: *The Last Days of Mankind, The Death of Tomorrow, The Doomsday Syndrome, The End of Affluence,* and *The Coming Dark Age.* Defenders of these books could point out that they anticipated some problems that bedevil the earth today. For example, Samuel Mines, author of *The Last Days of Mankind,* foresaw global warming. But what captured the public imagination and the critics' wrath were their prophecies of imminent disaster. John Loraine, in *The Death of Tomorrow*, thought that the earth would exhaust its supplies of natural gas and oil by the first decade or so of the twenty-first century. Paul and Anne Ehrlich warned that supplies of oil had only a few decades left and predicted, "We are facing within the next three decades, the disintegration of an unstable world of nation-states infected with growthmania."[6] The Club of Rome produced a work, *The Limits to Growth*, that used computer modeling to predict a massive population and industrial decline in the twenty-first century from overpopulation, limited agricultural production, industrial production, pollution, and a scarcity of resources. Critics pointed out flaws in the model and contended that the predictions were overly gloomy. Thirty years later the authors of *The Limits to Growth* continued to argue that their basic forecasts were correct. In retrospect, it is clear that the critics were mostly successful in winning the battle for public opinion. As a result, environmentalists were labeled as pessimists. But the fact that these books were popular indicated that Americans were far more uncertain about their future than they had been just a few years earlier.

The Antinuclear Movement and Appropriate Technology

Given the significance of energy to environmental issues, it was no coincidence that the largest movement of the era was against the construction of nuclear power plants. This was an unanticipated turn of events for a technology that had been widely popular in the 1960s. There were successful efforts to halt power-plant construction in California and New York early on, but the public met most proposals with open arms. Nuclear power grew enormously during what was known as the "Great Bandwagon Market" and displaced coal as the fuel of choice for the electric-power generation.

The first chinks in the nuclear industry's armor were revealed amid new concerns about thermal pollution. Although most power plants discharged hot water into lakes, rivers, and oceans, nuclear plants were particularly inefficient and emitted large quantities of it. Fish kills from thermal pollution were reported in the late sixties at the Oyster Creek plant in New Jersey. Activists intervened in a number of construction projects to force utilities to devise a solution. In a landmark ruling on the Calvert Cliffs plant in Maryland, federal courts ordered that the Atomic Energy Commission had to write Environmental Impact Statements for all new power plants. The thermal pollution issue was a short-lived controversy. The solution was simple, if expensive: the installation of cooling towers. Nevertheless, the episode opened up nuclear power to scrutiny and a generalized concern about the technology on the part of environmental groups.

Once the door to opposition opened, it never closed. Dissident scientists fanned the flames of opposition by raising new concerns about the threat of low-level radioactivity in the environment. Two scientists at the Lawrence-Livermore National Laboratory in California, John Gofman and Arthur Tamplin, argued that the Atomic Energy Commission (AEC) underestimated the risks of low-level radiation by at least a factor of ten. Gofman and Tamplin eventually left their positions at the lab and joined the antinuclear movement. On the East Coast, the Union of Concerned Scientists created apprehension about the adequacy of nuclear safety systems that guarded against a loss-of-cooling accident that might cause overheating and a reactor meltdown.

As new concerns sprouted like dandelions, the movement drew in a diverse array of organizations. United in their opposition to nuclear power, groups joined for varying environmental, anti-war, and political reasons. Environmental organizations such as

Friends of the Earth and later the Sierra Club became actively involved in nuclear opposition. The Sierra Club was active at both the national and local levels. Other organizations such as the National Wildlife Federation did not become actively involved but did pass resolutions in opposition to nuclear power. Generally, environmental groups feared a catastrophic accident or objected to the hazards posed by long-term storage of radioactive waste. Of the latter, they argued against leaving a legacy of wastes for future generations. Peace groups such as the Mothers for Peace joined the movement, fearing that fuel from civilian nuclear power plants could be turned into atomic weapons. Anticorporate crusader Ralph Nader became intimately involved in the movement, forming the first "Critical Mass" conference in 1974. The meeting demonstrated that the movement was growing beyond local opposition to some level of national organization.

In 1976, there was a great showdown over nuclear power. In half a dozen states, activists sponsored voter initiative drives to place a moratorium on the construction of nuclear power plants. Environmental organizations and countercultural activists campaigned for the initiatives. Former sixties activists were particularly drawn to the issue for the democratic flavor of voter initiatives and the opportunity to take on centralized government and corporate America. The initiative drives were all defeated by wide margins. The nuclear issue, it seemed, was still confined mostly to environmental and leftwing organizations. As one industry lobbyist noted, "We have broken the back of the opponents—that vast collection of food faddists, perennial bitchers, deep breathers, nature lovers, and anti-establishment counter-culturists who came together" for these initiatives.[7] For most Americans, who were not interested in social change or concerned about the environmental threat, nuclear power still seemed like a clean, cheap alternative to fossil fuels. That a vote was held at all, however, demonstrated that a significant minority had turned against what was once thought the energy solution of the future, even among environmentalists.

The 1976 defeats led to frustration within the movement and a resort to direct action protests. "We're feeling very disillusioned about the legal and legislative channels for stopping nuclear power," one activist concluded. "Our new method is disciplined, non-violent direct action."[8] Radicals were also attracted to the nuclear issue because it was the best symbol of the highly centralized, undemocratic system they hoped to change. Small direct-action protests started even before the 1976 initiatives. In February 1974, Sam Lovejoy, a member of a Massachusetts hippie commune, pulled down a utility tower as a protest against nuclear power. The act electrified the hippies and former antiwar activists in the New England region. This led to the formation of a direct-action movement to stop the construction of the Seabrook nuclear power plant in New Hampshire.

In 1976, the New England movement, called the Clamshell Alliance, took action against Seabrook. Inspired by a massive occupation of a proposed nuclear plant site in West Germany, eighteen activists occupied Seabrook with a sit-in in July, followed by 180 activists in August. The following April, 2,400 activists occupied the site temporarily, which gained the Alliance significant press coverage.

Despite the ever more successful protests, the Clams were riven with factionalism. This was due to the structure of the alliance. True to their democratic aspirations, the Clams were committed to maximum participation, decentralized governance, and consensus decision making. This structure led to endless debates to achieve consensus and disagreement over proper tactics. The movement generally emphasized protests and nonviolent direct action rather than political activism. But hardline groups within the alliance advocated more forceful confrontation and destruction of property. These affinity groups, as they were called, worked to block consensus when the group did not agree with them, leaving the Clams deadlocked.

The Clamshell Alliance inspired a host of copycats throughout the country. The most successful of these was the Abalone Alliance in California, organized to oppose the Diablo Canyon nuclear power plant near San Luis Obispo. Like the Clams, the Abalone Alliance sought to force political and social change through protest. The Abalone groups also operated without a formal leadership. After the nuclear accident at Three Mile Island in March

1979, where errors by the reactor operators led to a core meltdown, the Abalone Alliance gained tremendous press coverage. A protest against Diablo Canyon in San Francisco drew 25,000 participants. In June, 40,000 protesters gathered at the plant, which led to numerous arrests for civil disobedience. The direct-action phase drew particularly strong criticism from labor groups that the movement cared little for the needs of working families whose livelihoods depended on the jobs the nuclear industry provided. More than once, activist picket lines were disrupted by angry construction workers in hostile confrontations. These incidents did nothing to help the negative image of the environmental movement as being contemptuous of the needs of the working class. The movement was drifting far from the New Deal–emphasis on using conservation to achieve an equitable outcome in resource use for all Americans.

After Three Mile Island, the nuclear industry collapsed and took the antinuclear movement with it. The industry's ruin took away the immediacy of the nuclear issue. The antinuclear power movement was reincarnated as an antinuclear weapons movement, given the escalation of the Cold War under Ronald Reagan. This movement focused not only on weapons but on the environmental costs of weapons production. Activists led protests at the Hanford nuclear reservation in Washington and the Rocky Flats complex in Colorado. Both weapons facilities produced radioactive wastes that have yet to be fully cleaned up. But this movement, too, evaporated with the warming of relations between the Soviet Union and the United States.

The antinuclear movement nonetheless had an important influence. It badly weakened the federal government's control over nuclear power regulation, because state governments demanded more oversight in the licensing of nuclear plants. The antinuclear movement's most important contribution, however, came in the area of public opinion. Even without an active movement, the public retains such a negative view of nuclear power that no utility has attempted to build a new nuclear power plant since the Three Mile Island accident. The 1986 Chernobyl accident (in the Soviet Union) was the final blow that sealed an already dying industry's fate. Calling it "the largest managerial disaster in business history,"

Forbes magazine declared nuclear power "dead—dead in the near term as a hedge against rising oil prices and dead in the long run as a source of future energy."[9] More than twenty years after Chernobyl, the future of nuclear power is still uncertain. But despite *Forbes*'s prediction, the peaceful atom may revive, given the scarcity and expense of fossil fuels and concern for global warming. Fear of greenhouse gasses has even spurred some environmentalists to take a more positive view of nuclear power in recent years, especially since the movement is not as opposed to corporate control of energy sources as it had once been.

Growing up alongside the antinuclear movement was the appropriate-technology movement. Appropriate-technology advocates offered many of the same critiques of modern society that antinuclear activists did, but they also offered solutions. Appropriate technology, supporters believed, could solve environmental and social problems with smaller-scale technologies that rejected the kind of centralization that nuclear power and big government represented. Technology, they claimed, had values. Alternative technologists offered a critique of modern society's heavy emphasis on large, centralized technologies that required expert control. E. F. Schumacher, author of the widely read book *Small is Beautiful: Economics as if People Mattered*, wrote, "wisdom demands a new orientation of science and technology towards the organic, the gentle, the non-violent, the elegant and beautiful."[10] One supporter of the movement said that "soft" technologies were "ecologically sound, small energy input, low or no pollution rate, reversible materials and energy sources only, functional for all time, craft industry, low specialization . . . integration with nature, democratic politics, . . . decentralist."[11] The movement particularly appealed to former New Left and counterculture activists who appreciated its decentralizing tendencies. Since the 1960s, these groups had been developing a critique of industrial society that fit well with appropriate technology. The Vietnam War had led many to oppose the high-tech warfare being carried out in Southeast Asia, with a particular focus on the use of chemical weapons such as napalm (the chemical used in incendiary bombs). It seemed that technology, which had long been associated with human progress, was now being employed to undermine values of democracy and human decency.[12]

The alternative to such a world was best expressed in Stewart Brand's *The Whole Earth Catalog,* where one could find technology that Brand and his staff of hippies believed could empower the individual. In its statement of purpose, the *Catalog* declared "We are as Gods and might as well get good at it." It predicted that "a realm of intimate, personal power is developing—power of the individual to conduct his own education, find his own inspiration, shape his own environment, and share his adventure with who[m]ever is interested."[13] The *Catalog* appealed to a generation of the young who were returning to nature and forming independent communities. In it, a counterculture activist could find instructions on how to construct a geodesic domed house, an earth flag signifying that the wearer was a citizen of planet earth, windmills, tipis, a soybean cookbook, instructions on how to be a midwife, and kerosene lamps ('for those seeking an alternative to the ELECTRIC SOCIETY'). Their technology choices expressed their hostility toward high-tech, centralized entities such as the Pentagon, CIA, Nuclear Regulatory Commission, and major corporations. Amory Lovins's prescriptions for a soft-energy path of small-scale wind turbines and solar–water heaters fit in well with this worldview.

In the late 1970s, the appropriate-technology movement caught on with politicians. Governor Jerry Brown of California created the Office of Appropriate Technology. At the federal level Jimmy Carter promoted appropriate-technology catchphrases in poverty programs. Senate Majority Leader, Michael Mansfield, pushed through federal funding for a National Center for Appropriate Technology in his home state of Montana. A number of think tanks spent much time on the idea, and the *Journal of the New Alchemists* devoted its space to alternative forms of technology and philosophical musings about the place of science and technology in society.

Fundamentally, appropriate technology was appealing in the 1970s because, as Langdon Winner argued, it provided a solution to a full complement of public concerns, such as "'limits to growth,' the shortage of fossil fuels, worries about how to solve world population and hunger problems, a growing alienation from government, and suspicion of large public and private bureaucracies."[14] But when public apprehension shifted to other issues, as it did in the 1980s, the appropriate-technology movement was destined to failure. With the election of Ronald Reagan to the White House in 1980, government agencies became hostile to alternative technologies. Funding was cut for such programs, and California eliminated its appropriate-technology bureaucracy once Jerry Brown left office. The collapse in energy prices in the 1980s also contributed to the uneconomical nature of the "soft" path. Even in the twenty-first century, alternative energy sources such as wind power and biofuels often survive due to government subsidy.

The Endangered Species Act and Wildlife Preservation

Although energy and technology issues took center stage in the 1970s, the environmental movement faced challenges in its traditional areas of concern, such as wildlife protection. By the late 1970s, conservatives began to take on some sacred environmental laws. The Endangered Species Act underwent challenge in 1978. In 1973, a University of Tennessee professor, David Etnier, discovered a small fish called the snail darter—a kind of minnow—in the Little Tennessee River. The Little Tennessee, it turned out, was the only river known to be a spawning ground for the fish. The river was to be flooded by the Tellico Dam, a Tennessee Valley Authority project. The construction of Tellico Dam had been a controversial project. Landowners in the valley had fought the TVA from taking their land. Environmentalists had weighed in forcing an eighteen-month delay in the dam's construction while its Environmental Impact Statement was revised. But by 1973, it seemed that the opposition was dead in the water. But Etnier knew immediately the significance of what he had found in the snail darter. When someone asked him what kind of fish he was holding, he replied, "Mister, this is the fish that will stop the Tellico Dam."[15] He was almost right. The snail darter controversy became a major test of the effectiveness of the Endangered Species Act. It was a test that the act did not pass.

The Tellico Dam was an unsightly pork-barrel project (one that is funded as a political favor rather than on technical merit). The $116 million dam had almost no real benefits. It contributed just twenty-three megawatts of power to the area; a nuclear power plant by comparison often produces more than 1,000 megawatts. Neither did it offer flood control or irrigation benefits. Nonetheless, the TVA and powerful politicians such as Tennessee Senator Howard Baker wanted the project for the money it would bring to his state, and so it was built.

Environmentalists intervened. With the dam nearly completed, the Environmental Defense Fund filed suit to prevent construction. The EDF managed to get a ruling blocking the project on the grounds that it would destroy the snail darter's habitat. Politicians, the public and the press considered it a ridiculous ruling. Headlines around the country proclaimed "Hundred-Million-Dollar Dam Stopped by Three-Inch Fish."[16]

Proponents of the dam immediately amended the Endangered Species Act to create a cabinet-level committee to weigh the economic benefits of the project with the loss of a species. Clearly congressional backers expected that the need for a dam would easily outweigh the fate of a seemingly worthless fish. The committee, called by some the "God Committee," stunned the dam's supporters with a unanimous ruling that even with the dam 95 percent complete, it was not economically worth finishing. One committee member noted, "Frankly I hate to see the snail darter get the credit for delaying a project that was so ill-conceived and uneconomic in the first place."[17] The snail darter appeared to have been saved.

It did not turn out that way. In June 1979, the dam's supporters in the House sneaked a rider onto an appropriations bill exempting the Tellico Dam from environmental laws, including the Endangered Species Act. With Howard Baker's appeals, the bill passed the Senate. Environmentalists hoped for a presidential veto, but Jimmy Carter was already locked in a battle with Congress to pass an education bill and a treaty turning the Panama Canal back over to Panama. If he vetoed the appropriations bill, he might have no Panama treaty and stalled education legislation. Carter, "with regret," signed the legislation.[18]

Not only was snail darters' habitat destroyed, the Endangered Species Act had been weakened just five years after its passage. The fate of the snail darter has been more positive, however. More populations were discovered in nearby rivers, and transplants increased the darter's population sufficiently that the species was down-listed to "threatened" from "endangered" in 1984. The Tellico Dam controversy also represented the end of an era for the TVA. It had long justified its existence based on water projects and providing cheap hydroelectricity. The agency had represented the best of FDR conservationism. But the Tellico Dam was so ill-conceived and lacking in benefits that the only way it could be approved was through political hijinks. It was the end of the TVA's dam projects and raised questions about the value of resource conservation in general.

Despite the Tellico controversy, the Endangered Species Act retained some of its bite. This was evident in a controversy over saving the northern spotted owl in the Pacific Northwest. The Sierra Club Legal Defense Fund, the Audubon Society, and other environmental organizations executed a strategy that was, as one commentator noted, "one of the most successful legal campaigns in the history of American environmental law." The SCLDF's strategy was to have the spotted owl listed as a "threatened" species under the Endangered Species Act. The ulterior motive of environmentalists was to save old-growth timber stands from logging that were critical owl habitat. "The northern spotted owl is the wildlife species of choice to act as a surrogate for old growth protection," one environmental activist confessed. "And I've often thought that thank goodness the spotted owl evolved in the Northwest, for if it hadn't, we'd have to genetically engineer it." Believing that thousands of timber jobs were at stake, the Fish and Wildlife Service attempted to avoid the owl's designation as "threatened." The SCLDF sued and in November 1988 won a court order vacating the agency's position as "arbitrary and capricious."[19] In March 1989, the SCLDF also won a court injunction on timber sales in Oregon and Washington. A year and a half later, the FWS listed the owl as threatened.

The reaction to this coup was swift and angry. Protests erupted in logging towns throughout the Pacific Northwest. The persistent theme was that elitist environmentalists were contemptuous of the needs of working people. In Forks, Washington, the self-proclaimed logging capital of the world, loggers sported bumper stickers that said, "Are You an Environmentalist or Do You Work for a Living?"; "Save a Logger and Shoot an Owl"; and "I Like Spotted Owls: Baked, Broiled, or Fried." Sweatshirts sported sayings like "Support Your Local Spotted Owl: From a Rope" and "If we'd kicked the shit out of the preservationists, we wouldn't have this problem today."[20] Extensive rallies supporting logging were held in the region, some of which ended in violence. The congressional delegation from the Pacific Northwest fought back in seeking to put in riders on legislative bills that exempted logging from lawsuits. When riders did sneak through Congress, however, federal courts declared them unconstitutional. In federal court, the Audubon Society won an order in 1990 that directed the Forest Service to "proceed diligently" in revising its operations "to ensure the northern spotted owl's viability." The judge wrote that the case "exemplifies a deliberate and systematic refusal by the Forest Service and the Fish and Wildlife Service to comply with the laws protecting wildlife."[21] Environmentalists won by taking their case to federal courts and a national constituency, where support for saving the owl was high. In the Pacific Northwest opinion was evenly split, but most politicians supported the loggers whose livelihood was at stake. Had the controversy remained a regional issue, environmentalists would have lost. Sometimes, it seemed, centralized power could help the environment.

The environmental movement had won a great victory, or had it? Under a plan put forward by the Clinton administration, millions of acres of federal old-growth forestland were placed off limits to logging, with 2.4 million acres in Washington State alone. But preserving its habitat was not enough to save the spotted owl. In the last ten years, owl populations in Washington have dropped 50 to 60 percent. Natural competition with the barred owl, forest fires, and disease has decreased the spotted owls' numbers despite the rescue plan. Loggers have fared no better. The forest industry has lost 30,000 jobs in Washington and Oregon, by some estimates a 25 percent decline.[22] Environmentalists point out that many of these jobs were lost for reasons other than saving the spotted owl. Declining demand, modernizing of logging mills, and a shift to overseas markets also cost logging communities employment, but the spotted owl–protection plan has had an influence. Environmentalists, their opponents believed, cared more for the needs of animals than humans. Equity had been sacrificed for wildlife preservation. Neither side, then, has been happy with the result. Nevertheless, the effort to save the spotted owl and old-growth forests demonstrated the power of environmental laws. Even when saving a species hurt the economy, national opinion still supported protecting wildlife.

While the Endangered Species Act was a powerful weapon, the environmental movement lost historic allies in the fight to save wildlife: fishermen and hunters. The leftward drift of the movement led to alliances with animal rights groups and the antigun lobby. Some green groups including some local chapters of the Sierra Club passed antihunting resolutions. "To hear someone attack your grandfather's tradition—that stings," one hunting writer noted. "And they [hunters] don't forget." Culturally, too, there wasn't much affinity between the rural image of the "hook and bullet" community and liberal, countercultural types in the environmental movement. This provided conservatives the opportunity to widen the breach. By the mid-1980s, the campaign proved effective. Carl Pope of the Sierra Club realized how successful the campaign had been when he saw negative articles about the Sierra Club's position on hunting, even though the national branch of the club took no position on hunting. "At that point I realized we were dealing with a conscious political strategy to separate rural hunters and fishers from urban environmentalists," he noted. "It wasn't about hunting and fishing. It was about politics."[23] Organizations such as the National Rifle Association and Trout Unlimited became staunch GOP supporters. Earlier, environmentalists had lost traditional conservationists in battles over dams and forests. Now conservatives had managed to peel away another constituency from the movement.

Ecosystem Protection: The Everglades and Marjory Stoneman Douglas

As the spotted owl controversy indicated, the legal system had turned green, and the public had learned to think about environmental issues ecologically. The protection of the owl required safeguarding of the ecosystem in which it lived. Even if it cost other people their jobs, Americans were willing to protect ecologically sensitive areas. The shift from conservation's emphasis on efficiency and sustainable development at the turn of the twentieth century to environmentalism's focus on biodiversity and ecosystem protection represented a profound transformation.

One woman who exhibited this attitudinal shift was Marjory Stoneman Douglas, a leader in the efforts to save the Florida Everglades from development. Douglas was born in 1890 and lived until 1998, her life spanning the Progressive era to the modern movement. Her evolution as an activist and the development of her environmental philosophy is suggestive of the forces that led to an ecologically sensitive perspective and the alienation of the resource conservation and environmental wings of the movement. In essence, shifting ecological theory helped alter how activists like Douglas and the public viewed the landscape and questioned the neat division conservationists drew between a human-constructed environment and nature.

Douglas's background was typical of women conservationists at the beginning of the century. She grew up in Massachusetts, already a hotbed of conservation activity, in relative affluence and attended Wellesley College where she flourished as a writer. After a failed marriage, she moved to Florida in 1915 where her father, divorced from Douglas's mother, took her under his wing. He helped launch her into a career as a reporter and author, working for the *Miami Herald*, which her father had founded. An independent professional woman, Douglas was an ardent feminist. As she later noted, her free-thinking ways and liberal outlook came from her Quaker family background and liberal education, quite a contrast to Florida society. She arrived in Miami ten years after Governor Napoleon Bonaparte Broward called for a massive reclamation project of the Everglades. The governor hoped that government efforts could succeed where private enterprises had failed. Miami was still a frontier town of 11,000 with explosive growth but was hemmed in to the west by the Everglades. Once drained and diked, the area, as envisioned by Governor Broward, was to be an "Empire of the Everglades" filled with farms and cities. "Yes, the Everglades is a swamp;" he admitted. "So was Chicago sixty years ago."[24] Not everyone agreed with Broward's ideas. In the same year, the Florida Federation of Women's Clubs (FFWC) put out the first idea for creating an Everglades park to protect birds whose plumes were prized for fashion from market hunters. Douglas joined the FFWC, which had been active in other conservation work, including the establishment of the Sunshine State's first state park. When Douglas joined, she was put to work on publicity for women's suffrage in the state. She later supported the Equal Rights Amendment first proposed in 1923, seen as a radical amendment at the time even by many suffragists. Like many affluent, educated women of that period, her reform impulse ranged into other areas, such as urban renewal. As a journalist, she was quick to see the link between urban environmental decay and social problems as urban environmental reformers had seen in other cities. "Child welfare," she wrote, "ought really to cover all sorts of topics, such as better water and sanitation and good roads, and clean streets and public parks and playgrounds."[25] This social activism on her part continued into the postwar period when she campaigned for improving Miami's slums and crusaded for the rights of sugar-plantation workers in the state.

In this early period, she exhibited the traits of a typical conservationist. She did not oppose development as long as it was rationally done. In fact, she celebrated plans to reclaim the Everglades. In 1923 she wrote, "The wealth of south Florida, but even more important, the meaning and significance of south Florida, lies in the black muck of the Everglades and the inevitable development of this country to be the great tropic agricultural center of the world." She also supported the construction of a highway through the Everglades that connected Miami and Tampa, but impeded water flow in the wetlands.[26] She saw no contradiction in the fact that she also supported protection of the Everglades. Early on, she believed that conservation and preservation values were compatible. It was possible, she believed, to develop the wetlands and protect it too.

Her shift from this position took many years. Douglas eventually left the *Herald* and struck out on her own, publishing popular articles and books, both fiction and nonfiction. As a writer, she published many pieces with environmental themes relating to Florida, especially crusading articles to protect plumed birds. She first became involved in protecting the Everglades in 1930 when she served on a commission sent to scout out parts of the wetlands for inclusion as a national park. Her experience on this commission inspired her to write more articles in defense of the birds of the Everglades. She also joined activist Ernest Coe's Tropical Everglades National Park Association. Her interest in the Everglades as a whole, however, did not develop until the 1940s. After several years of research and mentoring under state ecologists, in 1947 she published *The Everglades: River of Grass,* a best-selling study of what until that time was considered a worthless swamp. In the book, she portrayed the Everglades as one large ecosystem that stretched from central to south Florida. Even the title, *River of Grass,* conveyed this changed view of the Everglades as something having intrinsic value. The book was also noteworthy for its portrayal of how human development had undermined the wetlands' ecosystem. Writing the book changed her. Douglas had developed an ecological sensibility and anticipated the themes of Aldo Leopold's *A Sand County Almanac* by two years. In the same year that *River of Grass* was published, Harry Truman signed a bill dedicating part of the Everglades as a national park, although it was a much smaller area than Ernest Coe argued was suitable to maintain the health of the ecosystem. Nevertheless, Douglas recognized that the park differed from previous ones that focused on places with unique geological scenic features, such as Yosemite. The Everglades will be, she wrote, "the only national park in which the wildlife, the crocodiles, the trees, the orchids, will be more important than the sheer geology of the country.'[27] The Everglades marked a shift in attitudes about the function of parks and wilderness.

In the same year that the park was established, a new threat loomed. Not all federal agencies had adopted a new ecological viewpoint. Hurricanes devastated Florida, and the Army Corps of Engineers proposed an extensive flood-control plan for the Everglades. Demonstrating that she had not made a full conversion to an environmentalist position, Douglas applauded as heroic the moves of the corps, an agency she would later excoriate. She called the project "second in all our history only to the majestic scope of the Panama Canal."[28] Even at this point, she saw no conflict between the corps' work and the health of the Everglades ecosystem.

In time, Douglas's views would shift further toward an environmental viewpoint, especially due to the fragile state of the river of grass. By the 1960s, the threats to the Everglades had increased so much that author Wallace Stegner wrote that "inertia, conflict of interests, competing land uses, natural disasters, and human mismanagement have combined to place an incomparable million-acre preserve in danger of imminent extinction."[29] The corps was diverting so much water from rivers that supplied the Everglades that the national park section of it had no water fed into it except for rainfall for four years. In 1969, environmental groups turned to Douglas to lead a new group against a proposed jetport in the Everglades, a project that the Interior Department predicted would destroy the wetlands. Douglas founded Friends of the Everglades. Dominated by women activists, FOE quickly garnered a membership of 3,000.[30] Responding to their lobbying, the Nixon administration killed the project.

After witnessing years of encroachment by cities and farms on the Everglades, Douglas finally concluded that her old views in favor of rational development had to be abandoned. "Conservation is now a dead word," she affirmed in 1982. "You can't conserve what you haven't got. That's why we [FOE] are for restoration." Rolling back expansion did not seem to be in the cards, but Douglas fought to limit incursions into the wetlands. Under the guidance of ecologists in Florida, her thinking developed further where she saw the urban environment and its natural hinterland as a connected system. Until she died in 1998, Douglas predicted ecological devastation for Florida's southern cities as the drying of the Everglades led to decreased rainfall. The urban areas, she claimed, depended on the water stored in the rock formations under the Everglades. South Florida, she feared, would become an arid wasteland. [31]

Douglas's campaign for restoration bore fruit in 1983 when Governor Bob Graham introduced a $100 million program labeled "Save Our Everglades." Demonstrating that he too saw the importance of protecting ecosystems, Graham said the function of the program was to "reestablish the natural ecological functions of the Everglades." Two years after Douglas's death, President Clinton signed the Comprehensive Everglades Restoration Act of 2000. Large sugar plantations that depended on the corps water system opposed the measures.[32] With economic interests opposed to restoration, the implementation of the bill is still uncertain. Nevertheless, Douglas's environmental conversion underscores the importance of shifting scientific theories in the evolution of what Aldo Leopold called a "land ethic."

The Love Canal and Toxic Wastes

Population growth and suburban expansion posed a dramatic threat to the Everglades, and, as Douglas argued, it could also pose a threat to the residents of South Florida. In a similar vein, that growth could harm the people who moved to the suburbs and came in contact with the ugly side of America's industrial development. As Adam Rome has argued, suburbanization created greater environmental awareness by forcing residents to confront the implications of America's postwar development. The issue of properly storing hazardous chemical wastes was mostly ignored until the late 1970s. For decades, chemical wastes had been disposed of in much the way other garbage was. Often fifty-five gallon drums full of chemicals were taken to a remote site and left there to rust. With suburban growth after 1945, the public came into contact with these sites, sometimes with tragic results.

That scenario was painfully evident in the city of Niagara Falls, New York. Its Love Canal neighborhood became the focus of one of the most famous environmental controversies of the postwar period. The story began when the Hooker Chemical Company used the unfinished Love Canal as a dump for some of its most toxic wastes. Between 1942 and 1952, Hooker filled the site with more than 21,000 tons of hazardous wastes, including caustics, benzene, toluene, trichloroethylene, carbon tetrachloride, and chloroform. When the canal filled, the company covered the dump with just a few feet of dirt over the drums. As the city grew, the school board purchased the Love Canal area in 1953 from Hooker for $1 with the understanding that the company was absolved from all responsibility and liability for the wastes. The school district built an elementary school on the land. During construction, builders excavating the site discovered a "pit filled with chemicals." Rather than being alarmed, the school board simply moved the school eighty-five feet away. By 1955, 400 children attended the school. The community continued to grow, adding new homes through the early 1970s. It was a working-class neighborhood in which homes cost roughly $20,000.[33]

By the early 1970s, residents realized that something was wrong in the neighborhood. The fields over the old canal were uneven. When a barrel underground disintegrated, holes opened up at the surface. Odors wafted up from below ground especially after rainstorms. Children played with "fire rocks," chunks of phosphorus, which exploded when dropped on the ground.[34] By 1976, resident complaints led to some investigative reporting by the *Niagara Gazette*. A reporter took a sample of a black oily residue that had been seeping into the basement of a resident near the canal and had it analyzed. The results traced it directly back to the wastes Hooker Chemical had dumped into the Love Canal. Over the next two years the city and state governments and the Environmental Protection Agency became more involved in the issue. They first tried to clean up the area, but recognized that it was impossible to halt, let alone to reverse, the seepage of chemicals underground. On August 2, 1978, the state commissioner of health announced that the Love Canal neighborhood constituted "an extremely serious threat and danger to the health, safety and welfare" of its residents. He declared a state of emergency and recommended the evacuation of all pregnant women and small children.[35]

As government officials tried to get a grip on the situation, residents organized. The key leader in the movement was a housewife, Lois Gibbs. Gibbs had moved to Love Canal in 1974 with her family. She seemed to have everything a middle-class family might want. "I had the picket fence," she recalled. "I had the swing set. I had the mortgage. I had two cars. I had HBO. I had a school three blocks away. It was literally the American dream."[36] Underneath the surface, however, something was amiss. Her son developed asthma, epilepsy, a blood disease, and a urinary-tract disorder. Her daughter came down with a rare blood disease. She started asking residents if they were having similar problems and discovered that there was a pattern of strange illnesses among them. Soon Gibbs was at the head of the Love Canal Homeowners Association demanding that the government purchase their homes.

Government reluctance to help the community only made Gibbs and other residents more determined. Officials had often told them there was nothing wrong with the area, and school officials refused to transfer afflicted students to other schools. Gibbs, who was often underestimated because she did not have a college degree, mastered scientific data, media relations, and political lobbying. The homeowners association took their case progressively higher, eventually reaching President Carter. Their bottom line was simple. They wanted the state of New York to buy their now worthless homes. To gain publicity, the homeowners' association resorted to militant tactics. Over 500 members surrounded two EPA officials and held them hostage in defiance of the FBI. Gibbs noted, "I mean, these are law-abiding citizens, blue-collar workers who pay their taxes."[37]

These tactics paid off. In 1979, the government bought out 237 families. By 1981, more than 500 families had accepted a government buyout. The federal government agreed to foot the $17 million price tag and brought suit against Hooker Chemical, slapping the company with heavy fines.

The events in Love Canal did not fit the mold for environmental activism. Most organizations focused on legislation and policy at the state or federal level. They were not well equipped to deal with community-based movements. Gibbs, in fact, went to local environmental organizations, but found that they knew little about chemical wastes. Moreover, people who rallied against wastes often did not conform to environmental stereotypes. Love Canal was a working-class community with many men working for chemical companies. They would not have joined an environmental movement if their communities had not been threatened. They were not interested in the political or social revolutions that the counterculture and former New Left activists advocated. What they created was new. As Robert Gottlieb argued, "Love Canal ultimately prefigured a new way of defining what it meant to be an environmentalist."[38] Thus, while the environmental movement was closing itself off to some blue-collar workers, it was recruiting others from suburban communities.

If there were to be new environmentalists, older environmental groups would have to adapt and there would have to be new organizations. Organizations with local chapters such as the Audubon Society and the Sierra Club moved to work with the new grassroots activism. The Sierra Club increased local organization and formed the National Toxics Campaign, which was spun off as a separate organization in 1984. Some activists decided to go it alone. Gibbs formed the Citizen's Clearinghouse for Hazardous Waste. Other organizations such as the Citizens for a Better Environment and Clean Water Action soon followed. These groups, Gibbs maintained, "are doing some terrific stuff. People are following the strategy. They're stopping landfills, stopping incinerators, and backing up the wastes. They're plugging up the toilet."[39]

This attitude led to charges that the new groups were NIMBY (Not In My Backyard) organizations that did not want to take on the responsibilities that went with modern life. One waste-disposal executive called NIMBYism "a major public health problem of the first order. It is a recurring mental illness that continues to infect the public." If that was the case, the disease was widespread. A 1980 poll found that 50 percent of respondents did not want a hazardous waste facility within fifty miles of their home. The movement was effective in preventing the construction of new hazardous waste dumps, "not because they're illegal," Gibbs pointed out, "but because people have lobbied at the grassroots."[40]

The antitoxics movement spawned by Love Canal, like the municipal housekeeping movement of the Progressive era, has been run largely by women seeking to protect their children. But these modern women differed from the Progressives because those who became involved came from all classes, not just the affluent. As a result, antitoxics activists were less genteel than their predecessors. "The women in the environmental justice movement have made it a movement known for its irreverence for the powerful, its willingness to take strong positions of principle, its unending persistence, and its impatience with token solutions," argued activist Penny Newman. "These women have refused to play by the old rules and have been the ones to insist that enough is enough. It has been women, for so long shut out of decisions affecting themselves and their children, who have stepped forward to demand a say."[41]

Love Canal also had an influence on politics on Capitol Hill. The fear that there would be many more Love Canals impelled politicians to act. Already there were additional incidents. Hooker Chemical was involved in a similar controversy in Michigan, and the Velsicol Chemical Company (singled out disapprovingly by Rachel Carson's *Silent Spring*) had a leaking landfill in Tennessee.[42] In December 1980 Congress passed the Comprehensive Emergency Response, Compensation, and Liability Act, known as Superfund. The Superfund budgeted $1.6 billion to clean up the country's contaminated sites. Superfund included mechanisms to identify polluted sites, prioritize their need for treatment, identify parties responsible for the pollution, and designate technologies to cleanup the sites. Superfund became a controversial piece of legislation. It was an open-ended commitment to clean up over 100,000 sites. The program's cost estimates have ranged up to $1 trillion. Far fewer sites have been cleaned up than anticipated, largely due to stalling by the Reagan administration in carrying out the Superfund mandate.

The Reagan Revolution

In 1977 at the beginning of the Carter administration, environmentalists held out great hope for major gains in environmental policy and legislation. Carter entered office by appointing important environmental players to key posts. For example, Gus Speth, founder of the Natural Research Defense Council, was appointed chairman of the Council on Environmental Quality. Carter proposed getting rid of useless dam projects. He supported the Alaska National Interest Lands Act, and right before he left office, signed the Superfund legislation into law.

The major organizations were confident of progress because their following had grown. Membership in the top five organizations rose 76 percent, from 841,000 to nearly 1.5 million by the end of the decade.[43] Notably this growth occurred in organizations that embraced the new environmental agenda. Those that remained wedded to a traditional preservationist ideal, such as the Wilderness Society, stagnated.

This affirmation of new environmental ideals translated into organizations that were more professional in their outlook, structure, and staffing. In Washington, environmentalists developed staffs that contained an array of experts who allowed them to compete with industries for the attention of Congress and the president. Dominating the environmental lobby was a loose coalition of ten major organizations (known as the Group of Ten): the Audubon Society, Defenders of Wildlife, Environmental Defense Fund, Environmental Policy Institute, Izaak Walton League, National Wildlife Federation, Natural Resources Defense Council, National Parks Conservation Association, Sierra Club, and Wilderness Society. The environmental establishment had arrived.

But as the 1970s drew to a close, the trend toward environmentalism that was launched by Earth Day began to wane. Hard times in 1979 forced Jimmy Carter to retreat on certain issues, such as air-pollution regulation. Environmentalists were increasingly exposed to conservative critiques that their policies hurt workers and that their scientific claims were dubious.

The election of Ronald Reagan halted environmental gains. Having resoundingly defeated Carter, Reagan and his staff saw the election as a mandate for their conservative ideology, which included an avowed desire to roll back environmental regulations and to "set business free again."[44] Reagan considered his victory as more than a defeat of the Democrats; he had also vanquished moderate Republicans, such as Nelson Rockefeller, who supported the environmental movement. Reagan's election signaled and end to bipartisan environmentalism. Anti-environmentalism became dear to conservatives who opposed the liberal state. Environmentalism, conservatives argued, served the interests of liberal elites and ignored the needs of "ordinary people."[45] After 1980, the movement found a home almost exclusively within the Democratic Party.

Reagan set the new tone immediately, painting environmentalists as extremists. When environmentalists criticized his policies, he responded, "I do not think they will be happy until the White House looks like a bird's nest."[46] He rejected a moderate proposal for environmental reform from Republican environmentalists, including former EPA administrators William Ruckelshaus and Russell Train. Instead he turned to conservative think tanks and the business community for advice. His overarching goals were to transfer power from the public sector to business and from the federal government to the states. Reagan also hoped to change policy by changing the heads of key agencies. He demanded that new appointees share his ideology. The chief administrator of the EPA, Anne Gorsuch, was a leading conservative in the Colorado legislature. John Crowell, who was appointed to oversee the Forest Service, had been general counsel for a leading timber company. In this position, Crowell opened up the national forests to a cutting spree by timber companies at cut-rate prices. Robert Burford, a Colorado rancher and legislator, was put in charge of the Bureau of Land Management.

No one in Reagan's administration better exemplified its anti-environmentalism than Department of the Interior Secretary James Watt. He was a Western lawyer who headed Colorado's Mountain State Legal Foundation, set up by business interests to bring lawsuits on their behalf. At the Interior Watt determined to open up the West's resources to development. His stated goal was to revise land management regulations radically and permanently. Permanently, he predicted, because not one of his successors "would ever change them back because he won't have the determination I do."[47]

Watt's main thrust was deregulation of resource management. He proposed turning over federal lands to private individuals or state governments. He called for the expansion of coal leasing on federal lands and increased offshore oil leases, especially along California's beautiful coastline. Watt also argued that the national park system had become too large and that some holdings should be transferred to the states.

Another aspect of Reagan's antienvironmental revolution was his effort to reduce public participation in a multitude of environmental decisions. Citizens were blocked on issues regarding transportation, water quality, and hazardous wastes, largely because Reagan opposed funding of legal intervenors in agency actions.

Reagan enjoyed some grassroots support for these proposals. The best-known effort was made by the Sagebrush Rebellion, a movement of ranchers and livestock raisers to turn federal lands over to the states—very fitting with Reagan's states' rights emphasis—or to sell them to private parties. The rebellion had been underway before Reagan's election, and the former actor embraced their goals during the campaign. Sagebrush activists argued that states should have more control over what happened within their borders. They claimed that Western states did not enjoy the same rights and powers as Eastern states because of large federal landholdings in the West. The movement had the strong backing of politicians such as senators Barry Goldwater and Dennis DeConcini of Arizona, Orrin Hatch of Utah, and Malcom Wallop of Wyoming. For residents of states like Nevada where the federal government held a majority of the state's land, the rebellion had a strong emotional appeal. Nevada, Wyoming, Utah, and New Mexico's legislatures all passed resolutions calling for the transfer of Bureau of Land Management properties to the states.

For the environmental movement, which relied on federal power for many policies, these proposals posed a grave threat. However, once in office Reagan ran into stiff opposition even from supposed beneficiaries of his policies. The proposal to turn lands over to the states foundered on the problem that states would have to shoulder the costs of managing them. Ranchers also woke up to the fact that if land were sold to private entities, they would be competing for it with major mineral and oil companies in the bidding process, a competition they were sure to lose. By 1984, the Sagebrush Rebellion was stalled, as divided Westerners could not agree on an acceptable political solution. But the rebels' protests gained them easier access to the use of federal land, their main goal in the first place.

The rest of Reagan's strategy did not fare much better. Timber-cutting increased, as did off-shore oil exploration. Some wilderness areas were opened to oil and gas exploration. But the tide began to turn after about two years. The removal of families from Times Beach, Missouri, because of dioxin contamination; thousands of deaths at a Union Carbide plant in Bhopal, India; ozone depletion; and the Chernobyl disaster in 1986 provided environmentalists with the ammunition to take the offensive. Movement organizations went on a recruitment drive and found ready converts. By 1985, total membership in environmental organizations reached 5 million, and 80 percent of the public wanted to preserve environmental regulations.[48]

Key leaders in the administration resigned in disgrace. Anne Gorsuch dragged her feet on enforcing the Superfund legislation and refused to testify before Congress about it. She resigned after being charged with contempt of Congress. Twenty other political appointees in the agency also resigned. Rita Lavelle, an EPA appointee, spent six months in prison for lying to Congress. James Watt was such a lightning rod for public discontent with the administration that he became ineffective. He made derogatory remarks about Indians, African Americans, Jews, the disabled, and even rock-and-roll fans. In October 1983, he was forced to resign after a storm of protest made him a political liability. To atone for its sins, the Reagan administration brought in William Ruckelshaus, the EPA's first administrator, to head up the agency and restore its integrity. The administration unwittingly proved that the social shifts behind the environmental movement were not a fad.

The Reagan years were a stalemate for environmental battles, at least in the short run. John Adams of the Natural Resources Defense Council noted that the 1980s were "absolutely thrown out the window with respect to environmental protection or any kinds of technological improvements in terms of energy conservation. All we did was hold our own and lots of times we thought it's wonderful that we held our own." William Ruckelshaus admitted of the Reagan White House, "They gave [the environment] the back of their hand; they told people it wasn't important. . . . They clearly didn't care about it—and people can figure that out. They're not stupid. And the American people said, 'We do care about it.'"[49] Because of public opinion, Reagan was foiled in his goals to tear down environmental agencies and distribute public resources to private interests.

The Third Wave and Alternative Movements

In response to the Reagan years, the environmental movement developed a split personality, becoming both more a part of the establishment and more radical. This in part reflected its strength. The movement had expanded so much during the 1980s that a variety of strategies and organizations were possible. The institutionalization of the movement was best exemplified by the major organizations. Managers were brought in from the outside, people with corporate executive experience who ran the organizations as they would a firm. "This is the big time," one Audubon official noted, "and we've simply decided to become more professional."[50]

The height of this professional drift was the formation of a loose federation of environmental groups shortly after Reagan came to power. The "Group of Ten" was a collection of the heads of the largest organizations in the movement. During the 1980s, they met regularly to discuss strategy and common interests. The Group of Ten tried to coordinate a defensive strategy to deal with the Reagan onslaught and became emboldened as James Watt and Anne Gorsuch stumbled. Eventually, the Group of Ten felt secure enough to reach out to corporations and discuss issues of interest.

The reaching out to corporate America indicated that professionalization also had a philosophical component. Advocates of "Third Wave" environmentalism—where the first wave was the Progressive era–conservation movement and the second the postwar movement—stressed that the movement's traditional tactics, such as litigation, lobbying, and protest, were insufficient. The movement, they argued, needed to adopt a less confrontational approach that allowed it to cooperate with corporations. Third Wave advocates talked in terms of incentives and profit to motivate industry. Jay Hair, head of the National Wildlife Federation, described the Third Wave: "Our arguments must translate into profits, earnings, productivity, and economic incentives for industry.

. . . Reaching out to the business world [and] enlisting the entrepreneurial zeal, the proven expertise, and the enlightened self-interest of America's private sector" would create more environmental progress than confrontational tactics.[51] "Corporate détente" in which environmentalists and corporate executives negotiated "the tough environmental issues together" was the new mantra of the movement. Because of the Reagan administration's emphasis on cost benefit analysis, environmentalists were under pressure to promote both the environment *and* economic growth.

Radical environmentalists rejected what they perceived as a lack of ideological purity in the Third Wave. Those who did not trust corporate America were particularly critical of the Third Wave. "I am not a big believer in the Third Wave," Douglas Scott, a former Sierra Club staffer said, "this idea that we'll sit down with our friends in industry and they will come to terms. I think they will come to terms only if we create a climate in which they're under such pressure that they don't have any damned choice!"[52] The anticorporate attitude of the movement made many environmentalists suspicious of negotiated deals. "The bigger these clubs get, the more conservative they get," one activist contended. "They go for quick, simple solutions. They love working with federal agencies, love getting crumbs from them. These guys become the government—there's no difference."[53] The radicals were not a unified group, but they did agree that the moderate reformers in the movement were not addressing the root causes of the environmental crisis and were not up to the task of saving the planet. What set the alternative movements apart from the mainstream groups was that many of them sought a fundamental change to the existing urban and industrial order to save the environment, while mainstream groups sought to merely reform capitalism.

From such idealists, the 1980s fostered a far different response than the mainline organizations. Direct confrontation with corporations and the government seemed the most logical response to the perceived failures of mainstream environmentalism. In the 1970s and 1980s a number of ever more radical organizations formed. Greenpeace, founded in 1971, had made a name for itself with its "save the whales" campaign by confronting commercial ships at sea and later efforts to protect other marine mammals. Its confrontational tactics owed a lot to the New Left and counterculture, and it attracted a number of former activists of this ilk. Its leadership was media savvy. "If crazy stunts were required in order to draw the focus of the cameras that led back into millions and millions of brains," one of its leaders said, "then stunts were what we would do." "Mass media," its president Robert Hunter said, "is a way of making millions bear witness at a time."[54] Greenpeace was not considered radical enough by member Paul Watson. He went on to form the Sea Shepherd Society, which disabled at least seven illegal whaling vessels and others using illegal gill nets. The group also tried to halt seal hunting in Canada and dolphin slaughter in Japanese waters. Their slogan was: "We don't talk about problems, we act."[55]

Radical organizations tended to draw their philosophy from the concept known as deep ecology. First developed by Norwegian philosopher Arne Naess, deep ecology tried to draw a distinction between two competing environmental views. Naess argued that traditional environmentalists practiced a shallow anthropocentric sort of ecology by placing the good of humans at the center of the environmental relationship. Such a philosophy allowed environmentalists to compromise with industry because they all shared the same human-first worldview. Deep ecologists, on the other hand, held a biocentric view. They believed that other flora and fauna had equal claims to existence as humans. Deep ecologists argued that a fundamental alteration of human society was necessary to bring it into harmony with the environment. Murray Bookchin, a radical environmentalist since the 1950s, argued that "liberal" environmentalists were more interested in "tinkering with existing institutions, social relations, technologies and values than on changing them. . . . [Moderate] environmentalists are simply trying to make a rotten society work by dressing it in green leaves and colorful flowers, while ignoring the deep-seated roots of our ecological problems."[56]

Radical environmentalists were also critical of each other. Various wings have faulted others for not perceiving the real root cause of environmental degradation. For example, social ecologists criticize deep ecologists for not seeing the social roots of environmental problems. Bookchin explained that environmental problems were the result of the nation's social structure. He was harshly critical of deep ecology. He said there was a conflict between a "vague, formless, often self-contradictory ideology called 'deep ecology' and a socially oriented body of ideas best termed 'social ecology.'"[57] Deep ecology "parachuted into our midst . . . from the Sunbelt's bizarre mix of Hollywood and Disneyland, spiced with homilies from Taoism, Buddhism, spiritualism, reborn Christianity, and, in some cases, ecofascism." Rather than see problems in nature as a result of social structures, Bookchin argued that deep ecologists reduced the problem to a vaguely defined "species called humanity." In reducing "humanity to a parasitic swarm of mosquitoes in a mystified swamp called "Nature,'" deep ecology demonstrated misanthropic tendencies. In essence, Bookchin and other critics of deep ecology argued that its adherents did not see the connections between the "global corporate-capitalist system" and environmental decline.[58] Neither side in this debate seemed to recognize in themselves that they were trying to boil down complex environmental problems to one all encompassing explanation. These debates over theory led to a number of alternative movements that prized their own version of truth over all others.

Synonymous with deep ecology was Earth First! (mentioned earlier), a movement that favored nonviolent direct action methods of protest and acts of sabotage against environmentally hostile technology. Like Greenpeace, this fringe element's emphasis on direct action represented environmentalism's debt to the civil rights and antiwar movements, as well as the antinuclear movement of the 1970s.

Earth First! began out of frustration with conventional political tactics. Dave Foremen, an organizer for the Wilderness Society, believed in the effectiveness of political lobbying until the 1979 RARE II process, which the Forest Service used to evaluate the appropriateness of its holdings for wilderness designation. Foreman had grown up in a devoutly religious military family of the fundamentalist sect the Church of Christ. Foreman wanted to be a preacher when he was young, which might explain his later gift of oratory. By college, he started to rebel. He became less religious, read Ayn Rand, and was attracted for a time to libertarian politics.

He campaigned in 1964 for Barry Goldwater. After being kicked out of the military—he claimed he was a communist to get out—Foreman spent a great deal of time backpacking in the Southwest. Not the typical counterculture environmentalist, Foreman liked to look the part of a cowboy and drank beer in large quantities. He eventually joined an anarchoenvironmentalist group called the Black Mesa Defense Fund, which was formed to stop a coal mine near Navaho and Hopi territory. The group used lawsuits but also went as far as sabotaging industrial equipment. As writer Susan Zakin put it, "Black Mesa Defense was to the Sierra Club what John Coltrane was to Bach. It was a hell of an introduction to the environmental movement."[59] The experience told Foreman what he wanted to do with his life and gave him a philosophical approach to environmental issues.

Foreman felt short-changed by the limited amount of land that was being designated wilderness. Through the RARE II process only 15 million acres were set aside, and half of that was seemingly worthless rocky and ice-bound areas. Howie Wolke, an activist who would help found Earth First! remembered, "We made moderate proposals. We showed up at the hearings with facts, data . . . I looked at the loggers who had organized. Didn't follow the Forest Service's parameters. They shouted down their buddies in the Forest Service. They bused loads of loggers down to public meetings, telling them, if this RARE II wilderness thing goes through, you'll lose your job. And they won. They kicked our butts." Foreman concluded, "When the chips were down, conservation still lost out to industry."[60] He was even more amazed when environmental groups tried to proclaim victory. Foreman left his position with the Wilderness Society and went out in search of an alternative to the Washington scene.

In 1980 after a drinking and whoring spree while camping in Mexico's Pinacate Desert, Foreman and four other "rednecks for wilderness," formed Earth First!, vowing to live by the inspiration of Edward Abbey's novel *The Monkey Wrench Gang*. In that story, a band of misfits decided that the best way to protect the environment was to commit acts of sabotage against earth-moving equipment used to clear the desert. Earth First! drew a distinction be-

tween sabotage and terrorism. Sabotage was violence against machines and property. Terrorism targeted humans. Their acts of
"monkeywrenching," members claimed, fit in the former category.
Foreman and company were not just trying to halt development of
wilderness; they wanted to roll it back. In the first issue of the
Earth First! Journal, the founders wrote, "It is time to recreate
wilderness: identify key areas, close roads, remove developments,
and reintroduce extirpated wildlife."[61] Their reasons for wilderness
protection differed from the anthropocentric approach of people in
the 1930s like Bob Marshall who wanted large tracts of land for
people to camp in. Earth First! sought to protect wilderness for its
own sake. "We identified all the ecosystems in the U.S.," Mike
Roselle, an Earth First! founder, remembered. "Then we identified
areas within each of those that would have to be protected in order
to maintain biological diversity so that no matter what happened
outside of those, there would still be genetic material to reconstruct
biota [flora and fauna]." [62] The group did have some minor practical successes. Their tactics helped stop oil exploration in the Gros
Ventre section of Bridger-Teton National Forest. But the group
was mostly responsible for raising awareness of key issues such as
protection of ancient forests in the Pacific Northwest. The Northwest became Earth First!'s battleground. Earth First! members
wrecked forest-removal equipment, guarded trees slated for the
logger's axe by sitting in them for weeks on end, and spiked trees
with long nails, making them too dangerous to cut down by crews.
Perhaps no other act by Earth First! got them so much attention
and trouble as tree-spiking. When a lumber mill worker was injured when, according to industry officials, a nail struck his saw,
Earth First! was blamed for the mishap. Earth First! denied it was
involved, but the damage was done.

Some of the unconventional tactics Earth First! used did prove
effective. Although other environmental groups won the legal
battle for old-growth forests, the radicals made it a national issue.
One activist who worked with Earth First! noted, "All of these
things, people sitting in trees and getting arrested, in my view were
very beneficial to the cause. Because they got attention of [the me-
dia]. They [the journalists] knew there was more to the story than

just these fringe dwellers . . . these people who live on the edge of society sitting in trees. But nonetheless that's what got attention. It wasn't administrative appeals, it wasn't rational discourse. It was somebody getting busted."[63]

Earth First! presented a militant image. Its slogan was "no compromise in defense of Mother Earth." Its guiding principle was biocentric, meaning "in any decision consideration for the health of the earth must come first."[64] "The central idea of Earth First!," the organization argued, "is that humans have no divine right to subdue the Earth, that we are merely one of several million forms of life on this planet. We reject even the notion of benevolent stewardship as that implies dominance. We believe, as did Aldo Leopold, that we should be plain citizens of the land community."[65] By the late 1980s, some members of the group had taken this logic to extremes and seemed even crazier than they were. Earth First!ers asserted that industrial society had to come to an end. As Bookchin rightly pointed out, the movement exhibited misanthropic tendencies. If deep ecology put humans on the same level as other creatures, some members concluded, perhaps a massive die-off of people was not such a bad thing, since it would save other species and ecosystems. One contributor to the journal, "Miss Ann Thropy," pointed to the positive aspects of the AIDS crisis, which would lead to a lowering of the world population. David Foreman said of a food crisis in Ethiopia that "the best thing would be to let nature seek its own balance, to let the people there just starve."[66] Darryl Cherney, an Earth First! leader in northern California, said during a *60 Minutes* segment on the group that if he were diagnosed with a fatal disease, "I would definitely do something like strap dynamite on myself and take out the Glen Canyon Dam. Or maybe the Maxxam [timber company] building in Los Angeles after it's closed up for the night."[67] Such positions, while probably flippant comments, hardly endeared Earth First! to the public and made the organization a pariah among some environmentalists. Bookchin derided the group for its "ecofascism."[68] Michael McCloskey, chair of the Sierra Club, dismissed the group as "just utopians." The Sierra Club, he said, "may be reformist and all, but we know how to work within the context of the basic institutions of the society—and they're just blowing smoke."[69]

Not everyone in Earth First! agreed with its misanthropic tendencies. Judi Bari led those who called for a more humanistic approach. Bari was a red-diaper baby, a child of communist parents, born during the 1950s. She inherited their leftist approach and was drawn to Maoism. In the late 1960s, she was a college radical campaigning for leftist causes at the University of Maryland. In the 1970s, she left college and worked as a labor activist in the post office. She married another labor organizer, and they moved to northern California in 1979, a haven of countercultural activity. She did carpentry work and was galled at the use of thousand-year-old redwoods in housing construction. She drew back from a commitment to Earth First! however. "I was against tree spiking and I was appalled by this male macho image and their anti-labor attitude. I thought it was disgusting."[70] But Darryl Cherney, her lover after her marriage broke up and co-activist, convinced her to join. Soon she was deeply involved in environmental activism, but she brought her labor and Marxist background to her analysis of environmental problems. "We don't have a chance of saving the world ecologically . . . if we don't overthrow capitalism," she argued. Socialism, she thought, was a more ecologically friendly system.[71] Unlike other Earth First!ers who looked at loggers as rapers of the land, Bari placed the blame for the overcutting of redwoods on corporate interests in the logging industry. She sought to create an alliance of loggers and environmentalists against corporations and actually had some luck with it. Bari worked to bring a feminist perspective to the movement as well.

Cherney and Bari pushed an idea of sponsoring a "Redwood Summer" in 1990, patterned after the Mississippi Summer project of the civil rights movement in which hundreds of college students from the North spent their summer vacations registering African Americans to vote in one of the most racist of Southern states. Redwood Summer was to consist of large protest rallies interspersed with more typical Earth First! activities, such as blocking logging roads and holding sit-ins. Foreman had his doubts about Redwood Summer. It came at the same time two environmental initiatives were on the ballot in California, and he feared that the lumber industry could lump Earth First! radicalism with the initiatives. With overwhelming activist support, however, Redwood

Summer moved forward without him. Bari was emphatic that the demonstrations be nonviolent. Nevertheless, she received numerous death threats. Despite their fear of being killed, Cherney and Bari did a number of road trips, speaking to college students to drum up support. On May 24, 1990, Bari and Cherney were in Oakland on their way to a speaking engagement in Santa Cruz when the Subaru she was driving was blown apart by a bomb. Bari was badly injured, suffering nerve damage and a crushed pelvis. Cherney was slightly injured. The Oakland police and the FBI announced that Bari and Cherney were their prime suspects in the explosion, speculating that they carried a bomb to be used in an act of sabotage. The incident heightened Earth First!'s militant image, and many assumed Bari and Cherney were guilty. There was enough in both activists' pasts for such suspicions. Cherney's comments on *60 Minutes* about blowing himself up certainly made him a candidate for violence. He had openly praised those who had brought down power lines near Santa Cruz saying that in twenty years "eco-terrorists will be looked upon as heroes." Bari, too, supported the saboteurs. "Desperate times demand desperate measures," she told a radio audience.[72] But as time went on it became clear that the two had not made the bomb, but the authorities did not make much effort to find who had tried to kill Bari and Cherney. It was a turning point for Earth First! Redwood Summer went forward without Bari. Thousands took part, and there was much media coverage, but it accomplished little in a practical sense. Perhaps related to the protests, the environmental ballot initiatives both went down to defeat. The group was coming up against its own limitations. Its protest activities could alert the public to important environmental issues, but its image of radicalism, deserved or not, alienated average voters and, despite Bari's efforts, working-class Americans.

Earth First!'s radicalism could not last indefinitely. The FBI infiltrated the group and, in a 1989 raid, arrested Foreman and others for plotting to sabotage power lines and nuclear power plants in Arizona and California. A number of members did time in prison. Foreman was paroled after a plea deal in which he disavowed monkeywrenching. He was finished with Earth First! anyway. He and other founders of the group had grown disenchanted with the influx of leftists and hippies from whom they felt culturally and politically alienated. They were stung by attacks from new members like Bari that they were sexist pigs. Foreman distanced himself from Earth First! in the 1990s as the organization became divided about its future role. The debate centered on whether the organization needed to develop a more humanistic agenda as Bari contended. Foreman rejected this drift and complained in an obvious jab at Bari that Earth First! was turning into an American version of the German Greens, "an ecological group [that was turned] into a leftist group. I also see a transformation to a wholeheartedly counterculture/antiestablishment style and the abandonment of biocentrism in favor of humanism." "I am not an anarchist or a Yippie," he announced in 1991. "I am a conservationist. I believe that human overpopulation is the fundamental problem on Earth today. . . . I am no longer part of the Earth First! movement. I no longer represent it and I am no longer represented by it."[73] With Foreman gone, Earth First! followed this more humanistic trend and tried to establish ties with community and labor groups. The organization continued on without its founders—Bari died of breast cancer in 1997. It now focuses on nonviolent protests such as tree-sitting. Elements of Earth First! that still supported sabotage joined more clandestine operations, such as the Earth Liberation Front, that continued carrying out criminal acts, what law enforcement officials label "ecoterrorism." In 1998, this group started a fire at the Vail, Colorado, ski resort to protest expansion plans there that the group claimed would wipe out "the last, best lynx habitat in the state." The fire destroyed three buildings and four ski lifts, causing $12 million in damage. While such groups have received only limited press coverage in recent years, the FBI estimates that between 1996 and 2002 the ELF and covert animal-rights groups committed 600 criminal acts and caused $43 million in damage.[74]

In some ways, the philosophical opposite of Earth First! and Deep Ecology was the environmental justice movement. Where Earth First! favored biocentrism, the environmental justice movement's central issues were human health, injustice, and institutional

racism. Deep ecologists rejected environmental justice's anthropocentrism, contending that the human race was the perpetrator of
environmental destruction. Environmental justice adherents' prime
motivation was to protect their families and neighborhoods from
environmental health hazards. Because of this focus on families
and community, a large number of environmental justice leaders
were women. Environmental justice advocates believed much
of the environmental crisis could be explained by racism or class
bias. They criticized the mainstream organizations for being "racially exclusive" and giving priority to saving wilderness over
dealing with human health hazards, especially in poor and minority communities. Leaders of the movement argued that marginalized communities had been systematically excluded from environmental decisions and policy by the Group of Ten and by
government regulators. This was due to the way mainline organizations drew a clear distinction between nature and the human-
built environment. Environmental justice advocates challenged
the Group of Ten to draw up a more inclusive view of the environment integrating these separate spheres. The environmental justice
movement brought the civil rights and environmental movements
together. The civil-rights movement came to believe that racism
had an environmental component, and some environmental organizations have begun to address the needs of minority communities.
For the first time in a long while, equity mattered again in the
movement.

Scholars have picked a number of starting places for the environmental justice movement. Some go as far back as Cesar Chavez
and the United Farm Workers Union's efforts in the 1960s to protect farm workers from pesticide exposure. Others point to the
1978 Love Canal episode. All agree, however, on the importance
of the 1982 protest in Warren County, North Carolina, a rural section of the state, which carried with it racial and class issues. There
African American and white residents banded together to protest
the location of a hazardous waste dump in their community, primarily for PCB-contaminated soil. Opponents suspected that the selection of the dump site was preordained. One protestor argued,
"The community was politically and economically unempowered;

that was the reason for the siting. They took advantage of poor people and people of color."[75] When the state decided to move forward with the dump anyway, residents resorted to nonviolent civil disobedience over a six-week period. Hundreds of arrests followed, and the protest received national coverage. Although residents failed to halt the disposal site, the episode was important for the involvement of civil rights leaders such as Benjamin Chavis. Chavis's arrest was particularly important because it involved the civil rights movement, especially the United Church of Christ (UCC) and the Southern Christian Leadership Conference, in environmental justice issues.

The participation of civil-rights leaders eventually led to political action. Walter E. Fauntroy, congressman from Washington, DC, was also arrested in Warren County. He pushed the Government Accountability Office to initiate a study of the correlation between race and toxic waste disposal sites. The study confirmed that there was a relationship between minority communities and the location of dump sites. In 1987, the UCC followed up on this study with an even more ambitious investigation, *Toxic Waste and Race*. Like the GAO study, the UCC report found that people of color suffered a "disproportionate risk" from toxic-waste disposal. African American and Latino communities had a 60 percent likelihood of having a toxic-waste site nearby. The report concluded that "the possibility that these patterns resulted by chance is virtually impossible, strongly suggesting that some underlying factors, which are related to race, played a role in the location of commercial hazardous waste facilities." The report's conclusions were challenged by other studies that disputed the racial correlation. Nevertheless the study had an important influence. Coining the term "environmental racism" for what the report showed, Chavis could assert what the Warren County protestors could only guess at: environmentalism had a racial and class component.[76]

The movement expanded rapidly in the wake of these studies. By 1990, a number of coalitions had formed around the country to push for environmental justice. These groups challenged the lack of interest in the movement on the part of the Group of Ten organizations. In a letter composed that year, the environmental justice groups demanded that the large organizations hire more people of color. They also claimed that the Group of Ten promoted "the cleanup and preservation of the environment on the backs of working people in general and people of color in particular."[77] There was some justification to this charge. The large environmental organizations had not involved themselves in issues relevant to people of color, largely at the instruction of their members. In the early 1970s, before there was much awareness of the problems defined in the two studies, the Sierra Club polled its members on the question, "Should the Club concern itself with conservation problems of such special groups as the urban poor and ethnic minorities?" Fifty eight percent said no.[78] Environmental organizations needed to change their approach.

A few members of the Group of Ten responded to such criticism with some programs to include marginalized groups. "It was a wake up call," said Sierra Club Director Michael Fischer. "They were saying 'you are getting lazy.'"[79] But some doubted the sincerity of the large organizations and even the wisdom of aligning with organizations that seem to care more about the environment than people. Lois Gibbs, director of the Citizen's Clearinghouse for Hazardous Waste (now the Center for Health, Environment, and Justice) complained that the "Big Ten" organizations were merely coopting environmental justice groups without providing much support. The large organizations helped the smaller groups largely to win publicity for themselves, she maintained, and to win foundation money that might have gone to smaller, more effective environmental justice organizations. Gibbs also was reluctant to admit she was part of the environmental movement because of the negative connotation it carries among the working-class and minority groups with whom she works. "Calling our movement an environmental movement," she said, "would inhibit our organizing and undercut our claim that we are about protecting people, not birds and bees."[80]

The letter to the Group of Ten environmental organizations had another important effect. In October 1991, 300 delegates arrived in Washington, DC, to convene the first People of Color Environmental Leadership Summit. Attendees came from all over the country to listen to discussions on issues of mutual interest. The key message of the conference to the Group of Ten organization was that the attendees wanted not a paternalistic relationship, but a "relationship based on equity, mutual respect, mutual interest, and justice." Attendees saw the movement in terms of "social, racial, and economic justice."[81] Responding to this activism, President Bill Clinton, in February 1994, ordered federal agencies to ensure that their programs did not unfairly degrade the environment of poor and minority communities. The environmental movement and the federal government admitted the connection between environmental justice and civil rights.

That admission was significant. Expanding the definition of environmentalism, as Environmental Justice advocates did, challenged suppositions about the origins and basis for the movement. Historians have long argued that the movement was largely the result of affluence. The environmental movement has been classed as a new social movement that emerged out of concerns with identity, nonmaterial issues, and quality of life. But the environmental justice movement emerged out of a very different context. The poor were environmentalists too; they just had different priorities. Oppressed classes cared about the environment for starkly different reasons than traditional environmentalists. Environmental justice advocates saw in toxic-waste protests a movement to address an array of issues, ranging from environmental quality to sources of oppression of downtrodden groups. The environmental justice movement has forced scholars to revisit their theories and expand their concept of what it means to be an environmentalist.

Just as the civil-rights movement of the 1960s fed into the environmental justice wing of the movement, feminism also contributed to the philosophical foundations of environmentalism creating a hybrid philosophy known as ecofeminism. More a set of ideas than a movement, ecofeminism rose to prominence in the 1980s and early 1990s. Although it drew inspiration from mainline feminism, it differed from it in two fundamental ways. Liberal feminists demanded equal and similar roles for men and women and did not seek to change society in any fundamental way. Equal opportunity for women, not social revolution, was their key demand. Moreover, liberal feminists believed in the domination of nature by humans. They accepted the idea that human reason made people superior to nature and its inhabitants; ecofeminists rejected both of these assumptions.[82]

Ecofeminists, as David Pepper wrote, believe that there is "an essential convergence between women and nature." Some more extreme members of the movement have beliefs that are essentialist, meaning that women's biological essence make them closer to nature than men because of their birthing and nurturing roles. Other ecofemists, however, think that such traits in women are socially created and reinforce women's inferior status in society. According to strict ecofeminists, women and nature share the fact that they are both dominated and objectified by men economically, politically, and culturally. This domination arose from the Enlightenment and industrialization, which elevated patriarchal values over matriarchal ones. They also believe that liberation will come to women and nature only when men accept a "women's culture," with traits that are more nurturing, peaceful, and cooperative. This would guide society toward a sustainable relationship with the environment.[83] Thus ecofeminists focus more on cultural change than political legislation and regulation as the environmental movement does now. Ecofeminists are also critical of the deep ecology movement. They argue that deep ecology did not recognize that the environmental crisis was caused largely by sexism.

Critics of ecofeminism contend that the philosophy is antimale and flawed. If women do have a special relationship with nature because of their birthing and nurturing roles, then men are, by implication, inferior because of their biology. The ecofeminist philosophy, they claim, also overlooks the reality that many men from minority groups and the lower classes are as oppressed as women. Can patriarchy explain the existence of racism and class oppression? Ecofeminists also assume that women and nature are both oppressed because of patriarchal values. But why is it that some traditional societies are seemingly both patriarchal and in harmony with nature?[84] Despite these critiques, ecofeminism has contributed to the assessment of the environmental movement as a white male–dominated bastion of elitism. Many of the alternative environmental movements have incorporated an ecofeminist perspective in their outlook.

The ideological debate between the different elements of the radical and alternative environmental movements has sharpened the analysis of the causes of ecological destruction, but it has come at a price. The deep ecologists, social ecologists, environmental justice advocates, and ecofeminists have not been able to unite around a coherent platform to effect radical social and economic change. Such diversity might have been considered a strength, if there were no organized opposition to environmentalism. But as the Reagan administration indicated, such was not the case.

Environmental Politics after Reagan

After eight frustrating years under Ronald Reagan, environmentalists were hopeful. Although a former oilman, George H. W. Bush entered the White House in 1989 pledging to be the "environmental president." Certainly, Bush's initial actions while in office were a positive indication to environmental leaders. He appointed a professional environmentalist, William Reilly, to head the EPA, and elevated the agency to cabinet status. He supported a 1990 agreement to limit ozone pollution in the atmosphere. He negotiated with Congress a major revision of the Clean Air Act and an agreement with Canada to limit pollutants that caused acid rain. Finally, he called for an international agreement to lessen harmful emissions of greenhouse gasses that contribute to global warming.

As Bush's term in office progressed, however, environmentalists accused him of backing away from his commitment to the environment to please conservative supporters. This was especially true of his indecision over whether to attend the United Nations Earth Summit in Rio de Janeiro in 1992. Although he did attend, he tended to oppose the international agreements put forward. Alone among representatives of other nations, Bush would not sign the Biodiversity Convention. He led opposition to establishing deadlines or targets for ameliorating greenhouse gasses. He also refused to commit much support for the Global Environmental Facility, a funding agency for global research projects on greenhouse gas emissions, ozone pollution, and biodiversity. Bush may have been green for a Republican president, but activists thought they could do better.

Environmentalists were heartened by the election of Bill Clinton in 1992. Although Clinton had demonstrated little interest in environmental issues as governor of Arkansas, his vice president, Al Gore, was a passionate environmentalist who had authored a popular book on the subject, *Earth in the Balance.* Clinton overrode Reagan and Bush policy in a number of areas. He provided support for the United Nations Population Fund and signed the Biodiversity Convention that Bush had refused to endorse. He approved the Law of the Sea Treaty, and supported the goal of stabilizing U.S. greenhouse gasses at 1990 levels. But virtually all these decisions needed Senate approval, which that body, controlled by Republicans after 1994, refused to give.

Another setback for environmentalists occurred on the issue of global warming. In 1997, the Kyoto Conference proposed a United Nations Framework Convention on Climate Change. The meeting sought to secure binding commitments to reduce greenhouse gas emissions in developed nations. Under pressure from business groups and Congress, the Clinton administration opposed binding agreements. The final treaty called for a 5 percent reduction of emissions from 1990 levels by all industrial nations (developing nations had no such restrictions) by 2012. Once again, Senate Republicans opposed the treaty. But even Carl Pope of the Sierra Club admitted that the Kyoto Conference document was a flawed one. It was "an attempt to start down the road that everyone knows will have a very large bill, without ever deciding who will pay for the bill. Which is why, in my view, Kyoto has gone nowhere in the U.S."[85]

The failure of environmental initiatives in the 1990s reflected the growing conservatism of America. In 1994, Republicans swept into power in Congress and offered a "Contract with America" to cut regulation, spending, and taxes. The regulatory power of the state seemed to many conservatives burdensome and anachronistic. A new movement similar to the Sagebrush Rebellion rode the conservative tide in what became known as the "Wise Use Movement." Its advocates borrowed their name from Gifford Pinchot, signifying their adherence to an older form of conservation. They claim to share Pinchot's emphasis on the efficient or "wise use" of resources. They did not, however, share Pinchot's support for an active regulatory state. Pinchot did not believe that it was possible to have wise use without government regulation. It was also doubtful that the chief forester shared their affinity for corporate interests, given his often hostile view of monopoly power. The Wise Use Movement favored individual and property rights as a check on community and federal power. These conservatives regarded environmentalists as "Green Nazis" bent on denying common Americans their livelihood and freedoms.[86] They believed that local control trumped Washington's authority in regulating federal land. This notion of interposition, giving state and local authorities veto power over federal laws, had been discredited by the Civil War and over a hundred years of legal decisions. Nevertheless, Wise Use adherents cited the Constitution as their authority to resist environmental laws.

The Wise Use Movement began to coalesce in the 1980s with the teaming of two right-wing activists, Alan Gottlieb and Ron Arnold from Seattle. Gottlieb came from a liberal Jewish family, but he switched over to conservatism under the influence of Barry Goldwater's political writings. Gottlieb became a fundraiser for conservative causes. Arnold worked for Boeing and was a member of the Sierra Club in the 1960s. He, too, rejected his early liberalism, based on his belief that the club knowingly launched a campaign to establish new wilderness areas on false pretenses. By the late 1970s, he was a hard-right conservative who tossed out lines to journalists like, "The National Park Service is an empire designed to eliminate all private property in the United States." Arnold came to the conclusion that the best way to fight environmentalism was with a countermovement funded by corporate interests. The two men formed the Center for the Defense of Free Enterprise (CDFE). The movement appealed to a constituency of conservative scientists, users of federally subsidized resources such as land and water, and those who favored property rights. These groups saw themselves as fighting environmentalists who were just one step removed from Lenin. They called environmentalists "watermelons," green on the outside and red on the inside. By 1994, the group had a mailing list of 125,000 and the backing of powerful politicians in Washington such as senators Jesse Helms and Ted Stevens and former Secretary of Defense Dick Cheney. [87]

Although the CDFE was a legitimate lobbying organization, the Wise Use Movement also had its share of those who favored illegal activity. These extremists attacked environmentalists and federal resource officials and bombed their homes and offices. One county commissioner in Nevada drove a bulldozer at a Forest Service ranger to force open a dirt road that had been closed by the service. With the 1995 terrorist bombing of the federal building in Oklahoma by right-winger Timothy McVeigh, however, the Wise Use adherents sought to distance themselves from the extreme margins of the movement.

The environmental movement tried to paint its foes as corporate lackeys. Jay Hair of the National Wildlife Federation said, "the self-proclaimed 'Wise Use Agenda' is merely a wise disguise for a well-financed industry-backed campaign that preys upon the economic woes and fears of U.S. citizens."[88] But Hair ignored the reality that his opponents enjoyed some popular support and were using the same grassroots organizing tools, such as mailing lists and letter-writing campaigns, that had been pioneered by environmentalists. The movement touched a nerve among middle-class voters, who prized private property rights and believed there was too much federal regulation.

The Wise Use Movement has had some important consequences. By at least appearing to emerge from the grassroots, it has effectively challenged environmentalists' claims to speak for the people. Wise Use advocates could cite their own polls indicating that the public supported their cause. One survey, for example, showed that more than half of all respondents agreed with the statement that "environmentalists care more about animals and habitats than about people's jobs."[89] Wise Use activists have strong support in Congress including former House Majority Leader Tom Delay, who in the 1990s railed with fascist imagery against the "Jackbooted EPA Gestapo."[90] Key support could also be found in the current Bush administration, where Interior Secretary Gale Norton was a powerful representative of the movement. The George W. Bush administration has assiduously courted conservative voters. It has proposed fossil fuel development in wilderness areas and the Arctic National Wildlife Refuge and withdrawn support for reducing greenhouse gasses through the Kyoto Accord on Climate Change. Some Republicans including George W. Bush even doubted the validity of the scientific community's consensus about the *existence* of global warming. Senator James Inhofe has called the global warming scare "the greatest hoax" ever forced on the American public.

Not all Republicans have accepted the Wise Use agenda. After the GOP takeover of Congress in 1994, some party members, led by Martha Marks, organized Republicans for Environmental Protection, known as REP America. Marks rejected the suggestion that she should become a Democrat. Although some see the REP's name as an oxymoron, its members seek to reclaim the conservation and environmental values that Theodore Roosevelt, Gifford Pinchot, Barry Goldwater (an REP America member), and Richard Nixon claimed. "We conservation-minded Republicans are the true conservatives in our party," Marks averred sounding very much like Roosevelt. "True conservatives protect the health and well-being of current and future generations." Operating by the slogan "conservation is conservative" the organization argues that the environment will only be protected when it becomes a two-party issue. The organization has grown substantially and has seen some of its members elected to state and federal offices, but it wages a lonely fight in trying to change the direction of the Republican party as a whole.[91]

In law, antienvironmentalists have also had some victories, particularly in using property rights to limit environmental regulations. They argue that, since the Constitution promises to compensate people whose land government agencies have seized by right of eminent domain (referred to as a "taking"), people whose land has lost value due to government regulations should be compensated for this "regulatory taking." The Supreme Court has agreed that when regulations make property worthless it is a taking, but the courts have not supported the idea of partial takings, where the regulated land still has commercial value. Nevertheless, this partial victory has emboldened property rights advocates to push takings laws in many state legislatures.

Their defeats, however, were as notable as their victories. Despite the Republican revolution of 1994, GOP politicians discovered they did not have a mandate to roll back environmental gains. Congressional losses by Republicans in 1996 and the reelection of Bill Clinton indicated that the 104th Congress had overreached in trying to gut environmental legislation. On the environment, the American people were moderates who would not accept radicalism whether it was from environmentalists or Wise-Use advocates.

Conclusion

The environmental movement stood at a crossroads at the end of the century. It still enjoyed widespread, if shallow, popular support. But with Al Gore's defeat in 2000 to George W. Bush, the movement confronted a situation that was unique. All three branches of government were openly hostile to the environmentalist agenda. The Bush administration might not rescind environmental legislation as the GOP hoped to do in 1994, but through administrative changes under Department of the Interior Secretary Gale Norton, a James Watt protégé, it hoped to accomplish nearly as much. Equally worrisome was the nation's insatiable appetite for oil that threatened its balance of payments and contributed to global warming. Even if the Bush administration were willing, a solution to damage by greenhouse gasses seemed to be beyond the grasp of any government.

It was in the context of this discouraging reality that dissent broke out among environmentalists in calls for drastic action. In October 2004, just before Bush's reelection, Michael Shellenberger and Ted Nordhaus, two young, experienced professional environmentalists, presented the provocative essay, "The Death of Environmentalism: Global Warming Politics in a Post-Environmental World," to a meeting of the movement's financial supporters.[92] "We have become convinced," the authors wrote, "that modern environmentalism, with all of its unexamined assumptions, outdated concepts and exhausted strategies, must die so that something new can live." After spending millions on pushing solutions to global warming, they wrote, the environmental movement had virtually nothing to show for it. The fault for this, they argued, lay with the movement's leadership and its historical development. It was in the heady days of the early 1970s, when environmentalists won so many victories, that the "seeds of failure were planted." Key leaders, the two activists complained, had narrowly defined the movement's mission and had not reached out to other "progressive" groups on the left to form effective coalitions. The movement had focused for thirty years on technical solutions, science, litigation, and lobbying. This kind of incrementalism, they believed, was foolish when the real battle was in marketing a coherent worldview that voters would accept, as conservatives had successfully done. As a result, environmentalism was seen by the public as "just another special interest." Shellenberger and Nordhaus were short on answers, but they did recommend that environmentalism should be subsumed into a broader progressive movement that focused on an array of intersecting issues, rather than maintain a separate identity.

Adam Werbach, the former and youngest president ever of the Sierra Club, dumped gasoline on the fire. "Environmentalism is dead," he announced. "Environmentalism has become a tradition, not a movement." Traditions, he explained, "hold on to the past for a sense of security." Movements take people forward. Werbach argued that environmentalism had never offered as compelling a vision as its enemies on the right. Its exclusive focus on environmental issues prevented the movement from a broader progressive vision. Rather than speak of doom, the movement needed to stress the positive outcomes of limiting global warming, including the jobs created for average Americans. "We were outflanked by Watt and his cohorts on the right, who infused corporate-driven anti-environmentalism with an anti-statist, populist energy. . . . We are now in a minority position, with a minority party as our advocate." Werbach's solution did not call for seeking middle ground with green conservatives. He wanted ideological purity. "If you're a conservative, and believe in dismantling our government, selling off our common assets, and endless war, but you still love nature, we wish you well, but we need you to leave this movement. . . . The Republican Party—as an institution—has declared war on us." Like Shellenberger and Nordhaus, he recommended a clean break with the movement's past. Environmentalists should merge their organizations with a broader progressive movement.

Columnist Nicholas Kristof of the *New York Times* agreed with their analysis of the movement's ineffective position and their concern about global warming, but he blamed the movement for being Chicken Little once too often. Environmentalists had so often predicted calamity in the past that they were "like car alarms, they are now just an irritating background noise."[93] They were "brimming with moral clarity and ideological zeal, but empty of nuance." They rightly suffered from a credibility problem, he concluded. Polls tended to agree, showing that public opinion had become more negative toward environmentalists. It was as if the jaded public had heard it all before, and they had. Every decade of the postwar period had its prophets of doom.

These assessments sparked a minor riot in the environmental community. One environmentalist called these relatively youthful activists "arrogant, self-indulgent, and wrong," arguing that they had not learned from the cyclical history of political movements and had "given up too early." Carl Pope, executive director of the Sierra Club, while agreeing that the movement had not made progress on global warming, blamed the rebels for "shoddy research," "patricide" and being "unfair, unclear, and divisive" in a way that "rendered their report nihilistic." The movement, he pointed out, had not been as narrowly focused as Shellenberger and Nordhaus suggested. The movement had, for some time, worked to build coalitions with other progressives and pursued multiple strategies for change. The movement managed to incorporate conventional lobbying strategies with direct action movements such as the antinuclear movement and Earth First! The fundamentals of the movement were sound, Pope asserted. Global warming was simply a far more obscure and long-term problem that the public could not see as an imminent threat as they had with far move visible and immediate water or air pollution. Pope also revealed another reason for the difficulty of solving the global warming problem. "The conversation we are having should be about an entirely different energy future, one which will mean a dramatic reconfiguration of the world's wealth." Such fundamental change had rarely occurred in world history.

Shellenberger, Nordhaus, and Werbach's message had considerable support, but in view of the movement's history, Pope's arguments seemed more compelling. Few disagreed with Werbach's recommendation for putting forward a more positive vision. Certainly conservationists and environmentalists were most successful when they combined their warnings with an optimistic vision of pristine beauty or ecological integrity. John Muir had done this in establishing national parks. Franklin Roosevelt sold conservation programs to the country based on the economic benefits they would bring. Howard Zahniser, too, had appealed to America's aspirations in his push for wilderness legislation. And everyone could agree that more effective coalition-building was essential. But the call for the dissolution of environmental groups, some that were over one hundred years old, underestimated the value of tradition and the capacity of these organizations had shown for adapting to political reality and value shifts. Shellenberger's and Nordhaus's essay was, perhaps, a reflection of their pessimism about breaking what seemed to be a "permanent majority," as Tom DeLay called it, for the GOP in Congress. The 2006 election and the Democratic resurgence suggest that neither party has the upper hand in an evenly divided nation. If such is the case, environmental organizations with a history of working with both parties will be more crucial than ever.

The call for environmentalists to embrace progressive ideology over bridge-building with Republican moderates overlooked the success the movement enjoyed when it had bipartisan appeal. While the far right is likely beyond reconciliation, it is doubtful that the movement could ever rebuild a political majority without appealing to GOP centrists. In one example of such a coalition, efforts to work with hunters and fishermen produced a successful alliance that engineered the defeat of a Republican effort in 2005 to open up public lands—prime hunting and fishing grounds—for purchase by mining companies. Leading the campaign was Trout Unlimited, an organization whose membership was two-to-one Republican. "The White House's pillaging of public lands has driven hunters and ranchers into the trenches with environmentalists," one Wilderness Society staffer said. Global warming may further solidify improved relations. Predictions that the greenhouse effect will dry up duck habitats and reduce trout populations that thrive in cold water have pushed some hook-and-bullet groups to take stands on carbon emissions. There may be a return of the historic alliance of these alienated groups.[94]

Efforts to appeal to union workers have also borne fruit. In June 2006, the Sierra Club and the United Steelworkers union announced the formation of the Blue/Green Alliance under the motto, "Good jobs, a clean environment, and a safer world." Like their efforts with the environmental justice movement, environmental organizations made headway in bridging its historical class divide. Steelworker David Foster noted, "We were born in different classes, for the most part—blue-collar workers on one side of the fence, environmental activists on another—but today we rely on almost exactly the same constituency to support our agendas. The Bush victory in 2004 made it very clear that green and blue values are under attack by exactly the same source."[95] Shellenberger, Nordhaus, and Werbach's call for alliances are occurring without the drastic restructuring they said was necessary.

The pronouncement of environmentalism's "death" and the substitution for it of a broad multi-issue progressive movement seemed to ignore the value that single-issue organizations have for the civil rights, feminism, and labor movements. The public has been attracted to the environmental movement for over a century because its leaders espoused an appealing vision and a set of values that explained why the environment was important to the nation. Organizations had made a difference by championing those values and integrating them into government institutions, laws, and the minds of the American people. Initiatives to clean up the air, land, and water had nearly universal endorsement, in part because environmentalists convinced the public of their importance. One poll in 2005 reported that 75 percent of respondents agreed with the statement, "Protecting the environment is so important that requirements and standards cannot be too high, and continuing environmental improvements must be made regardless of cost."[96] Because of public support, pollution was significantly less than it had been on the first Earth Day in 1970. America's park and forest system was the envy of the world, and natural-resource use was, with some exceptions, governed through scientific management. Will a broad "progressive" movement that sees the environment as just one of many issues succeed this well?

Where then did the movement stand? Considering the three activists' portrayal of environmentalism's death, its organizations were surprisingly energetic. After George W. Bush assumed office, fund-raising and membership surged among most major green groups. Between 1997 and 2005, the Audubon Society gained over 450,000 members, the Sierra Club 200,000, the Nature Conservancy 280,000, and Environmental Defense (formerly the Environmental Defense Fund) 100,000. Despite all the hand-wringing, a case could be made that environmentalism has, over the past fifty years, been the most resilient, popular, and successful progressive movement in the country.

Environmentalism could also boast that it was a true mass movement with a new outlook, something that John Muir could not claim at the turn of the twentieth century when the conservation ethic was confined to the well-to-do. With the expansion of the middle class after World War II, a broad constituency of Americans interacted with nature. They walked in it, camped in it, hunted and fished in it, and sought to protect it. And their reasons for protecting the environment evolved. Preservationists, for example, found the ground shifting under them. Preserving sublime vistas was once their raison d'être. Most of the national parks were preserved for their scenic qualities, and to this day much of the public visit them for the inspiration they provide. By the 1930s, however, change was afoot. Ecology came to have a significant influence on preservation efforts, such as the protection of the Everglades. More and more, science provided the reasons for preserving a certain patch of ground.

As Aldo Leopold had hoped, a significant portion of the public developed an ecological sensibility.

For alternative and radical environmental movements, success has been uneven. The fundamental restructuring of society that some groups sought has yet to occur, but in more subtle ways they have had an influence. The radicals have often proved to be keepers of a pure environmental vision that has inspired many within the movement. As a matter of practical policy, their influence has been muted but real. By taking strong stands on issues such as nuclear power, and protection of old-growth forests and endangered species, they have shifted the debate further to the left than mainstream organizations might have been willing to go. It is because of alternative groups that the larger movement pays attention to issues of race, class, and gender. After years of elite domination, the movement sought to return to its roots as a cross-class movement. The campaign against toxic-waste dumping and for environmental justice highlighted the needs of the working class and minorities. But progress has been slow. People of color, frustrated with the glacial pace of change in the larger environmental organizations, chose to establish their own organizations, diversifying the movement even more.

Perhaps the biggest winners in the environmental movement were those who rallied against the detrimental effects of modern life by improving public health and reducing pollution. Alice Hamilton and others had fought for an environmental understanding of health problems, and they succeeded. Rachel Carson alerted the public to the hazards of pesticides and pollution in general. Concern for pollution moved from a local issue to a central part of the environmental agenda in the 1960s. That concern lives on in efforts to control toxic wastes, such as the Superfund legislation of 1980 and the public preference for pesticide-free organic fruits and vegetables and opposition to genetically modified foods.

The movement, then, had a lot to be proud of, but also reason to worry. If the alarmists are right about global warming, environmentalists will have to convince the public to make dramatic lifestyle changes in a society founded on fossil-fuel consumption. That will require support across the political spectrum. Only a new sense of urgency seems likely to lead to another wave of environmental reform. It has happened before.

Endnotes

1 Susan Zakin, *Coyotes and Town Dogs: Earth First! and the Environmental Movement* (New York: Viking, 1993), 256–58.

2 Thomas Raymond Wellock, *Critical Masses: Opposition to Nuclear Power in California, 1958–78* (Madison: University of Wisconsin Press, 1998), 109.

3 Ibid., 95.

4 Ibid., 110.

5 Richard N. L. Andrews, *Managing the Environment, Managing Ourselves: A History of American Environmental Policy* (New Haven: Yale University Press, 1999), 298–99.

6 Paul R. Erlich and Anne H. Erlich, *The End of Affluence: A Blueprint for Your Future* (New York: Ballantine Books, 1974), 4.

7 Wellock, *Critical Masses,*169.

8 Ibid., 171.

9 Ibid., 243.

10 Langdon Winner, *The Whale and the Reactor: A Search for Limits in an Age of High Technology* (Chicago: University of Chicago Press, 1986), 62.

11 Ibid., 73.

12 Ibid., 64–65.

13 *Whole Earth Catalog: Access to Tools,* Fall 1970.

14 Winner, *The Whale and the Reactor,* 74.

15 William Bruce Wheeler and Michael J. McDonald, *TVA and the Tellico Dam, 1936–1979: A Bureaucratic Crisis in Post-Industrial America* (Knoxville: University of Tennessee Press, 1986), 156–57.

16 Marc Reisner, *Cadillac Desert: The American West and Its Disappearing Water,* 2d ed. (New York: Penguin, 1993), 326.

17 Wheeler and McDonald, *TVA and the Tellico Dam,* 211.

18 Hal Rothman, *Saving the Planet: The American Response to the Environment in the Twentieth Century* (Chicago: Ivan Dee, 2000), 161.

19 Robert J. Duffy, *The Green Agenda in American Politics: New Strategies for the Twenty-First Century* (Lawrence: University Press of Kansas, 2003), 73; and William Dietrich, *The Final Forest: The Battle for the Last Great Trees of the Pacific Northwest* (New York: Simon and Schuster, 1992), 85.

20 Richard White, "'Are You an Environmentalist or Do You Work for a Living', Work and Nature," in *Uncommon Ground: Rethinking the Human Place in Nature,* ed. William Cronon, (New York: W.W. Norton Co., 1995), 171; and Dietrich, *The Final Forest,* 29.

21 http://www.lib.duke.edu'forest/ Research/usfscoll/policy/ nothern_spotted_owl; and Dietrich, *Final Forest,* 213.

22 *The Olympian,* 9 September 2003, 1.

23 Christina Larson, "The Emerging Environmental Majority," *Washington Monthly,* May 2006, http://www. washingtonmonthly.com, 28 July 2006.

24 "Napoleon Bonaparte Broward," *Everglades Biographies,* http:// web.archive.org/web/2002121

8074854/everglades.fiu.edu/reclaim/ bios/broward.html (13 August 2006).

25 Jack E. Davis, "'Conservation is Now a Dead Word': Marjory Stoneman Douglas and the Transformation of American Environmentalism," *Environmental History* 8, no. 1 (January 2003): 58.

26 Jack E. Davis, "Green Awakening: Social Activism and the Evolution of Marjory Stoneman Douglas's Environmental Consciousness," *Florida Historical Quarterly* 80 (Summer 2001): 58–59.

27 Madelyn Holmes, *American Women Conservationists: Twelve Profiles* (Jefferson, NC: McFarland and Co., 2004), 92.

28 Davis, "Conservation is Now a Dead Word," 63.

29 Ibid., 64.

30 Holmes, *American Women Conservationists,* 95.

31 Davis, "Conservation is Now a Dead Word," 65.

32 Ibid., 66, 68.

33 Adeline Gordon Levine, *Love Canal: Science, Politics, and People* (Lexington, MA: D.C. Heath, 1982), 10–13.

34 Levine, *Love Canal,* 15; and Hal Rothman, *The Greening of a Nation?: Environmentalism in the United States since 1945* (Fort Worth, TX: Harcourt Brace, 1998), 149.

35 Levine, *Love Canal,* 28.

36 Philip Shabecoff, *A Fierce Green Fire: The American Environmental Movement* (New York: Hill and Wang, 1993), 234.

37 Ibid., 235.

38 Robert Gottlieb, *Forcing the Spring: The Transformation of the American Environmental Movement* (Washington DC: Island Press, 1993), 187.

39 Kirkpatrick Sale, *The Green Revolution: The American Environmental Movement, 1962–1992* (New York: Hill and Wang, 1993), 60; and Shabecoff, *Fierce Green Fire,* 237.

40 Mark Dowie, *Losing Ground: American Environmentalism at the Close of the Twentieth Century* (Cambridge, MA: MIT Press, 1995), 131; and Sale, *Green Revolution,* 60.

41 Dowie, *Losing Ground,* 130–31.

42 Samuel P. Hays, *Beauty, Health, and Permanence: Environmental Politics in the United States, 1955–1985* (Cambridge: Cambridge University Press, 1987), 201.

43 Sale, *Green Revolution,* 33.

44 Ibid., 49.

45 Benjamin Heber Johnson, "Conservation, Subsistence, and Class at the Birth of Superior National Forest," *Environmental History* 4, no. 1 (January 1999): 80.

46 Shabecoff, *Fierce Green Fire,* 207.

47 Rothman, *Greening of a Nation,* 174.

48 Sale, *Green Revolution,* 52–53.

49 Shabecoff, *Fierce Green Fire,* 229.

50 Sale, *Green Revolution,* 54.

51 Dowie, *Losing Ground,* 107.

52 Shabecoff, *Fierce Green Fire,* 259.

53 Dietrich, *Final Forest,* 84.

54 Gottlieb, *Forcing the Spring,* 193.

55 Sale, *Green Revolution,* 68.

56 Jeffrey C. Ellis, "On the Search for a Root Cause: Essentialist Ten-

dencies in Environmentalist Discourse," *Uncommon Ground: Rethinking the Human Place in Nature,* ed. William Cronon (New York: W.W. Norton, 1995), 264.

57 Ellis, "Search for a Root Cause," 264.

58 Ibid., 264–65.

59 Zakin, *Coyotes and Town Dogs,* 25.

60 Ibid., 113 and Rothman, *Greening of a Nation,* 183.

61 Dowie, *Losing Ground,* 209 and Zakin, *Coyotes and Town Dogs,* 131–33 and 145.

62 Rik Scarce, *Eco-Warriors: Understanding the Radical Environmental Movement,* 2d ed. (Walnut Creek, CA: Left Coast Press, 2006), 61–62.

63 Zakin, *Coyotes and Town Dogs,* 271.

64 Sale, *Green Revolution,* 66.

65 Christopher Manes, *Green Rage: Radical Environmentalism and the Unmaking of Civilization* (Boston: Little, Brown and Company, 1990), 74.

66 Carolyn Merchant, *Radical Ecology: The Search for a Livable World,* 2d ed. (New York: Routledge, 2005), 175.

67 Zakin, *Coyotes and Town Dogs,* 378.

68 Gottlieb, *Forcing the Spring,* 198.

69 Daniel J. Philippon, *Conserving Words: How American Nature Writers Shaped the Environmental Movement* (Athens: University of Georgia Press, 2004), 252.

70 Zakin, *Coyotes and Town Dogs,* 353.

71 Kate Coleman, *The Secret Wars of Judi Bari: A Car Bomb, the Fight for the Redwoods, and the End of Earth First!* (San Francisco: Encounter Books, 2005), 137.

72 Ibid., 146, 148.

73 Dave Foreman, *Confessions of an Eco-Warrior* (New York: Harmony Books, 1991), 219.

74 Douglas Long, *Ecoterrorism* (New York: Facts on File, 2004), 3.

75 Eileen Maura McGurty, "From NIMBY to Civil Rights: The Origins of the Environmental Justice Movement," *Environmental History* 2, no. 3 (July 1997): 302.

76 Dowie, *Losing Ground,* 142; and Giovanna Di Chiro, "Environmental Justice From the Grassroots: Reflections on History, Gender, and Expertise," in *The Struggle for Ecological Democracy: Environmental Justice Movements in the United States,* ed. Daniel Faber (New York: Guilford Press, 1998), 109–10.

77 Di Chiro, "Environmental Justice," 110.

78 McGurty, "From NIMBY to Civil Rights," 304.

79 Dowie, *Losing Ground,* 147.

80 Di Chiro, "Environmental Justice from the Grassroots," 112; and Gottlieb, *Forcing the Spring,* 318.

81 Gottlieb, *Forcing the Spring,* 5 and Dowie, *Losing Ground,* 151–52.

82 David Pepper, *Modern Environmentalism: An Introduction* (London: Routledge, 1996), 106.

83 Ibid., 106.

84 Ibid., 108.

85 Carl Pope, "And Now for Something Completely Different: An In–Depth Response to 'The Death of Environmentalism,'"13 January 2005, *Grist Magazine: A Beacon In the Smog,* http://www.grist.org 27 July 2006.

86 David Helvarg, *The War Against the Greens: The "Wise Use" Movement, the New Right, and the Browning of America,* 2d ed. (Boulder, CO: Johnson Books, 2004), 274.

87 David Helvarg, *The War Against the Greens: The "Wise Use" Movement, the New Right, and Anti-Environmental Violence* (San Francisco: Sierra Club Books, 1994), 130–31; and Phil Brick, "Determined Opposition: The Wise Use Movement Challenges Environmentalism," *Environment* 37, no. 8 (Oct. 1995): 36.

88 Brick, "Determined Opposition," 19.

89 Ibid., 38.

90 David Helvarg, *The War Against the Greens: The "Wise Use" Movement, the New Right, and the Browning of America,* 2d ed. (Boulder, CO: Johnson Books, 2004), 282.

91 Martha Marks, "Greening the Elephant: Republicans for Environmental Protection Need Not Be an Oxymoron," 13 May 2003, *Grist Magazine: A Becon in the Smog,* http://www.grist.org/comments/soapbox/2003/05/13/greening/, 21 July 2006.

92 For Shellenberger and Nordhaus essay and the debate that ensued, see *Grist Magazine*'s website, http://www.grist.org.

93 *New York Times*, 12 March 2005.

94 Christina Larson, "The Emerging Environmental Majority," *Washington Monthly,* May 2006, http://www.washingtonmonthly.com, 28 July 2006.

95 Amanda Griscom Little, "Labor Gains: New Green/Labor Alliance Brings Sierra Club and Steelworkers Together," *Grist Magazine: A Beacon in the Smog,* 16 June 2006, http://www.grist.org, 28 July 2006.

96 Christina Larson, "The Emerging Environmental Majority."

BIBLIOGRAPHICAL ESSAY

There are a number of general histories of the conservation and environmental movements. See Joseph M. Petulla, *American Environmental History: The Exploitation and Conservation of Natural Resources* (1977); Peter Coates, *In Nature's Defence: Conservation and Americans* (1993); Philip Shabecoff, *A Fierce Green Fire: The American Environmental Movement* (1993); John Opie, *Nature's Nation: An Environmental History of the United States* (1998); Hal Rothman, *Saving the Planet: The American Response to the Environment in the Twentieth Century* (2000); Ted Steinberg, *Down To Earth: Nature's Role in American History* (2002); Louis S. Warren, *American Environmental History* (2003); Benjamin Kline, *First Along the River: A Brief History of the U.S. Environmental Movement* (2002); Frank E. Smith, *The Politics of Conservation* (1966); Frank Graham, Jr., *Man's Dominion: The Story of Conservation in America* (1971); and Carolyn Merchant ed., *Major Problems in American Environmental History* (2005). On the development of environmental policy since colonization, see Richard N. L. Andrews, *Managing the Environment, Managing Ourselves: A History of American Environmental Policy*

(1999). The influence of nature writers on the movement has been studied by Daniel J. Philippon, *Conserving Words: How American Nature Writers Shaped the Environmental Movement* (2004).

Chapter One

In the 1950s, scholars accepted the notion that conservationists were democratic crusaders who sought to protect the public and resources from greedy impulses of major corporations. J. Leonard Bates' "Fulfilling American Democracy: The Conservation Movement, 1907–1921," *Mississippi Valley Historical Review* 44, no. 1 (1957): 29–57, is the best example of this interpretation. Two years later, Samuel P. Hays shattered the prevailing view with *Conservation and the Gospel of Efficiency: The Progressive Conservation Movement, 1890–1920* (1959). Hays argued that conservation was a top-down movement led by efficiency-minded experts who sought scientific management of resources, not democratic control. Conservation thus provided a window on to the nature of Progressive reform in general. Also useful from the same period is Elmo R. Richardson, *The Politics of Conservation: Crusades and Controversies, 1897–1913* (1962) and Henry Clepper, ed., *Origins of American Conservation* (1966). An interesting reformulation of Hays' thesis is Clayton R. Koppes, "Efficiency/Equity/Esthetics: Towards A Reinterpretation of American Conservation," *Environmental Review* 11, no. 2 (1987): 127–46.

Hays' interpretation remained the dominant view, but it underwent two significant challenges. John Reiger argued in *American Sportsmen and the Origins of Conservation* (1975, 2000) that it was sport hunters, especially among the wealthy, who provided the chief impetus for the conservation of wildlife. Daniel Justin Herman in *Hunting and the American Imagination* (2001) has found that the late nineteenth century was a critical period for hunters, breaking up the affinity that elite and subsistence farmers had for each other. The decline of game led to a growing rift between the two camps and game laws that favored the powerful elites over the less influential subsistence and market hunters. See also Thomas R. Dunlap, "Sport Hunting and Conservation, 1880–1920," *Envi-*

ronmental Review 12, no. 1 (1988): 51–60. James A. Tober, W*ho Owns the Wildlife?: The Political Economy of Conservation in Nineteenth-Century America* (1981) makes a similar argument in his study of the role of hunting clubs in wildlife protection. To understand the important role of organizations such as the Boone and Crockett Club to wildlife conservation see James B. Trefethen, *An American Crusade for Wildlife* (1975). The links between masculinity and wildlife preservation by clubs such as Boone and Crockett have been analyzed by Andrew C. Isenberg in *The Destruction of the Bison: An Environmental History, 1750–1920* (2000). The transformation of attitudes from one of plunder to conservation of wildlife has been studied for the state of Texas by Robin W. Doughty, *Wildlife and Man in Texas: Environmental Change and Conservation* (1983).

The other challenge to Hays' thesis came from Richard W. Judd who made a forceful case for the grassroots origins of conservation in *Common Lands, Common People: The Origins of Conservation in Northern New England* (1997) and "Grass-Roots Conservation in Eastern Coastal Maine: Monopoly and the Moral Economy of Weir Fishing, 1893–1911," *Environmental Review* 12, no. 2 (1988): 80–103. Judd argued that in New England, it was rural folk concerned about the loss of common resources to new economic forces and population growth that first called for state action in conservation. Steven Stoll makes a similar argument for east coast farmers in *Larding the Lean Earth: Soil and Society in Nineteenth-Century America* (2002). Steven Hahn, however, finds a less democratic outcome for the loss of common lands and resources in the South in "Hunting, Fishing and Foraging: Common Rights and Class Relations in the Postbellum South," *Radical History Review* 26 (1982): 37–64.

Recently, Hays' thesis has been challenged from another quarter. Some scholars have argued against the focus on American roots for the conservation movement. As early as 1977, Donald Worster had demonstrated the European origins in nineteenth-century ecological thought. His *Nature's Economy: A History of Ecological Ideas* (1977) saw ecology as a politically progressive science. It was in the administration of the British empire, however, that Richard H. Grove and Gregory Allen Barton contend was where American foresters found their chief inspiration for the establishment of the U.S. forest system. Conservation, apparently, had imperial origins. Grove's *Green Imperialism: Colonial Expansion, Tropical Island Edens, and the Origins of Environmentalism, 1600–1860* (1995) pointed to scientists working in European colonial holdings as chiefly responsible for environmental thought. Barton, in *Empire Forestry and the Origins of Environmentalism* (2002), argues that a broad community of experts throughout the globe influenced the imperial administration of Britain's forest empire and ultimately American foresters who came to study their trade in Europe. See also Richard H. Grove, *Ecology, Climate and Empire: Colonialism and Global Environmental History, 1400–1940* (1997), Ramachandra Guha, *Environmentalism: A Global History* (2000), and Tom Griffiths and Libby Robbin, *Ecology and Empire: Environmental History of Settler Societies* (1997).

Other scholars have also found conservation to have less than egalitarian goals, arguing that the conservation movement engaged in a form of class and racial warfare. In pushing to preserve resources and park land, conservationists made subsistence economies untenable, particularly among rural communities and Native Americans. See Mark David Spence, *Dispossessing the Wilderness: Indian Removal and the Making of the National Parks* (1999); Louis S. Warren, *The Hunter's Game: Poachers and Conservationists in Twentieth-Century America* (1997); Karl Jacoby, *Crimes Against Nature: Squatters, Poachers, Thieves, and the Hidden History of American Conservation* (2001), and Kevin DeLuca and Anne Demo, "Imagining Nature and Erasing Class and Race: Carleton Watkins, John Muir, and the Construction of Wilderness," *Environmental History* 6, no. 4 (October 2001): 541–560. Robert H. Keller and Michael F. Turek in *American Indians and the National Parks* (1998) also discuss the how the National Parks Service displaced Native Americans in establishing parks, but they also demonstrate that after World War II, tribes forced the Park Service to treat them with more sensitivity. For less than compelling studies of the links between the eugenics and conservation movements, see Alexandra Minna Stern, *Eugenic Nation: Faults and Frontiers of Better Breeding in Modern America* (2005) and

Gray Brechin, "Conserving the Race: Natural Aristocracies, Eugenics, and the U.S. Conservation Movement," *Antipode* 28, no. 3 (1996): 229–245.

The earliest conservation agencies began at the state level and regulated fisheries and pollution issues. John T. Cumbler's *Reasonable Use: The People, the Environment, and the State, New England 1790–1930* (2001) and "The Early Making of an Environmental Conciousness: Fish, Fisheries Commissions, and the Connecticut River," *Environmental History Review* 15, no. 4 (1991): 73–91, point to the origins of conservation in the grassroots efforts to get state regulation of fisheries and pollution issues. Unlike Richard Judd, Cumbler argues for urban and industrial origins of conservation in efforts to control water pollution. See also Joseph E. Taylor III, *Making Salmon: An Environmental History of the Norwest Fisheries Crisis* (1999); Donald J. Pisani, "Fish Culture and the Dawn of Concern over Water Pollution in the United States," *Environmental Review* 8, no. 2 (1984): 117–31; Margaret Beattie Bogue, *Fishing the Great Lakes: An Environmental History: 1783–1933* (2000); and Arthur F. McEvoy, *The Fisherman's Problem: Ecology and Law in the California Fisheries 1850–1980* (1986). McEvoy offers an insightful analysis of the interplay of values, law, and the state in creating environmental regulations.

David Lowenthal's fine biography, *George Perkins Marsh: Prophet of Conservation* (2000), has been reissued in a second edition. In the updated version, Lowenthal argues forcefully for the importance of Marsh's influence on conservation thinking against scholars who minimize his contribution. Marsh and John Muir are the subject of Robert L. Dorman's *A Word for Nature: Four Pioneering Environmental Advocates, 1845–1913* (1998). Two useful volumes that give numerous short biographies of conservation leaders is Peter Wild's *Pioneer Conservationists of Western America* (1979) and *Pioneer Conservationists of Eastern America* (1986). See also Douglas H. Strong, *Dreamers and Defenders: American Conservationists* (1988). Char Miller's *Gifford Pinchot and the Making of Modern Environmentalism* (2001) and "The Greening of Gifford Pinchot," *Environmental History Review* 16, no. 3 (1992): 1–20, offer a new interpretation of the forester in which he argues that the difference between conservation and preservation was never as distinct as scholars contend. Pinchot was both and thus an inspiration for the modern environmental movement. See also Harold T. Pinkett, *Gifford Pinchot: Private and Public Forester* (1970). For a look at how Pinchot engaged in state building activities see Brian Balogh, "Scientific Forestry and the Roots of the Modern American State: Gifford Pinchot's Path to Progressive Reform," *Environmental History* 7, no. 2 (April 2002): 198–225. Pinchot's conflicts with the Taft administration are best told by James Penick, *Progressive Politics and Conservation: The Ballinger-Pinchot Affair* (1968). Pinchot's views on conservation are best summed up in his two works *Breaking New Ground* (1947) and *The Fight for Conservation* (1910). Theodore Roosevelt's path to conservation has been chronicled by Paul Russell Cutright in *Theodore Roosevelt: The Making of a Conservationist* (1985).

Martin V. Melosi and Joel A. Tarr are the two pioneers in the study of urban sanitary and pollution problems. The starting point is Melosi's award winning work, *The Sanitary City: Urban Infrastructure in America from Colonial Times to the Present* (2000). Melosi argues that environmental issues were a key catalyst in the growth of municipal bureaucracy. Although most efforts to clean up the cities were carried out at the local level, an exception was when the Roosevelt and Taft Administrations involved themselves in the crusade to reduce smelter smoke in Montana. This was because the pollution affected national forest land. See Donald MacMillan, *Smoke Wars: Anaconda Copper, Montana Air Pollution, and the Courts, 1890–1924* (2000). Three other collections of essays are also essential: Melosi's *Pollution and Reform in American Cities, 1870–1930* (1980); Melosi's *Effluent America: Cities, Industry, Energy, and the Environment* (2001); and Tarr's *The Search for the Ultimate Sink: Urban Pollution in Historical Perspective* (1996). On refuse problems see Melosi's *Garbage in the Cities: Refuse, Reform, and the Environment, 1880–1980* (1981) and Daniel J. Zarin, "Searching for Pennies in Piles of Trash: Municipal Refuse Utilization in the United States, 1870–1930," *Environmental Review* 11, no. 3 (1987): 207–222. A case study of one city's efforts to clean up its environment is Judith Walzer Leavitt, *The Healthiest City: Milwaukee and the Politics of Health Reform*

(1982). Daniel Eli Burnstein has done a recent study of New York City refuse cleanup, including the activities of sanitarian George Waring. See *Next to Godliness: Confronting Dirt and Despair in Progressive Era New York City* (2006).

Air pollution up through the 1950s is covered very well by David Stradling's, *Smokestacks and Progressives: Environmentalists, Engineers, and Air Quality in America, 1881–1951* (1999). A more specific study of the Pittsburgh smoke problem is Angela Gugliotta, "How, When, and for Whom Was Smoke a Problem in Pittsburgh?," in *Devastation and Renewal: An Environmental History of Pittsburgh and Its Region,* Joel A. Tarr, ed. (2003). Pollution in the oil industry has been chronicled by Hugh S. Gorman in *Redefining Efficiency: Pollution Concerns, Regulatory Mechanism, and Technological Change in the U.S. Petroleum Industry* (2001). The role of industrial hygiene in creating a greater awareness of pollution problems is covered in Christopher C. Sellars' *Hazards of the Job: From Industrial Disease to Environmental Health Science* (1997).

The effort to reform cities with carefully designed parks has received extensive treatment. The best place to start is David Schuyler's *The New Urban Landscape: The Redefinition of City Form in Nineteenth-Century America* (1986). Schuyler demonstrates how nineteenth-century Americans reconciled America's agrarian past with its new urban reality in designing park systems. A broad overview of the subject may be obtained in Galen Cranz, *The Politics of Park Design: A History of Urban Parks in America* (1982). On Frederick Law Olmstead, see Anne Whiston Spirn, "Constructing Nature: The Legacy of Frederick Law Olmstead," in *Uncommon Ground: Rethinking the Human Place in Nature,* William Cronon, ed. (1995); Witold Rybczynski, *A Clearing in the Distance: Frederick Law Olmsted and America in the Nineteenth Century* (1999); Laura Wood Roper, *FLO: A Biography of Frederick Law Olmsted* (1973); Elizabeth Stevenson, *Park Maker: A Life of Frederick Law Olmsted* (1977); and Melvin Kalfus, *Frederick Law Olmsted: The Passion of a Public Artist* (1990). For more on Olmsted's contributions to the Boston park system, see Cynthia Zaitzevsky, *Frederick Law Olmsted and the Boston Park*

System (1982). For the essential role of Central Park in park design and its social impact see Roy Rosenzweig and Elizabeth Blackmar, *The Park and the People: A History of Central Park* (1992). After Olmstead, there emerged a "City Beautiful" movement that sought to systematically remake the urban environment. William H. Wilson's *The City Beautiful Movement* (1989) found that middle and wealthy class Americans sought to impose a middle-class environmentalism on communities and believed that by redesigning the urban environment they could imbue all classes with civic patriotism and make them more productive.

The history of the Forest Service had been chronicled in Harold K. Steen, *The U.S. Forest Service: A History* (1976). Another useful work is Glen O. Robinson, *The Forest Service: A Study in Public Land Management* (1975). The history of the American Forestry Association has been analyzed in a brief history by Henry Clepper, *Crusade for Conservation: The Centennial History of the American Forestry Association* (1975). For an overview of forestry see Thomas R. Cox and others, *This Well-Wooded Land: Americans and Their Forests From Colonial Times to the Present* (1985). The earliest years of professional forestry are covered in Char Miller, "The Pivotal Decade: American Forestry in the 1870s," *Journal of Forestry* 98, no. 11 (November 2000): 6–10. An excellent set of essays on forestry in general is Char Miller, ed., *American Forests: Nature, Culture, and Politics* (1997). William Robbins has written two books on the interplay between the lumber industry, legislators, and the United States Forest Service. See *Lumberjacks and Legislators: Political Economy of the Lumber Industry, 1890–1941* (1982) and *American Forestry: A History of National, State, & Private Cooperation* (1985). A more specific study of forestry practices in the Blue Mountains was conducted by Nancy Langston, *Forest Dreams, Forest Nightmares: The Paradox of Old Growth in the Inland West* (1995). A case study of the conflict over forest reserves in Colorado between anti-conservation and conservation forces is G. Michael McCarthy's *Hour of Trial: The Conservation Conflict in Colorado and the West, 1891–1907* (1977). Similarly Ronald F. Lockmann studies efforts to establish reserves in *Guarding the Forests of Southern California:*

Evolving Attitudes Toward Conservation of Watershed, Wood-lands, and Wilderness (1981) and Lawrence Rakestraw, *A History of Forest Conservation in the Pacific Northwest, 1891–1913* (1979).

There are two essential starting points in the battles waged over water development in the West. See Donald Worster, *Rivers of Empire: Water, Aridity, and the Growth of the American West* (1985) and Marc Reisner, *Cadillac Desert: The American West and Its Disappearing Water* (1986). From there it is useful to refer to Donald Pisani's series on reclamation. See *To Reclaim the Divided West: Water, Law, and Public Policy, 1848–1902* (1992) and *Water and American Government: The Reclamation Bureau, National Water Policy, and the West, 1902–1935* (2002). The early irrigation crusade was covered by Lawrence B. Lee, "William Ellsworth Smythe and the Irrigation Movement: A Reconsideration," *Pacific Historical Review* 41, no. 3 (1972): 289–311. Donald Pisani details the role of irrigation in the rise of agribusiness in California in *From Family Farm to Agribusiness: The Irrigation Crusade in California and the West 1850–1931* (1984). The Owens Valley–Los Angeles water controversy has been covered by Abraham Hoffman, *Vision of Villainy: Origins of the Owens Valley–Los Angeles Water Controversy* (1981) and William L. Kahrl, *Water and Power: The Conflict Over Los Angeles' Water Supply in the Owens Valley* (1982).

The appreciation of nature and scenic vistas as an essential form of leisure and the basis of American culture and citizenship has been chronicled by John F. Sears in *Sacred Places: American Tourist Attractions in the Nineteenth Century* (1989) and Marguerite S. Shaffer's *See America First: Tourism and National Identity, 1880–1940* (2001). Hal Rothman finds in *Devil's Bargains: Tourism in the Twentieth-Century American West* (1998) that tourism provided no panacea to postindustrial economic stagnation for communities throughout the West. See also David M. Wrobel and Patrick T. Long's anthology *Seeing and Being Seen: Tourism and the American West* (2001).

The essential role of women in conservation activities has been covered by several scholars. Glenda Riley's *Women and Nature: Saving the 'Wild' West* (1999) covers the multiple ways women interacted with the environment including political activism. Polly Welts Kaufman covers similar territory in *National Parks and the Woman's Voice: A History* (1996). For women's campaigns against the slaughter of birds, see Jennifer Price, *Flight Maps: Adventures With Nature in Modern America* (1999), Robin W. Doughty, *Feather Fashions and Bird Preservation: A Study in Nature Protection* (1975), and Mary Joy Breton, *Women Pioneers for the Environment* (1998). Carolyn Merchant surveys women's activism in "Preserving the Earth: Women and the Progressive Conservation Crusade" in *Earthcare: Women and the Environment* Carolyn Merchant, ed. (1995). Madelyn Holmes has produced brief biographies of major women conservationists throughout the twentieth century in *American Women Conservationists: Twelve Profiles* (2004). Kathy S. Mason describes the critical role of women in founding the Audubon Society in "Out of Fashion: Harriet Hemenway and the Audubon Society, 1896–1905," *The Historian* 65, no. 1 (2002): 1–14. Susan Flader discusses how the Progressive movement expanded the role of the state in environmental affairs at the expense of citizen organizations such as women's clubs in "Citizenry and the State in the Shaping of Environmental Policy," *Environmental History* 3, no. 1 (January 1998): 8–24. Adam Rome analyzes how what were perceived as feminine arguments used in saving nature and ending pollution undermined the position of male advocates for the environment. Ultimately, it led them to exclude women from alliances on environmental issues. See Adam Rome, "'Political Hermaphrodites,' Gender and Environmental Reform in Progressive America," *Environmental History* 11, no. 3 (July 2006): 440–63.

Women and pollution issues has also been studied by several scholars. Suellen M. Hoy argued that women used their traditional gender roles to justify a greater public role as "municipal housekeepers." They came to focus on pollution, beautification, and moral reform crusades long after the Progressive movement came to an end. See Hoy's *Chasing Dirt: The American Pursuit of Cleanliness* (1995). See also Maureen A. Flanagan, *Seeing with Their Hearts: Chicago Women and the Vision of the Good City, 1871–1933* (2002); Flanagan, "Gender and Urban Political Reform: The City Club and the Woman's City Club of Chicago in the Progressive Era," *American Historical Review* 95, no. 4 (1990): 1032–1050; and Harold L. Platt, "Jane Addams and the Ward Boss Revisited: Class, Politics, and Public Health in Chicago, 1890–1930," *Environmental History* 5, no. 2 (2000): 194–222.

The subject of wilderness and its preservation has undergone extensive study and controversy. The starting point for any study of wilderness politics is Roderick Nash, *Wilderness and the American Mind* (1967, fourth edition 2001). Nash argued that the traditional aversion to wilderness that Americans had faded with industrialization, urbanization, and the close of the frontier. No longer locked in a deadly struggle with nature, urbanized Americans came to appreciate pristine nature's restorative and inspirational qualities. They responded with a movement to preserve wilderness areas that led to the establishment of America's national parks and culminated in the 1964 Wilderness Act. A more specific study of the Progressive era–wilderness cult is Peter J. Schmitt, *Back to Nature: The Arcadian Myth in Urban America* (1969). Robert W. Righter has recently challenged Nash's emphasis on the preservationist's wilderness mission. He sees the preservationists as fighting to save places like Yosemite not for wilderness' sake, but to promote tourism. See *The Battle Over Hetch Hetchy: America's Most Controversial Dam and the Birth of Modern Environmentalism* (2005). On the Hetch Hetchy battle, see also John Warfield Simpson*, Dam! Water, Power, Politics, and Preservation in Hetch Hetchy and Yosemite National Park* (2006). See also Hans Huth, *Nature and the American: Three Centuries of Changing Attitudes* (1957). A ground breaking essay by William Cronon demonstrates the degree to which Americans' conception of wilderness is socially constructed can be found in William Cronon, "The Trouble with Wilderness; or, Getting Back to the Wrong Nature," in *Uncommon Ground: Rethinking the Human Place in Nature,* William Cronon, ed. (1996). J. Baird Callicott and Michael P. Nelson have edited a wonderful collection of essays on the meaning of wilderness in *The Great New Wilderness Debate* (1998). Thomas R. Dunlap has taken Cronon's wilderness controversy as a point of departure to explore environmentalism's religious aspects in *Faith* *in Nature: Environmentalism as Religious Quest* (2004). Susan Schrepfer has looked at how men and women interpreted their experiences in mountaineering in *Nature's Altars: Mountains, Gender, and American Environmentalism* (2005).

John Muir, the founder of the wilderness movement, has had several important biographies. Stephen Fox's *The American Conservation Movement: John Muir and His Legacy* (1981) and Frederick Turner, *Rediscovering America: John Muir in His Time and Ours* (1985) put Muir's contributions in a broad context. A new interpretation of Muir's early life is Steven J. Holmes, *The Young John Muir: An Environmental Biography* (1999). Michael P. Cohen offers an incisive analysis of Muir's philosophy in *The Pathless Way: John Muir and American Wilderness* (1984), as does Max Oelschlaeger in a chapter of his *The Idea of Wilderness: From Prehistory to the Age of Ecology* (1991). A useful anthology of Muir is Sally M. Miller, ed., *John Muir: Life and Work* (1993). Bill Devall has studied Muir's philosophy for its links to modern environmentalism in "John Muir as Deep Ecologist," *Environmental Review* 6, no. 1 (1982): 63–86. Muir's political acumen in dealing with the Southern Pacific Railroad has been pointed out by Richard J. Orsi in "'Wilderness Saint' and 'Robber Baron': The Anomalous Partnership of John Muir and the Southern Pacific Company for Preservation of Yosemite National Park," *Pacific Historian* 29, no. 2–3 (1985): 136–56. Orsi studied the Muir-Harriman relationship and the Southern Pacific's broader conservation efforts in *Sunset Limited: The Southern Pacific Railroad and the Development of the American West* (2005). The organization Muir founded to preserve the Sierra has its own history. See Michael P. Cohen, *The History of the Sierra Club, 1892–1970* (1988).

There are a number of studies on the drive to protect America's birds from the millinery trade. On the Audubon Society, see Frank Graham Jr., *The Audubon Ark: A History of the National Audubon Society* (1990). For other works on the subject, see Robin W. Doughty, *Feather Fashions and Bird Preservation: A Study in Nature Protection* (1975), Oliver H. Orr, Jr., *Saving American Birds: T. Gilbert Pearson and the Founding of the Audubon Movement* (1992), and Stuart B. McIver, *Death in the Everglades: The*

Murder of Guy Bradley, America's First Martyr to Environmentalism (2003).

The history of the national parks has been the subject of several broad studies and more specialized works on specific parks. Alfred Runte's *National Parks: The American Experience* (1979 3d ed., 1997) offers a political and intellectual study of the parks. See also John Ise, *Our National Park Policy: A Critical History* (1961), Kathy S. Mason, *Natural Museums: U.S. National Parks, 1872–1916* (2004), William C. Everhart, *The National Park Service* (1983), Joseph L. Sax, *Mountains Without Handrails: Reflections on the National Parks* (1980), and Thomas R. Cox, "From Hot Springs to Gateway: The Evolving Concept of Public Parks, 1832–1976," *Environmental Review* 5, no. 1 (1980): 14–26. Richard West Sellers in *Preserving Nature in the National Parks: A History* (1997) demonstrates how the park service altered its focus on the parks from scenic wonders to ecological systems worthy of study and management. Also useful is Donald Swain's biography *Wilderness Defender: Horace M. Albright and Conservation* (1970) and Robert Shankland, *Steve Mather of the National Parks* (1970). Many individual parks have histories on their establishment. One of the best is Susan R. Schrepfer's *The Fight to Save the Redwoods: A History of Environmental Reform, 1917–1978* (1983). Schrepfer's analysis is not just a history of the birth of Redwood National Park. It also shows how changing ideas of Darwinian evolution contributed to a growing militancy among some preservation organizations, such as the Sierra Club, after 1945. On the efforts to log Olympic National Park see Carsten Lien, *Olympic Battleground: The Power Politics of Timber Preservation* (2000). For Yellowstone National Park, see two books by Richard A. Bartlett, *Nature's Yellowstone* (1974) and *Yellowstone: A Wilderness Besieged* (1985). Also see Aubrey L. Haines, *The Yellowstone Story: A History of Our First National Park* (1977). For Grand Teton, see Robert W. Righter, *Crucible for Conservation: The Creation of Grand Teton National Park* (1982). Rocky Mountain National Park is chronicled in C. W. Buchholtz, *Rocky Mountain National Park: A History* (1983). For the first national park in Texas see John Jameson, *The Story of Big Bend National Park*

(1996). On the Great Smoky Mountain National Park, see Margaret Lynn Brown, *The Wild East: A Biography of the Great Smoky Moutains* (2000). The effort to establish America's first cultural park has been written by Duane A. Smith, *Mesa Verde National Park: Shadows of the Centuries* (1988). On the nation's national monuments see Hal Rothman, *Preserving Different Pasts: The American National Monuments* (1989) and "Second Class Sites: National Monuments and the Growth of the National Park System," *Environmental Review* 10, no. 1 (Spring 1986): 44–56.

State parks have undergone some study. A good starting point is Ney C. Landrum, *The State Park Movement in America: A Critical Review* (2004). On the history of the preservation of the Adirondacks, see Philip G. Terrie, *Forever Wild: Environmental Aesthetics and the Adirondack Forest Preserve* (1985) and Frank Graham Jr., *The Adirondack Park: A Political History* (1978). The founding of state parks in the Pacific Northwest has been analyzed by Thomas R. Cox, *The Park Builders: A History of State Parks in the Pacific Northwest* (1988). Arizona's parks have been studied by Jay M. Price in *Gateways to the Southwest: The Story of Arizona State Parks* (2004).

Other general studies of conservation include Charles T. Rubin, ed., *Conservation Reconsidered: Nature, Virtue, and American Democracy* (2000). A general history of public lands management is William K. Wyant, *Westward in Eden: The Public Lands and the Conservation Movement* (1982).

Chapter Two

Still the most important study of conservation during the Harding, Coolidge, and Hoover administrations is Donald C. Swain's *Federal Conservation Policy, 1921–1933* (1963). On the failure of game managers to think in ecological terms during this period see Jared Orsi, "From Horicon to Hamburgers and Back Again: Ecology, Ideology, and Wildfowl Management, 1917–1935," *Environmental History Review* 18, no. 4 (1994): 19–40. For a balanced account of the Teapot Dome Controversy see David H. Stratton's *Tempest Over Teapot Dome: The Story of Albert B. Fall* (1998). An extremely useful study of Herbert Hoover's immense contribution to the era is Kendrick A. Clements, *Hoover, Conservation, and Consumerism: Engineering the Good Life* (2000). Clements shows how Hoover saw conservation as an essential part of American prosperity and the spread of leisure. See also several helpful articles on Hoover: Kendrick A. Clements, "Herbert Hoover and Conservation, 1921–33," *American Historical Review* 89, no. 1 (1984): 67–88; Carl E. Krog, "'Organizing the Production of Leisure': Herbert Hoover and the Conservation Movement in the 1920s," *Wisconsin Magazine of History* 67, no. 3 (1984): 199–218; and Douglas C. Drake, "Herbert Hoover, Ecologist: The Politics of Oil Pollution Control, 1921–1926," *Mid-America: An Historical Review* 55, no. 3 (1973): 207–28. Hoover's critical role in the Colorado River Compact has been told by Norris Hundley, Jr., *Water and the West: The Colorado River Compact and the Politics of Water in the American West* (1975).

On the competition between the National Park Service and Forest Service see Hal K. Rothman, "'A Regular Ding Dong Fight': Agency Culture and Evolution in the NPS-USFS Dispute, 1916–1937," *Western Historical Quarterly* 20, no. 2 (1989): 141–61 and Richard Polenberg, "Conservation and Reorganization: The Forest Service Lobby, 1937–1938," *Agricultural History* 39, no. 4 (1965): 230–39. A case study of the Forest Service's efforts to fend off incursions from the Park Service can be found in Ben W. Twight, *Organizational Values and Political Power: The Forest Service Versus the Olympic National Park* (1983). The Park Service's history during the FDR administration has been detailed by Donald C. Swain, "The National Park Service and the New Deal, 1933–1940," *Pacific Historical Review* 41, no. 3 (1972): 312–32.

There have been a number of biographies completed of various leaders of the Wilderness Society and other conservationists. Larry Anderson's *Benton MacKaye: Conservationist, Planner, and Creator of the Appalachian Trial* (2002) is a fine study of the regional planner's conservation goals and social vision. Robert Marshall's life has been covered by James M. Glover in *A Wilderness Original: The Life of Bob Marshall* (1986) and "Romance, Recreation, and Wilderness: Influences On the Life and World of Bob

Marshall," *Environmental History Review* 14, no. 4 (1990): 23–39. Aldo Leopold had been the subject of some excellent biographies. See Susan L. Flader, *Thinking Like a Mountain, Aldo Leopold and the Evolution of an Ecological Attitude Toward Deer, Wolves and Forests* (1974) and Curt Meine, *Aldo Leopold: His Life and Work* (1988). See David Backes, *A Wilderness Within: The Life of Sigurd F. Olson* (1997) for a solid overview of Olson's ecological perspective and political activities.

There are quite a few organizational histories that are useful for this period. For the National Parks Association, see John C. Miles, *Guardians of the Parks: A History of the National Parks and Conservation Association* (1995). R. Newell Searle's *Saving Quetico-Superior: A Land Set Apart* (1977) covers the efforts of the Quetico-Superior Council to save this region in Northern Minnesota and Canada from 1927–1964. The National Wildlife Federation's history has been chronicled in Thomas B. Allen, *Guardian of the Wild: The Story of the National Wildlife Federation, 1936–1986* (1987). On the activities of Jay "Ding" Darling, chief of the Biological Survey and president of the National Wildlife Federation, see David L. Lendt, *Ding: The Life of Jay Norwood Darling* (1979).

The conflict between the Army Corps of Engineers and conservation groups in the years between 1920 and 1969 has been studied by Michael C. Robinson, "The Relationship Between the U.S. Army Corps of Engineers and the Environmental Community," *Environmental Review* 13, no. 1 (1989): 1–41. Given the conflict over the value of dams between preservationists and environmentalists on the one hand and conservationists on the other, it is useful to remember a time when dams were seen as an unalloyed good. See Wesley Arden Dick, "When Dams Weren't Dammed: The Public Power Crusade and Visions of the Good Life in the Pacific Northwest in the 1930s," *Environmental Review* 13, no. 3–4 (1989): 113–53.

A new work on New Deal conservation indicates a renewed interest in the era. See Henry L. Henderson and David B. Woolner, *FDR and the Environment* (2005). Most other New Deal histories of conservation are now a bit dated. A. L. Riesch Owen's *Conser-*

vation Under FDR (1983) is a useful, but too often uncritical reading of the era. More helpful is Clayton R. Koppes, "Environmental Policy and American Liberalism: The Department of Interior, 1933–1953," *Environmental Review* 7, no. 1 (Spring 1983): 17–53. Richard Lowitt in *The New Deal and the West* (1984) analyzes the influence of numerous conservation programs on the West. The Civilian Conservation Corps has several studies, but awaits a truly scholarly study of the program. Neil Maher should be rectifying that problem soon. For now, see Neil M. Maher, "A New Deal Body Politic: Landscape, Labor, and the Civilian Conservation Corps," *Environmental History* 7, no. 3 (July 2002): 435–461. See also his dissertation, Cornelius M. Maher, "Planting More Than Trees: The Civilian Conservation Corps and the Roots of the American Environmental Movement," (Ph.D. dissertation, New York University, 2001). Other studies include, John A. Salmond, *The Civilian Conservation Corps, 1933–1942: A New Deal Case Study* (1967); Leslie Alexander Lacy, *The Soil Soldiers: The Civilian Conservation Corps in the Great Depression* (1976); and Perry H. Merrill, *Roosevelt's Forest Army: A History of the Civilian Conservation Corps* (1981).

The Tennessee Valley Authority still awaits a full treatment, but there are several useful works on it. Especially helpful is a collection of essays edited by Erwin C. Hargrove and Paul K. Conkin, *TVA: Fifty Years of Grass-Roots Bureaucracy* (1983). A more personal and positive assessment of the agency can be found in North Callahan's *TVA: Bridge Over Troubled Waters* (1980). A more critical assessment of the TVA's contribution to the valley can be found in William U. Chandler, *The Myth of TVA: Conservation and Development in the Tennessee Valley, 1933–1983* (1984).

The importance of New Deal agricultural policy on conservation has been studied by Sarah T. Phillips. Her book is awaiting publication at present. In the meantime, refer to her dissertation, "Acres Fit and Unfit: Conservation and Rural Rehabilitation in the New Deal Era," (Ph.D. dissertation: Boston University, 2004). On the Soil Conservation Service see Neil Maher, "'Crazy Quilt Farming on Round Land': The Great Depression, The Soil Conservation Service, and the Politics of Landscape Change on the Great

Plains during the New Deal Era," *Western Historical Quarterly* 31, no. 3 (Autumn 2000): 319–339. On the influence of the Dust Bowl on conservation, see Donald Worster, *Dust Bowl: The Southern Plains in the 1930s* (1979, 2004), R. Douglas Hurt, *The Dust Bowl: An Agricultural and Social History* (1981), and Sarah T. Phillips, "Lessons From the Dust Bowl: Dryland Agriculture and Soil Erosion in the United States and South Africa, 1900–1950," *Environmental History* 4, no. 2 (April 1999): 245–266.

Of particular fascination to historians has been the career of FDR's Secretary of Interior, Harold Ickes. His work on behalf of the National Parks and efforts to create a Department of Conservation has been chronicled well by T. H. Watkins in *Righteous Pilgrim: The Life and Times of Harold L. Ickes* (1990). Especially useful is Part VII. Also useful on Ickes is Jeanne Nienaber Clarke, *Roosevelt's Warrior: Harold L. Ickes and the New Deal* (1996) and Graham White and John Maze, *Harold Ickes of the New Deal: His Private Life and Public Career* (1985).

The influence that ecological ideas had in altering thinking about nature in general is covered in Donald Worster's *Nature's Economy: A History of Ecological Ideas* (1977). The more specific role science played in altering wildlife management policy is the subject of Thomas R. Dunlap's *Saving America's Wildlife* (1988). The wildlife management failure on the Kaibab plateau is one that deserves its own book. Christian C. Young's *In the Absence of Predators: Conservation and Controversy on the Kaibab Plateau* (2002) explodes many of the myths surrounding this episode. Thomas R. Dunlap makes a similar argument in "That Kaibab Myth," *The Journal of Forest History* 32, no. 2 (1988): 60–68. Dunlap also studies the effect of ecologists on the perceptions the public had about predators in "The Coyote Itself"—Ecologists and the Value of Predators, 1900–1972," *Environmental Review* 7, no. 1 (1983): 54–70. Lisa Mighetto has studied the efforts of humanitarians to protect wild animals in *Wild Animals and American Environmental Ethics* (1991) and "Wildlife Protection and the New Humanitarianism," *Environmental Review* 12, no. 1 (1988): 37–49.

The 1920s and 1930s were critical decades in the intellectual formation of the modern wilderness movement. A ground breaking study on this subject is Paul S. Sutter's *Driven Wild: How the Fight Against Automobiles Launched the Modern Wilderness Movement* (2002). Sutter studies the lives of several of the founders of the Wilderness Society and argues that they favored preservation of the wilderness as an alternative to industrialization and modern ideas of leisure embodied in the growing use of automobiles and road building. Also helpful is Craig W. Allin, *The Politics of Wilderness Preservation* (1982) and Donald N. Baldwin, *The Quiet Revolution: Grass Roots of Today's Wilderness Preservation Movement* (1972). The automobile helped give rise to an anti-billboard, beautification movement in the 1920s. See Catherine Gudis, *Buyways: Billboards, Automobiles, and the American Landscape* (2004).

Chapter Three

There have been several general histories written of the post-1945 environmental movement. The starting place for any student of this period is Samuel P. Hays, *Beauty, Health, and Permanence: Environmental Politics in the United States, 1955–1985* (1987) and his "From Conservation to Environment: Environmental Politics in the United States Since World War II," *Environmental Review* 6, no. 2 (1982): 14–41. Hays demonstrated that suburban expansion, greater disposable wealth, education, and the rise of service industries encouraged particular elements of society to value physical and spiritual amenities whose monetary value is unclear, such as greater personal freedom and health, a protected ecosystem, and a pleasing environment that was scenic and free from pollution. These values gained popularity especially among young, well–educated white Americans who did not share their parents' concern with economic growth and technological advancement. When searching for solutions to the harmful effects of modern society such as pollution, these new environmentalists argued for a return to a simpler lifestyle, local amenities, and community power.

Hays' thesis has been challenged by Robert Gottlieb in *Forcing the Spring: The Transformation of the American Environmental Movement* (1993), one of the few scholars who traces environmentalism's lineage back to urban and industrial reformers. Gottlieb argued that historians have placed too much emphasis on conservationists, such as Gifford Pinchot, and wilderness organizations that followed the lineage of John Muir and have ignored those whose concentration was on urban and industrial issues. People who focused on occupation health issues for example have been slighted in favor of an exclusive emphasis on organizations such as the Sierra Club and Audubon Society. Gottlieb found a more diverse array of sources for the modern environmental movement. He sees the environmental movement as a "response to the urban and industrial changes" that has influenced society since the 1890s. Thus multiple responses to industrialization make for a broad based movement that has gender, class, and racial components. See also Robert Gottlieb, "Reconstructing Environmentalism: Complex Movements, Diverse Roots," *Environmental History Review* 17, no. 4 (1993): 1–19. In an excellent study, Adam Rome argues that suburbanization was a key ingredient in the rise of the environmental movement in the 1960s. In fact, Rome contends that a reaction against the environmental consequences of sprawl was a catalyst for the movement. See *The Bulldozer in the Countryside: Suburban sprawl and the Rise of American Environmentalism* (2001). Several other studies are also very useful. See Hal K. Rothman, *The Greening of a Nation? Environmentalism in the United States since 1945* (1998). Rothman has particularly strong sections on the Dinosaur National Monument controversy and the Wise Use Movement. Kirkpatrick Sale's *The Green Revolution: The American Environmental Movement, 1962–1992* (1993) picks up the story with Rachel Carson's publication of *Silent Spring* and does a nice job tracing the evolution of the movement particularly through the eyes of the major organizations in the movement. See also Samuel P. Hays, *A History of Environmental Politics Since 1945* (2000); Hays "Environmental Political Culture and Environmental Political Development: An Analysis of Legislative Voting 1971–1989," *Environmental History Review* 16, no. 2 (1992): 1–22; Victor B. Scheffer, *The Shaping of Environmentalism in America* (1991); and Marc Mowrey and Tim Redmond, *Not In Our Backyard: The People and Events That Shaped America's*

Modern Environmental Movement (1993). Adam Rome has produced a highly influential article that connects the environmental movement to intellectual and social currents in the 1960s in "'Give Earth a Chance': The Environmental Movement and the Sixties," *The Journal of American History* 90, no. 2 (September 2003): 525–54. See also Riley E. Dunlap and Angela G. Mertig, *American Environmentalism: The U.S. Environmental Movement, 1970–1990* (1992) and Donald Fleming, "Roots of the New Conservation Movement," in *Perspectives in American History,* Donald Fleming and Bernard Bailyn, ed. (1972).

Air pollution since 1945 has been the focus of Scott Hamilton Dewey, *Don't Breathe the Air: Air Pollution and U.S. Environmental Politics, 1945–1970* (2000), Dewey demonstrates the critical role of city efforts to come to grips with air pollution in their regions. When the problem crossed political boundaries, cities had to appeal to state and federal authority for help. This helped lead to the growing role of the federal government in what had been considered a local problem. On the Donora disaster see Lynne Page Snyder, "The Death-Dealing Smog Over Donora, Pennsylvania: Industrial Air Pollution, Public Health Policy, and the Politics of Expertise, 1948–1949," *Environmental History Review* 18, no. 1 (1994): 117–139. James E. Drier and Edmund Ursin studied the experience of California with smog in the postwar period in *Pollution and Policy: A Case Essay on California and Federal Experience with Motor Vehicle Air Pollution, 1940–1975* (1977). Pittsburgh's postwar smoke control movement has been analyzed by Sherie R. Mershon and Joel A. Tarr, "Strategies for Clean Air: The Pittsburgh and Allegheny County Smoke Control Movements, 1940–1960," in *Devastation and Renewal: An Environmental History of Pittsburgh and Its Region,* Joel Tarr, ed. (2003). See also Richard H. K. Vietor, *Environmental Politics and the Coal Coalition* (1980). For a conservative interpretation of the pollution issue see Indur Goklany, *Clearing the Air: The Real Story of the War on Air Pollution* (1999).

The Dinosaur campaign has been superbly recounted by Mark Harvey. His *A Symbol of Wilderness: Echo Park and the American Conservation Movement* (1994) demonstrates the profound influence this controversy had on the rising power of the conservation movement. The political implications of the Echo Park story are particularly important for water politics and the environmental movement. A book that covers the Echo Park, Glen Canyon, and Grand Canyon episodes is Russell Martin, *A Story that Stands Like a Dam: Glen Canyon and the Struggle for the Soul of the West* (1989). See also Jared Farmer, *Glen Canyon Dammed: Inventing Lake Powell and the Canyon Country* (1999). The history of Howard Zahniser's campaign for the Wilderness Act has been concisely recounted in Dennis Roth's "The National Forests and the Campaign for Wilderness Legislation," *Journal of Forest History* 28, no. 3 (July 1984): 112–125. Zahniser's life is the subject of a new book by Mark Harvey. See Mark Harvey, *Wilderness Forever: Howard Zahniser and the Path to the Wilderness Act* (2005). The Sierra Club's victory in the fight for the Grand Canyon has been taken for granted by scholars. Byron E. Pearson argues that environmental organizations have exaggerated their influence in *Still the Wild River Runs: Congress, the Sierra Club, and the Fight to Save Grand Canyon* (2002). The role of David Brower in these dam fights and the environmental movement in general has been the subject of Bill Devall's essay "David Brower," *Environmental Review* 9, no. 3 (1985): 238–53. Tim Palmer has written a history of efforts to save wild rivers from dam building. See *Endangered Rivers and the Conservation Movement* (1986). One of the great enemies of environmentalists was Congressman Wayne Aspinall. His career, especially the water battles have been well covered by Steven C. Schulte, *Wayne Aspinall and the Shaping of the American West* (2002) and Stephen C. Sturgeon, *The Politics of Western Water: The Congressional Career of Wayne Aspinall* (2002). For Aspinall's counterpart in the Senate, see Richard Allan Baker, *Conservation Politics: The Senate Career of Clinton P. Anderson* (1985). A critical Republican supporter of the environment in this period was John Saylor. See Thomas G. Smith, *Green Republican: John Saylor and the Preservation of America's Wilderness* (2006).

There have been other studies of specific environmental controversies. The long effort to provide national protection to the Indiana Dunes has been analyzed in Kay Franklin and Norma

Schaeffer, *Duel for the Dunes: Land Use Conflict on the Shores of Lake Michigan* (1983) and J. Ronald Engel, *Sacred Sands: The Struggle for Community in the Indiana Dunes* (1983). The important legal role of the Storm King hydroelectric project in New York to the birth of environmentalism has been told by Allan R. Talbot, *Power Along the Hudson: The Storm King Case and the Birth of Environmentalism* (1972). The management of water and the efforts to save water for the Florida Everglades is covered by Nelson Manfred Blake, *Land Into Water—Water Into Land: A History of Water Management in Florida* (1980).

The executive branch's role in conservation issues has been covered by Elmo Richardson, *Dams, Parks, and Politics: Resource Development & Preservation in the Truman-Eisenhower Era* (1973). Dwight Eisenhower's infamous Secretary of Interior, Douglas McKay has been analyzed by Elmo Richardson, "The Interior Secretary as Conservation Villain: The Notorious Case of Douglas 'Giveaway' McKay," *Pacific Historical Review* 41, no. 3 (1972): 333–45.

The Forest Services' role in over cutting since World War II has been analyzed by Paul W. Hirt, *A Conspiracy of Optimism: Management of the National Forests Since World War Two* (1994). The over cutting in the Alaska rainforests has been covered by Kathie Durbin, *Tongass: Pulp Politics and the Fight for the Alaskan Rain Forest* (1999).

The fallout controversy has been analyzed in Allan M. Winkler, *Life Under Cloud: American Anxiety About the Atom* (1993). See also Philip L. Fradkin, *Fallout: An American Nuclear Tragedy* (1989). On the important role of women in this movement see Amy Swerdlow, *Women Strike for Peace: Traditional Motherhood and Radical Politics in the 1960s* (1993).

Rachel Carson and the storm of protest surrounding her publication of *Silent Spring* has been the subject of a number of books. The best source is Linda Lear, *Rachel Carson: Witness for Nature* (1997). Lear's is a highly detailed and insightful analysis of Carson's life and her contributions to the environmental movement. Other works of value are: Paul Brooks, *The House of Life: Rachel Carson at Work* (1972); Carol B. Gartner, *Rachel Carson* (1983);

Frank Graham, Jr., *Since Silent Spring* (1970); Mary A. McCay, *Rachel Carson* (1993). Vera Norwood has an excellent article on Carson in *Made From This Earth: American Women and Nature* (1993). A useful article on the way gender was used in the controversy is Maril Hazlett, "'Woman vs. Man vs. Bugs': Gender and Popular Ecology in Early Reactions to Silent Spring," *Environmental History* 9, no. 4 (October 2004): 701–725. Ralph H. Lutts demonstrated the important influence of the atomic fallout controversy on the reception *Silent Spring* received. See "Chemical Fallout: Rachel Carson's *Silent Spring*, Radioactive Fallout, and the Environmental Movement," *Environmental Review* 9, no. 3 (Fall 1985): 210–225. Thomas R. Dunlap's *DDT: Scientists, Citizens, and Public Policy* (1981) is an excellent study that puts Carson's contribution in the context of the larger controversy over this pesticide. Early regulation of pesticides has been analyzed by James Whorton, *Before Silent Spring: Pesticides and Public Health in Pre–DDT America* (1974). The influence of DDT on the bald eagle population has been chronicled by Bruce E. Beans in *Eagle's Plume: The Struggle to Preserve the Life and Haunts of America's Bald Eagle* (1996).

Scholars have turned their attention to the critical role of women in the environmental and conservation movements. For short biographies on many activists see Mary Joy Breton, *Women Pioneers for the Environment* (1998). Hazel Wolf's activism has been chronicled in Susan Starbuck, *Hazel Wolf: Fighting the Establishment* (2002). Women active in preserving wild lands are covered by Anne LaBastille, *Women and Wilderness* (1980). Marjory Stoneman Douglas' fight to save the Florida Everglades has been studied by Jack E. Davis in "Green Awakening: Social Activism and the Evolution of Marjory Stoneman Douglas's Environmental Consciousness," *Florida Historical Quarterly* 80 (Summer 2001): 43–77 and "'Conservation Is Now a Dead Word': Marjory Stoneman Douglas and the Transformation of American Environmentalism," *Environmental History* 8, no. 1 (January 2003): 53–76.

Conservation politics and legislation during the Johnson administration has been well reviewed in Martin V. Melosi, "Lyndon Johnson and Environmental Policy," in *The Johnson Years Volume Two: Vietnam, the Environment, and Science,* Robert A. Divine, ed.

(1987), Lady Bird Johnson's critical influence on the Johnson agenda can been found in Lewis L. Gould, *Lady Bird Johnson and the Environment* (1988). The role of Stewart and Morris Udall in establishing environmentalism as a national issue has been studied by Henry B. Sirgo, *Establishment of Environmentalism on the U.S. Political Agenda in the Second Half of the Twentieth Century—The Brothers Udall* (2004). Morris Udall also has a biography by Donald W. Carson and James W. Johnson, *Mo: The Life and Times of Morris K. Udall* (2001). The changing nature of federal lands policy since the 1960s has been studied by Charles Davis, ed., *Western Public Lands and Environmental Politics* (2001).

Water pollution issues have been the subject of several studies. For a case study at the state level that shows that much of the impetus for reform came from the grassroots see Richard W. Judd, "The Coming of the Clean Waters Acts in Maine, 1941–1961," *Environmental History Review* 14, no. 3 (1990): 51–73. William Ashworth, *The Late, Great Lakes: An Environmental History* (1986) does a particularly effective job of describing the "death" of Lake Erie. William McGucken in *Biodegradable: Detergents and the Environment* (1991), tells the story of the controversy regarding washing detergents and pollution. On this topic see also Terence Kehoe, *Cleaning Up the Great Lakes: From Cooperation to Confrontation* (1997) and "Merchants of Pollution?: The Soap and Detergent Industry and the Fight to Restore Great Lakes Water Quality, 1965–1972," *Environmental History Review* 16, no. 3 (Fall 1992): 21–46. McGucken also tells the tale of the effort to clean up Lake Erie in *Lake Erie Rehabilitated: Controlling Cultural Eutrophication, 1960s–1990s* (2000). Howard R. Ernst chronicles the efforts to rehabilitate the Chesapeake Bay in *Chesapeake Bay Blues: Science, Politics, and the Struggle to Save the Bay* (2003). The Santa Barbara blowout story has been covered in two studies: Robert Easton, *Black Tide: The Santa Barbara Oil Spill and Its Consequences* (1972) and Carol E. Steinhart and John S. Steinhart, *Blowout: A Case Study of the Santa Barbara Oil Spill* (1972).

There is no history of Earth Day other than what is provided in general histories of the era. However, Bill Christofferson has produced a biography of its creator, Gaylord Nelson, in *The Man From Clear Lake: Earth Day Founder Senator Gaylord Nelson*

(2004). Related to Nelson is a superb study of the development of environmentalism in the important state of Wisconsin in the 1960s. See Thomas R. Huffman, *Protectors of the Land and Water: Environmentalism in Wisconsin, 1961–1968* (1994) and "Defining the Origins of Environmentalism in Wisconsin: A Study in Politics and Culture," *Environmental History Review* 16, no. 3 (1992): 47–69. Dave Dempsey completed a similar but more broadly based study for Michigan. See *Ruin and Recovery: Michigan's Rise as a Conservation Leader* (2001). Oregon and Maine's environmentalism has been studied by Richard W. Judd and Christopher S. Beach, *Natural States: The Environmental Imagination in Maine, Oregon, and the Nation* (2003).

The curious role of Richard Nixon in the environmental movement has left many historians speculating as to his motives. J. Brooks Flippen has produced an excellent study of the Nixon environmental record. He finds that Nixon's support of environmental causes was shallow—he recognized an important political issue and sought to moderate its impact—but important in allowing the passage of early laws. See *Nixon and the Environment* (2000). On the Johnson and Nixon era SST conflict see Mel Horwitch, *Clipped Wings: The American SST Conflict* (1982).

The passage and analysis of the effectiveness of the National Environmental Policy Act (NEPA) is well documented in Matthew J. Lindstrom & Zachary A. Smith, *The National Environmental Policy Act: Judicial Misconstruction, Legislative Indifference, & Executive Neglect* (2001). There is also useful history of the act in Ray Clark and Larry Canter, ed., *Environmental Policy and NEPA: Past, Present, and Future* (1997). On the twenty-fifth anniversary of Earth Day and NEPA, Robert Gottlieb did an assessment. See "Beyond NEPA and Earth Day: Reconstructing the Past and Envisioning a Future for Environmentalism," *Environmental History Review* 19, no. 4 (1995): 1–14. An earlier assessment of NEPA is Lettie McSpadden Wenner, "The Misuse and Abuse of NEPA," *Environmental Review* 7, no. 3 (1983): 229–254. The influence of the environmental movement on environmental law has recently been analyzed by Richard J. Lazarus, *The Making of Environmental Law* (2004).

The Endangered Species Act of 1973 is analyzed in Bonnie B. Burgess, *Fate of the Wild: The Endangered Species Act and the Future of Biodiversity* (2001); Jason F. Shogren, *Private Property and the Endangered Species Act: Saving Habitats, Protecting Homes* (1998); and Brian Czech and Paul R. Krausman, *The Endangered Species Act : History, Conservation Biology, and Public Policy* (2001). A popular history of the death and life of the wolf is Bruce Hampton, *The Great American Wolf* (1997).

Chapter Four

Unsurprisingly, the recent history of the environmental movement has not been studied closely by historians. Most of the accounts of the period come from scholars in other fields, activists, and journalists. A useful account of the period after Earth Day is Mark Dowie, *Losing Ground: American Environmentalism at the Close of the Twentieth Century* (1995). A study of the religious aspects of environmentalism is Thomas R. Dunlap, *Faith in Nature: Environmentalism as Religious Quest* (2004).

The antinuclear movement has been written about extensively. For a general overview of the struggle that attributes excessive importance to the movement see Jerome Price, *The Antinuclear Movement* (1982); Steven L. Del Sesto, *Science, Politics, and Controversy: Civilian Nuclear Power in the United States, 1946–1974* (1979); and Gerald H. Clarfield and William Wiecek, *Nuclear America: Military and Civilian Nuclear Power in the United States, 1940–1980* (1984). A number of studies have been done on individual nuclear power plants. A number chronicle futile efforts by activists. The Seabrook controversy has been studied by Henry F. Bedford, *Seabrook Station: Citizen Politics and Nuclear Power* (1990). The Shoreham plant on Long Island has been studied by David P. McCaffrey, *The Politics of Nuclear Power: A History of the Shoreham Nuclear Power Plant* (1991) and Joan Aron, *Licensed to Kill? The Nuclear Regulatory Commission and the Shoreham Power Plant* (1997). Daniel Pope concluded that in the Pacific Northwest the antinuclear movement had little influence. See "Antinuclear Activism in the Pacific Northwest: WPPSS and

Its Enemies" in *The Atomic West,* Bruce Hevly and John M. Findlay, eds. (1998). The Clamshell Alliance and Abalone Alliance have been studied by Barbara Epstein, *Political Protest and Cultural Revolution: Nonviolent Direct Action in the 1970s and 1980s* (1991). As might be expected of these episodes, the authors concluded that the regulatory system was badly flawed, helped lead the industry into catastrophe, and did not serve opponents well. Stories of more successful opposition movements paint a less negative portrait of the regulatory process. See Dorothy Nelkin, *Nuclear Power and Its Critics: The Cayuga Lake Controversy* (1971) and Daniel Pope, "'We Can Wait. We Should Wait.' Eugene's Nuclear Power Controversy, 1968–1979," *Pacific Historical Review* 59, no. 3 (1990): 349–73. Thomas Wellock's study of opposition to nuclear power in California demonstrates the important influence activists had at the state level and how they ultimately undermined the authority of the Nuclear Regulatory Commission. See Thomas Raymond Wellock, *Critical Masses: Opposition to Nuclear Power in California, 1958–1978* (1998). A number of scholars have studied the movement from an international comparative perspective. See James Jasper, *Nuclear Politics: Energy and the State in the United States, Sweden, and France* (1990); John L. Campbell, *Collapse of an Industry: Nuclear Power and the Contradictions of U.S. Policy* (1988); and Christian Joppke, *Mobilizing Against Nuclear Energy: A Comparison of Germany and the United States* (1993). The Three Mile Island accident has been studied well by J. Samuel Walker, *Three Mile Island: A Nuclear Crisis in Historical Perspective* (2004). Walker has also produced a study that covers the thermal pollution issue and other issues of the 1960s and 1970s in *Containing the Atom: Nuclear Regulation in a Changing Environment, 1963–1971* (1992). The story of the disposal of nuclear wastes in Nevada has been told by Gerald Jacob, *Site Unseen: The Politics of Siting a Nuclear Waste Repository* (1990). Thomas V. Peterson has written a popular account of a case study of opposition to a nuclear waste site in New York. See *Linked Arms: A Rural Community Resists Nuclear Waste* (2002).

Toxic wastes have been studied from a number of angles. No historian has taken a crack at the Love Canal episode, but sociologist Adeline Gordon Levine did chronicle the story in *Love Canal: Science, Politics, and People* (1982), as did Allan Mazur in *A Hazardous Inquiry: The Rashomon Effect at Love Canal* (1998). Levine's and Mazur's books can also be supplemented with activist Lois Gibbs's account, *Love Canal: My Story* (1981). In the rural South, activist and historian Suzanne Marshall studied Appalachian environmentalism in *"Lord, We're Just Trying to Save Your Water": Environmental Activism and Dissent in the Appalachian South* (2002). The passage and fate of Superfund legislation has been told by Harold C. Barnett in *Toxic Debts and the Superfund Dilemma* (1994) and John A. Hird, *Superfund: The Political Economy of Environmental Risk* (1994).

The acid rain controversy has been studied by Robert Lovely in "Wisconsin's Acid Rain Battle: Science, Communication, and Public Policy, 1979–1989," *Environmental History Review* 14, no. 3 (1990): 21–48. The campaign for bottle bills and study of a failed Washington, DC, initiative can be found in Joy A. Clay's "The D.C. Bottle Bill Initiative: A Casualty of the Reagan Era," *Environmental Review* 13, no. 2 (1989): 17–31. Jeffrey K. Stine has studied the politics of canal building in *Mixing the Waters: Environment, Politics, and the Building of the Tennessee-Tombigbee Waterway* (1993) and "Environmental Politics in the American South: The Fight Over the Tennessee-Tombigbee Waterway," *Environmental History Review* 15, no. 1 (1991): 1–24. The story of the Snail Darter and the Tellico Dam has been studied by William Bruce Wheeler and Michael J. McDonald in *TVA and the Tellico Dam, 1936–1979: A Bureaucratic Crisis in Post-Industrial America* (1986).

Although no one has written a book on Third Wave Environmentalism, a number of books devote significant sections to it. See Mark Dowie, *Losing Ground: American Environmentalism at the Close of the Twentieth Century* (1995); Philip Shabecoff, *A Fierce Green Fire: The American Environmental Movement* (1993); and Robert Gottlieb, *Forcing the Spring: The Transformation of the Environmental Movement* (1993).

Radical movements have elicited a great deal of attention. A general overview of radical movements can be found in Carolyn Merchant, *Radical Ecology: The Search for a Livable World*

(1992) and David Pepper, *Modern Environmentalism: An Introduction* (1996). Greenpeace's story has been told by Jim Bohlen, *Making Waves: The Origins and Future of Greenpeace* (2001). Earth First! has been superbly chronicled by Susan Zakin, *Coyotes and Town Dogs: Earth First! and the Environmental Movement* (1993) and Christopher Manes, *Green Rage: Radical Environmentalism and the Unmaking of Civilization* (1990). See also Dave Foreman, *Confessions of an Eco-Warrior* (1991) and Rik Scarce, *Eco-Warriors: Understanding the Radical Environmental Movement* (1990). Judi Bari's activism has been studied in a negative biography by Kate Coleman in *The Secret Wars of Judi Bari: A Car Bomb, the Fight for the Redwoods, and the End of Earth First!* (2005). Coleman's book, however, has been heavily criticized for inaccuracies and unfounded conclusions. See http://www.colemanhoax.com/ for a list of errors. The Deep Ecology movement has been studied by Bill Devall and George Sessions in *Deep Ecology: Living as if Nature Mattered* (1985). See also Sessions' article "The Deep Ecology Movement: A Review," *Environmental Review* 11, no. 2 (1987): 105–25. Jeffrey Ellis has written about the essentialism of the radical environmental movement in "On the Search for a Root Cause: Essentialist Tendencies in Environmentalist Discourse," *Uncommon Ground: Rethinking the Human Place in Nature,* ed. William Cronon (1995). Raymond Dominick has completed a comparative analysis of the rise of the Greens. See "The Roots of the Green Movement in the United States and West Germany," *Environmental Review* 12, no. 3 (1988): 1–30. Ecoterrorism has been studied recently by Douglas Lang in *Ecoterrorism* (2004).

Battles over the saving of Redwoods and old growth forests have been documented by David Harris, *The Last Stand: The War Between Wall Street and Main Street over California's Ancient Redwoods* (1995). In the Pacific Northwest see Kathie Durbin, *Tree Huggers: Victory, Defeat, & Renewal in the Northwest Ancient Forest Campaign* (1996). The spotted owl story has been marvelously recounted in William Dietrich, *The Final Forest: The Battle for the Last Great Trees of the Pacific Northwest* (1992). A more up-to-date study is Benjamin B. Stout, *The Northern Spotted Owl: An Oregon View* (2003). On the campaign to save wilderness in Alaska, see Daniel Nelson, *Northern Landscapes: The Struggle for Wilderness Alaska* (2004).

There are a number of studies on environmental controversies in Alaska. Peter A. Coates has studied the fight over the Alaska pipeline in *The Trans-Alaska Pipeline Controversy: Technology, Conservation and the Frontier* (1991). The Exxon Valdez disaster has been studied by Art Davidson in *In the Wake of the Exxon Valdez: The Devastating Impact of the Alaska Oil Spill* (1990) and John Keeble, *Out of the Channel: The Exxon Valdez Oil Spill in Prince William Sound* (1991).

Traditionally, labor and environmentalism have been seen as at odds with each other. See for example Chad Montrie, "Expedient Environmentalism: Opposition to Coal Surface Mining in Appalachia and the United Mine Workers of America, 1945–1977," *Environmental History* 5, no. 1 (January 2000): 75–98. However, researchers have studied a number of cases where labor and environmental activists allied. See Brian K. Obach, *Labor and the Environmental Movement: The Quest for Common Ground* (2004); Richard Kazis and Richard L. Grossman, *Fear at Work: Job Blackmail, Labor, and the Environment* (1982); Timothy J. Minchin, *Forging a Common Bond: Labor and Environmental Activism During the BASF Lockout* (2003); Scott Dewey, "Working For the Environment: Organized Labor and the Origins of Environmentalism in the United States, 1948–1970," *Environmental History* 3, no. 1 (January 1998): 45–63; Robert Gordon, "'Shell No!': OCAW and the Labor-Environmental Alliance," *Environmental History* 3, no. 4 (October 1998): 460–87; and Richard White, "'Are You an Environmentalist or Do You Work For a Living?': Work and Nature," in *Uncommon Ground: Toward Reinventing Nature,* William Cronon, ed. (1995). Heinrich Siegmann completed a comparative study of West German and American environmental-labor relations in *The Conflicts Between Labor and Environmentalism in the Federal Republic of Germany and the United States* (1985).

The literature on the Environmental Justice Movement is quite large. A good place to start is with Michael Egan's review essay "Subaltern Environmentalism in the United States: A Historiographic Review," *Environment and History* 8, no. 1 (2002): 21–41 and the seminal work in the field Robert D. Bullard's *Dumping in Dixie: Race, Class, and Environmental Quality* (1990). Bullard has also edited two anthologies on the topic. See *Confronting Environmental Racism: Voices From the Grassroots* (1993) and *Unequal Protection: Environmental Justice and Communities of Color* (1994). Martin Melosi produced essays that question the extent of environmental injustice in America and the claim by some of its adherents that it has little in common with the environmental movement. See his article "Environmental Justice, Political Agenda Setting, and the Myths of History," in *Environmental Politics and Policy, 1960s–1990s,* Otis L. Graham, Jr., ed (2000) and "Equity, Eco-Racism and Environmental History," *Environmental History* Review 19, no. 3 (1995): 1–16. In a similar vein, Andrew Hurley argues that the siting of toxic wastes in minority neighborhoods had less to do with environmental racism and more to do with the dynamics of the real estate market. See *Environmental Inequalities: Class, Race, and Industrial Pollution in Gary, Indiana, 1945–1980* (1995) and "The Social Biases of Environmental Change in Gary, Indiana," *Environmental Review* 12, no. 4 (1988): 1–19. The importance of the Warren County protests has been analyzed by Eileen Maura McGurty, "From NIMBY to Civil Rights: The Origins of the Environmental Justice Movement," *Environmental History* 2, no. 3 (July 1997): 301–23. Many studies have tended to focus on urban and black communities. Laura Pulido breaks this mold in *Environmentalism and Economic Justice: Two Chicano Struggles in the Southwest* (1996). This book contains an account of the United Farm Workers efforts to limit farm workers' exposure to DDT. An excellent article on the reluctance of mainstream groups to support UFW strikes is Robert Gordon, "Poisons in the Fields: The United Farm Workers, Pesticides, and Environmental Politics," *Pacific Historical Review* 68, no. 1 (1999): 51–77. The effort of farmers and working-class whites to stop surface coal mining has been well studied in Chad Montrie's, *To Save the Land and People: A History of Opposition to Surface Coal Mining in Appalachia* (2003). The environmental justice movement in Louisiana's "cancer alley" on the Mississippi River has been analyzed by Barbara L. Allen, *Uneasy Alchemy: Citizens and Experts in Louisiana's Chemical Corridor Disputes* (2003). Other useful works include Andrew Szasz, *Ecopopulism: Toxic Waste and the Movement for Environmental Justice* (1994); David E. Camacho, ed., *Environmental Injustices, Political Struggles: Race, Class, and the Environment* (1998); Daniel Faber, ed., *The Struggle for Ecological Democracy: Environmental Justice Movements in the United States* (1998); Kristin Shrader-Frechette, *Environmental Justice: Creating Equality, Reclaiming Democracy* (2002); Edwardo Lao Rhodes, *Environmental Justice in America: A New Paradigm* (2003); Jim Schwab, *Deeper Shades of Green: The Rise of Blue-Collar and Minority Environmentalism in America* (1994); Ellen Stroud, "Troubled Waters in Ecotopia: Environmental Racism in Portland, Oregon," *Radical History Review* 74 (1999): 65–95; and Luke W. Cole and Sheila R. Foster, *From the Ground Up: Environmental Racism and the Rise of the Environmental Justice Movement* (2001).

As an introduction to ecofeminism, it is best to start with Carolyn Merchant, *Earthcare: Women and the Environment* (1996). In it, Merchant lays out the several schools of ecofeminism, differentiating between liberal, Marxist, cultural, and socialist forms. Also helpful is Karen J. Warren, *Ecofeminist Philosophy: A Western Perspective on What It Is and Why It Matters* (2000); Greta Gaard, *Ecological Politics: Ecofeminists and the Greens* (1998); and Michael E. Zimmerman, *Contesting Earth's Future: Radical Ecology and Postmodernity* (1994).

A number of studies have been completed on anti-environmental movements. R. McGreggor Cawley has studied the Sagebrush Rebellion in *Federal Land, Western Anger: The Sagebrush Rebellion and Environmental Politics* (1993), as has C. Brant Short, *Ronald Reagan and the Public Lands: America's Conservation Debate* (1989). The Wise-Use Movement has had several good studies done on it. David Helvarg's highly readable but slanted *The War Against the Greens: The "Wise-Use" Movement, the New Right, and Anti-Environmental Violence* (1994) has been reissued in 2004 with an updated text. It details the more sinister side of the movement and the acts of violence that have been carried out in its name. There are three useful anthologies that are more balanced in their treatment of the movement. Benjamin Heber Johnson traces anti-environmentalism at the turn of the century in his study of class divisions in the town of Ely, Minnesota near Superior National Forest. He finds that the town elite used conservation in ways that led to resentment by lower classes, resentment that continues to the present. See "Conservation, Subsistence, and Class at the Birth of Superior National Forest": *Environmental History* 4, no. 1 (January 1999): 80–99. See John D. Echeverria and Raymond Booth Eby, *Let the People Judge: Wise Use and the Private Property Rights Movement* (1995); Philip D. Brick and R. McGreggor Cawley, eds., *A Wolf in the Garden: The Land Rights Movement and the New Environmental Debate* (1996); Judith Scherff, ed., *The Piracy of America: Profiteering in the Public Domain* (1999); and Phil Brick, "Determined Opposition: The Wise Use Movement Challenges Environmentalism," *Environment* 37, no. 8 (Oct. 1995): 16–20, 37–42. A more general study of anti-environmental activism can be found in Jacqueline Vaughn Switzer, *Green Backlash: The History and Politics of Environmental Opposition in the U.S.* (1997).

Information on Republicans for Environmental Protection can be found on their website and Martha Marks, "Greening the Elephant: Republicans for Environmental Protection Need Not Be an Oxymoron," 13 May 2003, *Grist Magazine: A Becon in the Smog,* http://www.grist.org/comments/soapbox/2003/05/13/greening/, 21 July 2006.

The United State's role in international environmental treaties has a number of important studies. The starting point is Lynton Keith Caldwell, *International Environmental Policy,* 3rd ed. (1996). Also useful is Ken Conca and Geoffrey Dabelko, ed., *Green Planet Blues: Environmental Politics From Stockholm to Johannesburg,* 3rd ed. (2004). Individual studies have been done of the Earth Summit in Rio and the Kyoto Accords. See Ranee K. Panjabi, *The Earth Summit at Rio: Politics, Economics, and the Environment* (1997) and David G. Victor, *The Collapse of the Kyoto Protocol and the Struggle to Slow Global Warming* (2001).

INDEX

Abalone Alliance, 200–1
Abbey, Edward, 226
Acadia National Park, 116
Adams, John, 221
Addams, Jane, 69, 71
Adirondack State Park, 26
aesthetics
  blending with ecology, 126–27
  economic issues vs., 62–65
  efficiency vs., 40, 144–49
  equity vs., 157
  as feminine approach to environ-
    mental issues, 70
  as goal of preservationists, 5
  as goal of wildlife/wilderness
    preservation, 1, 5–6, 45, 157
  open-space fight and, 168
  postwar affluence and, 7
  reality vs., 115
  wilderness movement and, 121, 122
affluence, 7, 9–10, 81, 129, 138–39
agriculture
  balance of field and forest, 19, 21–
    22
  defense of Forest Service, 86
  grazing rights, 40, 64, 98, 123, 154
  irrigation management programs,
    35, 41–42, 90–91, 98

New Deal policies regarding, 99,
    101, 104–8
use of pesticides, 9, 138, 157, 161–
    65, 169, 177–79, 248
air pollution
  agreements with Canada regarding,
    237
  federal legislation regarding, 139,
    170, 179, 181
  government controls of, 111–13
  postwar issues, 138–43
  women's fight against, 166–67
Air Pollution Control District
  (APCD), 140
Air Quality Act (1967), 170
Alaska, 13, 43–44, 94, 98, 218, 241
Alaska National Interest Land Act,
    218
Albright, Horace, 85, 101
algae blooms, 173
Alpine Club of Williamstown,
    Massachusetts, 50
American Forestry Association, 65
American Game Protection Associa-
    tion (AGPA), 88
American Ornithologists Union, 53
American Planning and Civic
    Association, 96

aminotriazole scare, 162
Anderson, Harold, 121
animal rights groups, 208, 231
anthropocentric motivations, 5–6, 56, 118–19, 224, 231–32
anticapitalist attitudes, 137, 138, 174–75, 229
anticorporate attitudes
  alienation of GOP by, 10, 192
  antinuclear movement and, 199–200
  of appropriate-technology movement, 203
  Earth Day 1970 and, 176–77
  of sixties activists, 175, 183
  Third Wave environmentalism and, 223
  youth activism, 138–39
anti-environmentalism, 10, 219, 238–41
antifeather campaign, 52–53, 210, 211
antigun lobby, 208
antinuclear movement, 190–91, 197–202
Antiquities Act (1906), 38
Anti-Stream Pollution Act (PA), 110
antitoxics movement, 213–17
antiwar activists, 4, 174–75. See also counterculture; New Left
appropriate-technology movement, 192, 202–4
Arctic National Wildlife Refuge, 241
Arctic Village (Marshall), 120
Army Corps of Engineers, 111, 146, 147, 157, 212
Arnold, Ron, 239–40
Aspinall, Wayne, 153–54
Association of Civilian Conservation Corps Alumni, 102
Atomic Energy Commission, 145, 158, 176, 198
atomic weapons, 135, 136, 137, 138, 157–58, 201–2. See also antinuclear movement
Audubon Society

antifeather campaign and, 52–53
approach to conservation, 72
defense of Carson, 177–78
Earth Day 1970 and, 177–78
fight for northern spotted owl, 206–8
as member of Group of Ten, 218
membership of, 178, 247
on open space, 168
Republican domination of, 96
response to grassroots environmentalists, 216
Wilderness Act and, 153
automobiles
  abuse of environment and, 7, 9, 81, 85, 94
  access to hunting and, 87
  call for energy efficiency in, 196
  camping craze and, 81, 114–15, 129, 150
  emissions control, 139, 140–41, 181
  wilderness movement and, 122

Baird, Spencer, 20
Baker, Howard, 205
Ballinger, Richard, 13–15, 43–45
Ballinger-Pinchot controversy, 13–15, 43–44
Balogh, Brian, 39
Bari, Judi, 229–30
Bay of Pigs, 159
Bennett, Hugh Hammond, 105–7
Benson, Ezra Taft, 164
Bentham, Jeremy, 30, 39
Berry, Phillip, 195
biocentric worldview, 6, 56, 193, 224, 228
Biodiversity Convention, 237, 238
Black Mesa Defense Fund, 226
Blue/Green Alliance, 246
Bookchin, Murray, 224, 225, 228
Boone and Crockett Club, 40, 47–48
Boston Fens, 32
Boundary Waters Canoe Area, 119–20

Bowditch, Henry Ingersol, 31
Boy Scouts, 49
Bradley, Harold, 150
Bradley, Richard, 151
Brand, Stewart, 203
Brandis, Dietrich, 24, 35
Bravo test, 158
Bridge Canyon, 146, 154
Bridger-Teton National Forest, 227
Broome, Harvey, 121
Broward, Napoleon Bonaparte, 209–10
Brower, David, 147, 148–49, 150, 151, 155, 178
Brown, Harrison, 136, 137, 171, 172, 197
Brown, Jerry, 203
Bureau of Land Management, 219, 220
Bureau of Reclamation, 42, 91–92, 143–51, 154–57
Bureau of Smoke Control (BSC), 142
Bureau of Soils, 106
Burford, Robert, 219
Burroughs, John, 47–48
Bush, George H. W., 193, 237–38
Bush, George W., 241, 242, 246

Caldwell, Lynton, 179
California Motor Vehicle Pollution Act (CA, 1960), 141
Calvert Cliffs nuclear plant, 198
camping craze, 81, 114–15, 129, 150
Cannon, Joe, 38, 58
Canyonlands Park (Utah), 170
capitalism, 4–5, 34, 138, 139, 174–75, 229
Carhart, Arthur, 117–18, 119
Carson, Rachel, 71, 138, 161–66, 177, 217, 248
Carter, Jimmie, 192, 203, 205, 215, 217–18
Carter administration, 180
Cather, Willa, 49
CCC, 100–102, 115–16, 129

Center for Health, Environment, and Justice. See Citizen's Clearinghouse for Hazardous Waste
Center for the Defense of Free Enterprise (CDFE), 239–40
Central Arizona Project, 156
Central Park, New York City, 32–33
CEQ, 180, 218
Chadsey, Mildred, 70
Chadwick, Edwin, 30, 32, 65, 67
Challenge of Man's Future, The (Brown), 136
Chapman, Oscar, 145, 146–47
Chavez, Cesar, 232
Chavis, Benjamin, 233
chemical industry, 157, 162–63, 164
chemical warfare, 202–3
Cheney, Dick, 240
Cherney, Darryl, 228, 229–30
Chernobyl nuclear accident (USSR), 201–2, 221
Chicago sewage treatment (IL), 110–11
Citizen's Clearinghouse for Hazardous Waste, 216, 234
Citizens for a Better Environment, 216
citizenship, 49–51
Civilian Conservation Corp (CCC), 100–102, 115–16, 129
civil rights movement, 4, 174–75, 233, 235
Clamshell Alliance, 200
class
    conservation movement and, 2–3, 4, 16
    environmental bridge-building and, 246
    environmental movement and, 4, 6, 7–8, 72, 193, 231–35, 248
    game laws and, 45–47, 48, 87–88
    irrigation management programs, 35, 41–42, 90–91, 98
    New Deal programs and, 81–82, 98–108, 191

parks system and, 32–34
preservation movement and, 73, 157
radical environmentalists and, 191–92
restriction of commons and, 27–29
sanitation issues and, 30, 31, 66–67, 69, 71–72
Warren County, North Carolina waste-dump and, 232–33
Clean Air Act (1963), 170
Clean Air Act (1970), 181, 237
"Clean Streams for Health and Happiness" campaign, 110
Clean Water Action, 216
Clements, Kendrick, 83, 93–94
Cleveland's Cuyahoga River fire (OH), 173
climbing clubs, 50
Clinton, Bill, 213, 235, 238, 242
Clinton administration, 180, 207, 213, 238
Club of Rome, 197
coal burning, 112–13
Coe, Ernest, 126–27, 211
Cold War, 9, 145, 157–58, 201
Coleman Company, 115
colonialism, 16–17, 23–24
Colorado Cliff Dwellings Association, 51
Colorado Environmental Rapist of the Year award, 176
Colorado Federation of Women's Clubs, 51
Colorado River, 91–93, 143–51, 154–57
Colorado River Compact, 92, 95, 96, 145, 148
Colorado River Storage Project (CRSP), 143–51
commercial growth, 7. See also consumerism
Committee for Nuclear Information, 158–59
Commoner, Barry, 159
commons, 18–21, 26–29, 165
communes, 174

Comprehensive Emergency Response, Compensation, and Liability Act, 217, 218, 221, 248
Comprehensive Everglades Restoration Act (2000), 213
Conference of Governors (1908), 43
conservation, definition of, 6, 44
conservation movement/conservationists
American vs. European, 16–18
approach of, 124, 128
centralization of, 34
characteristics of, 4–6, 57
conservative Republican policies and, 82–96
division over Hetch Hetchy Dam, 2, 60–65
Earth Day and, 177–78
eastern formulation/western application, 28
elitist image of, 2, 8, 16, 26–28, 80–81, 102, 107–8, 138
emergence of, 19, 23–24
environmentalism and, 7, 138, 191
estrangement from preservationists, 144
expansion of constituency, 3, 9, 81–82, 102
expansion of federal government and, 2–4, 8–9, 15, 19–21, 38–39, 106–7
fish restoration projects, 19–21
foundations of, 2–3
goals of, 1–2, 3, 4–5
grassroots beginnings of, 16, 18–29
Hoover's approach to, 93–94
international aspects of, 3, 7–8, 9, 16–17, 23–24, 29, 35–36, 48
loss of elitist control, 108
as means of reinforcing class and racial inequality, 27–29
nationalization of, 34–45
New Deal policies for, 3–4, 98–108
place in twentieth century politics, 13–15

practical economics of, 15–16
preservationism vs., 2, 60–65, 143–51, 157
racism and, 58–60
reinforcement of class and racial inequality, 26, 28–29
Republican approach to, 82–84, 93–96
shift in focus to environmentalism, 209, 210–11, 213
as source of job opportunities, 81–82, 84, 97, 99–101
transfer of initiative to Democrats, 102, 108
World War II as watershed of, 129
consumerism, 7, 81, 94, 114–15, 129, 174
Contract with America, 238
Coolidge, Calvin, 82
cooperative pragmatism, 182
corporate average fuel efficiency (CAFÉ) standards, 196
corporate détente, 223
Council of Conservationists, 147–49
Council on Environmental Quality (CEQ), 180, 218
counterculture
  antinuclear movement and, 199–200
  appropriate-technology movement and, 202–3
  Earth Day 1970 and, 174, 176
  Greenpeace and, 224
  radicalization of environmental movement, 190
Crater Lake National Park, 86
Critical Mass conference, 199
Crowell, John, 219
Cuban Missile Crisis, 159–60
Cumbler, John, 30
Cuyahoga River, 173

dams
  Bureau of Reclamation's plans for Colorado River, 143–51
  Colorado River Storage Project

(CRSP), 143–51
  Echo Park controversy and, 145–51, 157
  Glen Canyon dam, 151
  goal of, 35
  government control of water flow and, 20
  Hetch Hetchy Dam, 2, 45, 53, 60–65
  Hoover Dam, 91–93
  of Tennessee Valley Authority, 102–4, 204–6
Daughters of the American Revolution, 59–60
DDT, 162
"Death of Environmentalism: Global Warming Politics in a Post-Environmental World, The" (Nordhaus/Shellenberger), 242–43
Death of Tomorrow, The (Loraine), 197
DeConcini, Dennis, 220
deep ecology, 193, 224–32, 236
Defenders of Wildlife, 218
deforestation, 22, 23–25, 26, 97
DeLay, Tom, 240, 245
democracy, 17, 32–33, 42
Democrats
  election of Franklin Roosevelt, 96–98
  New Deal expansionism, 81–82, 98–108
  as party of environmentalists, 10, 102, 108, 192, 219
  victory in 2006, 245
  See also specific Democrat or Democratic administration by name
Department of Agriculture, 38
Department of Interior
  aid for Dust Bowl regions, 105
  attempt to transfer Forest Service to, 86
  Ballinger-Pinchot controversy, 13–15, 43–44
  Carson as writer for, 161

Echo Park dam and, 145, 146–47
under George W. Bush, 241, 242
Hetch Hetchy Dam and, 62
irrigation management programs,
90–91
Johnson's conservation policies and,
153–55, 169
under Reagan, 193, 219–20
removal of National Forests from,
38–39
on roads in national parks, 122
under Franklin Roosevelt, 98
under Theodore Roosevelt, 13–15
under Taft, 45
Teapot Dome scandal, 82, 95
view of Everglades flood control
plan, 212
Desert Lands Act (1877), 41
Dewey, Scott Hamilton, 139, 141
Diablo Canyon nuclear power plant
(CA), 200–201
Dinosaur National Monument, 143–51
disease, 29–32, 65–66, 109, 167. *See
also* epidemics
domesticity, 68–70, 160, 166–67
Dominy, Floyd, 155, 156
Donora disaster (PA), 113, 142
Douglas, Marjory Stoneman, 209–13
Douglas, Paul, 148
drinking water purification, 109–10,
167
Driven Wild (Sutter), 114
drought, 104, 105, 106
Drury, Newton, 85–86, 145–47
Dunlap, Thomas, 73
Dust Bowl, 101, 104–8

Earth Day 1970, 10, 139, 174, 175–
78, 192
Earth First!, 189–92, 193, 225–31
Earth in the Balance (Gore), 238
Earth Liberation Front, 231
Echo Park controversy, 145–51
ecofeminism, 193, 209–13, 229, 235–
37

ecological change, human actions
and, 22, 23, 24–25
Ecological Society of America (ESA),
116–17, 119, 124
ecologists, 116–17, 119, 124–27, 128
ecology, 19, 80, 82, 126–27, 128, 247
economic issues
aesthetics vs., 40, 62–65
endangered species, 204–8
as environmentalists' concerns, 222–
23
equity vs., 13–16
Everglades restoration and, 213
expansion and conservation, 16–17
pollution and continued growth,
195–96
radical environmentalists and, 191–
92
unchecked economic expansion, 4,
7
See also Great Depression; New
Deal
ecosystem protection, 209–13
ecotage, 176, 191, 200, 227, 231. *See
also* nonviolent direct-action
movements
ecoterrorism, 227, 231
EDF, 205, 218, 247
Edge, Rosalie, 80, 116, 117, 146,
166
efficiency
aesthetics vs., 40, 144–49, 150
equity vs., 5, 15–16, 40–41, 44, 82
Forest Service's claim to, 39, 140
as goal of conservation, 3, 5, 6–7,
35
Ehrlich, Anne, 197
Ehrlich, Paul, 171–72, 190, 197
EIS, 180, 198, 204
Eisenhower, Dwight David, 153, 159,
181
elitism
of conservation movement, 2, 8, 26–
28, 80–81, 102, 107–8, 118–19, 138
of environmental movement, 206–7

game laws and, 87–88
of Group of Ten, 232
of preservationists, 45–46
sanitation reforms and, 67
of Theodore Roosevelt, 73
of wilderness movement, 118–19,
    121, 122
Emergency Conservation Committee,
    80, 116, 146, 166
Emerson, Ralph Waldo, 53
Endangered Species Act (1973), 183,
    204–8
energy consumption, 138, 172–73,
    194, 195–97, 242
energy crisis, 194–97
England, 17, 24, 48
environment
  automobiles and, 139, 140–41, 181,
      196
  lack of understanding of balances in,
      72
  pesticides damage to, 161–65
  recreational abuse of, 7, 81, 85, 87,
      94, 114–15, 129
  See also Environmental Protection
      Agency (EPA); nuclear power
      plants; nuclear weapons testing;
      oil spills; pesticides; pollution;
      toxic-waste disposal
Environmental Defense Fund (EDF),
    171, 205, 218, 247
Environmental Impact Statements
    (EIS), 180, 198, 204
environmental justice movements, 69,
    213–17, 231–35, 248
environmental movement, 9–10
  after Reagan administration, 237–42
  alienation of hunters and fishermen,
      208
  alleged death of, 11, 242–43, 244
  alternative movements within, 223–
      37, 248
  antinuclear movement, 197–202
  appropriate-technology movement,
      202–4

broadening of constituency, 9–10
Carter administration and, 217, 218
CCC foundations of, 102
class and race and, 8, 215–16, 231–35
coalition building, 245–48
current status of, 247–48
Earth Day 1970, 175–78
Echo Park fight and, 143–51
elitism of, 206–7
emergence of, 135–39
energy crisis and, 194–97
factionalism in, 10–11, 191–93, 200
fallout controversy and, 157–61
fight for the Grand Canyon, 154–57
focus of, 4, 6–7, 209, 213
foundations of, 2–3
grassroots support of, 102, 138
impact of Silent Spring, 161–65
institutionalization of, 183–84, 218,
    222–23
Johnson administration and, 169–71
legislative victories, 178–83
Leopold's land ethic and, 126–27
open-space crusade, 168–69
political support of, 10
pollution issues and, 139–43
push for limitations on utilitarian
    use of national parks, 65
Reagan administration and, 217,
    218–22
redefinition of, 129
split from conservationists, 7, 157,
    159, 190–92
strategies of, 189–90
unifying nature of, 176, 183
use of litigation, 171
water pollution issues, 167, 172–73
Wilderness Act of 1964 and, 151–54
wildlife preservation and, 204–8
women in, 166–67
youth involvement in, 174–75, 176
See also environmental justice
    movements; urban environmen-
    talism; specific organization,
    person, or issue

Environmental Policy Institute, 218
Environmental Protection Agency
  (EPA), 215
  Bush appointee, 237
  creation of, 139, 180–81
  Love Canal and, 214
  under Nixon, 139, 180–81
  Reagan appointees to leadership of,
    219, 221
epidemics, 29–30, 32–34, 66–72, 109.
  See also disease
equity
  aesthetics vs., 121, 157
  antinuclear movement and, 201
  economic issues vs., 13–15
  efficiency vs., 15–16, 40–41, 82,
    144–49
  environmental justice movements
    and, 232, 234–35
  European forestry practices and, 36
  games laws as means of enforcing
    class and racial discrimination,
    27–28
  as goal in resource allocation, 5, 16,
    35
  New Deal policies and, 98, 99
  Pinchot's concern for, 44
  TVA aims for, 102–4
  wildlife preservation vs., 207–8
  women's desire for, 50
erosion, 24–25, 101, 104–7, 108, 135,
  137
Etnier, David, 204
eugenics, 59, 60, 136
Europe
  conservation efforts in, 7–8, 16–17,
    23–24
  control of common resources, 18
  forest management in, 22, 23–24,
    35–36, 125
  Migratory Bird Treaty (1916) with
    England, 48
  park systems in, 32
  pioneering of fish culture, 20
  urban environmentalism in, 29, 31

Everglades National Park, 126–27,
  209–13, 247
Everglades: River of Grass, The
  (Douglas), 211
experts
  agrarian reforms and, 106
  disease transmission theories, 29–
    30, 66, 71–72, 167
  domination of conservation, 3, 5,
    65, 80, 81, 128, 248
  domination of pollution reform, 65,
    108–13
  on environmental organizations'
    staffs, 190, 218
  forecast of energy consumption, 196
  game management and, 124–27
  international exchange of ideas, 8,
    29–30
  Newlands Reclamation Act and, 42
  oversight of natural resource
    consumption, 9, 34–35
  pesticide pollution and, 162, 163
  pollution control and, 112, 128, 167
  required to control complex
    technology, 202
  sanitation reforms and, 65–72, 128
  warnings of global calamity, 24–25,
    135–38, 171–73, 197
  wilderness preservation and, 128
  women and, 70–71, 166

Fall, Albert, 82
fallout shelter craze, 159, 160
farmer reformists, 19
farming/farmers. *See* agriculture
Federal Oil Conservation Board, 96
Federal Water Pollution Control
  Administration, 171
feminism, 8, 167, 209–10, 235–37
fence laws, 27
Fernow, Bernard, 37
FFWC, 210
fire prevention in forests, 84, 101–2,
  123
Fischer, Michael, 234

Fish and Wildlife Service, 183, 206–7
fish commissions, 20–21, 23
fish culture, 20–21, 23, 94
fishermen/fishing
  alienation from environmental
    movement, 208, 246
  fish restoration projects, 19–21, 23,
    94
  Hoover's view of, 93–94
  as sport of common man, 46, 81, 94
  as sport of elite, 45
  water pollution and, 110
  See also Izaak Walton League
Fleming, Donald, 125
Florida Federation of Women's Clubs
  (FFWC), 210
Forcing the Spring (Gottlieb), 177
Foreman, Dave, 189–90, 225–28,
  229, 230–31
forest conservation and forestry, 21–
  22, 23, 25–26, 35–38, 41
Forest Homestead Act, 40
Forest Reserves Act (1891), 25–26
forest reserve system. *See* National
  Forest system
Foster, David, 246
Fox, Stephen, 57, 81
France, 17, 23–24, 35–36
Friends of the Earth, 178, 199
Friends of the Everglades, 212
frontier heritage, 5, 17, 45, 47–51, 58
Future of the Great Plains, The, 105

game management
  by Biological Survey, 87–89, 90
  class issues with, 45–47
  in early America, 18
  ecological philosophy of, 124
  Franklin Roosevelt's approach to, 97
  as means of reinforcing class and
    racial inequality, 26, 28–29
  Migratory Bird Treaty Act and, 87
  reforms in, 89–90, 128
game reserves, 40
garbage disposal. *See* solid-waste

disposal; toxic-waste disposal
Gardner, John, 170
gender, 8, 50, 72, 236–37. *See also*
  ecofeminism; feminism; women
General Federation of Women's
  Clubs, 51, 86, 116, 153
genetically modified foods, 248
German forest management, 17, 23,
  24, 35–36
germ theory, 30, 66
Get Oil Out (GOO), 172–73
Gibbs, Lois, 215, 216, 234
Gila National Forest, 118
Glacier National Park, 57, 58, 146
Glen Canyon dam, 151
Global Environmental Facility, 237–
  38
global warming
  death of environmentalism and,
    242–43
  doubts about, 241
  greenhouse gases and, 202, 237
  Kyoto Conference, 238, 241
  need for dramatic social change,
    244–45, 248
  prediction of, 137, 138, 197
  revival of nuclear power and, 202
global worldview, 137
Glover, James, 119
Gofman, John, 198
Goldwater, Barry, 220, 239
Gore, Al, 238, 242
Gorsuch, Anne, 219, 221, 222
Gottlieb, Alan, 239–40
Gottlieb, Robert, 177, 216
government
  broadening involvement in
    conservation, 34–35, 81–83
  centralization of, 34
  expansion into environmental issues,
    4, 8, 69, 128
  expansion of authority over
    resources, 2–4, 5, 8, 15, 38–39,
    73, 81
  expansion of tourism and, 114

growth of power through sanitation reforms and parks system, 34
involvement in pollution control, 108–13, 139–40, 141, 143
New Deal expansion of, 98–108
regulation of commons, 19–21, 73
responsibility for sanitation, 29–30
weakening of controls over nuclear power, 201
women in environmental positions, 69–70
Government Accounting Office study, 233
Graham, Bob, 213
Grand Canyon National Park, 38, 86, 146, 154–57
Grant, Madison, 59
grazing rights, 40, 64, 86, 98, 123, 154
Great Bandwagon Market, 198
Great Depression, 7, 9, 81, 91, 96–108. *See also* New Deal
Greeley, William B., 83, 84, 119
greenhouse gases, 202, 237, 238, 242–43
Greenpeace, 223–24
Grinnell, George Bird, 46–47
Group of Ten, 218, 222, 232, 233–35
gun industry, 88

habitat protection, 87, 183, 206–8
Hair, Jay, 222–23, 240
Hamilton, Alice, 69, 71, 248
Hardin, Garret, 18
Harding, Warren, 82, 95
Harriman, Edward H., 57, 58, 92
Hartford nuclear reservation, 201
Harvey, Mark, 149–50, 151
Hatch, Orrin, 220
Hayes, Dennis, 176
Hays, Samuel, 6, 36, 178
health issues
  class and race and, 29–31, 71–72
  as environmental focus, 3, 4, 7, 9, 231–32, 248

fallout controversy and, 157–61
inventories of public health, 43
open-space crusade and, 32–34, 168, 169
outdoor activities and, 45, 93–94, 100–101, 114
pesticide threat to, 162
pollution, 109–10, 112, 113, 128, 138, 139–43, 167, 170, 181
sanitation reforms and, 29–31, 67–72, 109
toxic-waste disposal and, 213–17
work environment and, 71
Helms, Jesse, 240
Herman, Daniel, 45–46
Herrin, William F., 57
Hetch Hetchy Dam, 2, 45, 53, 60–65
Hoberg, George, 182
Holyoke Waterpower Company, 20
Hooker Chemical Company, 213–17
Hoover, Herbert, 81, 82, 83, 92, 93–96
Hoover Dam, 91–93
Hornaday, William, 87–88, 127
Housewives to End Pollution, 166
Humphrey, Hubert, 152
Hunter, Robert, 224
hunting/hunters
  alienation from environmental movement, 208, 246
  defense of Forest Service, 86
  environmental movement and, 208, 245–46
  frontier heritage and, 5
  as leisure sport of common man, 81, 87
  as leisure sport of elite, 26, 28, 45–47, 48
  masculinity and, 46–47
  Pinchot and, 40
  regulation of, 87, 88
  for subsistence, 26–28, 45–47, 87
  in wilderness areas, 123
  See also Boone and Crockett Club; game management

Hunt v. *The United States,* 89
husbandry, 19
hydrogen bomb testing, 136, 158. *See also* antinuclear movement

Ickes, Harold, 98, 122
Imperial Irrigation District, 92–93
India, 24
Indian Forest Department, 24
industrialization/industry
   American male virility and, 47
   conservation and environmentalism
      and, 3, 7, 9
   conservationists' position on, 4–5
   contribution to pollution, 81, 109–
      10, 128, 137, 139, 140, 142
   emergence of international
      conservation programs and, 16–
      17
   exposure of environmental risks of, 71
   government control of resources
      and, 19–20
   limitation of pollution from on
      Mauritius, 23
   Pinchot and, 16
   sanitary reforms and, 66–72
   urban environmentalism and, 3
Inhofe, James, 241
irrigation management programs, 35,
   41–42, 90–91, 98, 148
Isle Royale Park, 126
Izaak Walton League
   Boundary Waters Canoe Area
      protection, 120
   founding of, 80
   game laws and, 87
   Hoover as president of, 93
   involvement in water pollution
      issues, 178
   as member of Group of Ten, 218
   mistrust of Department of Interior, 86
   study of stream pollution, 110
   Wilderness Act and, 153

Jackson, Henry, 156, 179

Johnson, Ladybird, 153
Johnson, Lyndon Baines, 108, 153,
   154, 156, 169–70
Johnson, Robert Underwood, 57
Johnson administration, 183
Judd, Richard, 16, 18, 28

Kaibab National Forest, 89–90, 125
Kehoe, Terence, 182
Kennedy, John F., 153, 159–60, 164,
   170
Kent, William, 63
Knopf, Alfred, 148
Koppes, Clayton, 5
Kristoff, Nicholas, 244
Kyoto Accord on Climate Change,
   241
Kyoto Conference, 238

L-20 regulations, 119, 123
Lacey Act (1900), 53
Ladies Health Protective Association,
   68–69
Lake Erie, 173
land ethic, 126–27
Land Water Conservation Fund Act
   (1964), 169
Last Days of Mankind, The (Mines), 197
Latrobe, Benjamin Henry, 29
Lavelle, Rita, 221
Law of the Sea Treaty, 238
lawsuits. *See* litigation
Lear, Linda, 161
leisure time
   affluence contributing to, 81, 138
   attitudes toward in interwar years, 114
   automobile and, 114
   camping craze and, 81, 114–15,
      129, 150
   demand for healthy environment
      and, 138, 139
   effect of on conservation movement,
      7, 9, 150
   growth of hunting and fishing and,
      46–47, 81, 87

Hoover's view of, 93–94
parks development and, 83, 85, 114–15, 116
preservationists' motivations and, 7, 45, 150
Leopold, Aldo
    as advocate of ecological preservation, 124–28
    balanced environmental philosophy of, 165
    campaign for wilderness areas, 118–19, 121, 122
    environmental philosophy of, 79–80, 125–26, 248
    on Forest Service, 84
    on game management, 88–89
    influence of, 136, 137, 151, 164, 228
Limits of Growth, The (Club of Rome), 197
listing, 105
litigation
    as defense of Navaho and Hopi territories, 226
    of Environmental Defense Fund, 171
    fight for northern spotted owl, 206–7
    as means to change, 182
    over Siskiyou road building, 190
    over Tellico Dam construction, 205
    against polluters, 180–81
    Sierra Club's use of, 178
Lodge, Henry Cabot, 47
logging. *See* timber industry
Loraine, John, 197
Los Angeles smog problems (CA), 139–40, 141, 143
Love Canal episode (NY), 213–17, 232
Love Canal Homeowners Association, 215–16
Lovejoy, Sam, 200
Lovins, Amory, 196

lumber industry. *See* timber industry
Lynd, Helen, 114
Lynd, Robert, 114

MacKaye, Benton, 121
Maher, Neil, 102, 107
Malthus, Thomas, 138, 172
Mammoth Cave National Park, 146
Man and Nature; or, Physical Geography as Modified by Human Action (Marsh), 24–25
Mansfield, Michael, 203
Marble Canyon, 146, 154
Marks, Martha, 241
Marsh, George Perkins, 21–23, 24–25, 26, 43, 138
Marshall, Louis, 120
Marshall, Robert, 120–22, 123–24, 227
masculinity culture, 5, 47–50, 65, 70
Massachusetts Board of Health, 29
Mather, Stephen, 64, 85, 86, 115
Mauritius, 23–24
Mazamas, 50
McCloskey, Michael, 177, 178, 228
McVeigh, Timothy, 240
Mead, Margaret, 174
media, 200–201, 224, 227–28, 230
Melosi, Martin, 109
Mesa Verde cliff dwellings, 51
Migratory Bird Treaty Act (1916), 48
Migratory Bird Treaty Act (1918), 87
Miller, Char, 37
Mines, Samuel, 197
mining interests, 86, 123, 153, 154
modernization, 3, 4, 7, 34, 48
Monkey Wrench Gang, The (Abbey), 226
Moore, Les, 189–90
morality, 15–16
Morgan-Guggenheim syndicate, 13, 44
Mothers for Peace, 199
mountaineering, 49–50

Mountain State Legal Foundation
(CO), 219
Mount Rainer National Park, 57, 86
movie industry, 159
Muir, Daniel, 54
Muir, John
approach to preservation politics of,
1, 2, 245, 247
background of, 54–56
creation of Yosemite National Park,
56–58
cultivation of women's clubs, 53
fame of, 53–54
as founder of Sierra Club, 45
Hetch Hetchy Dam conflict and, 2,
60, 62–63
Pinchot and, 1–2, 60–61
Mumford, Lewis, 171
municipal housekeeping, 68–70
Muscle Shoals Dam, 103
Muskie, Edmund, 170

Nader, Ralph, 199
Naess, Arne, 224
Nash, George, 93
Nash, Roderick, 49, 64
National Academy of Sciences,
158
National Agricultural Chemicals
Association, 164
National Center for Appropriate
Technology (MT), 203
National Coast Anti-Pollution
League, 109
National Committee for a Sane
Nuclear Policy (SANE), 160
National Conservation Commission, 43
National Environmental Policy Act
(NEPA), 139, 179–80
National Forest system, 1, 25–26, 38,
39, 40, 84, 86, 101–2, 169, 227
National Lumber Manufacturing
Association, 40
national parks and monuments system

Dinosaur National Monument fight,
143–51
effects of New Deal projects in, 101–2
Everglades preservation and, 126–
27, 209–13, 247
expansion of, 115–16, 122, 170–71
fight for the Grand Canyon, 154–57
increased tourism in, 143, 146
institution of, 1, 247
Muir's contribution to, 53–54, 56–
58, 62
racism and, 58–60
Theodore Roosevelt's contribution
to, 38
threats to Dinosaur National
Monument, 143–51
utilitarian element of, 62–65
Watt's view of, 219–20
See also National Parks Service
(NPS); parks system; specific
national park by name
National Parks Association, 96
National Parks Conservation
Association, 218
National Park Service Act, 146
National Parks Service (NPS)
battle with Forest Service, 84–86,
119, 122–23
CCC projects and, 101–2
Dinosaur National Monument and,
145–47
expansion for campers, 115–16
first Democratic head of, 98
function of, 64, 73
goals/methods of, 85
Ickes and, 122
Republican domination of, 96
Wilderness Act and, 153
wildlife policy of, 48, 89, 90
National Parks Service Act (1916), 64
National Rifle Association, 208
National Toxics Campaign, 216
National Wholesale Lumber Dealers
Association, 40

National Wildlife Federation, 80–81,
110, 177, 178, 199, 218, 222, 240
National Woolgrowers Association, 86
Native Americans, 45, 58–59
natural gas, 113
natural resources
concerns about depletion of, 3, 4–5,
9, 35, 84, 137
conservationists' position on, 4–5, 9,
82–96
deregulation of, 219
European conservation programs
and, 16–17
government control of, 2–4, 8, 13–
16, 19–21, 38–39
interwar attitudes toward, 83
movements developed in response to
depletion of, 3–5, 18
Taft's view of, 13–14
See also conservation movement/
conservationists
Natural Resources Defense Council,
171, 218, 221
nature, attitudes toward, 45, 114, 236
Nature Conservancy, 247
Nelson, Gaylord, 175
NEPA, 139, 179–80
New Conservation, 169. *See also*
environmental movement
New Deal
CCC projects, 100–102, 115–16, 129
conservation programs of, 3, 5, 9,
98–108
environmental movement and, 102,
138
legacy of, 139
programs dealing with pollution
control, 109, 110, 111–12
WPA projects, 111
Newlands, Francis, 41–42
Newlands Reclamation Act (1902),
42, 90, 98
New Left, 174–75, 176, 190, 202, 224
Newman, Penny, 217
New York (city), 113, 140, 141–43

New York (state), 26, 215
NIMBYism, 216
Nixon, Richard, 139, 179, 180, 192,
195
Nixon administration, 139, 180, 192,
212
nonviolent direct-action movements
agenda of, 192
of alternative environmental
movements, 223–24
of antinuclear power movement,
190–91, 199–201
Earth First! and, 225
of Love Canal Homeowners
Association, 215
at Siskiyou National Forest, 189–90
Nordhaus, Ted, 242–43, 245, 246
North Cascades Park (WA), 170
Norton, Gale, 241, 242
NPS. *See* National Parks Service (NPS)
nuclear power plants, 194, 195, 197–
201, 202
Nuclear Regulatory Commission, 203
nuclear weapons testing and fallout,
9, 138, 157–60, 162, 163, 166

Oelschlaeger, Max, 54
Office of Appropriate Technology
(CA), 203, 204
oil industry. *See* petrochemical
industry
Oil Pollution Control Act (1924), 95,
111
oil spills, 94–95, 172–73
Olmstead, Frederick Law, 32–33
Olson, Sigurd, 150
Olympic National Park, 80, 123
Olympic peninsula (WA), 38
On the Beach (Shute), 159
Open Space Action Institute, 168
Open Space Council, 168
open-space crusade, 167–69, 178
organic foods, 174, 248
Osborn, Fairfield, 135–36, 137, 171,
172, 190, 197

Our Plundered Planet (Osborn), 135–36

Outdoor Cleanliness Association, 142

outdoor recreation
  health issues and, 93–94
  increased opportunities for in interwar years, 83, 94, 114–15, 116, 143, 146
  regenerative powers of, 45
  wilderness cult and, 49
  See also camping craze; climbing clubs; fishermen/fishing; hunting/hunters

overpopulation. *See* population growth

ozone depletion, 221

ozone pollution, 237

Pacific Southwest Water Plan, 154–57

parks system
  epidemics leading to institution of, 32
  European concepts of, 17
  increased tourism in, 143, 146
  interwar tourism and, 115
  Johnson's additions to, 169–70
  Muir's contribution to, 53–54, 56–58
  postwar tourism in, 143, 146
  threats to Dinosaur National Monument, 143–51
  See also national parks and monuments system; National Parks Service (NPS); open-space crusade

Passing of the Great Race, The (Grant), 59

patriarchy, 236

Pauling, Linus, 158

Pearson, Byron, 156

People for Open Space, 168

People of Color Environmental Leadership Summit, 234–35

Pepper, David, 236

pesticides

Audubon Society on, 177–78
  Carson on, 138, 161–65, 248
  as central concern, 9, 248
  federal legislation regarding, 178–79
  Johnson administration and, 169
  uniting of environmentalists and preservationists, 157

petrochemical industry
  contribution to pollution, 81, 94–95
  Earth First! and, 227
  energy crisis and, 194–97
  overproduction in, 95–96
  Reagan administration and, 219, 221
  Teapot Dome scandal, 82, 95
  Wilderness Act and, 153

Phelan, James, 63

Phillips, Sarah, 99

phosphates, 173

physicians, 67, 112, 113, 128

Pinchot, Gifford
  accomplishments of, 1–2, 38–39
  approach of, 1–2, 5, 99, 104
  background of, 35, 36
  call for mandatory regulation of timberlands, 83–84
  cultivation of women's clubs, 53, 65
  development of forestry service, 35–41
  goals of, 35
  Hetch Hetchy Dam conflict and, 2, 45, 60, 62, 63
  influence of, 238–39
  influence of Brandis on, 24, 35
  interest in settlement houses, 35, 66
  as member of Boone and Crockett Club, 47
  Muir and, 60–61
  racism of, 59
  relationship with Theodore Roosevelt, 37–38
  Franklin Roosevelt and, 97, 98
  study of European forestry, 17, 35–36
  Taft administration and, 13–15, 43–44

unification of conservation efforts,
42–43
Pittsburgh, Pennsylvania, 71–72, 113,
166
Pluralist Regulator Regime, 182
Poivre, Pierre, 23, 36
political conservatives, 10, 179, 218–
20, 238–41
pollution
broadening of view of, 109–10, 165
as central concern, 9, 128, 138, 167,
169, 170, 171, 248
control of as government responsibility, 29, 30–31
energy aspects of, 195–96
Europe as source of ideas for clean-
up, 17, 29–31
federal legislation regarding, 108–
13, 139, 170–71, 178–79, 181–82
Hoover's response to, 94–95
industrial growth and, 81
interwar governmental policies
regarding, 83
isolation of women from reforms
concerning, 70, 71
Johnson administration and, 169
limitation of on Mauritius, 23
nuclear power plants and thermal
pollution and, 198
oil spills, 94–95, 172–73
overpopulation and, 137, 195
postwar issues with air pollution,
139–43
as result of urbanization, 65–68
Silent Spring and, 138
pollution bill (1878, MA), 31
Pope, Carl, 208, 238, 244–45
Population Bomb, The (Ehrlich), 171–
72
population growth
environment and overpopulation, 4,
136, 137. 195–96
increased demand on commons, 19
prediction of mass famine, 171–72
sanitary reforms and, 66–72

urban blight and, 3
postwar period
air pollution issues, 139–43
Carson's Silent Spring published,
161–65, 177–78
Earth Day 1970, 174–77, 178
Echo Park dam and, 139–40
fight for Grand Canyon, 154–57
New Conservation, 169–71
nuclear fallout fears, 157–61
open-space crusade, 168–69, 178
water pollution controls, 167, 173,
178, 181–82
Wilderness Act of 1964, 151–54,
177–78
women in environmental movement,
166–67, 216–17, 235–37
predator control, 8, 64, 79–80, 88–90,
124–25, 128
preservation movement/preservation-
ists
addition of scientific argument, 127
approach of, 157
characteristics of, 57
definition of, 5–6
Dinosaur National Monument and,
143–51
division over Hetch Hetchy Dam, 2,
45, 60–65
Earth Day and, 177–78
elitism of, 45–46
emergence of, 4
fight for the Grand Canyon, 154–57
goals of, 1, 3, 5–6
habitat protection as method of,
204–8
motivations of, 247
Muir and, 53–54
racism in, 58–60
tourism and, 9
utilitarian conservationists vs., 2,
60–65, 129, 143–51, 154–57
white supremacy and, 59–60
Wilderness Act of 1964 and, 151–54
wilderness movement and, 117–24

President's Science Advisory Committee, 164
Progressive era, 124–25
  Hetch Hetchy Dam conflict, 60–65
  Roosevelt/Pinchot conservation policies, 9, 28, 34–45
  sanitation reforms, 65–72
  wildlife and wilderness preservation, 45–60
Project Independence, 195
property rights, 72, 241–42
public opinion
  antinuclear movement and, 201
  collapse of support for Appropriate Technology, 192
  concerning the energy crisis, 195, 197
  economic issues vs. environmental issues, 193–94
  environmentalist warnings and, 137
  Reagan revolution and, 220–22
  shift toward conservation, 15, 16
  water pollution controls and, 109, 110
  on wildlife preservation, 208
Public Works Administration, 111

Quiet Crisis, The (Udall), 169

race
  conservation/preservation movement and, 2–3, 4, 58–60, 73
  environmental justice movements and, 232–35, 248
  environmental movement and, 4, 8, 60, 72, 193, 232, 234
  national park system and, 58–60
  New Deal programs and, 102
  restriction of commons and, 27–29
  Warren County, North Carolina waste-dump and, 232–33
Race Betterment Foundation of Battle Creek, 59
RARE II process, 225, 226
Reagan, Ronald, 176, 180, 193, 201, 204, 218–22

Reagan administration, 217–22
Redwoods Park (California), 170
Redwood Summer (1990), 229, 230
reforestation, 25, 51, 84, 101
Refuse Act (1899), 111
Regional Planning Association of America (RPAA), 103
Reiger, John, 26–27
Reilly, William, 237
Report on the Sanitary Commission, 31
Report on the Sanitary Conditions of the Labouring Population of Great Britain, 30
republicanism, 32–33
Republicans
  Ballinger-Pinchot controversy, 13–15
  conservative conservation policies of, 44, 82–96, 108, 281–92
  domination of conservation organizations, 96, 97–98
  Earth Day 1970 and, 177
  environmentalists bridge-building with, 245–46
  NEPA and, 179
  REP America and, 241
  rightward drift, 179
  turn from environmental issues, 177
  withdrawal of support for environmentalism, 4, 10, 183, 192–93, 218–19, 220, 237–41, 242, 244
  See also specific Republican or Republican administration by name
Republicans for Environmental Protection, 241
Righter, Robert, 62
"Road Not Taken, The" (Lovins), 196
Road to Survival (Vogt), 135, 137
Rockefeller, Nelson, 218
Rocky Flats complex (CO), 201
Rocky Mountain National Park, 86
Rogers, Daniel, 17
Rome, Adam, 213

Roosevelt, Eleanor, 153
Roosevelt, Franklin D.
  approach to conservation, 96–99,
    191, 245
  approach to game management, 89
  background of, 96–97
  expansion of Dinosaur National
    Monument, 144
  New Deal, 3, 9, 81, 98–108
Roosevelt, Theodore
  challenge to Taft administration, 14,
    44
  commitment to conservation, 13, 28,
    38
  elitist attitudes of, 73
  fluid environmental activism of, 66
  founding of Boone and Crockett
    Club, 47
  Hetch Hetchy Dam and, 2
  increase in forest reserves, 26
  irrigation management programs
    and, 41–42
  as police commissioner, 70
  racism of, 59
  relationship with Muir, 1, 57–58
  relationship with Pinchot, 1, 37–38
  restraint of capitalism through
    regulation, 34
Root, Elihu, 47
Roselle, Mike, 227
Roth, Dennis, 153
Rothman, Hal, 99, 177
RPAA, 103
Ruckelshaus, William, 180–81, 219,
  221
rural areas, 3. See also agriculture
Russell Sage Foundation, 71, 72

sabotage, 176, 191, 200, 227, 231
Sagebrush Rebellion, 192, 220, 238
Sale, Kirkpatrick, 197
Sand County Almanac, A (Leopold),
  80, 125–26, 211
sanitation reforms, 29–31, 65–72,
  109–11, 166

Save Our Everglades program, 213
Save the Redwoods League, 59, 85–
  86, 108
save the whales campaign, 223–24
Saylor, John, 152
Schlesinger, Arthur, Jr., 169
Schrepfer, Susan, 50
Schumacher, E. F., 202
Schuyler, David, 33
Schweitzer, Albert, 126, 152, 163
science
  fish culture and, 20–21, 23
  Forest Service and, 84
  game management and, 88–90
  land ethic and, 126–27, 128
  preservationism and, 6, 128, 247–48
  urban environmentalism and, 4
  women in urban environmentalism
    and, 66, 70–71
Scott, Douglas, 223
Sea Around Us, The (Carson), 162
Seabrook nuclear power plant (NH),
  200
Sea Shepherd Society, 224
septic tanks, 167
Sequoia National Park, 86
sewage systems, 17, 29–31, 69, 70,
  110–11. See also septic tanks;
  wastewater issues
sexism, 236–37
Shabecoff, Philip, 165
Shaffer, Marguerite, 50–51
Shellenberger, Michael, 242–44, 245,
  246
Shipstead-Newton-Nolan Act (1930),
  120
Shute, Nevil, 159
Sierra Club
  activity on racial/class-based issues,
    234
  alienation of hunters and fishermen,
    208
  antinuclear movement and, 199
  Blue/Green Alliance, 246
  camping craze and, 115

on changes in energy consumption, 195, 196
Dinosaur National Monument and, 144, 147, 148, 150
Earth Day and, 177
founding of, 50, 54
Glen Canyon Dam and, 151
Grand Canyon fight and, 155, 156
Hetch Hetchy Dam conflict and, 62
litigation of, 178
as member of Group of Ten, 218
membership of, 178, 247
nuclear power debate and, 178
response to grassroots environmentalists, 216
Wilderness Act and, 151
Sierra Club Legal Defense Fund, 171, 206–8
Silent Spring (Carson), 138, 161, 163–65, 177, 217
Siskiyou National Forest, 189–90
Small is Beautiful: Economics as if People Mattered (Schumacher), 202
smog, 139–40
snail darter, 204–6
social ecologists, 224–25
Soil Conservation Service, 98, 101, 105–7
soil desiccation, 22, 23–25, 97
Soil Erosion Service, 105
solid-waste disposal, 17, 29–31, 68–69, 70, 171, 178, 232–33
Solid Waste Disposal Act (1965), 171
Sons of Daniel Boone, 49
Southern Christian Leadership Conference, 233
Southern Pacific Railroad, 56–57
Speth, Gus, 217–18
sportsmen, 5, 20–21, 26–27, 45–48, 52, 59–60, 208, 245, 246. *See also* fishermen/fishing; hunting/hunters
state-building, 8–9, 39. *See also* government
state parks system, 115

Stegner, Wallace, 148, 150, 212
Stern, Alexandra, 59, 60
Stevens, Ted, 240
Stevenson, Adlai, 153
Stimson, Henry, 47
St. Louis, Missouri, 110–11, 112–13, 166
stock laws, 27–28
Stoll, Steven, 19
subsistence practices, 18–19, 21, 26–28, 45–47, 87
suburbanization
emergence of environmental movement and, 4, 7, 9, 137, 138
expansion of conservation movement and, 129
open-space crusade and, 168–69
septic tanks and, 167
toxic-waste disposal and, 213–17
wilderness movement and, 4, 138
Superfund, 217, 221, 248
Superior National Forest, 119
Sutter, Paul, 114

Taft, William Howard, 13–15, 43–44
Tamplin, Arthur, 198
Taylor Grazing Act (1934), 98
Teapot Dome scandal, 82, 95
technology, 202–4. *See also* appropriate-technology movement; automobiles; nuclear power plants
Tellico Dam, 204–6
Tennessee Valley Authority (TVA), 102–4, 204–6
Term Permit Act, 117
terrorism, 227, 231, 240
thalidomide tragedy, 163
Thanksgiving Weekend episode (1966), 142–43
thermal pollution, 198
Third Wave environmentalism, 222–23
This is Dinosaur: Echo Park Country and Its Magic Rivers, 148
Thoreau, Henry David, 53, 56, 57
Three Mile Island accident, 200–201

Timber Conservation Board, 95
timber industry
  cooperation with Forest Service,
    40–41, 83–84
  Earth First! and, 227
  fight for northern spotted owl, 206–
    208
  L-20 regulations and, 123
  overproduction in, 95
  RARE II process and, 226
  Reagan administration and, 219, 221
  Wilderness Act and, 152, 153
Times Beach dioxin contamination
  (MO), 221
Tobago, 24
tourism
  camping craze and, 81, 114–15,
    129, 150
  citizenship and, 50–51
  effect on Native Americans, 58–59
  during interwar period, 81
  national parks system and, 64
  wilderness movement and, 114–24
Toxic Waste and Race (UCC), 233
toxic-waste disposal, 8, 193, 199,
  213–17, 232–33, 248
"Tragedy of the Commons, The"
  (Harding), 18
Train, Russell, 219
Trapper's Lake, Colorado, 117–18
Treaty Banning Nuclear Weapons in
  the Atmosphere, in Outer Space,
  and Underwater, 160
Tropical Everglades National Park
  Association, 126, 211
Trout Unlimited, 208, 246
Truman, Harry S., 127, 147, 211
Tucker, Raymond, 112
Turner, Frederick Jackson, 48
TVA, 102–4, 204–6

U-2 affair, 159
Udall, Morris, 156
Udall, Stewart, 153, 154, 156, 169

Under the Sea Wind (Carson), 161–62
Union Carbide plant disaster in
  Bhopal, India, 221
Union of Concerned Scientists, 198
Union Oil Company spill, 172–73
union workers, 246
U.S. Biological Survey, 87–88, 90
U. S. Commission on Fish and
  Fisheries, 20–21
U.S. Forest Service (USFS)
  battle with Parks Service, 84–86,
    119, 122–23
  clash with environmentalists, 189–
    90, 191
  control of game, 89
  Department of Interior's attempted
    takeover, 86
  first Democratic head of, 98
  founder of, 1
  goals/methods of, 39–41, 85
  interwar policies of, 83–84
  L-20 regulations, 119, 123
  Pinchot's accounting for, 37
  place in twentieth century politics,
    15
  RARE II process, 225, 226
  Reagan appointee to leadership of,
    219
  Republican domination of, 96
  transfer of National Forest to, 38–39
  U regulations for wilderness areas,
    123
  wilderness movement and, 117–19,
    121–23, 152, 153
  wildlife management policies of,
    79–80
U.S. Public Health Service, 110, 111
United Church of Christ (UCC), 233
United Farm Workers Union, 232
United Nations Earth Summit (1992),
  237
United Nations Framework Conven-
  tion on Climate Change, 238
United Nations Population Fund, 238

United Steelworkers union, 246
Unruh, Jesse, 176
urban environmentalism
    approach of, 6–7
    creation of open space in cities, 32–34
    emergence of, 4
    environmental justice movement and, 232–35
    goals of, 3, 29
    international social policy exchanges, 17
    rise of, 129
    sanitation reforms, 29–31, 65–72
    traits of, 67–68
urbanization, 4–5, 29, 47, 66–72
U regulations for wilderness areas, 123
USFS. See U.S. Forest Service (USFS)
utilitarian conservationists, 1–2, 34–45, 60–65, 143–51, 157, 191. See also conservation

Vanderbilt, George, 36
Vaux, Calvert, 32–33
Velsicol Chemical Company, 217
Vietnam War, 202–3
Vogt, William, 135, 136–37, 171, 172, 197

Wallace, Henry, 97–98
Wallop, Malcom, 220
Waring, George, 68, 70
Warren County waste-dump protest (NC), 232–33
waste management. See also toxic-waste disposal
wastewater issues, 30, 31, 70, 110–11, 167, 171, 181, 182. See also septic tanks; sewage systems
water pollution
    federal legislation regarding, 139, 171, 179, 181–82
    government control of, 109–11
    Hoover's response to, 94–95
    of Lake Erie, 173
    oil spills, 172–73
    prohibited in Massachusetts in 1878, 31
    public demand for controls, 138
Water Pollution Control Act (1948), 111
Water Pollution Control Act Amendments (1972), 181–82
water reclamation projects, 41–42, 90–91, 92
watershed protection, 25–26
Watson, Paul, 224
Watt, James, 193, 219–20, 221, 222, 243
Werbach, Adam, 243–44, 245, 246
White, E. B., 161
white supremacy, 27–28, 59–60
Whole Earth Catalog, The (Brand), 203
Wilderness Act (1964), 124, 151–54, 169
wilderness cult, 49–51, 64–65
wilderness movement
    Dinosaur National Monument battle, 143–51
    frontier heritage and, 5
    increased public support for, 138
    increased tourism and, 9, 114–24
    Johnson administration and, 169
    scientific rationale for, 124–27, 128
    Wilderness Act of 1964 and, 124, 151–54
wilderness refuges, 1, 83, 114–24, 225, 226
Wilderness Society
    Dinosaur National Monument and, 144, 146, 147, 149–50
    Earth Day and, 177
    fight for wilderness preservation, 122–24
    founding of, 81, 121–22, 124

as member of Group of Ten, 218
membership of, 178
wildlife preservation
Boone and Crockett Club and, 47–48
challenge to methods, 81
class issues with, 45–47, 48
Endangered Species Act (1973), 183, 204–8
expanding government involvement in, 83
frontier heritage and, 5
game laws/refuge establishment, 87–89
Leopold's revelations on, 79–80, 125
Marsh's influence on, 22–23
New Deal projects and, 101
sportsmen vs. subsistence hunters, 26–27
Willard, Frances, 68
Wilson, Woodrow, 14–15, 44, 144
Winner, Langdon, 203
Wise Use Movement, 238–41, 242
Wolke, Howie, 226
women
antifeather campaign, 52–53
antitoxics movement and, 215, 216–17
in environmental justice movement, 232
in environmental movement, 80, 166–67
fight against nuclear testing, 160, 166
fight against pesticide use, 161–65, 166–67
in fight for Everglades, 209–13
fluid environmental activism of, 66
mountaineering and, 50
in preservation movement, 53, 65
role in air pollution control, 112, 142

role in urban environmentalism, 8, 68–70, 71
wilderness preservation and, 51
women's clubs
air pollution control and, 112
decline of, 80
experts and, 70–71
preservation movement and, 51–53, 65, 72
support for environmental controversies, 166–67
urban environmentalism and, 66, 68–70
Women's Organization for Smoke Abatement, 112
women's rights movement, 51
Women Strike for Peace (WSP), 160
Work, Hubert, 91
Works Progress Administration, 111
World War II, 7, 9, 113, 129, 145–46
Worster, Donald, 127
WPA, 111
Wright, Mabel Osgood, 73

Yard, Robert Sterling, 122
Yellowstone National Park, 48, 57, 58, 86
Yom Kippur War, 194
Yosemite National Park, 1, 2, 56–58, 60–65
youth
anticorporate attitudes, 138–39
CCC projects for, 100–101
entrance into environmental movement, 10, 174, 203. *See also* counterculture; New Left
wilderness cult and, 49

Zahniser, Howard, 146, 147, 149, 151–54, 176, 245
Zakin, Susan, 22

Preserving the Nation: The Conservation and Environmental Movements, 1870–2000
Developmental editor: Andrew J. Davidson
Copy editor and Production editor: Lucy Herz
Proofreader: Claudia Siler
Indexer: Pat Rimmer
Printer: Versa Press, Inc.